French Film

Texts and contexts

Edited by

Susan Hayward

and

Ginette Vincendeau

Routledge
London and New York

First published in 1990 by
Routledge
11 New Fetter Lane, London EC4P 4EE

Simultaneously published in the USA and Canada
by Routledge
a division of Routledge, Chapman and Hall, Inc.
29 West 35th Street, New York, NY 10001

Laser-printed by
Aston University Modern Languages Publishing Services
Printed in Great Britain by
Richard Clay Ltd. Bungay Suffolk

British Library Cataloguing in Publication Data

French film: Texts and contexts.
  1. French cinema films, 1920–1980.
  Critical studies
  I. Hayward, Susan II. Vincendeau, Ginette
  791.43′0944

  ISBN 0–415–00130–7 (Hardback)
  ISBN 0–415–00131–5 (Paperback)

Library of Congress Cataloging in Publication Data

French film, texts and contexts / edited by Susan Hayward and Ginette
  Vincendeau.
    p. cm.
  Bibliography: p.
  Includes index.
  ISBN 0–415–00130–7. – ISBN 0–415–00131–5 (pbk.)
  1. Motion pictures – France – History. I. Hayward, Susan.
II. Vincendeau, Ginette.
PN1993.5.F7F74 1990
791.43′0944–dc.19 89–6038

CONTENTS

,

NOTES ON CONTRIBUTORS

RICHARD ABEL teaches film studies in the English Department at Drake University, Des Moines. He is the author of *French Cinema: The First Wave, 1915-1929* and the two-volume history/anthology, *French Film Theory and Criticism, 1907-1939*. He has also contributed to many film journals, including *Cinema Journal, Framework, Film Quarterly, Wide Angle,* and *Les Restaurations de la Cinémathèque française*. He is President of the Society for Cinema Studies (1987-1989).

DUDLEY ANDREW directs the Institute for Cinema and Culture at the University of Iowa where he is the Angelo Bertocci Professor of Critical Studies. He has written widely on film theory and film criticism, and is the author of *The Major Film Theories, Film in the Aura of Art*, and *André Bazin*. He is currently finishing a study entitled: *Poetic Realism: The Cultural Hermeneutics of a Style*.

JACQUES AUMONT worked as a critic for *Cahiers du cinéma* for several years and now teaches film aesthetics in the Film Department of the University of Paris III at Censier. He edited the French version of the works of S. M. Eisenstein and is the author of a book on the Soviet director (*Montage Eisenstein*). He has just completed *L'Oeil interminable,* a book on the relationship between cinema and painting.

SANDY FLITTERMAN-LEWIS is Assistant Professor in the English Department at Rutgers University in New Jersey where she teaches courses in literature, film, and women's studies. A co-founder of *Camera Obscura: A Journal of Feminism and Film Theory*, she remained with the journal until 1978. She has published articles in such journals as *Screen, Wide Angle, Enclitic, Literature and Psychology,* and *Discourse* among others. Her work is anthologized in *Theories of Authorship*, *Regarding Television*, *Dada and Surrealist Film*, *Visibly Female: Feminism and Art Today*, and *Framing Feminism*. Her book, *To Desire Differently: Feminism and the French Cinema*, is on French women directors.

ANNE GILLAIN teaches film and literature in the French Department at Wellesley College, Massachussetts. She is completing two books on François Truffaut: a critical study of his films and a collection of his interviews in France and North America.

SUSAN HAYWARD teaches film and television in the Modern Languages Department at Aston University in England. Her articles on film and television have been published in such journals as *Language and Style*, *SubStance*, *Le Monde Diplomatique*, and *CinémAction*.

JEAN-PIERRE JEANCOLAS teaches history and is a film critic for *Positif*. He is the author of two books on French cinema: *15 ans d'années trente* and *Le Cinéma des Français, la Ve République, 1958-78*. He is at present working on French cinema during the years 1945-1958. His most recent book, on the new Hungarian cinema, is shortly to be published in Budapest in French. He is the vice-president of the French Association for Research in Film History.

NORMAN KING is Senior Lecturer in Film and Television Studies at Glasgow University. He has published a book on Abel Gance, *Abel Gance, a Politics of Spectacle*, and written extensively on early Romantic French Literature.

MICHELE LAGNY teaches film and history in the Film Department of the University of Paris III at Censier. She is the author, with Marie-Claire Ropars and Pierre Sorlin, of *Générique des années 30*. She is currently working on the relationship between cinema and society as seen through French cinema, on the relationship between time, film, and history, and on Visconti.

MICHEL MARIE is a lecturer in film history and aesthetics in the Film Department of the University of Paris III at Censier. His numerous publications include contributions to *Muriel, Histoire d'une recherche, Lectures du film,* and *L'Esthétique du film,* and the forthcoming *L'Analyse des films.* He is currently co-ordinating (with Michèle Lagny) a research group on early cinema and the coming of sound.

CLAIRE PAJACZKOWSKA trained in art and design at Goldsmith College, University of London. She has worked with the Heresies Collective, and with the Jay Street Collective, making films, including *Sigmund Freud's Dora.* She is a lecturer in women's studies and cultural history at Middlesex Polytechnic, London, and she also teaches film theory and practice at St Martin's School of Art. She has recently completed postgraduate research on women's relation to science, to emotions, and to the body.

KEITH A. READER is Senior Lecturer in French at Kingston Polytechnic. He is the author of a number of articles and reviews on French cinema, as well as of the books *Cultures on Celluloid* and *Intellectuals and the Left in France since 1968.* He is co-author and editor, with Ginette Vincendeau, of *La Vie est à nous: French Cinema of the Popular Front, 1935-1938.* He is currently working on Simone Weil and on a book on the May 1968 events in France.

BERENICE REYNAUD is an independent film scholar, critic, and curator, whose work has been published in many journals, including in *Afterimage, American Film, October, Screen, Cahiers du Cinéma, CinémAction,* and *Libération.* She is currently completing the third volume of *The Front Line,* a series of essays on independent cinema. A regular correspondent for international women's film and video festivals in Créteil (Paris) and Montreal, she has also curated film and video series for the Festival d'Automne in Paris, the Jerusalem Cinémathèque, The Collective for Living Cinema, and Artists Space in New York.

MARIE-CLAIRE ROPARS-WUILLEUMIER lectures at the University of Paris VIII at Saint-Denis. Her research field is the analysis and theory of filmic and literary *écriture.* Her numerous publications include over 50 articles. She has also worked on seven books, four of them as part of a team (notably *Générique des annés 30* with Michele Lagny and Pierre Sorlin), and three as a single author, including *Le Texte divisé: essai sur l' écriture filmique*. She is one of the founders of the interdisciplinary journal *Hors Cadre*.

PIERRE SORLIN lectures in contemporary history and video at the University of Paris VIII at Saint-Denis. His numerous publications include books on French history and on the sociology of the cinema. He is currently working on a comparative theoretical study of late twentieth-century European cinemas in their social context. His applied research is in documentary and historical film, and at the moment he is working on a documentary on Carpi, a small Italian town near Modena, as well as on a historical film on the Jews in France at the time of the French Revolution.

MAUREEN TURIM is Associate Professor in Theatre and Film Studies at SUNY-Binghamton. She is the author of *Abstraction in Avant-Garde Cinema* (1985) and has recently completed a book entitled *Flashbacks in Films: Memory Processes and the Subjectivity of History*. Her work on a number of topics has appeared in *Enclitic*, *Semiotica*, the AFI monograph *Cinema Histories*, *Cinema Practices*, and the anthology *New German Film Makers: From Oberhausen through the Seventies*.

GINETTE VINCENDEAU teaches in the Film Studies Department at the University of Warwick and is a member of the Editorial Board of *Screen*. She has published articles on French cinema and on women's films in *Screen*, *Framework*, *The Monthly Film Bulletin*, *Positif*, and *CinémAction*, and is the co-author and editor with Keith Reader of *La Vie est à nous: French Cinema of the Popular Front 1935-1938*. She is the British correspondent of the International Women's Film Festival in Créteil (Paris).

A nos amours...

Our particular thanks go to Simon Caulkin for his invaluable editorial advice, and to Valerie Swales and Simon Caulkin for their intellectual stimulation and special support; the editors would also like to thank Thomas Elsaesser for his initial advice; our heartfelt thanks to Françoise Bannister and Claire Turner for all their secretarial expertise and assiduity; finally, our thanks to Peter Graham, Marianne Johnson and Carrie Tarr for their talented gifts of translation.

S.H. & G.V.

Introduction

SUSAN HAYWARD and GINETTE VINCENDEAU

The study of French cinema in English-speaking countries presents something of a paradox. Whereas, undoubtedly, 'the landscape of film studies in Britain and the United States has been transformed by post-1968 developments in French film theory' (Harvey 1978, 1), the study of the cinema of France has in the main seemed to be by-passed by these developments and remained the province of rather conventional approaches: the study of film as 'reflection' of society on the one hand, and traditional auteurism on the other.

This paradoxical situation is clearly related to institutional and historical factors, starting with the fact that French cinema courses in Britain and America are often located within Modern Languages departments, with the primary aim of giving students an increased access to French *culture*, filtered through the work of individual artists on a literary analogy. As a result French film *as film* and French cinema as an institution tend to be neglected. Within Film Studies departments, French cinema is — for different reasons — also often narrowed down to the work of a few 'masters' such as Renoir and Godard. In addition, contemporary film studies (particularly in the UK) tend to subsume French cinema under the label of 'European art cinema'. As theorized by David Bordwell (1979) and Steve Neale (1981), 'European art cinema' has been defined as a set of institutional practices and as a coherent body of stylistic and narrative strategies, such as ambiguity and narrative looseness, commonly used by European 'art' filmmakers in a bid to distinguish their films from Hollywood products. Though such work has usefully taken European/French cinema away from the excessive canonization of individual artists, it has also in our view lost sight of the films' cultural specificity and has tended to obscure important differences between films as well as directors, and to make European/French cinema appear simply as Hollywood's 'other'.

Within its contemporary academic context, French cinema thus sits uneasily between French and film studies, and it seemed pertinent at this stage to attempt to bridge this gap by turning some of the concerns and methods of current film studies (hitherto overwhelmingly preoccupied with Hollywood) towards French cinema, while at the same time remaining attentive to French films' cultural inscription, a dual objective reflected in our title *French Film: Texts and contexts*.

* * *

Several sets of choices and constraints determined the format of this book and the corpus of films examined in it. The decision to concentrate on single-film essays was both methodological and practical: to provide a forum for detailed analyses, and to offer a useful format for lecturers, scholars, and students. More than any other discipline, film studies is materially bound to the availability of single texts, which is why our final list of films, beyond personal choices and contingencies, reflects a desire to concentrate on works that are easily available on 16mm hire and on video or as part of cinema repertories (although unfortunately films go in and out of distribution in an apparently random way; sometimes even 'classics' are unavailable, as Dudley Andrew points out in his essay on *Casque d'or*). Our selection, also, inevitably speaks of *auteur* cinema in a way which might seem to contradict our opening statements. But recognizing the centrality, in the French context, of *cinéma d'auteur* as a mode of production and a mode of film practice does not necessarily entail adopting an auteurist stance. Our project is, precisely, to approach significant French *auteur* films from perspectives that do not equate authorship with the personal in a narrow sense, even in instances which exemplify a very individualistic approach to filmmaking, to the point of autobiography. As Anne Gillain puts it in her essay on *Les 400 coups*, 'autobiographies, even the least sophisticated, involve elements of stylization. By turning experience into language, autobiographical narration injects it with meaning.' Similarly, the essays on films notoriously 'authored' by more than one person — Dulac/Artaud for *La Coquille et le clergyman*, Carné/Prévert for *Le Jour se lève* and *Les Enfants du paradis*, Resnais/Duras for *Hiroshima mon amour* — respectively by Sandy Flitterman-Lewis, Maureen Turim, Jean-Pierre Jeancolas, and Marie-Claire Ropars-Wuilleumier, are not concerned with unravelling the relative parenthood of the films in any anecdotal-biographical sense.

This book does not claim to offer a 'representative' portrait or history of French cinema. For one thing mainstream popular cinema is largely absent from it, and for another too many important works are perforce missing. We would be the first to agree that *L'Atalante*, *Le Corbeau*, *Le Roman d'un tricheur*, *Le Ciel est à vous*, *Bob le Flambeur*, *Lacombe Lucien*, *Céline et Julie vont en bateau*, and many others, are as central to French cinema as the works represented here. We are also acutely aware that two periods (early cinema and the 1970s) are not represented. We can only hope at this point that a second volume will give us the opportunity to continue the work contained in the present book. Looking at the titles that *are* contained in this book, there is little doubt however that the films analysed in these pages are — as the essays make abundantly clear — central texts within the canon of French cinema. Whether unavoidable 'monuments' like *Napoléon*, critical cult films like *Hiroshima mon amour* and *Le Mépris*, popular classics such as Pagnol's *Marius*, *Fanny*, and *César*, *Les Enfants du paradis*, or *Les Vacances de M. Hulot*, or recent works of the calibre of *Sans toit ni loi* and *Les Nuits de la pleine lune*, they have become part of an essential French repertory.

But our decision to concentrate on single films also relates to more fundamental questions concerning the nature of film history. If Georges Sadoul could still confidently write in 1960 that 'the most obvious constant element of French cinema since its origins, since Zecca (*Les Victimes de l'alcool*) and Méliès (*Le Voyage dans la lune*), is its faithfulness, in one way or another, to our great novelists of the last century' (Sadoul 1979, 210), the difficulties now recognized in approaching film history as a globalizing 'grand narrative' have made us more tentative in our definitions. Nineteenth-century French Realist and Naturalist literature is undoubtedly a major intertext of French cinema, but one that is very much mediated in the case of each film by a multitude of factors, among them ideological and generic constraints and the period (the difference between, say, *L'Argent*, *La Bête humaine* and *Casque d'or*). Close studies of individual texts thus seemed more useful than wide-scale generalizations, and a finer intertextual scrutiny a potentially rewarding methodology — to which we shall now turn.

* * *

Historically, French films have tended to be analysed either as privileged expressions of their *auteur*, or as direct symptoms of historical or sociological factors. Films, however, are placed within a far more complex network of determinants which include their 'makers', but also industrial and financial constraints, historical circumstances and discourses about history, the presence (or absence) of stars, generic expectations in their contemporary audience, etc. To investigate the various ways in which films textually inscribe and rework these contexts *as other texts*, the way they can be seen as 'tissue[s] of quotations drawn from the innumerable centers of culture' (Barthes 1977, 146), is the methodological project of this book. Within this overall framework, different emphases and points of entry are possible, determined by the texts themselves, as well as by the positions of their analysts. The diversity of disciplines — history, literary studies, semiotics, psychoanalysis — that forms the background of our contributors' work (and which is itself representative of the way film studies have developed in the last 20 years), guarantees such a variety of approach, which we hope will also go some way towards bridging the gaps, outlined above, between 'French' theory and the study of French cinema on the one hand, and between the methodologies employed in Film and French departments on the other. For example, the chapters by Jacques Aumont, Michel Marie, and Claire Pajaczkowska — all three on Godard's films, respectively *Le Mépris*, *A bout de souffle*, and *Sauve qui peut (la vie)* — show such a plurality in their widely different approaches. Aumont, Marie, and Pajaczkowska add new chapters to the considerable literature on Godard. Norman King and Bérénice Reynaud enter much less well charted territory and both demonstrate, in very different ways, that it is possible to speak rigorously about Rohmer's work, which has suffered as a rule from being simultaneously liked and dismissed as 'lightweight'. King's tracing of the literary connections in *Ma nuit chez Maud* goes far beyond the usual nods in the direction of Rohmer's 'literary' dialogues, while Reynaud's recourse to Lacanian psychoanalysis illuminates the sexual relationships of *Les Nuits de la pleine lune*. These are only a few examples.

The strength of the intertextual approach in our view is twofold. First it provides a theoretical framework with which to articulate the relationship between a particular textual system (a film) and texts outside it, beyond notions of influence, reflection, or faithfulness. Second, it extends the definition of these 'other texts' beyond the traditional notion of published literary works. Thus, although a number of films examined in this book are based on actual novels or plays (L'Herbier's *L'Argent*, Dulac's *La Coquille et le clergyman*, the Pagnol 'trilogy' of *Marius*, *Fanny* and *César*, Renoir's *La Bête humaine*, Cocteau's *La Belle et la Bête*, Bresson's *Le Journal d'un curé de campagne*, and Resnais' *Hiroshima mon amour*), others are not, but are nevertheless analysed for the way they quote, rework, come to terms with, and inscribe, a variety of other cultural and historical 'texts'. These range from popular and learned discourses on historical figures such as Napoleon (in *Napoléon vu par Abel Gance*), to autobiography (*Les 400 coups*) and patriarchal definitions of family and gender in films as different from each other as *Marius*, *Fanny* and *César*, *Sauve qui peut (la vie)*, *Casque d'or* and *A nos amours*; from the technological and aesthetic changes brought by the coming of sound that form a crucial sub-text as well as the main textual strategy of *Sous les toits de Paris*, to filmic allusions found in *A bout de souffle* and *Le Mépris*, or the ones, at once more oblique and more violent, in *A nos amours*; from changing leisure patterns in early 1950s France (*Les Vacances de M. Hulot*), to the very principle of literary adaptation (*Le Journal d'un curé de campagne*). They include myth and fairy tale, whether in Cocteau's rendering of *La Belle et la Bête* or in the contemporary settings of *Sans toit ni loi*. But crucially, these various texts/sub-texts/pre-texts are reworked in, deeply dependent on, and at the same time created by, cinematic forms. As Richard Abel shows in his analysis of *L'Argent*, L'Herbier's film is predicated as much on the contemporary 'modern studio spectacular' genre and on the overlap between avant-garde and commercial narratives in the 1920s, as on Zola's novel. On another Zola 'adaptation', Michèle Lagny's close analysis of *La Bête humaine* demonstrates how Renoir's textual system, and particularly disruptions in narrative causality and 'implication' on the one hand, and the ambiguous relationship between the Jean Gabin hero and the gaze on the other, inscribe Zola's notorious *fêlure* (usually assigned to purely sociological factors) in the film, and consequently create ambivalent spectator positions. Many more examples could be mentioned here, as all the essays in this book in their own way address the question of intertextual inscription. Rather than detailing them further, it seems preferable to leave their discovery to the reader.

All the essays in this book are original contributions. In our desire to combine the best developments in film studies with rigorous scholarship in French cinema, we were fortunate to be able to draw on the expertise of writers (from France, Britain, and the United States) who are not only reputed scholars in French film, but also major names in film theory and history. We wish to thank them all here for their contributions, but also for giving the book their immediate and enthusiastic commitment and support.

* * *

A few words remain to be said about the practical organization of this book. It contains 21 chapters, each focusing on one particular film; each contains a selected bibliography of works in French and in English on the film and director discussed, as well as a filmography. In addition, a general bibliography of works (also in French and in English) on French cinema will be found at the end of the book. Titles of French films are given in French within the text; the filmographies at the end of each chapter indicate English/American release titles. American spelling has been retained in contributions from American writers. Throughout the book the Harvard system of references has been used, that is to say that a short mention of author and publication details is indicated in brackets within the text, with a fuller citation in the bibliography at the end of each essay.

BIBLIOGRAPHY

Barthes, Roland (1977) *Image, Music, Text*, London, Fontana/Collins.
Bordwell, David (1979) 'The art cinema as a mode of film practice', *Film Criticism*, IV, 1, Fall 1979.
Bordwell, David, and Thompson, Kristin and Staiger, Janet (1985) *The Classical Hollywood Cinema*, London, Routledge and Kegan Paul, chapter 30.
Harvey, Sylvia (1978) *May '68 and Film Culture*, London, British Film Institute.
Neale, Steve (1981) 'Art cinema as institution', *Screen*, 22 (11).
Sadoul, Georges (1979) *Chroniques du cinéma français: 1 1939-1967*, Paris, UGE (10/18).

1. 'Poetry of the unconscious': circuits of desire in two films by Germaine Dulac: *La Souriante Mme Beudet* (1923) and *La Coquille et le clergyman* (1927)

SANDY FLITTERMAN-LEWIS

In discussions of the filmmaking career of Germaine Dulac there is often a certain tendency to contrast what are perceived as the two poles of her work, to compare two conflicting — and consecutive — cinematic practices.[1] The first is represented by *La Souriante Mme Beudet*, in which a fairly traditional narrative sequence is amplified by a whole range of suggestive poetic and cinematic techniques to evoke the inner world of its main character. The other, exemplified by a kind of anti-narrative experimentation which borders on abstraction, is seen in Surrealism's first film, *La Coquille et le clergyman*. However, from the standpoint of Dulac's own preoccupation with what constitutes an alternative language of desire 'in the feminine', there is a remarkable consistency. On the surface, it is true, no two films could be farther apart. Indeed it is just the sort of artistic and technical 'navel contemplation' demonstrated by Dulac in *Beudet* that comes under attack by the Surrealists.[2] However, the deeper commitment to feminist issues — a commitment which characterizes all of Dulac's work, from her explicitly feminist articles and interviews for such publications as *La Fronde*, to the more subtle challenges to patriarchal authority demonstrated by her continued resistance to the aesthetic domination of the mainstream commercial fiction film — strongly connects such superficially divergent projects.

Another connection between Dulac's apparently contradictory aesthetic concerns can be found in the feminist reappraisal of the notion of fantasy as a staging or performance of unconscious desire,[3] for Dulac's enthusiasm for the cinema as an expressive medium is rooted in her belief in its capacity to powerfully render the processes of the human psyche: 'The cinema is marvelously equipped to express the manifestations of our thought, of our hearts, of our memories.'[4] Contemporary feminist film theory has looked to the structures of psychoanalysis in order to better grasp both the spectator's psychical involvement in the cinema and the role of sexual difference within that. Seen from this perspective, Dulac's shift in interest from the *representation* of fantasy (through the portrayal of the intensely active and imaginative mental world of her heroine in *Beudet*) to the actual *generation* of the fantasmatic process (through the seemingly arbitrary and irrational depiction of those processes themselves in *Coquille*) can be understood as an entirely consistent evolution in her search for a new cinematic language capable of expressing female desire. At the heart of both films is an interest in the psychical mechanisms of the unconscious, an exploration of subjective reality which — whether determined by the specific confines of fictional characterization or liberated by the unmediated play of the logic of dreams — is capable of revealing not only productive insights into our deepest longings but the manner in which these might be cinematically conveyed.

The unsmiling protagonist of *Beudet*, whose revolt against the stifling constraints of a bourgeois marriage is demonstrated by a desire for liberation through fantasy, provides the point of focus for both narrative articulation and spectator identification. The film's slim plot involves one day in the life of a cultured and sensitive provincial housewife (Germaine Dermoz) and her oppressively vulgar fabric-merchant husband (Arquillière). One evening, having found her piano locked by M. Beudet, who is at a performance of *Faust*, Mme Beudet loads the gun which her husband — in a jokingly sadistic parody of suicide — often puts to his head. The next morning, overcome by guilt, fear, and remorse, she unsuccessfully tries to empty the chamber prior to the habitual joke's repetition, but before she can do so Beudet impulsively aims the gun at her instead. The film climaxes and resolves ironically, as the egotistical husband mistakenly interprets the loaded gun as his wife's suicide attempt, and his renewed appreciation of her is matched by Mme Beudet's resignation — and the implied closing off of any future possibilities for her fertile imaginative world.

Yet it is the very interiority of this world which comprises the majority of the film's 40 minutes. Dulac uses a whole range of experimental cinematic techniques in order to represent Mme Beudet's dreams and desires, to filmically render female subjectivity through the metaphoric figuration of her character's fantasies. Through a battery of technical devices ranging from dissolves, punctuating fades and irises, soft-focus and superimpositions to both slowed-down and accelerated motion, distorting lenses, camera manipulations and unusual angles, Dulac creates a highly charged visual atmosphere for these mini-scenarios of the fantasmatic. The actual narrative action of the film, as I've noted, is relatively sparse; it is in the visual orchestration of the memories, dreams, hallucinations, and fantasies which constitute Mme Beudet's inner world that Dulac's prime interest in cinematic experimentation can be found. In her desire to eliminate those constraints on expression implied by the logic of narrative causality and of character development through action, Dulac turned to music as a model for cinematic composition. For her, the unmediated directness of the visual image could best be conveyed through a musical form:

> Shouldn't the cinema — an art of vision, as music is an art of hearing — lead us … toward the visual idea, made of movement and of life, toward a conception of an art of the eye composed of emotional inspiration, evolving in its continuity and attaining, just as music does, our thoughts and feelings? [5]

Thus for the 'imaginary' sequences in *Beudet* images are chosen for their evocative power, for their ability to suggest a state of mind or feeling, rather than for their strict application to dramatic or causal requirements of the narrative, and this accounts for what can be considered the visual richness of this relatively uncomplicated story.

Yet, although a universalist assumption of consciousness might be inferred from Dulac's formulation of the musical analogy, it is not simply a generalized notion of fantasy that interests her here; clearly, in *Beudet*, she is concerned to articulate what might be called a feminine 'imaginary', as she makes the exploration of *female* subjectivity the very core of her film. For this reason, the fantasy sequences — organized in each instance by a relay of mental associations — are anchored in the particulars of the woman character which she creates, a frustrated, imprisoned housewife who longs for some sort of romantic evasion. Thus a focus on the *content* of the representation of fantasy is necessary as Dulac finds metaphoric equivalents and subjective distortions for each of Mme Beudet's imaginings. The most complete realization of this filmic rendering of unconscious processes is found in what can be called the 'fantasy-solitude' sequence of the film, a series of seven segments in which Mme Beudet's fantasies take hold and overpower her in the moments preceding her decision to load her husband's gun.[6] However, although this sequence is virtually the longest in the entire film, comprising roughly one-fifth of its shots, Dulac is careful to prepare this cinematic explosion of perception, fantasy, and desire by a number of shorter subjective sequences, momentary indications of the power of Mme Beudet's imaginative capacities.

This 'prologue' to the fantasy sequence has a trajectory of its own, for it moves from a purely mental representation of Mme Beudet's thoughts, through a metaphoric image signifying her wish for escape, to an imagined scenario of desire in which a fantasm of her creation actually interacts with the space of the room where the Beudets sit. This gradation in the type of mental or unconscious operation is matched by an increase in duration, as each of the three sequences furthers the demonstration of Dulac's interest in combining the experimental techniques of the 'First Avant-Garde' with a cinematic elaboration of female desire. There is in this progression a movement from a more conventionally accepted icon of feminine resistance, through a momentary display of the power of the female imagination, to a situation which locates the productive capacity to dream (and thereby enact the possibility of liberation) within the female psyche itself. In this way the prologue prepares the more extensively developed fantasy sequence, whose conclusion to the complex visual chain of associations results in the ultimate act of resistance, a fantasy of murder.

The first of these sequences is a simple exchange of two pairs of shots, each representing the Beudets' part in a conversation. M. Beudet tries to convince his wife to see *Faust* and she replies with a polite shake of her head. A close-up of M. Beudet singing (fade to black) is followed by a shot of the opera chorus, while Mme Beudet's close-up (again, fade to black) leads into a glowering Mephistopheles, large in the left foreground, and a resisting Marguerite, arm stretched out to fend off his intrusion. Although the first of these has been attributed to Dulac's attempt to give some small measure of subjectivity to other characters,[7] I maintain, instead, that Dulac's chief interest is in the subjective experience of her female character and the possibilities it represents for expressing feminine desire. From this standpoint, M. Beudet's shot simply illustrates what he is saying (a silent film convention), while Mme Beudet's shot — a representation of her thoughts — is a first indication of the interiority that will control our identification with her throughout the film.

This is an appropriate preparation for the sequence which follows, the first demonstration of Mme Beudet's ability to imaginatively call up an image of something longed-for, and thus a mark of the shift from a mental image to the representation of a wish. The five shots of this sequence cluster around a subjective inversion of the reverse-shot structure, a cinematic figure conventionally used to indicate perceptual point-of-view. Instead of the traditional alternation of character seeing/object seen, Dulac gives us a sequence transformation from *perception* to *imagination* as a close-up of a car advertisement (for a Sizaire-Berwick) in a journal dissolves to a profile close-up of Mme Beudet reading, and its fade to black then opens on a shot of the miniature car gliding across a background of clouds. The sequence ends on an extreme close-up of Mme Beudet's eyes (reminiscent of a subsequent use of this ethereal and haunting shot in *Coquille*, to which I will return), as the frame is filled with eyes that close — in resignation or in satisfaction. Thus the momentary insertion of two anti-naturalistic shots within the context of the narrative development serves to illustrate Dulac's interest in mental processes and her related belief in the close-up as a powerfully evocative expressive tool: she called the close-up a 'psychological shot' because of its peculiar ability to materialize 'the very thoughts, souls, emotions, and desires of the characters projected on the screen'.[8] But more importantly, this first indication of Mme Beudet's fantasmatic capacity to escape what she cannot leave in reality reflects Dulac's own desire to cinematically represent the psychic force of the human mind as well as her uncanny ability to designate such subtle distinctions as those between thought, imagination, and, ultimately, unconscious fantasy.

The last preparatory sequence depicts precisely that latter process of the unconscious, for in it Mme Beudet advances from a picture that she imagines to a fantasmatic scenario which she directs. Having succeeded in mentally projecting an image of a vehicle for escape (if only for an instant), she is now able to envision a little *mise-en-scène* of action in the form of a confrontation between an imaginary lover and the oppressive husband who sits across from her. In no fewer than twenty-four shots the sequence depicts a phantom tennis player (come to life from the pages of the magazine by means of a superimposition) who waltzes over to M. Beudet's desk, lifts him bodily and carries him off. To Mme Beudet's spontaneous — and exceptional — eruption of laughter, M. Beudet responds in mimicked glee, taking the gun from the

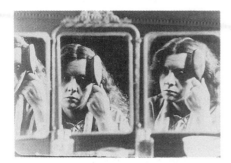

La Souriante Mme Beudet — above left: Mme Beudet (Germaine Dermoz); above right: Mme Beudet and M. Beudet (Alexandre Arquillère).
La Coquille et le clergyman — below left: the clergyman (Alex Allin); below right: the general (Lucien Bataille).

drawer as a title-card explains: 'A stupid and oft-repeated joke, dear to M. Beudet: The suicide-parody.' A subjective shot of the blanched and contorted face of M. Beudet in large close-up (Dulac's cinematic distortion to suggest Mme Beudet's emotional attitude toward her husband) is matched by a profile shot of Mme Beudet wincing. The return to a more 'realistic' shot of M. Beudet as he places the gun back in the desk and shrugs, is followed by alternation of similar shots and shrugs.

This sequence is notable for a number of reasons. First, it is the introduction of the suicide joke which will generate the central dramatic action of the film. But, and this is the second point, this joke is not presented in the form of a simple narrative event. Rather, it is prefaced by the first example of Mme Beudet's mental ability to 'create' a character of her own who performs in a fantasmatic scene enacted within the *actual* space of her life, a fictive character capable of representing (through action) her desire to rebel against her despotic husband. And so powerful is this imaginary scene that it can accomplish what nothing else in her oppressive existence can do — it makes her laugh. A smile that explodes in one single moment of the film thus gives renewed ironic substance to its title, for it is not simply that Mme Beudet *never* smiles; she is, in fact, quite capable of smiling — even laughing — but only as a result of the power of her own fantasmatic capability. Thirdly, the conclusion of the sequence is a foreshadowing of the film's ending itself. The two shots of the back of Mme Beudet's head function in direct contrast to her interaction with the fantasy tennis player. In the moments when we see her face, we observe her as the sole member of an audience reacting to a scenario of her own creation, and are thus given access to her interiority. But when the *back* of her head is depicted, there is a sealing off of this capacity to fictively interact, and of our capacity to identify as well. Therefore, just as these last shots of the sequence represent a temporary cessation of Mme Beudet's imaginative activity, the final images of the film itself signify a similar — and this time permanent — closure. The film's ending shot depicts M. and Mme Beudet in American-shot, seen from the back, as they continue down the provincial cobblestone street toward the vanishing point of the frame. Mme Beudet's resignation to the suffocating trap of bourgeois marriage is signified by the narrative action; the impossibility of future flights of fantasy is equally emphasized by the symbolic 'closed door' of the back of the head. To return to the sequence under analysis, then, the hostile sarcasm of the exchange between the couple which concludes this fantasized scene (of the tennis player's triumph) is a forceful indication of the power of Mme Beudet's painful reality to limit and confine her imagination's play.

But because Dulac's *character* can no longer fantasize, this does not mean that the filmmaker herself ceases to be concerned with the representation of unconscious processes in her subsequent work. Quite the contrary; what is significant about precisely those passages which signify subjectivity in *Beudet* is the fact that they represent one stage in Dulac's sustained exploration of the processes of the psyche which is to continue, at another level, in *La Coquille et le clergyman*. As I indicated at the outset of this essay, Dulac's interest in the mechanisms of the unconscious remains constant throughout her filmmaking career. What marks the difference between the earlier and the later films is a modification in the type of spectatorial involvement required by each text. Whereas the spectator is made to identify with a specific character whose thoughts, dreams, and fantasies are represented within the confines of a fiction in *Beudet*, what *Coquille* elicits is the spectator's actual participation in the *experience* of those psychic processes themselves.

In order to better understand this distinction it is necessary to take a closer look at what is meant by 'psychic processes' in discussions of the cinema. Contemporary film theory posits that the film spectator is in some sense 'constructed' in and by the viewing experience, and that fictive participation in the film's events has its roots in fantasy. The notion of fantasy runs through all theoretical work on the cinema, for fantasy — in its definition as a wish-fulfilling staging of desire — is at the base of all 'stories told in images', all moving visual representations such as dreams, films, and the like. In the words of French post-Freudians Jean Laplanche and J.-B. Pontalis, 'Unconscious ideas are organized into phantasies or imaginary scenarios to which the instinct becomes fixated and which may be conceived as true *mise-en-scènes* of desire', and 'even where they can be summed up in a single sentence, phantasies are still scripts ... of organized scenes which are capable of dramatization — usually in a visual form'.[9] Within this framework, desire is understood not as a relation to a real object, independent of a subject and capable of being satsified, but as a relation to a representation, a relation of the subject which circulates in an infinite process. And it is the intersection of film and unconscious fantasy in a notion of performance which accounts for the mobilization of the spectator's desire in the viewing situation.

It can be successfully argued that *La Coquille et le clergyman* represents one of the first attempts to cinematically render these unconscious forces in a way that engages the viewer in a process of identification with the film-text *itself*, rather than with any specific fictional construct in the form of characters. Acknowledged as the first example of Surrealist cinema — both chronologically and aesthetically — Dulac's film is based on a script by the revolutionary poet and dramatist Antonin Artaud. This double authorship has been the source of much critical confusion, for the riot which accompanied the film's inaugural screening on 9 February 1928 has led to extensive debates concerning artistic theory, intentionality, and cinematic transcription from verbal to visual text.[10] What interests me here, however, is the way that *Coquille*'s articulation of hallucinations, dream-images, fantasms and obsessions is consistent with Dulac's exploration of unconscious processes throughout her career, and how, in fact, this suggests possibilities for the conceptualization and expression of feminine desire. It is within this context that I consider both Dulac and Artaud as having similar conceptions of the film and compatible impulses behind its realization. For purposes of the present analysis, I thus emphasize the correspondence of authorial voices.[11]

To attempt to describe the 'plot' of *Coquille* is immediately to situate oneself within its central problematic, for the film consists of a series of moments which are connected associatively without any regard for narrative logic or causality. It is precisely the unpredictability and confusion of dreams which Artaud sought in his scenario, a succession of images 'in a film constructed according to the dark and hidden rules of the unconscious', images which would follow each other despotically, arbitrarily, relentlessly in a 'poetry of the unconscious ... which is the only poetry possible'.[12] This pure poetry of visual elements was intended to approximate subjectivity by recreating the impact of the dream *as it is being dreamed*:

> [*La Coquille et le clergyman* attempts] to find, in the occult birth and wanderings of feeling and thought, the deep reasons, the active and veiled impulses of our so-called lucid acts [.] [This] scenario can resemble, can be related to *the mechanism of a dream* without actually being a dream itself. [It seeks to] restore the pure work of thought.[13]

Thus a simple outline of the visual situations which follow each other for no apparent reason is the closest one can come to a narrative description, for the significance of each sequence of images comes from its suggestive relationships (its representation of thought processes) rather than from its content (its motivation through character development).

A clergyman (Alex Allin) fills beakers with a black liquid from an oyster-shell, then lets them shatter on the floor; a general (Lucien Bataille) arrives and brandishes his saber; the clergyman follows him through the city-streets to a church, where an astonishingly beautiful woman in eighteenth-century attire (Génica Athanasiou) suddenly appears; there is a confrontation in the confessional, as the officer abruptly becomes a priest; after tossing the priest from a cliff, the clergyman takes the latter's place in the confessional, then, confronting the woman, rips off her bodice, which turns into a carapace of shell-shaped armor. There is next a wildly dancing society-crowd into which a royal couple (the general and the woman) arrive, followed by the clergyman brandishing first the seashell and then the carapace; as he drops the carapace, which disappears in flames, all of a sudden his coat-tails grow and expand across the parquet floor; suddenly, he is chasing the woman down a country road, as she metamorphoses (through close-ups) into a series of facial distortions; he continues to chase her through several hallways with closing doors until, finally, he enters a room where there is a large globe on a pedestal; he beckons to the (unseen) woman, captures her head and places it inside the ball; now jauntily trying his key on a number of doors, the clergyman again sees the royal couple and this time pursues them both through the hallways and on the country road. Pounding fists wake the clergyman who is asleep on a hammock on a ship; he spies the general and the woman kissing, a sight which prompts an attempt to strangle her fantasized neck in a movement which initiates a series of dream-like images of glittering stalactites, islands, shimmering water, a tiny sailing ship, mist. Abruptly, a corps of maids emerges into a room, busily dusting as the woman, now a governess, takes charge; there is a couple (the clergyman and the woman) playing tennis, then a return to the maids who clean the globe as a group of butlers arrives; a return to the tennis scene precedes the arrival in the room of the clergyman and the woman, now as a wedding couple; a close-up of the clergyman's head initiates a series of dream-images which are displayed on four different portions of his face; suddenly the headless clergyman descends the stairs, holding the glass ball; he then arrives in the room as the servants line up; a panning shot of their eyes causes the clergyman to drop the globe, which shatters on the floor, his face emerging among the shards; he stands, now with the oyster-shell in his hand, then drinks from the shell which has his head in it, and the film ends as he drinks the black liquid — and his own image — which pours from the seashell.

Again it is Artaud's words which clarify this apparent narrative confusion and indicate the profound systematicity at work beneath the film's surface disorientation.

> *La Coquille et le clergyman* does not tell a story, but develops a series of states of mind, just as one thought derives from another, without needing to reproduce a logical sequence of events. From the clash of objects and gestures, true psychic situations are derived, and from these rational thinking, trapped, can only seek a subtle escape.[14]

What is particularly illuminating for the purposes of this article is the manner in which an emphasis on psychic processes eliminates the distinction between internal and external necessitated by the conventional fiction film, for it is precisely this latter kind of film which must develop narrative alibis and rational explanations for the appearance of every one of its images. In the traditional film a veneer of narrative complications acts as an explanatory frame for the arbitrariness of the subjective images, while in *Coquille* the absence of this frame allows the spectator him/herself to actually participate in the fantasmatic process. Once liberated from the constraints of these narrative conventions, the unconscious forces of desire which circulate in the cinematic text are available to the spectator who is, in fact, psychically positioned as the *producer* of the fiction. Far from being a facile depiction of dream associations on the screen, therefore, *Coquille* attempts to reproduce — *for the spectator's active engagement* — the actual production process of desire, its perpetual metamorphoses as it circulates from representation to representation. And it is no coincidence that this is associated specifically with the representation of the female figure, for throughout the text the elusive quality of the female figure is equated with that of desire in its evanescence. The woman's image is repeatedly generated as a fantasm of vision throughout the film, as femininity is thematized as desire.[15] Therefore it can be said that conceptions of the 'feminine' do not disappear from *Coquille*, but are reoriented in such a way as to associate them more fundamentally with unconscious processes.

In addition to the plot, the concept of 'character' is equally under assault, for while in *Beudet* it is the female protagonist who occasions the cinematic representation of fantasy, in *Coquille* it is the spectator who is the subject of vision and desire. Thus in *Beudet* we find a continual use of character to mediate the textual work, as each representation of the fantasm is anchored in a notion of individual psychology; each depiction of thoughts and internal longings, each transformation of objective reality into the fantastic, amplifies our understanding of Mme Beudet's desires. But in *Coquille* the concept of character is obviated altogether. Instead of a single protagonist used to focus and organize the identificatory processes of the spectator, there is a multiplicity of positions available within the fantasmatic scenario, and this fantasy, in fact, comprises the entire film. Again, this form of dispersed subjectivity expands the notion of 'fiction' in the film, for it puts the viewer rather than the character in the place of the desiring producer of the fantasm. There are thus numerous relations of identification with both characters and functions as the film's 'story' becomes a series of dramatized relationships and narrative moments and the spectator perpetually slides between and among them.

This is made clear both from the opening words of the scenario and the inaugurating images of the film. 'The camera-lens discovers a man dressed in black...'[16] writes Artaud, as Dulac presents several subjective point-of-view shots (before any 'character' has been introduced) which advance, in dissolves, down a dark corridor toward a lighted doorway with stairs. This has the effect of installing the spectator immediately in the midst of an undifferentiated image-flow, a series of orchestrated visions which, from this point on, will negotiate the viewer through the generalized dream-consciousness which is the film: this is *not* the fantasy of an individual character. In this way both filmmaker and scenarist recreate the *experience* of the dream, permitting the viewer to psychically interact with each successive visual transformation as it circulates through — and thus constructs — the dream-space of the film. This latter space, a generalized everywhere of the unconscious, is matched by a temporal dislocation in which association replaces chronology, for characters appear in several places at once, actions lack consequences, and day and night intermingle unexpectedly. It is as if the very projection of the film is a materialization of Artaud's words on the capacity of cinema to approximate the logic of unconscious desire:

> Dreams have a logic of their own — but more than that, they have a life of their own in which nothing but dark and intelligent truths appear. This scenario seeks out the sombre truth of the mind, in images emerging uniquely from

themselves, images which do not draw their meaning from the situation in which they develop, but from a sort of powerful inner necessity which projects them in the light of merciless obviousness ['évidence sans recours'].[17]

A quick tracing of the manner in which the notion of character gives way to a dispersed spectatorial subjectivity throughout the film will demonstrate the power of the Surrealist text to engage the viewer's participation in the meaning-making process. The opening sequence just mentioned — an oneiric succession of Expressionistically-lit camera pans from top to bottom and a dolly forward — suggests a vertiginous, disorienting plunge into a realm in which spatial and temporal coordinates have been dissolved: this can be seen to represent the scene of the unconscious where the dramas of the psyche are played out, and it thus signifies the replacement of traditional characters with ones who symbolize, in a more general way, the forces of subjectivity. As for the 'clergyman' of the film's title, he is introduced to us from the back of the head, for the viewer does not see his face (and thus distinguishing characteristics) until well into the sequence of shattered vials and the officer's apparition. But even as a frontal close-up reveals an ecclesiastical collar, the written screenplay still refers to him as 'the man dressed in black', and continues to do so until he follows the officer through the city streets. Even at this point, Artaud is hesitant to be too specific; he slides, instead, from 'the man in black who looks very much like a clergyman ...' to a final solidification of meaning when he describes this character *being seen*: 'We see the clergyman on all fours trotting along the cobblestone street.'

It is precisely this passage through the urban landscape which provides the next spectatorial experience, for what appears on the screen is a succession of street corners to indicate the transit on city streets, all from different (low) angles, all dissolving or superimposed, and all emphatically marked as point-of-view shots. Importantly, the absence of a character — a fictional perceiving subject from whom this point-of-view might emerge — reinforces the position of the spectator as the site of viewing subjectivity, as it simultaneously recalls the film's opening shots and their concomitant suggestion of psychic space. This type of experiential sequence — or rather, subjective sequence without a subject — recurs throughout the film, each time representing a state of psychic reality which places the viewer at the center of the process. The wild party which precedes the entry of the royal couple is filmed in such a way as to render the experience of delirium and intoxication suggested by the scene: accelerated motion, unusual angles, circular camera movement, superimpositions, images which border on abstraction — all are used to convey a sense of psychic participation in the event. Likewise, the clergyman's later action of opening successive doors occurs in undifferentiated darkness, in a materialization of the experience of the hermeneutic process. In each of these sequences, precisely because of their relative undecipherability and their placement at the limits of abstraction, something of Artaud's vision of the spectator is achieved: 'The mind is affected outside of all representation. This sort of virtual power of the image finds hitherto unutilized possibilities in the very depths of the mind.'[18]

There are numerous other sequences in the film which actualize psychic processes, and they can be categorized (in addition to the sequences of dispersed subjectivity just discussed) in terms of: [1] the use of characters as cultural constructs, symbolic representations of masculinity and femininity, of patriarchal authority and female sexuality; [2] the use of shots or sequences which foreground vision, such as the staging of the primal scene or the emphatic elaboration of the gaze and structures of looking; [3] the representation of a dreaming consciousness as evidenced by the apparition of metamorphosing objects and fantastic visions; [4] the depiction of a subjectivity turned in on itself, as exemplified by the film's conclusion, which repeats its beginning in a parable of film spectatorship, the clergyman consuming his own image in an act of narcissistic absorption. The limits of this article do not permit detailed elaboration of each of these, but one tiny moment — an exchange of two shots — condenses all five categories with striking clarity and bears some discussion here.

This pair of shots is the 'eyeline match' *par excellence*, for it is, quite simply, the alternation of two large close-ups of eyes (gauzily masked to render everything else in the image a hazy blur) — first the woman's, then the clergyman's. This exchange, embedded within sequences which dramatize religious hypocrisy and erotic violence, seems, by its very energy, to erupt from the more narrational instances which surround it. This is how Artaud's scenario describes the action:

> The woman and the clergyman are praying in a confessional. The clergyman's head quivers like a leaf, and all of a sudden it seems that something begins to speak inside him. He pushes up his sleeves and gently, ironically, knocks three times on the partition of the confessional. The woman gets up. Then the clergyman bangs with his fist and opens the door like a fanatic. The woman stands before him and looks at him. He throws himself on her and tears off her bodice as if he had wanted to lacerate her breasts.[19]

In keeping with her usual practice, Dulac renders — in detailed images and gestures — each action described. Yet for one small moment she diverges from the written scenario to depict these eyes, and this is highly significant. For it is precisely in their capacity to act as *signs* that these haunting, elusive images function to evoke exactly those processes of unconscious figuration which are central to the film in its effort to create, *for the spectator*, the experience of the fantasm. In their isolation, their fragmentary status, they aid the dissolution of character and the redirection toward psychic processes by emphasizing vision itself. In so doing, these pairs of eyes create an ambiguous space of interpretation for the viewer, a site in which character psychology is only one option among many others in determining the symbolic value of the shot. It is possible, for example, to regard this exchange of glances as one instance in the circulation throughout the film of cultural signifiers of femininity and masculinity — hers the alert and watchful eyes of a female victim, his the lustful eyes of a violent brute. This is, after all, a confrontation with an extensive representational heritage. From another standpoint, these shots can be seen to take their place in a paradigm of subjective images and dream distortions; it is generally this sort of close-up which is linked to the flow of glistening castles, shimmering water, and the like in the film.

Yet there is something different about these shots as well, a difference that recalls the slide of subjectivity back into itself. Although Artaud's script specifies only the gaze of the woman (as opposed to that of the man), Dulac chose to emphasize the actual fact of looking in a reciprocity of vision that blurs the distinction between characters. This slippage is characteristic of a film whose very textual processes have worked to establish an association between the woman and the clergyman's identity, between his pursuit of her and his quest for himself. But more important than that, here Dulac is able to give both characters the privilege of visuality, and in so doing she reaffirms the psychic reality that is the mainspring of the film. You will remember that there is a similar close-up of eyes in *La Souriante Mme Beudet*, a shot which was used to amplify our understanding of the character, her desperate need for escape and her imaginative capacity to envision flight. When this type of shot reappears in *Coquille*, in what amounts to an echo of the earlier film, it reinforces the latter film's project, not of recounting the dream or the daydream, but of portraying the unconscious figural processes of dreams themselves. And this gives new significance to those three knocks that the clergyman makes on the confessional panel. In the tradition of French theater, three knocks were sounded at the beginning of each performance in order to signal that the play was about to begin. A preparatory gesture, it set the scene and focused the attention of the audience toward the stage. In the context of the clergyman's three knocks, a narrative reading would suggest that this denotes the end of the confessional session. However, from a *textual* standpoint, this minute gesture, with a historical tradition of theatricality, subtly suggests something more profound, and more in keeping with the problematic of the film: a scene is about to be played out, to be sure, but it is a drama of vision on the stage of the psyche, a staging of desire for both 'character' and spectator.

And this brings us back to my original discussion of Dulac. For it is with just such a notion of fantasy as an unconscious staging of desire that the requirements of Dulac's triple project — experimentation with cinematic language and its constructions of the spectator, exploration of the structures of unconscious fantasy, and research into the possibilities for representing (female) desire — can be met. Dulac took the first important steps in *La Souriante Mme Beudet*, where she used an imaginative battery of technical devices to illustrate the content of her female character's fantasies. *La Coquille et le clergyman*, however, offered the process of desire itself in a move which shifted from a fictional character as subject of the fantasy to the spectator as subject of the fantasmatic process. The implication of every viewer's direct affective access to the film via the unconscious and the concomitant power of interpretation is something echoed by Artaud: 'To understand this film it is only necessary to look deeply into oneself. To give in to this sort of plastic, objective, attentive examination of the internal I...' ('**MOI** interne').[20] Mme Beudet's mental universe (shared with the spectator, though not with other characters) becomes the generalized collective fantasm of *Coquille*, a realm of desire in which each unexpected, incongruous image affords the unconscious of the spectator free rein.

For Dulac, *Coquille* marked a step toward the kind of film she most desired — an abstract cinematic poem which worked with a circulation of figures and connotations in order to elicit the spectator's own participation in the meaning-process. In what amounts to a short manifesto, she claimed a priority for the spectator in the cinematic process:

> Yes, lines, volumes, surfaces, light, envisioned in their constant metamorphoses, are capable of taking hold of us by their rhythms if we know how to organize them in a construction capable of responding to the needs of our imagination and our feelings ...[21]

To the feminist critic looking for easy answers, this seems to pose a problem at first, for the notion of a generalized collective fantasm has nothing gender-specific about it. However, too abrupt a conclusion in this vein overlooks the powerful implications of an alternative form of cinematic discourse conceived to articulate something utterly new. It is not a question of what is 'feminine' about the fantasy — for all of us, women and men, partake of subjective processes — but of a mode of engagement in the cinema that works with each individual's interpretative capacities in a liberating way. The feminist import of such a project can be found in the creation of a new language of desire. In cinematic terms this suggests the multiple positionalities offered by the text. Cinematic identification is an immeasurably complicated process. *Coquille* contributes to a progressive formulation by offering to its spectators the position of 'a look', a series of possible identifications, rather than the fixity of an identity. For we are never (or perhaps always) in the film simply one character or another — the clergyman or the woman. We are only, or above all, a perceiving subjectivity, among their avatars and between the two. An understanding of female fantasy is only possible if we have some idea of how that fantasy comes about, what produces it, and how it engages significations for the subject. In this respect, both *La Souriante Mme Beudet* and *La Coquille et le clergyman* suggest the critical nexus of psychoanalysis and the cinema, sexuality and representation crucial to feminist thinking, for the question of feminine desire is the question of desire itself.

NOTES

1. This article is a version of part of a larger study of Dulac's work (in relation to the work of two other filmmakers, Marie Epstein and Agnès Varda), entitled *To Desire Differently: Feminism and the French Cinema*, forthcoming from the University of Illinois Press. I would like to dedicate the present article in memory of Claire Johnston, whose work continues to be an inspiration.

2. Here are two examples of the Surrealist critique regarding the aestheticizing of the so-called 'First Avant-Garde'. In a lecture given at the Vieux Colombier Theater on 14 June 1930, filmmaker Jean Vigo stated: 'To aim at a social cinema would be to consent to work a mine of subjects which reality ceaselessly renews.... It would be to avoid the overly artistic subtlety of a pure cinema which contemplates its super-navel from one angle, yet another angle, always another angle, a super-angle; technique for technique's sake.' (This manifesto, entitled 'Toward a Social Cinema', is translated in *Millenium Film Journal*, 1977, I, 1, 21-24.) And in a polemical statement of purpose, Luis Buñuel is quite explicit about the object of his attack: 'Historically, [*Un Chien andalou*] represents a violent reaction against what was at that time called 'avant-garde ciné', which was directed exclusively to the artistic sensibility and to the reason of the spectator, with its play of light and shadow, its photographic effects, its preoccupation with rhythmic montage and technical research, and at times in the direction of the display of a perfectly conventional and reasonable mood. To this avant-garde cinema group belonged Ruttmann, Cavalcanti, Man Ray, Dziga-Vertov, René Clair, Dulac, Ivens, etc.' (This is from 'Notes making *Un Chien andalou*', collected in Frank Stauffacher, ed. [1947] *Art in Cinema*, San Francisco Art Institute, 29.) While the grouping of Vertov, Clair, Man Ray, and, of course, Dulac within this a-political avant-garde is debatable, the clarity with which Buñuel defines the aesthetic enemy is not.

3. See in particular Elisabeth Cowie (1984) 'Fantasia', *m/f*, 9, 70-105, and Elisabeth Lyon (1980) 'The Cinema of Lol V. Stein', *Camera Obscura*, 6, 7-53.

4. Germaine Dulac (1924) 'Les Procédés expressifs du cinématographe', *Cinémagazine*, 28, 68. This is a transcript of a talk given by Dulac on 17 June 1924, at the Musée Galliera. All translations from the French are my own unless otherwise noted.

5. Dulac (1925) 'L'Essence du cinéma, l'idée visuelle', *Les Cahiers du mois*, 16/17, 64. Another translation of this article, by Robert Lamberton, can be found in P. Adams Sitney, ed. (1978), 36-42.

6. I discuss this sequence in detail in my book, where I concentrate on the different types of subjective image used to render Mme Beudet's thoughts and fantasies.

7. See Richard Abel's insightful discussions of Dulac in Abel (1984).

8. Dulac (1924), 68.

9. Jean Laplanche and J.-B. Pontalis (1974) *The Language of Psychoanalysis*, New York, W.W. Norton, 475 and 318 respectively.

10. When the film was shown, a riot broke out in which Dulac and the film were violently insulted. There is some confusion as to whether Artaud himself participated in the commotion and, in fact, several of the protesters believed that they were attacking Artaud. For a complete account, in French, see Artaud (1978) *Les Oeuvres complètes d'Antonin Artaud*, Paris, Gallimard, III, 326-327. It is this volume which contains all of Artaud's film scenarios, letters and texts concerning the cinema; the edition date is important as each edition of *Les Oeuvres complètes* contains new material and different pagination. As with the Dulac texts, all translations are my own. Richard Abel (op. cit.) also describes the event in some detail. For discussion of the film, I refer the reader to my two articles (Flitterman [1984] and [1987]). In the first article, I concentrate on representations of the woman as a counter to traditional feminist arguments about the misogyny of the film. The second article deals in depth with the Dulac-Artaud debate in terms of conflicting aesthetic theories of Symbolist poetic fusion and Surrealist juxtaposition.

11. Although Dulac's film follows the scenario, image for image, with extreme precision, there is still a very complex relation between the two texts (I explore this in detail in Flitterman [1987] and in my forthcoming book).

12. Artaud (1978) 'Letter to Jean Paulhan, 22 January 1932', 259-260; there is a translation by Helen Weaver in Artaud (1976), 281.

13. Artaud (1928) *La Coquille et le clergyman, Cahiers de Belgique*, 8, and in Artaud (1978), 71.

14. Artaud (1927) 'Le cinéma et l'abstraction', *Le Monde illustré*, 3645, and in Artaud (1978), 68. A translation can be found in Sontag (1976),149-150, as well as in *Tulane Drama Review*, 1966, XI, 1, 166-185, where a number of Artaud's scenarios and texts on the cinema have been collected in English.

15. I treat this representation of the female figure in depth in Flitterman (1984).

16. The scenario for *Coquille* is reprinted in Artaud (1978), 18-25. There is a translation by Victor Corti in *Tulane Drama Review* (op. cit.), 173-178.

17. Artaud (1927) 'Cinéma et réalité', *La Nouvelle revue française*, 170, and Artaud (1978), 19. This article functioned as an introduction to the scenario for *Coquille*, which was published in the same issue. English translations are in Sontag (1976), 150-152, and *Tulane Drama Review* (op. cit.).

18. Artaud (1978) 'Sorcellerie et cinéma', 66. Written at the time of the shooting of *Coquille,* this article does not appear to have been published until 1949, when it appeared in the catalogue of the Festival du Film Maudit, Biarritz, 29 July-5 August,1949. Translations are in *Tulane Drama Review* (op. cit.), 178-180, Sitney (1978), 49-50, and Paul Hammond, ed. (1978), 63-64.

19. Artaud (1978), 67. Translations in Hammond (1978), 64, and Sitney (1978), 50.

20. Artaud (1978), 67. Translations in Hammond (1978), 64, and Sitney (1978), 50.

21. Dulac, 'Du Mouvement, des harmonies, et du rythme: A la symphonie visuelle', 6, chapter VIII of an unpublished manuscript of texts collected by Marie-Anne Colson-Malleville, Dulac's close personal friend and assistant from the time of Dulac's divorce in 1920.

SELECTED BIBLIOGRAPHY

Included in this bibliography is only a selection of Dulac's (prolific) writings which have been translated into English; the same goes for Artaud. For an extensive list of Dulac's articles in French, consult Abel (1984); for the French texts of Artaud's writings on the cinema see Artaud (1978).

Abel, Richard (1975) 'The Contribution of the French Literary Avant-Garde to Film Theory and Criticism', *Cinema Journal*, 14.
Abel, Richard (1984) *French Cinema: The First Wave 1915-1929*, Princeton, Princeton University Press.
Artaud, Antonin (1976) in Susan Sontag (ed.) *Antonin Artaud: Selected Writings*, trans. Helen R. Weaver, New York, Farrar, Strauss and Giroux.
Artaud, Antonin (1978) *Les Oeuvres complètes d'Antonin Artaud*, III, Paris, Gallimard.
Cornwell, Regina (1979) 'Maya Deren and Germaine Dulac: Activists of the Avant-Garde', in Patricia Erens (ed.) *Sexual Stratagems*, New York, Horizon Press.
deMiro, Ester Carla (1979) 'Germaine who?' (Excerpts and translation of Dulac's 'Du sentiment à la ligne' by Felicity Sparrow) in *Film as Films: Formal Experiment in Film 1910-1975*, London, Arts Council of Great Britain.
Dozoretz, Wendy (1979) 'Dulac Versus Artaud', *Wide Angle*, 3 (1).
Dorozetz, Wendy (1982) 'Mme Beudet's Smile: Feminine or Feminist?', *Film Reader*, 5.
Dulac, Germaine (1978) 'Visual and Anti-Visual films', 'The Essence of Cinema: The Visual Idea', and 'The Avant-Garde Cinema', in P. Adams Sitney (ed.) *The Avant-Garde Film: A Reader in Theory and Criticism*, New York, New York University Press.
Dulac, Germaine (1982) 'The Aesthetics. The Obstacles. Integral Cinegraphie', trans. Stuart Liebman, *Framework*, 19.
Flitterman, Sandy (1974) 'Heart of the Avant-Garde: Some Biographical Notes on Germaine Dulac', *Women and Film*, 1 (5-6).
Flitterman, Sandy (1980) 'Montage/Discourse: Germaine Dulac's *The Smiling Mme Beudet*', *Wide Angle*, 4 (3).
Flitterman, Sandy (1984) 'Theorizing 'The Feminine': Woman as Figure of Desire in *The*

Seashell and the Clergyman, *Wide Angle*, 6 (3).
Flitterman, Sandy (1987) 'The Image and the Spark : Dulac and Artaud Reviewed', in Rudolf E. Kuenzli (ed.) *Dada and Surrealist Film*, New York, Willis Locker and Owens.
Hammond, Paul (ed.) (1978) *The Shadow and its Shadow*, London, British Film Institute
Sitney, P. Adams (ed.) (1978) *The Avant-Garde Film: A Reader in Theory and Criticism*, New York, New York University Press.

SCRIPTS

Artaud, Antonin (1966) *The Seashell and the Clergyman*, in *Tulane Drama Review*, 11 (1).
Artaud, Antonin (1978) *La Coquille et le clergyman*, in *Les Oeuvres complètes d'Antonin Artaud*, 18-25.

APPENDIX:

Germaine Dulac (1882—1942): filmography

1916 *Géo le mystérieux (La Vraie richesse)*
1916 *Dans l'ouragan de la vie*
1916 *Les Soeurs ennemies*
1916 *Vénus victrix*
1917 *Ames de fous*
1918 *Le Bonheur des autres*
1919 *La Cigarette*
1919 *La Fête espagnole*
1920 *La Belle dame sans merci*
1920 *Malencontre*
1921 *La Mort du soleil*
1922 *Werther* (unfinished)
1923 *Gosette*
1923 *La Souriante Mme Beudet* (*The Smiling Mme Beudet*)
1924 *Le Diable dans la ville*
1925 *Ame d'artiste*
1925 *La Folie des vaillants*
1926 *Antoinette Sabrier*
1927 *Le Cinéma au service de l'histoire* (compilation)
1927 *La Coquille et le clergyman* (*The Seashell and the Clergyman*)
1927 *L'Invitation au voyage*
1928 *Germination d'un haricot*
1928 *La Princesse Mandane*
1929 *Etude cinégraphique sur une Aaabesques*
1929 *Disque 927*
1929 *Thèmes et variations*

2. History and actuality: Abel Gance's *Napoléon vu par Abel Gance* (1927)

NORMAN KING

> '*Napoléon* [...] will show what the
> historical film can and must be, a
> living lesson for the future.'(Abel
> Gance, 1924)[1]

Napoléon, Gance was still proclaiming in 1971,[2] was one of only two filmic *chansons de geste* in the whole history of cinema, the other being *Birth of a Nation*. And he went on to define the *chanson de geste* as a poetry of action — which, being interpreted, could be said to mean the lyrical and heroic actualization of the past, what we might now call pertinence. Whatever recent enthusiasts may claim, *Napoléon* is *not* a rediscovered masterpiece that was misunderstood because it was ahead of its time. Nor can it easily be dismissed as an example of proto-fascism on the basis of a general theory of fascism which takes no account of conditions of production in mid-1920s France. Innovatory it certainly is, as well as authoritarian. Essentially, though, it is a film of and for its own time. Marked by its immediacy and its relevance, it interpellates a specific audience — or rather audiences since, being so specific, it needed to be revised and updated. In that sense it is indeed a *chanson de geste*, the archetypal French epic.

All historical reconstructions are of course themselves historically inscribed. In the Latin sense of the word, they *invent*, they *re*-discover. Whether they claim to be imaginative fictions or straight presentations of hard facts, historical narratives tell at least as much about their own material conditions of existence as they do about a past which can never be entirely available. They organize, rework and polemicize.

If this basic fact of historiography has not received the attention one would expect in cinema studies, that is perhaps because it seems self-evident. Before they can narrate or analyse, films have first of all to show. Their images have to be acceptable to audiences of their time, to seem appropriate. The Springfield of *Young Mr Lincoln* has to correspond to how a 1930s viewing public imagines it rather than to how it actually was. And Henry Fonda has to conform to preconceptions of what the youthful Abe Lincoln might have looked like, as well as to accepted notions of his character. Given the immediacy of the image, popular mythology and iconography matter more than authenticity.

There is also a problem of critical method. Film specialists are not always good historians and, even when they are, they have tended to focus on cinema as apparatus and as institution. Recent studies on representation have shifted the perspective, recognizing cinema as a process of mediation, but a great deal of basic work still needs to be done if we are more adequately to understand how films re-work history as well as being themselves historical products. Even the seminal *Cahiers du cinéma* analysis of *Young Mr Lincoln* ultimately fails because it takes too narrow a view of political inscription. As a Republican picture, it may indeed seem to be inconsistent and thus to show up ideological gaps. As an example of American populism of the late 1930s, it is on the other hand remarkably coherent in the way it presents a legendary hero who unites the human and the natural, sensibility and the need for order. As with Renoir's *La Marseillaise*, the link between the historical and the actual can indeed be assumed to be self-evident for a 1930s audience, even without the speeches which, in both films, spell out the immediacy of the message. Whether any specific member of a given audience did or did not fully grasp the coherence of that message is beside the point. What matters is how the film positions the imagined audience of its time.

These are the criteria which have to be taken into account in an analysis of *Napoléon* as a film for its time, as a re-working not of 'facts' but of a legend that is re-actualized, drawing, in the way *Young Mr Lincoln* does, on the convenient anecdote and extrapolating from it a 'poetic' truth and a punctual lesson.

Authenticity is of course important, as the film's intertitles frequently proclaim (referring back to Griffith), but the film's hold on history is actually very tenuous. Albert Dieudonné may have had to go on a crash diet to make himself look like idealized portraits of the young Bonaparte (popular iconography) and Gance may have felt it necessary to lace his text with quotations from Bonaparte's letters and speeches. The film is, even so, almost entirely fictional. The whole of the Brienne prologue is the elaboration of a legend. The Marseillaise sequence is pure invention. The 'double tempest', with its parallel montage and superimposition linking Bonaparte to the fate of the Revolution in crisis, is a chronological juxtaposition which has no historical justification. And so on, through to the courtship of Josephine (historical romance), the ghosts of the Convention (affabulation) and the arrival at Albenga (popular mythology). Even the Corsica sequence (Bonaparte's return to home and nature, his struggle against Pozzo di Borgo and escape to France) shot, as Gance proudly announces, in the actual places where these events took place, owes at least as much to traditions of the melodrama and the western as to the dubious memoirs that Gance gives as his sources. And there are, of course, characters who are entirely figments of Gance's imagination, like the Fleuris, the naive, sentimental and enthusiastic family which reappears throughout the film, often in the most unlikely circumstances.

This is not even an economical use of the truth, it is an embroidery, the interweaving of multifarious strands to form a design which presents itself as a true picture. Authenticity is a form of packaging, imprinted with a seal of approval guaranteeing the quality of the product and its usefulness.

*   *   *

Gance's original intention had been to make a single film encompassing the whole of Napoleon's career, a project which was soon expanded to four feature-length films and then to six. As a 1923 outline shows,[3] the complete cycle would have been an evocation of the 'greatest drama of all time', rigorously historical but appealing to the heart as well as the mind. To sustain this dual impact, Gance proposed to give the Fleuris a role that was almost as important as Napoleon's. They would be the representatives of the ordinary people, sharing obscurely in the destiny of the great man, understanding him intuitively and providing points of identification for the audience. Institutional constraints soon led to major changes of emphasis. When, for example, the production syndicate insisted on the completion of three screenplays before filming could begin, Gance simply upped the total number of films to eight and divided the Revolutionary period into two — *Bonaparte et la Terreur*, and *Arcole*. Then, after Westi, the principal backers, went into liquidation in 1925, he welded them back together, incorporating as much of the existing footage as possible but cutting or revising a number of major scenes and leaving only the beginning of *Arcole* as the film's conclusion.[4]

The result of this stretching and shrinking was a major change of emphasis. The Fleuris remained central characters (since many of the scenes in which they figure are now lost, their importance is not always apparent in the restored version) but the Revolutionary leaders assumed a much greater significance. The drama had become a tripartite one, in which Bonaparte was the unifier preventing a divide between the leaders and the ordinary people of France.

Gance claimed in 1927[5] that his view of Napoleon was a bioptical one: Bonaparte was a liberator; Napoleon as Emperor was the victim of a system, trapped by his family, his advisers and the self-interested machinations of the great powers. And when, in the autumn of 1927, he began work on a sequel, Gance opted not for *Arcole*, which was already written, nor for *Brumaire*, the next film in the series, but for *Sainte-Hélène*, the last episode in the original project, showing a Napoleon in exile reflecting on his amazing career and exploring its lessons.[6] In his insistence on the bioptical, Gance was, though, mostly responding to criticisms like those of Léon Moussinac and Emile Vuillermoz[7] who claimed that he had produced in *Napoléon* a travesty of the Revolution and its aftermath. For them, there was no doubt about the film's actuality or its relevance. As Vuillermoz wrote, by making light of the history of yesterday, Gance was, without realizing it, helping to write the history of tomorrow.

Such strictures, made by critics who were on the whole sympathetic towards Gance, are not difficult to understand. Van Daele's Robespierre with his solemnity, studied gestures, powdered wig and dark glasses, Koubitsky's brazen and eloquent Danton, holding the crowds by his magnetic power,

Gance's effeminate Saint-Just and Artaud's 'hideous' Marat,[8] writing shopping lists for the guillotine and drinking blood in his bath, are at once great performances and pernicious caricatures. They conform so closely to popular mythology that it is difficult now to imagine them otherwise. Yet these objections are, in some respects, grossly unfair. Gance's portrayal of the Revolution is an ambivalent one: its leaders are both monsters and heroes, and the mob is both depraved and magnificent. Whatever its faults, the Revolution marks the beginning of a new social order. It is unfortunate in this respect that when the screenplay was cut back in 1925, Gance omitted several major sequences which did not directly involve Bonaparte except as an onlooker. The most interesting of these is the 'Tenth of August 1792',[9] in which scenes of the bloodshed occasioned by the storming of the Tuileries are followed by an idealized view of the Revolutionary programme, as the leaders assembled in Louis XVI's office each propose some major reform — the Civil Code, the decimal system, state hospitals, primary schools, the abolition of all surviving feudal privileges... . Though he did keep Saint-Just's speech at the Convention, in which he reviews the achievements of the Revolution and its 12,000 decrees — before, like all good prophets and men of principle, he is sent off to be executed.

The problem, as Gance presents it, is that during the Reign of Terror and the Directory the Revolution had lost its way. Rivalry among the leaders and quarrels about strategy had brought about a situation in which factions were fighting each other instead of confronting a common enemy. Only a strong unified power could save the Revolution from itself and preserve what it had accomplished. Gance does not, then, condemn out of hand the Robespierres, the Dantons and the Marats but merely criticizes their weaknesses and their rivalries. Although they are indeed caricatures, it is Robespierre who insists on the national will, and Danton who unites a disparate mass of bourgeois and sans-culottes in the Cordeliers sequence.

Even though he is usually seen as a pacifist of sorts, Gance does not condemn violence — Saint-Just's final speech is a reminder of that. Instead, he argues throughout the film that violence has to be proved to be necessary. Disorder and factionalism lead to needless bloodshed, discipline and unity lead to violence only as a last resort, in defence of fundamental principles. It is, after all, Marat who, in one of the Convention scenes, first recognizes that the Revolution can only be saved from its self-inflicted violence by a powerful leader, a dictator who will restore order, a man of war who will establish peace.

Enter Bonaparte, whose presence in the Revolutionary sequences was much more prominent in the original screenplay. In the incomplete reconstruction we still see him in the sidelines thanking Rouget de Lisle in the name of France for writing an anthem which will save many a cannon, as the impoverished lieutenant who deplores the gratuitous slaughter in the streets of Paris, and as 'Général Vendémiaire' quelling a royalist revolt with a maximum of efficiency and a minimum of bloodshed, more than enough to convince us

Napoléon — above: Battle scene (the siege of Toulon); centre: Map of Italy with silhouette of Napoleon (Albert Dieudonné) and the face of Josephine (Gina Manès) superimposed; below: Italian campaign scene in triptych with silhouette of Napoleon.

of his commitment to France and its future. What we do not see quite enough of is his love for the people and his commitment to the Revolution, as the one person who could understand it and bring it to fruition. Gance's Bonaparte is a Saviour, a visionary and man of action, afraid of violence only when it is an act of vengeance. Without his intervention, all that the Revolutionaries had accomplished would have been lost.

In reaching this view of Bonaparte, Gance had drawn extensively on the work of academic historians like Albert Sorel and especially Alphonse Aulard, whose affirmation that the young Bonaparte was a Revolutionary and a Republican is quoted on the dedicatory page of the published screenplay.[10] But like Godard, he was using the document only as a starting point in the search for a truth of fiction, a truth Gance presents as immortal and hence, like the myth and the epic, always actual — although pertinent might again be a better term, given the urgency of the film's message and the complexity of the cross-references between the political situation in post-1918 Europe as seen by Abel Gance and the French Revolution as seen by Napoleon Bonaparte.

* * *

In broad terms, *Napoléon* picks up where *J'accuse* had left off. Released in 1919, *J'accuse* was an interrogation of the First World War and its purpose. At the end, Jean Diaz, the visionary poet driven mad by the horrors of the war, raises up the men who had died on the battlefields and calls them home to see if their sacrifice has been justified. Their appearance so terrifies their families and friends that they all faithfully promise to change their lives. Already, then, it is suggested that the Great War had indeed not served its purpose since a new order is brought about only through fear and only in the imaginary.

By the mid-1920s it was clearer still that the War to end all wars had not led to the creation of a pacified and unified Europe. France had perhaps avenged itself and regained its territorial integrity, but it was still governed by weak centre-right coalitions which seemed to have forgotten much and learned only a little. Like the Congress of Vienna, the new Europe 'dansait mais ne marchait pas'. Hence the articulation of *Napoléon* around the Reign of Terror and its aftermath. Within the film, Saint-Just's justification of the Terror is quickly forgotten and instead the French bourgeoisie celebrates the fall of Robespierre by dancing, if not on the graves of the dead, in the places where the victims had been incarcerated. The *Bal des victimes* sequence is in this respect the most visually actual of the whole film. It presents a society which is stylish, elegant, innovatory, exciting — and effete. A decadent world of the 1790s and of the 1920s, subject to the whims of a Barras or a Josephine, to mediocre politicians and to cartels. A world which merges past and present even in the flimsy costumes worn by the dancers. Bonaparte is appalled, but he too is captivated, by the calculated charm of Josephine. Yet it is clear that his calling is to sweep away all this effrontery and to regenerate that 'genuine' enthusiasm and patriotism he had witnessed at the Club des Cordeliers. Order, discipline, a strict morality and devotion to a cause are what he stands for.

Not surprisingly, the immediacy of Gance's message was quickly recognized by critics who condemned the film as an apologia of dictatorship. To quote Moussinac again, Gance had produced 'a Bonaparte for budding fascists'.[11] Once more, though, the castigation is too hasty to be entirely convincing. It is indeed possible to read the film as an urgent appeal for strong leadership so that France will once again find a sense of direction and Europe a sense of unity. Of course that is in many ways what the film is about. But to read it as being only about that, you have to leave out all the scenes which show Bonaparte learning from the virtues and the failings of others. In the 'ghosts of the Convention' sequence, Bonaparte is interrogated not just by the Dantons and the Robespierres but by representatives of all the great Republicans. His promise is to continue their work, and their response is to remind him of the fate that will befall him if he forgets that promise. One contemporary critic[12] compared the sequence to a Workers' Institute giving lessons to Mussolini, but that too is overemphatic. Gance's Bonaparte, for all his solemnity, is Saviour not just because he creates a new order but because he builds on the ideas of his predecessors, realizing what they could not achieve. As such he is a unique figure in the process of history. Inheritor and precursor, he supplied the impulsion that others had lacked and remained present in popular memory as an example for the future. It is that vision of the future that counts most in a Gancian world that is full of prophets. Not perhaps a 'historical' Bonaparte, but not a Mussolini either. Bonaparte *vu par Abel Gance* was much greater than that. He may have been impetuous and, when necessary, authoritarian, but never cynical, not at least before 1799.

* * *

In this evocation of 'a Bonaparte as great leader', as the man who took over the Revolution and brought it to fulfilment before external forces, his family, corrupt ministers and misguided calculations brought him to his downfall, Gance was not just re-working Romantic and Republican traditions which date back to the beginning of the nineteenth century. He was particularly influenced by two quite recent and highly controversial books: *L'Ame de Napoléon*, published by Léon Bloy, a liberal Catholic, in 1912, and more particularly by Elie Faure's *Napoléon*, begun in 1918 and published on 5 May 1921, the Centenary of Napoleon's death. Although Gance quotes both books in the various texts he wrote to present his film to the public, intertextuality becomes quite complex here since it is Faure's redefinition of Bloy's basic argument which is the motive force of Gance's film — the idea of Napoleon as poet of action.[13]

All three are troubled by Napoleon's imperialism — he is, like the Revolutionary leaders, both heroic and monstrous — but they also see in him a great artist. To summarize Faure, Napoleon had made more impact on the way we see the world than any man since Jesus. In placing himself above the law, he had destroyed forever the feudal system and brought the Revolution back to the path traced for it by the *philosophes* and the *Constituants*. For that, he needed 'superhuman' powers of energy and concentration. Both Faure and Gance develop these points at length. But, like Bloy, they see his essential impact in his hold on the imagination. As man of destiny, military genius and fusion of art and science, he is *the* continuing presence. Napoleon is important less for what he accomplished than for what he made possible. As Faure suggests, to change the world you have first of all to change mentalities, and without Napoleon the Romantic imagination, as fusion of the political and the aesthetic, would not have existed.[14]

Faure, as an art historian, a doctor and a left-wing populist, could afford to be outrageously polemical, dedicating his book to the future leader of the universal revolution, 'whoever he might be'. Gance, however much he may have been in sympathy with Faure's view, could not. His immensely expensive film had to please his backers as well as his audiences. He could, on the other hand, actualize Bonaparte's appeal to the imagination much more powerfully than Faure could in a rather rhetorical essay. Gance could exploit the power of the image to produce in the spectator a new sense of recognition and identification.

These terms have to be used with caution. It could be said, for example, that both Faure and Gance recognize themselves as men in the same mould as Napoleon and thus identify with him.[15] Gance's hold over his extras is well known, and Vuillermoz's suggestion[16] that if he had asked them to, they would have stormed the National Assembly may be only a mild exaggeration, since they were so engrossed in their roles. But recognition and identification have, in narrative and in spectacle, to refer principally to the construction of an audience. It is from that emplacement that a film like *Napoléon* derives its impact. The spectator is led to identify not with Bonaparte who, like the Robespierres and the Saint-Justs, is 'too great for us', but with the onlookers, the enthusiastic crowds who recognize his power, his ability to fuse the eloquence of Danton, the austerity of Robespierre, the populism of Marat and the intellectual rigour of Saint-Just into a coherent vision of the future.

That is the film's immediacy, the construction of an audience desiring specific forms of change, the removal of factionalism, and of decadence, the establishment of a new order and a new unity founded on enthusiasm and a sense of mission. In one of his presentations of the film, Gance quotes a sentence from Paul Valéry: 'The idea of the past is meaningful and has value only for a person who finds within himself a passion for the future.'[17] That is as good a summary as one could find of *Napoléon*. It is a film which by reactualizing the past seeks to construct spectators who want to change the world, enthusiastically. That involves an authoritarian process, a merging of the intuitive and the rational, of past and present, of document, invention and spectacle. We might call that political Romanticism.

* * *

So important was actuality that when Gance was invited to produce a sonorized version of *Napoléon* in 1934, he did not just re-edit the film, he completely restructured it, adding new footage and considerably changing its impact. A complex framing narrative is set in March 1815 (just before the return from Elba) in a covert Bonapartist club in Grenoble, and all the major events in Bonaparte's early career are told in flashback. As the narrators — Tristan Fleuri, Santo Ricci and other minor characters from the 1927 version, along with Théroigne de Méricourt — recount these events to an inscribed audience (Crécy, Stendhal and Béranger), they lament Napoleon's downfall and pray for his return. Asked whether he really believes Napoleon will come back, Crécy responds that he does not think so but that you have to make people believe that he will because France is dying from a lack of enthusiasm. The tone of the film is nostalgic, evoking lost opportunities. It is also, in its way, more authoritarian, ending with a celebration of Napoleon's victories inscribed on the Arc de Triomphe, very actual in the patriotic and militarist circumstances of 1935 when the film was released. Certainly not Popular Front, Pétainist might be the best description, although Pétain, like the young Bonaparte, was still waiting in the sidelines to be asked to take control of the destinies of France. It was not until 1941 that Gance could explicitly dedicate a film to him,[18] although well before the outbreak of the Second World War, he had not concealed his sympathies for the Pétainist movement.

The final remake is also a very different film. Due to be completed in time for the bicentenary of Napoleon's birth (1969) but not released until 1971, *Bonaparte et la Révolution* incorporates footage from both the 1927 and 1935 versions plus a few scenes from *Valmy*, a television film directed by Gance in 1967. There is extensive new footage consisting mostly of dialogues and speeches, shot cheaply using Gance's pictograph, a device which made it possible to use photographs and engravings as 'backdrops' instead of elaborate sets. The main difference is a spoken commentary which explains in more detail the significance of the images within the context of the years 1792-1796. The result, as the new title suggests, is a broader and less caricatured view of the events which took place between the fall of the monarchy and the fall of Robespierre, along with a more assertive statement of Bonaparte's response to these events.

The Brienne prologue is replaced by a preface, filmed in colour and spoken straight to camera, in which Gance spells out the relevance of this ultimate re-ordering of old images. As always he claims that everything in his film can be justified by documentary evidence although he admits, once again, to having sometimes 'extrapolated historical truth on the wings of poetry'. He particularly insists on the parallels between the critical years of the Revolution and the political situation in post-1968 France. Bonaparte remains a saviour and a precursor but the visionary who, according to Gance, had advocated a fusion of minds, ambitions, customs, interests and hopes has become the *contestataire* of his day. The appeal for enthusiasm, unity and orderly change is thus addressed to a generation which, in its attempt to come to terms with the events of 1968, should set aside factionalism and anarchy, and be attentive instead to the message of the young Bonaparte as seen by Abel Gance.

Although it does not quite deserve the blistering critiques it has received, particularly since the release of the restored silent version, *Bonaparte et la Révolution* is inevitably a very odd film, a hybrid which does not quite belong anywhere — as for example when an ageing Dieudonné with a slightly quivering voice lip-synchronizes silent footage which has been speeded up to 24 fps. Yet in its own estranging way it illustrates the complexity of the intertextual in historical films. In the 1927 version Gance had reworked a legend, using historians of the political and of the aesthetic as guarantors of a poetic truth, conforming in that sense to the basic 'principles' of the *chanson de geste*. In *Bonaparte et la Révolution*, he reworks his own 'fixed' images of a Napoleon for the 1920s and 1930s, reactualizing them within a new mythology. What we mostly see, as a result, alongside this multi-layered fictionalization of the past, is a fictionalization of the present. Gance's spectators are constructed as 'amazed victims' but his equivalent of the famous 'Français, je vous ai compris!' is as much a figment of the imagination as Bonaparte's appearance before the ghosts of the Convention.

That is what the Vuillermozs and the Moussinacs objected to in 1927: a discourse of truth acting upon an audience positioned within a fictional process, led to believe that a fictional past could indeed provide lessons for the future. They may not have defined the problem quite in those terms, but they did see that the notion of actuality was itself a construct, a passage between one moment of 'truth' and another.

NOTES

1. Letter to Charles Pathé, quoted from Gance's copy of the original typescript (Paris, Centre National de la Cinématographie).
2. Prologue to the 1971 remake of *Bonaparte et la Révolution*.
3. Published in *Cinématographe*, 82 (1982) 5-7.
4. For the production history of *Napoléon*, see Brownlow (1983), Icart (1983a) and King (1984).
5. 'Aux spectateurs de *Napoléon*', a text printed in programmes issued for the general release of the film in November 1927 (translated in Brownlow [1983], 163-166). Gance had taken a somewhat similar line in 'La porte entr'ouverte', *Paris Soir*, 17 March 1925 (not 1927 as indicated by King [1984], 251).
6. Gance was not able to make the film himself. A modified version (*Napoléon auf Ste Hélène*) produced by Peter Ostermayer and directed by Lupu Pick was released in Germany in 1929.
7. For translations of the Moussinac and Vuillermoz articles referred to here, see King (1984), 34-49.
8. 'Hideux' is Gance's description (see note 9).
9. Gance subsequently published this sequence in *Le Rouge et le noir*, July 1928, 7-17 (translated in King [1984], 96-105).
10. *Napoléon vu par Abel Gance. Epopée cinégraphique en cinq époques. Première époque: Bonaparte*, Paris, Plon, 1927. For an analysis of Gance's borrowings from academic historical writings, see Icart (1983b).

11. See above, note 7. Moussinac's phrase is 'un Bonaparte pour apprentis fascistes'.

12. See King (1984), 32. It should be noted that most critics of the time either accepted that Gance's representation of Bonaparte was 'artistically' true or took the view that political readings of the film were irrelevant.

13. Gance acknowledges his debt in his letters to Faure (see Norman King's preface to the reprint of Elie Faure's *Napoléon*, Paris, Denoël-Gonthier, 1983).

14. This view of Napoleon had already been expounded in Faure's *Histoire de l'art* (see his *Oeuvres complètes*, edited by Yves Lévy, Paris, Pauvert, 1964).

15. Faure is explicit on this point in his correspondence (*Oeuvres complètes*, 3).

16. See King (1984), 48. Other critics of the time made similar observations, notably Jean Arroy in *En tournant 'Napoléon' avec Abel Gance*, Paris, La Renaissance du Livre, 1927.

17. In the prologue to *Bonaparte et la Révolution* (1971).

18. *La Vénus aveugle* which was given a gala presentation at Vichy in 1941.

SELECTED BIBLIOGRAPHY

Abel, Richard (1982) 'Charge and countercharge: coherence and incoherence in Abel Gance's *Napoleon*', *Film Quarterly*, 35, 2-12.

Abel, Richard (1985) *French Cinema: The First Wave*, Princeton, Princeton University Press.

Brownlow, Kevin (1968) *The Parade's Gone By*, London, Secker & Warburg.

Brownlow, Kevin (1983) *'Napoleon', Abel Gance's Classic Film*, London, Cape.

Eisenschitz, Bernard (1980) 'Abel Gance' in Richard Roud (ed.), *Cinema, a Critical Dictionary*, London, Secker & Warburg, I, 404-415.

Icart, Roger (1983a) *Abel Gance*, Lausanne, L'Age d'Homme.

Icart, Roger (1983b) 'La Représentation de Napoléon dans l'œuvre d'Abel Gance', *Cahiers de la cinémathèque*, 35/36.

Jeanne, René and Ford, Charles (1963) *Abel Gance*, Paris, Seghers.

King, Norman (1981) 'Poètes de l'action: les *Napoléon* d'Elie Faure et d'Abel Gance' *Cahiers Elie Faure*, I, 52-71.

King, Norman (1982) 'Une Epopée populiste', *Cinématographe*, 83, 8-10.

King, Norman (1984) *Abel Gance, a Politics of Spectacle*, London, British Film Institute.

Kramer, Steven and Welsh, James (1978) *Abel Gance*, Boston, Twayne.

Pappas, Peter (1981) 'The superimposition of vision: *Napoleon* and the meaning of fascist art', *Cineaste*, 11 (2), 4-13.

Philpott, Richard (1983) 'Whose *Napoleon*?', *Framework*, 20, 8-12.

For a more extensive bibliography, see Abel (1985) and King (1984). The latter gives summary details of the principal Gance archives.

SCRIPT

Gance, Abel (1927) *Napoléon vu par Abel Gance*, Paris, Plon.

APPENDIX

Abel Gance (1889—1981): filmography

For a more detailed filmography, see King (1984).

1912 *La Digue*
1912 *Il y a des pieds au plafond*
1912 *Le Nègre blanc*

1912   *Le Masque d'horreur*
1915   *Un Drame au château d'Acre*
1915   *La Fleur des ruines*
1915   *La Folie du docteur Tube*
1915   *L'Enigme de dix-heures*
1915   *L'Héroïsme de Paddy*
1915   *Strass et compagnie*
1915   *Fioritures*
1915   *Le Fou de la falaise*
1915   *Le Périscope*
1915   *Ce que les flots racontent*
1916   *Les Gaz mortels*
1916   *Barberousse*
1916   *Le Droit à la vie*
1916   *Mater dolorosa*
1917   *La Zone de la mort*
1917   *La Dixième symphonie*
1918   *Ecce homo*
1918-19   *J'accuse*
1920-2   *La Roue*
1923   *Au secours*
1925-7   *Napoléon vu par Abel Gance*
1925-7   *Autour de Napoléon*
1925-8   *Marine*
1926-8   *Danses*
1925-8   *Galops*
1928   *Cristallisation*
1930   *La Fin du monde*
1930   *Autour de La Fin du monde*
1932   *Mater dolorosa*
1934   *Poliche*
1934-5   *Napoléon Bonaparte*
1935   *Le Roman d'un jeune homme pauvre*
1935   *Jérôme Perreau, héros des barricades*
1935   *Lucrèce Borgia*
1936   *Un Grand amour de Beethoven*
1937   *J'accuse*
1937   *Le Voleur de femmes*
1938   *Louise*
1939   *Le Paradis perdu*
1940-1   *La Vénus aveugle*
1942-3   *Le Capitaine Fracasse*
1944   *Manolete*
1953   *14 juillet 1953*
1954   *La Tour de Nesle*
1956   *Magirama*
1959-60   *Austerlitz*
1963   *Cyrano et d'Artagnan*
1965-6   *Marie Tudor*
1967   *Valmy*
1969-71   *Bonaparte et la Révolution*

Other films cited in the text

Birth of a Nation, D. W. Griffiths (1915)
La Marseillaise, Jean Renoir (1927)
Young Mr Lincoln, John Ford (1939)

3. Discourse, narrative, and the subject of capital: Marcel L'Herbier's *L'Argent* (1929)

RICHARD ABEL

Near the end of the silent cinema period, at opposite ends of Europe, two films were being planned on the subject of money or capital: Sergei Eisenstein's project for a film based on Karl Marx's *Capital*, and Marcel L'Herbier's film adaptation of Emile Zola's *L'Argent*. Eisenstein's project, unfortunately, never got beyond the preliminary stage of diary notes (12 October 1927-22 April 1928), recorded discussions with G. V. Alexandrov, and the rough outline of a scenario.[1] But these clearly indicate how Eisenstein meant to extend the discursive and narrative strategies he had developed in *October*, strategies that were soon deflected or abandoned in the face of specific technological and cultural changes — the worldwide sound film's 'revolution' and the Soviet imposition of a 'social realist' aesthetic. L'Herbier's project, of course, was completed and released as *L'Argent*, in the midst of controversy, critical condemnation as well as acclaim, and uncertain commercial success, at least in France. This project, too, is revealing, not only of L'Herbier's thinking, but, more important, of those issues and practices that most characterized the French cinema in the late 1920s. The shimmering silver letters of the film title itself point to some of those issues and practices that will be explored in this essay — the extent and limits of adapting 'classic' literary texts to film, the international financing and casting of big-budget productions, the dazzling array of available stylistic techniques in the discursive practice of French filmmakers, and the unusual relationship between style and ideology that comes from directly representing an intrigue of capitalist exploitation. Together these provide the critical context for a radical re-reading of *L'Argent* which the film itself seems to demand.[2]

The French cinema had become dependent on fiction films whose scenarios were adapted from popular literary texts well before the Great War — as early as the 1908-1909 adaptations of Film d'Art and S.C.A.G.L. — principally as a means for the new industry to establish a continuous clientèle that would include the bourgeoisie and to legitimate the 'spectacles' it produced as art. During the war and continuing into the early 1920s, a loosely linked circle of scriptwriters and filmmakers challenged this practice with the first manifestation of a *politique des auteurs*, by promoting original scenarios as opposed to adaptations as one of several bases for distinguishing the cinema from the other arts. This group initially included Louis Delluc, Abel Gance, Marcel L'Herbier, Germaine Dulac, and critic Léon Moussinac — with the later addition of Jean Epstein, René Clair, and others. The French film industry seems to have encouraged this alternative, as well as the independent production companies which supported it, in a desperate effort to resist the

American attempt to penetrate every sector of the industry. As that effort increasingly led, however, to big-budget international co-productions, especially with German firms, and a concentration of fewer production companies, by the middle and late 1920s, adaptations became almost necessary for commercial success.

L'Herbier's own career exemplifies this shift, as he worked through a series of companies: Eclipse, Gaumont (Séries Pax), his own Cinégraphic, and, finally, the largest French film producer of all, Jean Sapène's Cinéromans.[3] During the war, for instance, he wrote original scenarios, directed by Louis Mercanton and René Hervil as *Le Torrent* and *Bouclette*. Of the first eight feature-length films he himself then directed, five were original scenarios: *Rose-France*, *Villa Destin*, *El Dorado*, *Don Juan et Faust*, and *L'Inhumaine*. Thereafter, L'Herbier was forced to confine himself exclusively to adaptations, all of them produced in conjunction with Cinéromans — shifting again from the work of an unfamiliar author like Luigi Pirandello, *Feu Mathias Pascal*, to safer, more marketable names and titles such as playwright Charles Méré, *Le Vertige*, and Emile Zola, *L'Argent*.

Scenario adaptations of Zola's novels had been a staple of French film production before and especially after the war — e.g. Victorin Jasset's *Au pays des ténèbres*, Albert Capellani's *Germinal*, André Antoine's *La Terre*, Henri Pouctal's *Travail*, Jacques de Baroncelli's *Le Rêve*. And they were returning to prominence in the late 1920s — e.g. Jean Renoir's *Nana*, Jacques Feyder's *Thérèse Raquin,* Julien Duvivier's *Au bonheur des dames*. So, given this 'tradition', as well as Feyder's recent rationale for the adaptation strategy,[4] it was not unusual for L'Herbier to choose to write and direct a scenario drawn from Zola's *L'Argent*. What was somewhat unusual, however, was his decision to update the novel's story from 1868 to 1928, a decision that raised the ire of the celebrated ex-theatre director and ex-filmmaker, André Antoine.

In his film column in *Le Journal* (12 March 1928), Antoine denounced L'Herbier for 'tampering' with Zola's work, for betraying the spirit and intent of the author. He demanded, in effect, an accurate, detailed reconstruction of what Zola intended as a scathing representation of the French banking milieu under the Second Empire. Soon after, in several pieces published in *Cinéa-Ciné-pour-tous*, L'Herbier argued in response that he meant to use *L'Argent* as a pretext to express, in all its 'modern virulence' his own contempt for money and capitalist speculation, despite his obvious dependency on them.[5] He rejected Antoine's demand for a literal adaptation in order to avoid the risk of creating an unwitting parody of Zola's work, much as René Clair had rejected the idea of retaining the by then nostalgic Second Empire setting for *Un Chapeau de paille d'Italie*. Besides, he added, transposing or modernizing a literary text through adaptation was widely accepted in France as well as the United States — witness Feyder's *Thérèse Raquin* and even Antoine's own versions of *La Terre* and especially *L'Arlésienne*. Although L'Herbier's argument located authority in the film's author rather than, as Antoine assumed, in the author of the source text, he also gave further credence to the practice of film adaptation as a uniquely creative act, a practice which would become even more dominant in the 1930s.

It is instructive to glance briefly at Zola's novel in order to clarify the 'modernizing' strategy of L'Herbier's scenario as well as, unexpectedly, to find support for his transpositions. In *L'Argent* (1891), according to his letters, Zola sought to write a novel about the Bourse (the Paris Stock Exchange) through which he could equate the economic and political crises of the late 1860s that preceded the collapse of the Second Empire.[6] His central character is Saccard, an impulsive, ingenious financier who, though recently ruined by speculation, now plans to exploit several little-known iron and silver mines in Palestine, in a joint venture with his own Banque Universelle and an engineer, Jacques Hamelin. His antagonist is Gundermann, a sober, methodical financier who gradually undermines Saccard's scheme and gets him arrested, with the help of Baroness Sandorf, whose 'frigid beauty' is matched by a passion for gambling on the stock market, and the engineer's ambitious sister, Caroline Hamelin. Saccard evades prison, however, through the intervention of his brother, a minister in the government, and slips off to Holland and a new speculative scheme.

Zola uses several historical events as primary source material for this intrigue — e.g., the catastrophic collapse of the Union Générale (1878-1885), which is transposed into the failure of Saccard's Banque Universelle, and the 1867 Paris Exposition, which provides a celebratory backdrop for his near triumph. This transposition of a financial scandal from the period of the Third Republic back to the late years of the Second Empire may seem disingenuous (since Zola condemns the earlier regime as an advocate of the later one), but critics generally contend that the French economic system continued unchanged through the two periods, despite the political change.[7] Critics are less than unanimous, however, on the locus and extent of Zola's alleged critique of capital. Whereas some, like André Wurmser, argue that the novel's ambivalent attitude never really puts the political economy of capitalism in question, others suggest that it actually defends capitalism — all that is needed are certain moralistic measures to curb or eliminate its excesses. Yet more than one critic perceives a contradictory impulse here, in that a distinct form of anti-Semitism shapes the conflict between Saccard and Gundermann (modelled on Baron James de Rothschild) — the sub-text of a financial struggle between Catholic and Jewish groups and institutions

In *L'Argent*, L'Herbier retains the major characters from Zola's novel and generally follows the main lines of its action, but with crucial modifications, partly because the narrative is now set in the late 1920s rather than the late 1860s. Saccard's scheme, for instance, involves the more contemporary colonial exploitation of oilfields in French Guyana and a deceptively publicized solo flight across the Atlantic by Jacques Hamelin, whose heroic status as a French aviator is modeled on the fame of Charles Lindbergh. Hamelin has a young wife, Line Hamelin, rather than a sister; and her fascination for the trappings of wealth proves useful to Saccard — who attempts to make her his mistress as well — in securing and sustaining the aviator's consent to his scheme. Saccard celebrates his expected triumph at a lavish private party (complete with a pool and a stage full of dancers and musicians), but it is there that Line, now ashamed of her complicity, comes close to shooting him. Soon after, manipulated by the enigmatic Baroness Sandorf and Gundermann, she initiates a stock-selling spree that leads to the Banque Universelle's collapse and the arrest of Saccard as well as, briefly, her own husband.

In one sense, the film's rival financiers are represented much as they were in Zola's novel. Saccard is a 'bad' capitalist whose appetite exceeds all bounds — vulgar, devious, impulsive, and immoral. Gundermann is his exact opposite — sophisticated, ascetic, coldly calculating, calmly sinister in demeanor. Yet here, too, Saccard's energy and ingenuity make him the much more appealing figure of the two. And L'Herbier changes the beginning and ending of the narrative, dissolving certain differences defining the narrative antagonism, to undermine any notion that Gundermann can be taken as a 'good' capitalist. It is Gundermann who, behind the scenes at the Bourse, directs the maneuvers of his allies, Massias and La Méchain, that almost ruin Saccard at the outset. And it is Gundermann who, having acquired a controlling body of stock in the Banque Universelle, can step in at the end as a *deus ex machina* to dismiss the charges against Jacques Hamelin and allow the case against Saccard to proceed to the point where he is sent to prison.[8] As a bonus, he reconciles the Hamelins as a couple through an ironic repetition — they play even more naïvely into his hands than they did earlier into Saccard's — which hardly restores the value and integrity of a 'transcendent' romantic love. If Gundermann, no less than Saccard, is representative of the capitalist system of speculation and accumulation, his deceptive ability to play the supposedly compassionate judge, again behind the scenes, ultimately leaves that system unchallenged and unchanged.

As this brief narrative analysis suggests, L'Herbier's decision to situate *L'Argent* in the luxurious milieu of high finance in the late 1920s depended on more than a rationale for and a 'tradition' of adapting Zola's novels or any other 'classic' literary texts. It was also determined by the increasingly international character of French film production in the late 1920s and, coincidentally, by a new genre of film, the modern studio spectacular, to whose development L'Herbier himself had contributed. The international financing and casting that characterized the French cinema came primarily from two sources: Russian émigrés, who initially helped the French resist the hegemony of the American cinema and then German film companies, in a series of co-productions that quickly led to an unequal balance of power disadvantageous to the French. This French/Russian émigré/German axis of investment was particularly evident in the big-budget historical reconstruction films produced by the consortium of Westi/Ciné-France/Pathé-Consortium

L'Argent — Baronness Sandorf (Brigitte Helm) and Saccard (Pierre Alcover).

— e.g. Henri Fescourt's four-part *Les Misérables*, Victor Tourjansky's *Michel Strogoff*, and Abel Gance's *Napoléon* — and the Société Générale des Films — e.g. Alexandre Volkoff's *Casanova* and Carl Dreyer's *La Passion de Jeanne d'Arc*. The co-producers of *L'Argent*, Cinéromans and Ciné-Mondial (an affiliate of L'Herbier's own company, Cinégraphic), seem to have operated slightly outside this axis, although both had been involved previously in French-German co-productions.[9] Instead, in order to maximize the potential market for the film, they relied on the corollary strategy of casting the major character roles with both French and non-French actors.

In *L'Argent*, this casting strategy took on particular ideological significance. Most of the French actors — e.g., Antonin Artaud (Saccard's secretary Mazaud), Alexandre Mihalesco (Salomon Massias), Pierre Juvenet (Baron Defrance), Jules Berry (Saccard's ally, the journalist Huret), Yvette Guilbert (La Méchain) — were asked to perform generally according to type. As Saccard, however, Pierre Alcover seemed cast against the grain of the role. His stocky, solid physique and heavy, bluntly hatchet-like face gave to Saccard what one leftist reviewer described as a 'plebeian profile' that suggests one of two contradictory readings: casting Alcover either constituted a deliberate misrepresentation in order to foment a class-based attack from within capitalism, or else it simply reflected the desire for a vigorous new breed of capitalist. By contrast, Mary Glory, in her first starring role, brought the expected *ingénue*'s sense of vulnerable innocence to the pivotal, victimized character of Line Hamelin. Similarly, the choice of an unfamiliar English actor, Henry Victor, emphasized the lonely alienation and ineffectual heroism of Jacques Hamelin. Finally, the German actors, Alfred Abel and Brigitte Helm, both of whom had most recently starred in Fritz Lang's *Metropolis*, were effectively typecast as Gundermann and Baroness Sandorf, respectively. Abel turned Gundermann into a tall, thin, tight-lipped 'aristocrat' whose finicky, repressive manner contrasted sharply with that of Alcover's 'nouveau riche' Saccard. In turn, Helm embodied Sandorf (the role was expanded when the actress agreed to work on the film) as a cool blonde seductress whose lithe figure was equally at ease in either the stylized jungle luxury of her apartment or the formally abstract spaces of Gundermann's office. The casting of Abel and Helm may well have contributed to the film's apparent commercial success in Germany, but it also redefined the economic antagonism of the narrative in pointedly nationalistic rather than, as in Zola, in ethnic or religious terms. Here, whatever the contradictions of class, distinctly French characters seem to suffer defeat at the hands of Germans.

Another important, related context for L'Herbier's decision to 'modernize' *L'Argent* was provided by the modern studio spectacular. In a sense, this new genre emerged in the middle and late 1920s to serve as a further marketing strategy to exploit international film co-productions and the increasingly elaborate studio sets designed in France and Germany, as well as the cultural internationalism that was beginning to characterize urban life in the industrialized centers of Europe. Early evidence of the genre's emergence can be seen in the ultra-modern decors (by Robert Mallet-Stevens, Alberto Cavalcanti, Fernand Léger, and Claude Autant-Lara) of L'Herbier's own *L'Inhumaine* and especially in Germaine Dulac's *Ame d'artiste*. Although ostensibly set in London and using French, English, and Russian émigré actors, *Ame d'artiste*, for instance, effectively neutralized cultural differences to the point where its setting and action were nearly indeterminate. The genre then quickly gelled in a series of box office successes, most of them based on familiar melodramatic plays and novels — e.g., L'Herbier's *Le Vertige*, Léonce Perret's *La Femme nue*, Julien Duvivier's *L'Homme à l'Hispano*, Jean Renoir's *Marquitta*, Perret's *La Danseuse orchidée*, and L'Herbier's *Le Diable au coeur*.[10] These films, according to Gérard Talon, represented the good life of a new post-war generation and helped define what was 'modern' and 'à la mode' in fashion, sport, dancing, and manners in general.[11] Given the genre's socially and aesthetically neutral milieu, however, the overall effect of the modern studio spectacular was a fantasy of internationalism that tended to deny the specificity of French culture and accede to the new ideology (principally

American in origin) of consumer capitalism or conspicuous consumption.

If Gance's *Napoléon* and Dreyer's *La Passion de Jeanne d'Arc* constitute the apex of big-budget historical reconstruction films in the French silent cinema, then *L'Argent* certainly can be taken as the culmination of the modern studio spectacular. With a five-million franc budget, L'Herbier was given privileged access to the Paris Bourse for three days of shooting (with 1,500 actors and over a dozen cameramen) and was permitted to electrify the Place de l'Opéra in order to shoot a night scene of the huge crowd awaiting news of Hamelin's solo transatlantic flight. At the newly opened Studios Francoeur, Lazare Meerson and André Barsacq constructed immense set decors, including an enormous bank interior, several large offices and vast apartments, a dance stage for Saccard's celebration party, and an unusual circular room next to Gundermann's office whose entire wall length was covered with a giant world map.

Many of these studio spaces have smooth, polished surfaces and are stylized to the point of exhibiting little more than walls, ceilings, and floors. This stark simplicity, especially in such monumental designs, undermines any appeal to verisimilitude (a principle crucial to Antoine's concept of adaptation) and tends to dissolve the boundaries differentiating one space from another, so much so that the rightist critic, Jean Fayard, complained — in an unconsciously apt equation for a consumer society — that the Banque Universelle 'might just as well be a department store' (Burch 1973, 132). The indeterminacy of these decors, although exemplary of the modern studio spectacular, thus specifically functions to further abstract the film's capitalist intrigue. Together with the crowds of extras that often traverse the frame and chief cameraman Jules Kruger's selection of slightly wide-angle lenses and high- and low-angle camera positions, especially for the frequent long shots or extreme long shots, they produce a consistently deep-space *mise-en-scène* and exaggerated sense of dynamism that perfectly complement the rivalry between larger-than-life capitalists (Marie 1978, 5). Furthermore, the highly stylized or generalized milieu of the film actually serves to foreground the nationalistic and class-based terms of the intrigue, articulated through the casting, and allows them to read all that more clearly.

The 'modernizing' strategy that shapes *L'Argent*'s set decors and deep-space *mise-en-scène* was also governed, finally, by a loosely systematic discursive practice which many French filmmakers shared in the late 1920s. This practice had developed in partial opposition to the dominant American system of representation and narrative continuity that was fixed in place by the end of the war. Generally, the French tended to privilege the specifically 'cinematic' elements of framing and editing — e.g. close-ups (especially of objects), unusually high and low camera positions, extensive camera movement, superimpositions and dissolves, various forms of rhythmic montage, associative editing. These elements, along with others common to the American continuity system, served to break with, redirect, and reconstitute the parameters of conventional narrative film discourse. Within French film practice, for instance, description was given as much weight as narration; the representation of the subjective re-oriented the diegetic flow of a film from action to perception, feeling, and thinking; and various syntactical forms of conjunctive and disjunctive simultaneity attained co-equal status with 'classical' spatio-temporal continuity editing. The particular significance of this alternative or 'deviant' French paradigm, however, was hardly fixed or immutable; rather, that significance depended on its function within the textual system of any one specific film. Jean Epstein's *La Glace à trois faces* provides an exemplary model of this paradigm at work, in a 40 minute film that narrates three separate past stories, each embedded within separate present stories, all of which are then encompassed within a fourth, also narrated in the present. But L'Herbier's *L'Argent* offers another, perhaps even more interesting model for the way its reflexive style ultimately helps to articulate the film's critique of capital.

At least two particular features of this film practice loom large in *L'Argent*, one of which received a good deal of attention in Jean Dréville's unique documentary study, *Autour de L'Argent*. This first feature Noël Burch has described as an 'absolutely unprecedented mobile camera strategy', whose high visibility and extreme dynamism render its effect peculiarly ambiguous.[12] The range and extent of the film's camera movement is unmatched except perhaps by that in Gance's *Napoléon* (for which Kruger was also chief cameraman). Both at the Bourse and the Banque Universelle, for instance, cameramen were strapped to various low-slung vehicles and plunged into the crowds or pulled rapidly alongside them. At Saccard's party, camera and operator glided back and forth over performers and guests on a platform suspended by ropes and pulleys from the ceiling. Finally, at the moment of Hamelin's departure by plane, the frenzied activity at the Bourse was recorded by an automatic camera descending on a cable from the dome toward the central stock exchange ring.

The virtuosity of this mobile camera strategy often produces a sense of energy that seems to charge a character like Saccard — e.g. the frequent quick dollies and combination track-pans which exaggerate his moves — as well as render the film's deep-space *mise-en-scène* even more dynamic. But sometimes, its effect is much more blatantly unconventional. Instead of adjusting to the movement of characters, in order to reposition them in the frame, for instance, the camera itself does the repositioning. The most unusual instances of this occur in and around Gundermann's office. One such track-pan, moving counter to a servant gliding across the office at a distance, creates a strangely drifting yet anchored sense of space that accentuates the easy inevitability of his movement. Soon after, a 180° track-pan around Massias, standing in the circular map room, reveals the opening of an invisible door in the wall, through which he then disappears. The world literally seems to revolve around him — at Gundermann's command, as we discover by the end. Largely because of such unusual camera movements, in *L'Argent* space oscillates uncannily between the fixed and the fluid.

A second feature of the film's discursive practice is its rather unconventional editing patterns, which sometimes work in tandem with camera movement. One of these editing patterns depends on 90° shifts in camera position, coordinated with the rotation or lateral movement of actors, to create a kind of dance — as in the 'chess piece' choreography of Saccard and Sandorf on the large black and white squares of a spacious hall adjacent to Gundermann's office. Another joins shots in elliptical associative series — as in the short scene that succinctly defines the separately slumbering Saccard and Line in relation to an alertly seductive Sandorf, whose movement, in turn, seems controlled by the off-screen presence of Gundermann. Yet another is predicated on the counterpoint of cross-cutting — as in the 'center pivot' of the film, the sequence that intercuts shots of Hamelin's plane's take-off and ascent with aerial shots plunging directly toward the Bourse stock exchange ring (L'Herbier 1979, 157). At the original screening, this 'montage of attractions' — in which the mass tumult of speculation threatens to 'drag down' Hamelin's flight — was accompanied by sound-disk recordings of 'crowd noises at the Bourse and the motorized roar of the plane', not synchronized and kept distinct, but overlaid one on top of the other, in order to underscore the interrelationship between the two disparate activities. Finally, there is the uniquely persistent pattern of cutting a stable shot just as a sudden camera movement becomes perceptible, which creates a slightly jarring effect in the film's rhythm that ruptures its sense of spatio-temporal continuity and foregrounds the very construction of filmic space-time.[13]

The reflexivity of this discursive practice marks *L'Argent* as a Modernist text, of course, at least to the extent that the materials of the film medium and their deployment as a disruptive system become an ancillary subject of the film. In this, *L'Argent* differs radically from the other concurrent film adaptations of Zola — Feyder's *Thérèse Raquin*, which apparently sought (more in line with Antoine's argument) to recreate the novel's sordid, oppressive atmosphere, within which psychological details accumulated to propel the action, and Duvivier's *Au bonheur des dames*, whose synthetic style emphasized the pathos of a small family clothing shop being supplanted by a modern department store (modelled on the Bon Marché). Instead, *L'Argent*'s framing and editing techniques, in conjunction with set design and acting style or casting, more closely resemble those of Renoir's *Nana* or Dreyer's *La Passion de Jeanne d'Arc*, both of which serve to subvert the conventions of another genre, the historical reconstruction. Yet reflexivity here bears a subversive significance that exceeds the genre of the modern studio spectacular precisely because the subject of *L'Argent* is a story of capital.

L'Argent's achievement, in the end, rests on the correlation it makes between discourse, narrative, and the subject of capital. Capital is both everywhere and nowhere, as Pierre Jouvet argues, echoing Marx; it motivates nearly every character in the film and is talked about incessantly, but it is never seen or — as 'the dung on which life thrives' — even scented.[14] Capital remains invisible, and yet, in its ideological manifestation, produces a surplus of effects. At the level of narrative, that surplus informs the melodramatic conflict between Saccard's scheming, duplicitous passion and Gundermann's 'unnaturally' omniscient suppression. At the level of discourse, it swells into a magnificent excess of technique, whose inflated dynamism reaches the point of intense disequilibrium or imbalance. In the reflexivity of that discourse, however, through a correspondence of terms, the film reflects on and critiques that which it cannot represent directly — the crucial reference point of a crisis in capitalist exploitation or, more specifically, the condition of western capitalist society on the brink of the Great Depression.

This critique is perhaps most strikingly articulated in the excess of a further correspondence of terms — the fascinating nexus of rhetorical figuring that links Saccard, Line, and Sandorf along sexual and economic axes. Crucial to this figuring is the concept of fetishization, which is introduced as Saccard initially is concocting his scheme. In a restaurant and, soon after, in the Hamelin apartment, through several series of point-of-view shots, Saccard's gaze seems to fragment and objectify Line's body as a prelude to possession. That fetishization later becomes literal when Saccard offers Line an expensive bracelet and a checkbook, then obsessively gazes at one of her slips, and finally caresses the silken garment as a superimposition dissolves in of her reclining nude figure. Through the exchange of objects, or the promise of exchange, and the parallel figuring of what is and is not represented, the scene condenses Saccard's desire for a woman's body and for capital into a single obsession.[15] In a related pattern of figuring, the film increasingly inscribes Line's body on or behind glass surfaces, images over which Sandorf, through a deceptive pattern of doubling, gradually seems to gain control. The climax of this figuring comes at Saccard's party where Line appears in a sort of waiting room reflected in a wall mirror, a virtually immobile *femme de glace*. And when she threatens to shoot Saccard, Sandorf is there to control the reverberations of this mirror image, suppressing the expected gunshot for a later, more damaging (and more profitable) discharge. As a fetishized object that stands in for capital, Line follows Sandorf in circulating from one 'master' to another, all within a political economy where the hierarchy of capitalist relations is synonymous with that of patriarchy.

Given this framework of reflexivity, perhaps inevitably, *L'Argent* includes traces of its own production. Jacques Hamelin's uneasy, compromised relation to the world of finance as an aviator hero, for instance, seems to parallel L'Herbier's own as a filmmaker/artist within the French film industry. Like Daedalus or, more precisely, Icarus, neither can escape the labyrinth of capitalist speculation that sustains their creative efforts. But there is another, even more tantalizing trace. In the elliptical sequence which links Saccard, Line, and Sandorf to the off-screen presence of Gundermann, the latter is associated with a copy of *Le Matin* that he seems to be reading. *Le Matin* was then a right-wing mass circulation Paris newspaper which served as the financial base for Jean Sapène, who ran Cinéromans, the company that co-produced *L'Argent*. Relations between Sapène and L'Herbier were far from cordial at the time of the film's release. According to L'Herbier, in fact, a personal feud between the two, involving verbal insults and physical assaults, led Sapène to cut and re-edit *L'Argent* drastically between the time of its December 1928 preview for critics and its premiere one month later at the Max Linder Cinema. Despite pressure from several quarters, Sapène refused to let L'Herbier re-edit the film; and the cut version went into general release in April 1929.[16] It was not until the early 1970s that L'Herbier finally had his revenge, in personally helping the Archives du Film to restore his original version of *L'Argent*.[17] But the filmmaker's attitude toward Sapène, as the source of capital for the film's production, is already there in the film text itself — in the conjunction, through the image of *Le Matin*, of the two unrepresented figures most in control of capital, both inside and outside the film. In this reflexive trace, one can read the film's own demand for a process of re-reading counter to that of Gundermann/Sapène, a re-reading which this essay has attempted to articulate and extend.

NOTES

1. Sergei Eisenstein (1976) 'Notes for a Film of Capital', trans. Macie J. Sliwowski, Jay Leyda, and Annette Michelson, *October*, 2, 3-26. See, also, Annette Michelson (1976) 'Reading Eisenstein Reading *Capital*', *October*, op. cit., 26-38.
2. This essay constitutes a reconceived, rewritten, and sometimes condensed version of the description and analysis of *L'Argent* in my (1984) *French Cinema: The First Wave, 1915-1929*, 513-526. For further information on the French silent cinema as a context for L'Herbier's film, see Abel (1985) 'On the Threshold of French Film Theory and Criticism, 1915-1919', *Cinema Journal*, 25, 12-22; and Abel (1988) *French Film Theory and Criticism, 1907-1929*.
3. Jean Epstein and Germaine Dulac were the principal exceptions to this kind of shift, for both directed a number of original scenarios in the middle and late 1920s.
4. Jacques Feyder (1925) 'Transpositions visuelles', *Cahiers du mois*, 16/17, 67-71, trans. in Abel (1988).
5. For further information on L'Herbier's response to Antoine, see Jean-André Fieschi (1968) 'Autour du cinématographe', *Cahiers du cinéma*, 202, 38, 40; Claude Beylie and Michel Marie (1978) 'Entretien avec Marcel L'Herbier', *Avant-Scène Cinéma*, 209, 36x; and Marcel L'Herbier (1979) *La Tête qui tourne*, 150.
6. Emile Zola in Robert Judson Niess (ed.)(1940) *Letters to J. Van Santen Kolff*, St Louis, Washington University Studies, 37.
7. André Wurmser, 'Préface à *L'Argent*', in Zola (1967) *Oeuvres complètes*, 6, Paris, Cercle du livre précieux; reprinted in Emile Zola (1974) *L'Argent*, Paris, Garnier-Flammarion, 494-498; Emilien Cararsus 'Introduction' to Zola (1974) *L'Argent*, 18-32; Joanna Richardson, *Zola* (1978) New York, St Martin's Press, 141-143. See, also, Zola's own notes in 'Extraits de l'Ebauche', in Zola (1974) *L'Argent*, 458.
8. Noël Burch was the first to notice Gundermann's role as *deus ex machina* at the end of *L'Argent*, in Burch (1973)'*L'Argent*', *Marcel L'Herbier*, Paris, Seghers, 132.
9. The year before, L'Herbier and Cinéromans had teamed up on *Le Diable au coeur* (1928), which was produced jointly with UFA (Germany) and Gaumont-British.
10. Besides playwright Charles Méré, the authors of these source texts included playwright Henri Bataille and novelist Pierre Frondaie. An even greater number of these films were drawn from Maurice Dekorba's novels and scenarios.
11. Gérard Talon (1975) 'Cinéma français: La Crise de 1928', *Synchronismes: 1928*,

Paris, Editions du signe, 109.

12. Burch (1973) 141-142. Burch argues that the singularity of the film's camera movements, and hence its originality, lies principally in their 'arbitrariness', a position with which I cannot agree.

13. Similarly, Nicole Schmitt calls attention to the consistent ellipses produced by the intertitles which interrupt shots involving actor and/or camera movement in 'Avertissement', *Avant-Scène Cinéma*, 209, 7.

14. Pierre Jouvet (1977) '*L'Argent* de Marcel L'Herbier', *Cinématographe*, 27, 8. L'Herbier quotes Zola's famous remark, 'money is the dung on which life thrives' in Beylie and Marie (1978) 36x.

15. Jouvet first makes this connection (1977) 8.

16. For information on the release of L'Herbier's *L'Argent*, see 'Les Nouveaux Films', *Cinéa-Ciné-pour-tous*, 125, 15 January 1929, 7; 'Les Nouveaux Films', *Cinéa-Ciné-pour-tous*, 130, 1 April 1929, 6; and L'Herbier (1979) 159-162.

17. My analysis has been based on this restored version of *L'Argent*, copies of which are available at the Archives du Film (Bois d'Arcy), the National Film Archive (London), the Museum of Modern Art (New York), and elsewhere. A complete shot log or *découpage* of *L'Argent* is published in *Avant-Scène Cinéma*, 209. Unfortunately this restored version has been stretch-printed so that it now runs slightly slower and longer than when the film was first projected, at close to sound speed, in 1929.

SELECTED BIBLIOGRAPHY

Abel, Richard (1984) *French Cinema: The First Wave, 1915-1929*, Princeton, Princeton University Press.

Abel, Richard (1988) *French Film Theory and Criticism, 1907-1929*, Princeton, Princeton University Press.

Beylie, Claude and Marie, Michel (1978) 'Entretien avec Marcel L'Herbier', *Avant-Scène Cinéma*, 209, 9-26, 43-60.

Bordwell, David (1980) *French Impressionist Cinema: Film Culture, Film Theory, and Film Style*, New York, Arno.

Brossard, Jean-Pierre (1980) *Marcel L'Herbier et son temps*, Locarno, Cinédiff.

Burch, Noël (1973) *Marcel L'Herbier*, Paris, Seghers.

Burch, Noël (1980) 'Marcel L'Herbier', in Richard Roud (ed.), *Cinema: A Critical Dictionary*, II, New York, Viking, 621-628.

Catelain, Jaque (1950) *Jaque-Catelain présente Marcel L'Herbier*, Paris, Jacques Vautrain.

Fescourt, Henri (1959) *La Foi et les montagnes*, Paris, Paul Montel.

Fieschi, Jean-André (1968) 'Autour du cinématographe', *Cahiers du Cinéma*, 202, 26-42.

Jouvet, Pierre (1977) '*L'Argent* de Marcel L'Herbier', *Cinématographe*, 27, May, 7-9.

L'Herbier, Marcel (1979) *La Tête qui tourne*, Paris, Belfond.

Marie, Michel (1978) 'Modernité de *L'Argent*', *Avant-Scène Cinéma*, 209.

Mitry, Jean (1973) *Histoire du cinéma*, III, Paris, Editions Universitaires, 377-378.

Sadoul, Georges (1975) *Histoire générale du cinéma*,VI, Paris, Denoël, 328-332.

SCRIPT

L'Herbier, Marcel (1978) '*L'Argent*', *Avant-Scène Cinéma*, 209.

APPENDIX

Marcel L'Herbier (1890—1979): filmography

1918 *Phantasmes*
1919 *Le Bercail* (short)

1919 *Rose-France*
1920 *Le Carnaval des vérités*
1920 *L'Homme du large*
1920 *Villa Destin*
1921 *El Dorado*
1922 *Prométhée banquier*
1922 *Don Juan et Faust*
1924 *L'Inhumaine*
1925 *Feu Mathias Pascal (The Late Matthew Pascal)*
1926 *Le Vertige*
1927 *L'Homme à l'Hispano*
1928 *Un Chapeau de paille d'Italie (The Italian Straw Hat)*
1928 *Le Diable au coeur*
1928 *Nuits de prince*
1929 *L'Argent*
1930 *L'Enfant de l'amour*
1930 *La Femme d'une nuit*
1931 *Le Mystère de la chambre jaune*
1931 *Le Parfum de la dame en noir*
1933 *L'Epervier (Bird of Prey)*
1934 *L'Aventurier*
1934 *Le Scandale*
1935 *Le Bonheur*
1935 *La Route impériale*
1935 *Veille d'armes*
1936 *Les Hommes nouveaux*
1936 *La Porte du large (The Great Temptation)*
1937 *La Citadelle du silence (The Citadel of Silence)*
1937 *Forfaiture (The Cheat)*
1937 *Nuits de feu (The Living Corpse)*
1938 *Adrienne Lecouvreur*
1938 *Children's Corner*
1938 *La Tragédie impériale*
1938 *Terre de feu*
1939 *La Brigade sauvage (Savage Brigade)*
1939 *Entente cordiale*
1939 *La Mode rêvée* (short)
1941 *Histoire de rire (Foolish Husbands)*
1942 *La Comédie du bonheur*
1942 *La Nuit fantastique*
1943 *L'Honorable Catherine*
1945 *La Vie de bohême*
1946 *Au petit bonheur*
1946 *L'Affaire du collier de la Reine (The Queen's Necklace)*
1948 *La Révoltée (Stolen Affections)*
1950 *Les Derniers jours de Pompéi (The Last Days of Pompeii)*
1953 *Le Père de mademoiselle.*
1963 *Hommage à Debussy*
1967 *Le Cinéma du diable* (documentary)
1978 *La Féerie des fantasmes* (documentary)

Other films cited in the text

Ame d'artiste, Germaine Dulac (1925)
L'Arlésienne, André Antoine (1921)
Au bonheur des femmes, Julien Duvivier (1929)
Autour de L'Argent, Jean Dréville (1928)

Bouclette, Louis Mercanton and René Hervil (1918)
Casanova, Alexandre Volkoff (1927)
La Danseuse orchidée, Léonce Perret (1928)
La Femme nue, Léonce Perret (1926)
La Glace à trois faces, Jean Epstein (1927)
Germinal, Albert Capellani (1913)
Marquitta, Jean Renoir (1927)
Metropolis, Fritz Lang (1927)
Michel Strogoff, Victor Tourjansky (1926)
Les Misérables, Henri Fescourt (1925-26)
Nana, Jean Renoir (1926)
Napoléon vu par Abel Gance, Abel Gance (1927)
October, Sergei Eisenstein (1928)
La Passion de Jeanne d'Arc, Carl Dreyer (1928)
Au pays des ténèbres, Victorin Jasset (1912)
Le Rêve, Jacques de Baroncelli (1921)
La Terre, André Antoine (1919)
Thérèse Raquin, Jacques Feyder (1928)
Le Torrent, Louis Mercanton and René Hervil (1918)
Travail, Henri Pouctal (1919-20)

4. 'Let's sing it one more time': René Clair's *Sous les toits de Paris* (1930)

MICHEL MARIE

René Chomette, who called himself René Clair when he started out as a film actor in 1920 under such directors as Loïe Fuller and Louis Feuillade, had just turned 30 when the film-going public's overwhelming enthusiasm for the talkies buried the silent cinema for good. By 1929, Clair was an internationally famous *auteur*-director: he had made an avant-garde short which caused something of a scandal in fashionable society (*Entr'acte*) and six silent feature films, including *Paris qui dort* (shot in 1923 but distributed in February 1925 after *Entr'acte*), and, most recently, his two adaptations of vaudeville plays by Eugène Labiche and Marc Michel, *Un Chapeau de paille d'Italie* and *Les Deux timides* respectively. Within the space of five years Clair had established himself as one of the few genuine *auteurs* among the new generation of filmmakers; he was recognized as having a personal universe and an idiosyncratic style, and obtained highly favourable production conditions when making his last three silent features for Alexandre Kamenka's Films Albatros.

But in 1926, Warners had already used the Vitaphone sound system for *Don Juan*, a film with sound and singing; and October 1927 saw the box-office triumph of the celebrated *The Jazz Singer*, which Parisian filmgoers saw only in January 1929, 15 months later. French companies lagged almost two years behind their American counterparts in the production of sound films. *L'Eau du Nil*, which, on its release on 18 October 1928, was presented as 'the first French sound film' (a Vandal & Delac production directed by Marcel Vandal), was merely a silent movie with music and songs, and caused considerable disappointment among the public. Three months later, filmgoers responded enthusiastically to the few sentences spoken by Al Jolson in a film which in fact contained only a few snatches of synchronized dialogue.

In 1929, there were only eight French sound productions or co-productions. The new techniques had had the effect of stepping up competition between the American and German industries (RCA and Western Electric in the United States, and Tobis Klang Film in Germany), both of which were trying to impose their patents on Europe. Gaumont-Franco-Film-Aubert put a soundtrack on *Le Collier de la Reine* and *Quand nous étions deux*. Etablissements Jacques Haïk produced *Le Mystère de la Villa Rosa* in England, a solution also adopted by Pierre Braunberger and Roger Richebé for *La Route est belle* and by Pathé-Natan for *Les Trois masques*; all these productions relied on American sound systems. German techniques were used, on the other hand, by the three following films: *Mon béguin*; *La Nuit est à nous*, which was shot in Germany in two versions and presented as 'the first major full-talking French super-production with sound recorded during shooting' (produced by Films P. J. de Venloo, Carl Froelich Film and Lutèce Film); and *Le Requin*, a Société des Films Sonores Tobis production made at the Epinay studios, near Paris, by René Clair's brother, Henri Chomette — Albert Préjean, who played the male lead, Lazare Meerson, who designed the sets, and Frank Clifford, who was production manager, all appear on the credits of *Sous les toits de Paris*.

In 1929, Sofar asked Clair to go to Berlin, where he wrote the original screenplay of *Prix de beauté*; but production got under way only a year later with the Italian director Augusto Genina. The film has a remarkably inventive final sequence in which the heroine, played by Louise Brooks, is murdered by her lover in a viewing theatre while on the screen she continues to sing — a fine metaphor for the death throes of the silent film and its metamorphosis into the singing and talking cinema. Throughout the year 1929, Clair, who began as a journalist on *L'Intransigeant*, wrote articles siding with those who were furiously resisting the invasion of cinema screens by the talkies.

But on closer inspection it can be seen that Clair did not condemn the sound cinema outright:

> It is not the invention of the talking picture that frightens us, it is the deplorable use our industrialists will not fail to make of it.
>
> The sound film or, more precisely, the synchronization between the reproduction of images and sounds, could be useful in the musical accompaniment of films, in newsreels, in educational cinema, etc. It is not even out of the question that an art peculiar to the talking film might be created, an art the object and laws of which we cannot foresee any more than those of the film in general were foreseen around 1900. (Clair 1972, 128)

Clair looked at the transition from silent to sound cinema from the viewpoint of an artist who condemned the commercial constraints which, with the massive backing of the big electric companies, were about to change radically the still 'artisanal' conditions of filmmaking:

> 1929. Second birth, or death? If chance — a few grains of sand in the industrial machine — does not come along to foil the plans of the financiers of the cinema, *we must place our wager on death, or at least on a long sleep that resembles it.* What is the cinema for us? A new medium of expression, a new poetry and dramaturgy. What is it for them? Fifty thousand theaters all over the world that must be supplied with a show — film, music acts or a sheep with five legs — capable of making the spectator's money pour into the box

office. It is only by chance that our interests and theirs have sometimes coincided. The stand taken by American finance, and soon by European finance, on the question of talking pictures finally enlightens us in this regard. (Clair 1972, 129-130)

But Clair himself added in 1970 that 'during the early period of the sound and talking picture, the spirit of invention was stimulated by the novelty of the technology' (Clair 1972, 130). At the time what he condemned was the talking film as opposed to the sound film, and *Sous les toits de Paris* served as the manifesto film for that aesthetic revolution: a sound cinema which would be musical, part-talking and part-sung, but in which synchronized dialogue would never play a dominant dramatic role.

> ... It is unnecessary to pay attention to the bad talking pictures, which are not rare; *Give and Take* and *The Strange Cargo* are perfect examples of these.
> Here, the image is reduced precisely to the role of the illustration of a phonograph record, and the sole aim of the whole show is to resemble as closely as possible the play of which it is the 'cinematic' reproduction. In three or four settings there take place endless scenes of dialogue which are merely boring if you do not understand English, but unbearable if you do. (Clair 1972, 137)

In May 1929, Clair was bowled over by two American musicals, *The Broadway Melody* and *Show Boat*, whose aesthetic innovations he described in detail in an article:

> The actors move around, walk, run, talk, shout and sigh, and the equipment reproduces their movements and voices with a suppleness that would be like a miracle if we did not know that science and meticulous organization will lead us to see many more wonders like these. [...] The immobility of the shots — that flaw of the talking picture — has disappeared. The camera is as mobile, the shots as varied, as in a good silent film. (Clair 1972, 138)

He went on to mention a number of sound effects that we find in *Sous les toits de Paris*:

> For example we hear the sound of a car door being shut and the car pulling away, which is heard while, on the screen, the anguished face of Bessie Love watches this unseen departure from a window. This brief scene — in which all the effect is

concentrated on the actress's face, and which the silent film would have had to break up into several shots — owes its success to the 'unity of place' obtained by the use of sound.

In another scene, Bessie Love is in bed, sad and pensive; you feel that she is about to cry: she puckers up her face, but it disappears into the shadow of a fade-out, and from the screen, which has turned black, issues the sound of a single sob.

In these two examples it will be noted that at the right moment sound has replaced the image. It seems that it is in this economy of its means of expression that the sound cinema has a chance to find some original effects. (1972, 138-139)

Clair's article resembles in many respects the celebrated 'manifesto' signed by Eisenstein, Pudovkin and Alexandrov — and with which he was not acquainted at the time — in favour of a counterpoint, or non-coincidence, of image and sound (or, as they put it, of 'sight-images', and 'sound-images'); and, interestingly enough, in his comments on *Close Harmony*, '*Broadway Melody*'s kid brother', Clair remarks on:

> [...] a fight scene in a nightclub in which the battle of the two men remains invisible [they are hidden by the spectators crowding around them], but is suggested by shouts and noises. (Clair, 1972, 139)

Sous les toits de Paris, which Clair shot in January 1930, was, then, the work of a man who had been looking at talkies for two years, first in London, then in Paris. He opted for European backing (Tobis) and geared his choice of scenario closely to the constraints of the medium: since American talkies contained singing and dancing, *Sous les toits de Paris* would have as its central character a street singer who is in love with a *midinette* — characters that were crucial (one entertaining, the other being entertained) to the great success of the ever-growing record industry of the time. Clair's last two silent films had been set around the turn of the century and depicted the quaintly old-fashioned cardboard characters of Labiche's farces. In the sound films he was then planning to make, he decided to focus once again on the daily lives of the very kind of people that would see his films, and showed a keen interest in real-life stories. He wrote the screenplays first of *Prix de beauté*, whose central character is a young typist fascinated by the cinema, then of *Une Enquête est ouverte*. The sound cinema came into being not in a vacuum, but at a time when the sound media — records and radio — were expanding considerably. At the same time, the end of the 1920s was a period when filmgoers in France were coming from an appreciably wider social background, including the working-class suburbs of large cities. Clair's stroke

Sous les toits de Paris — above: Albert (Albert Préjean) with Pola (Pola Illéry); below: Pola and Louis (Edmond T. Gréville).

of genius was to work this development into the fabric of his film by taking a street singer as his central character. Most of the action takes place in the street, in working-class cafés and in attic lodgings, in contrast with the many American films set behind the scenes of Broadway musical theatres. With *Sous les toits de Paris* Clair initiated the populist vein which was to inspire the French sound cinema of the decade up until its most tragic and pessimistic manifestation, *Le Jour se lève*.

Its story line is reduced to essentials. It is no more complex than the kind of theme or dramatic situation customarily evoked by popular songs with three verses and a chorus. Clair's aim in doing this was to give free rein to the emblematic sound effects that were characteristic of what he regarded as the true talking film. But his deliberate shunning of synchronized dialogue meant he could not embark on the kind of psychological analysis required by complex characters. So they had to be easily identifiable figures, pre-constructed social types: the good-natured, engaging street singer (Albert/Albert Préjean), his rather impulsive young friend (Louis/Edmond T. Gréville), the flighty foreign *midinette* (Pola/Pola Illéry), the gang leader (Fred/Gaston Modot), the pickpocket (Bill, played by an actor called, of all things, Bill-Bockett), as well as the grumpy neighbour, the fat woman, the bowler-hatted policeman, and so on — a whole cast of stock characters on whom Clair repeatedly drew until *Le Dernier milliardaire*, at which point he set off on a ghost-raising venture in England (where he shot *The Ghost Goes West* in 1935).

Miraculously for the film, Albert Préjean turned out to be the ideal person to play the popular singer. In 1930, though, he was by no means at the beginning of his career. After a walk-on part in *Les Trois mousquetaires*, the 'Douglas Fairbanks of the Paris suburbs' had dazzled filmgoers with his physical feats in *Le Miracle des loups*, and in *Paris qui dort*, in which he casually lit a cigarette while standing perched on the top of the Eiffel Tower. Clair had also directed him in *Le Voyage imaginaire* and *Un Chapeau de paille d'Italie*, where he played the bourgeois Fadinard decked out for a wedding. In Henri Chomette's *Le Requin*, he played the skipper of a freighter sunk by its crooked owner because he wants to pocket the insurance money. Audiences had not yet had the opportunity to hear him sing. 'In 1929, what this good-natured, cocky, ever-smiling character still lacked was a voice and a chance to appear in a film with a genuinely populist theme' (Cadars 1982, 90). That is why *Sous les toits de Paris* marked a turning point both in Préjean's career and in the history of the French sound cinema. In the role of Albert, 'Préjean just had to play himself — he was perfectly at ease in what was his own milieu' (Cadars, 1982, 92). Like Maurice Chevalier, Préjean could sing: he then began a tour of all the European capitals, and he became a popular star as much because of his song recitals as because of his films. *Sous les toits de Paris* marked the first encounter between the French sound cinema and popular song. The two songs by René Nazelles and Raoul Moretti, 'Sous les toits de Paris' and 'C'est pas comme ça', became worldwide hits and resulted directly in the film's success. Initially did it much better abroad than in France: it was acclaimed not only in Berlin (August, 1930), New York and London (December, 1930) but in Tokyo and Buenos Aires, whereas its Paris release at the Moulin Rouge in May 1930 had drawn rather low attendances.

When Albert, in the film, addresses his listeners in the street and says 'And now for the latest hit, "C'est pas comme ça", as sung in all Paris concert-halls — words and music, one franc', he is also promoting Clair's movie, whose musical theme was hummed by people the moment they emerged from the cinema.

> I observed the spectators leaving after hearing a talking picture. They seemed to be leaving a vaudeville theater. They were not plunged into that comfortable numbness which a trip to the land of pure images used to bestow on us. They were talking, laughing and humming the last refrain they had heard. *They had not lost the sense of reality.* (Clair 1972, 141)

This was a perfect example of how the sound medium — the song relayed by radio broadcasts — could serve the purposes of the film industry and turn a poor first run into an international triumph.

The film's secret resides precisely in the simplicity of its narrative and its situations, and in the way the signifying function of words is, so to speak, interfered with. Whenever a character has something verbal to express, his or her action is hindered by the dramatic situation or by a deliberate directorial device. Thus, at the beginning of the film, when Albert wants to warn Pola about the pickpocket's designs, he can only use mime or speed up the tempo of the song he is singing, for he cannot stop his performance without attracting the attention of those who are giving him a vocal accompaniment.

More specifically, Clair chooses, whenever possible, to eschew the classical style which frames the person who happens to be talking. This *parti pris* is particularly noticeable when the gang leader Fred goes to see Pola in her attic room. All we see at first are his feet climbing the stairs; when he opens the door of her room, a high-angle shot from outside the building shows the room through the skylight, revealing part of Fred's body but not his face. So we do not actually see him speak when he says 'I came to say hello'. This voice-over effect accentuates the sequence's voyeuristic approach, which began with an earlier shot that lingered lovingly on Pola's legs as she put on her stockings while singing the chorus of the song: it is 'Sous les toits de Paris' ('beneath the roofs of Paris') that the prettiest legs can be admired, even those of a Romanian *ingénue* (she makes her nationality clear in the opening sequence when knowingly exploiting her accent to eroticize her voice).

People's memory of the film very often occults its prologue-like opening sequence.[1] Instead they tend to remember the celebrated panoramic/tracking shot (shot 32 in the shooting script published by *Avant-Scène Cinéma* 1982,

10) which descends from the rooftops to show Albert, in medium close-up, singing and beating time, thus ensuring the 'diegetization' of the musical theme first heard during the credits, then repeated as the camera begins its downward journey.

But the prologue, which has virtually no dialogue, pays homage to the aesthetic possibilities of the silent cinema, and divides up the filmic space with a variation in the choice of camera angles that makes the sequence a classic: a high-angle shot of a shop awning framed diagonally, a high-angle shot of a gutter, a lateral tracking shot of passers-by whose faces are hidden by their umbrellas, and who bump into each other and exchange *silent* insults. Throughout the prologue, it is Armand Bernard's continuous musical score, which is very like the music of Chaplin's silent films, that comments on and even signifies the action instead of words (as in the altercation between Fred and one of the members of the gang, played by Aimos, who has just come out of the café). The first piece of synchronized dialogue in the movie — and therefore in Clair's sound films — comes in a very unusual low-angle shot of Albert, Pola and Louis, who occupy the lower part of the frame and are shown only from the waist upwards; and the language used consists partly of slang (of a type known as 'javanais'):

> Albert: 'Elle est rien bavath, la môme du haut' ('She ain't half a bit of all right, that bird from upstairs')
> Louis: 'Et gaffe un peu les mirettes ...' ('and watch those minces')[2]

Pola cannot understand their exchange, and answers in Romanian. Albert then asks her to speak French — a request that is not without irony in the contemporary context of mainly English-speaking talkies. This linguistic imbroglio clearly heralds the film's aesthetic programme, which is to call into question the communicative function of speech, or at least to disrupt it as systematically as possible.

The film's structure hinges on an ironic repetitive saturation of the title song, which is relentlessly reiterated until it even begins to irritate some of the characters, such as the grumpy tenant who washes his feet in a bowl. After the musical prologue, a long sequence of over seven minutes is devoted to a demonstration of Albert's vocal talents. As the camera slowly moves down from the rooftops to the cobbled street, there is an increase in the volume of the sound and, consequently, of space; the camera homes in on Pola, who is leaning against the door of a building, then moves towards the source of the singing, drawing her in its wake. After a brief cut to a high-angle shot showing the face of the young woman, whose own curiosity stimulates that of the audience at the beginning of the film, Albert is shown face-on, and in medium close-up, giving a pep talk to his interlocutors — who in this case include not only the diegetic audience but the spectators of Clair's film: 'That wasn't too bad this time. We'll try the chorus one last time together, and it'll be much better, won't it? Here we go!'. This one last time is in fact the first, and will be repeated in the closing sequence of the film: 'Come on, that's not bad, we'll just sing it one more time' — a device which enables Clair to tie up the narrative neatly and lead straight into the next projection of the film, producing a kind of loop, as is suggested by an orchestral repetition of the theme when 'The end' and the name Tobis come up on the screen.

The 'working to death' of the theme tune is emphasized immediately after the sequence where the pickpocket steals purses: a very straight descending tracking shot (shot 109 in *Avant-Scène* script) — the opposite of the ascending tracking shot (shot 40) which immediately followed Albert's first performance — comes down the façade of the building from the rooftops to the pavement. The tune is being hummed, sung or played by the tenants, who are shown one after the other during the tracking shot and later in a series of medium shots (shots 112-114): a woman seated at a piano on the ground floor stumbles through the score while her husband tries to read his newspaper; another woman, the fat lady on the first floor whose purse was stolen, hums the tune while doing her hair, much to the exasperation of her neighbour on the second floor, who is himself singing with his feet in a washbowl, but protests by banging on the floor when he hears her: 'Oh! that song!' (very irritatedly).

Meanwhile, we have also seen Fred, who is whistling the same tune, and an obviously inebriated Albert at a café counter, who starts singing again, this time fortissimo:

> 'Mais t'as compris un peu plus chaque jour
> ce que c'est que l'bonheur mon amour!
> Sous les toits de Paris ...'

> 'But more and more, every day, you've realized
> what happiness is, my love!
> Beneath the roofs of Paris ...'

Louis then interrupts him: 'Okay, okay, we've heard it before'; and Albert replies: 'Very well, you won't hear it any more' — a neat filmic denial referring to the heated controversy that followed the release of the first French talkies in 1930.

A second and equally famous song, which comes exactly half way through the film, divides the narrative into two symmetrical sections and marks a new stage in Pola and Albert's budding but thwarted romance.

The first section closes with the long sequence in Albert's room, when both characters end up sleeping on the floor, one on either side of the bed, after their celebrated row in the dark (which Godard recycles in *Une Femme est une femme*, a film dedicated to Lubitsch and Clair — the credits also quote Clair's *Quatorze juillet*) followed, in the morning, by Bill's visit to plant his bag of stolen goods in Albert's room.

Then, after a fade-out, we are given another very spectacular panoramic/tracking shot, which reaffirms the mobility of the *mise-en-scène* and, like its predecessor, leads us to the singing Albert, this time accompanied by Pola who is selling scores of a new song, 'C'est pas comme ça'. The musical performance lasts for more than four minutes, and is abruptly brought to an end by the neighbour on the second floor, who throws a pitcher of water over the fat police inspector. This sequence, like the first, is completely articulated around the characters' inability to conduct a dialogue (clearly, they would like to talk but cannot because they are singing!). The breakdown of shots in both sequences is governed entirely by the directions and alternations of the characters' gestures and looks, as in the best moments of the silent cinema. It is as if Clair, in a direct homage to the style of Charlie Chaplin, were trying to prove that the sound cinema can be hummed, sung and mimed, but that it has absolutely nothing to gain from synchronized dialogue.

The three street-singing sequences (at the beginning, middle and end of the film) alone account for over 12 minutes and 30 seconds of a movie whose total length is only 80 minutes (according to existing copies). What is more, two long sequences take place in a popular dance hall where an accordion can be heard almost continuously, playing very well-known waltzes and *javas* (dances in fast three-four time). On each occasion, the music is so loud as to prevent verbal communication between the characters. The first dance hall sequence, which introduces Fred's gang and reveals the existence of rivalry between Louis and Albert, consists of three *javas* and two waltzes with a total length of 7 minutes and 40 seconds; the last dance hall sequence, where Albert meets Pola again after his release from prison, comprises two waltzes and one *java*, or 3 minutes 10 seconds of music, which is interrupted in the middle of the second waltz by the departure of Fred's gang and the preparations for the fight with Albert. In both sequences, there is a long succession of brief shots contrasting the attitudes and expressions of the characters, which signify alternately defiance, provocation, threats, seduction, feigned absent-mindedness and so on.

Thus, the diegetic songs and dance tunes alone take up over 23 of the film's 80 minutes; in addition to this series there is the recorded music the drunk customer listens to in the café at the end of the film, during the final showdown between Louis and Albert (the theme of 'The Charge of the Light Brigade'); the record is so badly scratched that at one point the same musical motif is repeated again and again. It emerges, then, that, even without taking into account the non-diegetic musical score (themes orchestrated by Armand Bernard, which themselves occupy large sections of the film), there remain very few sequences or fragments of sequences where the characters are able to exchange a few words without a musical background.

But music was not the only method Clair used to cut the power of synchronized speech down to size. Many critics and filmgoers in 1930 noted his directorial strategy of filming characters from outside the glass door of the café. Thus, when Pola goes to fetch Louis, we hear the noise inside the café when she opens the door, but the camera remains outside and we cannot catch the heated conversation between the two characters, whose gestures can be seen through the window; at other times background music spills out from one place to another and completely drowns the animated conversations between Albert and his friend Louis. Speech is also 'masked' by whispering. During Albert and Pola's first walk through the dark streets, a series of close shots of their feet on the cobblestones is followed by a shot of Albert whispering a few words in the ear of the young woman, who replies several times: 'No, no, no!' Then Albert echoes her: 'So it's no?' Pola: 'No.' True, it is not difficult to imagine the gist of what Albert was whispering to her, but the important thing here is Clair's use of a talking situation where the audience is once again prevented from hearing the actual words.

Conversely, Clair at other times plays on 'acousmatic' voices, to use the term recently taken up by Michel Chion. This time we hear the voice but cannot see where it comes from. First there is a gag based on a repeated situation. The pickpocket knocks on Albert's door very early in the morning, after the eventful night with Pola. Albert hears, 'Open up in the name of the law! Open up, will you please!', without seeing the speaker of the words. The same verbal situation is repeated in a later sequence, but this time it is the real police inspector who barks, out of shot: 'Open up in the name of the law!' The gag was not a new one, but it did require recorded sound, at least in this form.

Two equally famous sequences demonstrate the originality of the *mise-en-scène*, which this time exploits the soundtrack at the expense of the image: in both cases the screen remains dark for several minutes.

The first scene takes place in Albert's room. He has just had an increasingly acrimonious row with Pola, who wants to sleep — alone — in the room's one and only bed. Albert, dressed in striped pyjamas, gets into bed and turns off the light. At this point all that can be seen are two shadowy figures in the dark, and it is the sound track that occupies all the filmic space: the two characters exchange a series of insults and cries of rage, which are intentionally allowed to overlap on the soundtrack. The light comes back on when Pola says 'I'm fed up' and we see Albert sitting on the bed with his hair ruffled.

Such inventiveness in the manipulation of the sound parameters of film was not to be found again until the appearance of Godard and the New Wave, for traditional cinema had a phobia of darkness or any temporary disappearance of the image. The whole effect here is achieved by the pace of the altercation and the editing, by the discrepancy between the image and the axis of the soundtrack, and by the play on Pola's Romanian accent, which Albert mocks ('But I *am* leaving you alone!', he says in a falsetto voice).

The second sequence also takes place at night, but this time outside, in a dark alley. Albert has been tailing Fred and his gang so they can have a proper physical showdown this time, and not just a verbal one. The scene is shown in high-angle long shots. A few wan streetlamps selectively illuminate two or three areas of the alley. In addition, the brawl takes place near a railway line, and a steam train swathes in smoke the few areas of the night landscape still visible. The sound of the scuffling is drowned by the cries of the gang, the whistling of the policemen who arrive on the scene, and the mounting clatter of a train as it passes off-screen. To cap everything, Louis arrives on the scene with a revolver and fires at a streetlamp, which shatters, plunging the screen into utter darkness. We cannot see which of the characters is actually speaking ('Here, take that!'), and the darkness of the alley is dispelled only by the headlamps of a police car.

It can be seen, then, that without this simplicity and circularity of story line Clair would not have been able to experiment with such stylistic figures. The primacy given to formal experimentation is largely responsible for the modernity of Clair's first sound film, which is hardly narrative at all, and which adopts a descriptive approach that was rediscovered only by the innovatory cinema of the 1970s.

But it was not just in this respect that *Sous les toits de Paris* broke new ground. Thematically, it marked the first appearance of a working-class milieu that was subsequently exploited, as Raymond Chirat has rightly pointed out (*Avant-Scène Cinéma*, 281, 6) by UFA's Berlin musical comedies, whose central characters included garage mechanics (*Le Chemin du paradis*), window-cleaners (*Un Rêve blond*), and nightwatchmen (*A moi le jour, à toi la nuit*).[3]

Marcel Carné, who was Clair's assistant on the film along with Georges Lacombe and Jacques Houssin, later recalled the peculiarly Parisian flavour of the district described in *Sous les toits de Paris*; and the cobbled streets along which Préjean walks in *Jenny* are a clear reference to his stroll with Pola.

I have concentrated on the soundtrack of the film at the expense of its photographic style. Its rich visual qualities, though, would alone merit a separate study. Any such study would have to discuss the parallels between the very specific style of the images produced by Clair, Georges Périnal and Lazare Meerson (the lighting formed an integral part of the set design) and Brassaï's photographs of the same milieu at the same period (see his book *The Secret Paris of the 1930s*), and in particular the chapter on popular dance-halls. I shall restrict myself here to mentioning one particularly remarkable visual composition in Clair's film.

After the first dance hall sequence, where she is harrassed by Fred and has her key stolen, Pola goes out, leans against the door of a building and weeps. The street is shown in a general shot with considerable depth of field. A pan right reveals Albert in the foreground leaning against a wall. He is watching Pola, who is in the far distance, standing in a pool of light. He walks towards her. The lighting divides the space up into several distinct areas, and exploits the strongly contrasting blacks, greys and whites. There is certainly material here for further and more detailed study in another essay.

Jean-Luc Godard had Clair's visual style in mind when he exploited Franscope and Eastmancolor in his filming of the emotional involvements of another trio, Angela, Emile and Alfred, in the working-class milieu of Faubourg Saint-Denis in *Une Femme est une femme*.

Translated from the French by Peter Graham (except René Clair's quotes, from Clair [1970], which are here reproduced from the published translation of the book: Clair [1972]).

NOTES

1. Most prints of the film in distribution (in the UK and USA) omit this first sequence and begin with the panoramic/tracking shot described here. For a description of the special apparatus devised by Clair for this technically advanced shot (for the period), see Dale (1986), II (eds).

2. The US translation given by Dale (1986, II, 109) is 'Glim the Jane'; 'Not a bad looker' (eds).

3. These films were shot in several languages. *Le Chemin du paradis*: German version, *Die Drei von der Tankstelle* (Wilhelm Thiele, 1930). *Un Rêve blond:* German version, *Ein blonden Traum* (Paul Martin, 1932); English version, *Happy Ever After* (Paul Martin, 1932). *A moi le jour, à toi la nuit:* German version, *Ich bei Tag und Du bei Nacht* (Ludwig Berger, 1932); English version, *Early to Bed* (Ludwig Berger, 1932) (eds).

SELECTED BIBLIOGRAPHY

Amengual, Barthélémy (1963) *René Clair*, Paris, Seghers.

Barrot, Olivier (1985) *René Clair ou le temps mesuré*, Paris, Hatier.

Brassaï (1976) *The Secret Paris of the 1930s*, New York, Random House; London, Thames & Hudson.

Cadars, Pierre (1982) *Les Séducteurs du cinéma français (1928-1958)*, Paris, Henri Veyrier.

Charensol, Georges, and Régent, Roger (1952) *Un Maître du cinéma, René Clair*, Paris, La Table Ronde.

Charensol, Georges and Régent, Roger (1979) *Cinquante ans de cinéma avec René Clair*, Paris, La Table Ronde.

Chion, Michel (1982) *La Voix au cinéma*, Paris, Cahiers du cinéma, Editions de L'Etoile.

Clair, René (1951) *Réflexion faite*, Paris, NRF, Gallimard.

Clair, René (1970) *Cinéma d'hier, cinéma d'aujourd'hui*, Paris, NRF, Gallimard.

Clair, René (1972) *Cinema Yesterday and Today*, trans. Stanley Applebaum, New York, Dover Publications.

Dale, R.C. (1986) *The Films of René Clair*, I: *Exposition and Analysis*, II: *Documentation*, Metuchen, New Jersey, Scarecrow.

Edelmann, Marc and Giret, Noëlle (1983) *René Clair*, Catalogue of the retrospective season held 19 January-15 March, 1983, Paris, Cinémathèque Française.

Fillier, Jacques (1932) *Sous les toits de Paris*, Paris, *Le Film Complet du Mardi*, 1155.

Greene, Noemie (1985) *René Clair; A Guide to References and Resources*, Boston, G. K. Hall.

McGerr, Celia (1980) *René Clair*, Boston, Twayne, G. K. Hall.

Marie, Michel (1985) 'La Bouche bée', *Hors Cadre*, 3, 115-130 (the issue is devoted to the use of voice-over and studies the soundtrack of Alan Crosland's *The Jazz Singer* in detail).

Mitry, Jean (1960) *René Clair*, Paris, Editions Universitaires.

Thiher, Allen (1979) '*From Entr'acte* to *A nous la liberté*: René Clair and the Order of Farce', in *The Cinematic Muse*, Columbia and London, University of Missouri Press, 64-77.

SCRIPT

Clair, René (1982) *Sous les toits de Paris*, *Avant-Scène Cinéma*, 281.

APPENDIX

René Clair (1898—1981): filmography

1923   *Paris qui dort (The Crazy Ray)*
1924   *Entr' acte*
1925   *Le Fantôme du Moulin Rouge*
1926   *Le Voyage imaginaire*
1927   *La Proie du vent*
1927   *Un Chapeau de paille d'Italie (The Italian Straw Hat)*
1928   *La Tour* (short)
1928   *Les Deux timides*
1930   *Sous les toits de Paris (Under the Roofs of Paris)*
1931   *Le Million*
1931   *A nous la liberté*
1932   *Le Quatorze juillet*
1934   *Le Dernier milliardaire*
1935   *The Ghost Goes West*
1938   *Break the News*
1941   *The Flame of New Orleans*
1942   *I Married a Witch*
1943   *Forever and a Day* (one episode)
1944   *It Happened Tomorrow*
1945   *And Then There Were None* (US); *Ten Little Indians* (UK)
1947   *Le Silence est d' or (Man about Town)*
1950   *La Beauté du diable (Beauty and the Devil)*
1952   *Les Belles de nuit (Beauties of the Night)*
1955   *Les Grandes manoeuvres (The Grand Manoeuvers)*
1957   *Porte des lilas (Gates of Paris)*
1960   *La Française et l' amour (Love and the Frenchwoman*, episode)
1961   *Tout l' or du monde*
1962   *Les Quatre vérités (Three Fables of Love: Les Deux pigeons*, episode)
1965   *Les Fêtes galantes*

Other films cited in the text

The Broadway Melody, Harry Beaumont (1929)
Le Collier de la Reine, Gaston Ravel and Tony Lekain, (1929)
Le Chemin du paradis, Wilhelm Thiele and Max de Vaucorbeil (1930)
Close Harmony, John Cromwell and Edward Sutherland (1929)
Don Juan, Alan Crosland (1926)
L'Eau du Nil, Marcel Vandal (1928)
Une Femme est une femme (A Woman is a Woman), Jean-Luc Godard (1961)
Give and Take, William Beaudine (1928)
The Jazz Singer, Alan Crosland (1927)
Jenny, Marcel Carné (1936)
Le Jour se lève, Marcel Carné (1939)
Le Miracle des loups, Raymond Bernard (1924)
A moi le jour, à toi la nuit, Ludwig Berger and Claude Heymann (1932)
Mon béguin, Hans Behrendt (1929)
Le Mystère de la Villa Rosa, Louis Mercanton and René Hervil (1929)
La Nuit est à nous, Carl Froelich and Henry Roussell (1929)

Prix de beauté, Augusto Genina (1930)
Quand nous étions deux, Léonce Perret (1929)
Le Requin, Henri Chomette (1929)
Un Rêve blond, Paul Martin (1932)
La Route est belle, Robert Florey (1929)
Les Trois masques, André Hugon (1929)
Les Trois mousquetaires, Henri Diamant-Berger (1921)
Show Boat, Harry Pollard (1929)
Strange Cargo, Benjamin Glazer and Arthur Gregor (1929)

5. In the name of the father: Marcel Pagnol's 'trilogy': *Marius* (1931), *Fanny* (1932), *César* (1936)

GINETTE VINCENDEAU

Marcel Pagnol's series of three films, *Marius, Fanny,* and *César,* usually referred to as 'the trilogy', has conformed to the fate of many truly popular classics: adored by the public — they were all box-office hits — the films were put down by contemporary critics as bad boulevard theatre or Marseillais melodramas (Bardèche and Brasillach 1948, 411). Pagnol did not seem to care and would blithely declare 'I only write about clichés' (Leprohon 1976, 388). Such professed candour, however, was underpinned by considerable intellectual and economic assets.

Pagnol was a forceful participant in the debates surrounding the coming of sound cinema in France, and particularly the question of 'filmed theatre'. He launched his own (short-lived) film magazine *Les Cahiers du film* in 1933 partly to publicize his provocative views on the primacy of dialogue over image, such as 'any sound film that can be projected silently and still remain comprehensible is a very bad film' (Pagnol 1933, 293). But Pagnol's contribution to the filming of theatrical texts was far more sophisticated than such bravado remarks would credit. If Pagnol the intellectual could give as good as he got, Pagnol the businessman could afford to brush off criticism. Between the release of *Marius* in 1931 and that of *César* in 1936, Pagnol, already the latest prodigy among France's playwrights and an experienced literary editor, made his name also as a filmmaker, a novelist, and a journalist. In addition, he became a producer, first with Rocher Richebé in 1932, then with his own company in 1933, *Les Auteurs associés* (changed in 1934 to *Les Films Marcel Pagnol),* and the owner of a studio in Marseilles — almost his home town as he came from nearby Aubagne — complete with labs, editing rooms, viewing theatres, and a regular staff. In 1935, he was the first to publish the full dialogue of one of his films *(Merlusse)* and two years later, he started his own publishing company, *Les Editions Marcel Pagnol.*

Pagnol had complete control over the technical side of his productions and his collaborators have testified that his equipment was, in many ways, the most advanced in France. This technological state of the art, as well as exceptional financial freedom — unheard of in 1930s French cinema — allowed him, for example, to experiment with direct sound and multiple re-takes, going as far as shooting both *Merlusse* and *Cigalon* twice over in 1935. Unlike Sacha Guitry, the other 'theatrical' director with whom he is often compared, and who would shoot a film like *Le Mot de Cambronne* in an afternoon, Pagnol always showed a keen interest in the cinematic process —

thus belying his (part self-fostered) image as a despiser of film as a 'minor art'. The completion of Pagnol's vertically integrated film 'empire' came with the opening of his own cinema in Marseilles, the Noailles, for the release of *César* in 1936, used as a 'sneak preview' theatre for his productions until 1938. Pagnol went on to make films until 1954 and subsequently published autobiographical works, among which *La Gloire de mon père* and *Le Château de ma mère* now figure on many schoolchildren's set book lists both in France and abroad.

Though it has had passionate defenders (Bazin, the *Cahiers du cinéma* editors in the late 1960s), Pagnol's work has generally suffered from critical discredit, with the exception of the Giono-inspired trio of *Jofroi, Angèle,* and *Regain*, which have been hailed, by Rossellini for instance, as precursors of Neo-Realism. Together with *La Femme du boulanger* (also based on Giono), it is the trilogy, however, which has remained the most popular part of Pagnol's oeuvre, regularly repeated on French television as well as in film clubs, its outrageously 'melodramatic' plot still bringing tears to the most cynical eyes, despite a cast of comic actors. Yet it is also the trilogy which has contributed most to the derogatory label of 'Pagnolade' given to anything set in Marseilles — a tribute, if anything, to its iconic power. Outside France, the trilogy has suffered from its association with a certain notion of quaint populist French film, evoking dusty film clubs, or, worse, holidays in the south of France and French cuisine (publicity material for one of the trilogy's American remakes advised local exhibitors to 'link the film with all local off-licences, wine importers, and hotels'); more recently, an expensive gourmet restaurant near San Francisco, 'Chez Panisse', has taken the name of one of the trilogy's key characters, a *panisse* in Marseillais patois being also a type of bread loaf. Thus Pagnol's films have acquired, in film studies, a somewhat debased cultural image. Their enduring popularity, however, remains, and we only need to look at the international success of Claude Berri's *Jean de Florette* and *Manon des sources*, both based on Pagnol's scripts, to perceive the centrality and actuality of Pagnol's work to a definition of French film.

* * *

The plot of the trilogy is disarmingly simple. In Marseilles' Vieux Port, Fanny (a shellfish seller) and Marius (who works in his father's bar) love each other, but Marius longs for the sea. After he sails away Fanny, now pregnant, has to marry the older and wealthier Panisse to save the family's honour. Marius later comes back to claim his 'wife' and son Césariot, but his father, César, sends him away. When Panisse dies twenty years later, Césariot learns the truth about his paternity and seeks out his real father. Fanny and Marius are finally reunited.

Equally disarming is the explicitness of these three films. The mechanics of desire, repression, and economics that propel the narrative along are practically spelt out by the dialogue. Furthermore, the *mise-en-scène* of the trilogy is what might be called 'exoteric'. Camera set-ups, predominantly static, are unashamedly put to the service of the dialogue, and the editing — bar a couple of montage scenes — simply juxtaposes one episode after another, and this whether the films were technically directed by Alexandre Korda (*Marius*), Marc Allégret (*Fanny*), or Pagnol himself (*César*). Does this mean, as some would claim, that the trilogy is 'the end of cinema' and, pushing the image further, the end of analysis? Perhaps not quite. While Pagnol's cinema is far from experimental, it is nonsense to describe it as 'utterly anti-cinematic' (IDHEC 1958, 31). For one thing, as Claude Beylie points out (1986, 56), the trilogy makes imaginative use of *sounds*, not just dialogue. And if it is not quite a documentary on Marseilles, the iconography of the city is present in all three films, and most effectively in Fanny's long walk to Notre-Dame de la Garde in *Fanny*. Pagnol's views on the grounding of authorship in the written word have been publicized well enough, and the debates on 'filmed theatre' sufficiently aired[1] for me not to have to rehearse them here. More importantly, Pagnol's works owe their genesis and appeal to a variety of intertexts that go beyond their dramatic basis: cast, performances, and iconography create a strong identity, in excess of a simple illustration of the written texts. The trilogy, however, because of its close relationship to a set of plays, is also a good test-case for a study of the interaction of the theatrical and the filmic.

Though conceived with a perfect ending for sequels (Marius sailing away), *Marius* was written as a single play for the stage, first performed in March 1929. Its filming in 1931, however, belongs to the early history of sound cinema in France, during which playwrights — including the most prestigious — turned out play adaptations and 'original' material, notably for the infamous Parisian branch of Paramount.[2] It is in this context that, in harmonious collaboration with Alexander Korda who was drawn in by Bob Kane (the head of Paramount in Paris) to palliate Pagnol's lack of experience in filmmaking, Pagnol adapted his stage hit for the screen, with almost the same cast: Raimu as César, Pierre Fresnay as Marius, Orane Demazis as Fanny, Charpin as Panisse. In line with the contemporary practice of making multiple-language films, German and Swedish versions were shot at the same time, with, according to Pagnol, much tinkering with the narrative compared with the French original (Pagnol 1981, 242).

The triumph of *Marius* prompted Pagnol to write a follow-up, *Fanny*, also for the theatre but clearly with a film in mind. Though Harry Baur (a considerable name and talent then) took the part of César on stage, a questionnaire among audiences showed overwhelming demand for the return of the same cast for *Fanny* (the film) as in *Marius*, the intertext already sliding from a theatrical to a filmic one. As André Bazin remarked, 'even though Marius triumphed at the Théâtre de Paris, its essential form is now and forever cinematic. Any new production of it on stage can only be a theatrical adaptation of the film' (Bazin 1975, 181). As would be expected, *Fanny* (the film) shows far fewer changes compared to the play than *Marius* does. As for

César, it was written directly as a screenplay and only performed on stage after the release of the film. The fact that *César* took a directly cinematic form is, paradoxically, a function of the success of *Marius* and *Fanny*: the cast, and in particular Raimu and Pierre Fresnay, had become far too expensive as film stars for them to be immobilized for months in a theatre. The published text of *César* does away with the traditional theatrical divisions into acts and tableaux present in the first two works. The gradual evolution away from the stage play is echoed in the increasing amount of outdoor shooting. Pagnol moves from the earlier, studio-bound *Marius* to *César*, where almost a quarter of the film is shot on location, and which, significantly, ends on a long open-air scene. These technical distinctions between 'play' and 'screenplay', between stage and cinema, are not, however, the only way the trilogy articulates the theatrical with the filmic.

Though the importance of performance is a feature of French 1930s cinema as a whole, the primacy of the cast in the trilogy is unique and works on several levels: as a marketing strategy (Raimu and Pierre Fresnay were stars of the Parisian stage before *Marius* was shot), as a way of consolidating the coherence of the narrative across three films, and as a way of successfully blending different generic codes. Alongside its obvious references to classical tragedy (the trilogy structure, the unity of space and action and, for the most part, time, and the 'chorus' formed by M. Brun, Panisse, Escartefigue and friends), Pagnol's trilogy has recourse to thematic and structural patterns that belong to melodrama, such a conjunction — of tragedy and melodrama — connecting it to the tradition of specifically *French* stage melodrama (Turim 1987). The cast of characters includes a suffering mother, an illegitimate child, a wealthy tutor, and an overbearing father. Marius' sudden return in the middle of the night at the end of *Fanny*, to reclaim woman and child from the clutches of the older man, bears the hallmark of stage melodrama (as well as modern soap opera), as does his alleged involvement with smugglers in *César*. Something else links the trilogy to specifically French melodrama: that is the constant juxtaposition of comic and tragic modes. Structurally, this informs the trilogy throughout, where a comic episode almost invariably follows, or is interspersed with, a 'tragic' one, as in the burlesque orange episode after the writing of the letter to Marius in *Fanny*, or the comical arguments in the kitchen while Panisse is dying at the beginning of *César*. The same principle works at the level of practically each scene and rests not just on dialogue and situation but on performance.

The cast of the trilogy is largely composed of actors whose range included music-hall revue and boulevard plays (Raimu), and classical tragedy (Charpin), and it mixes specific comic types (Dullac, Maupi) with an archetypal Comédie Française actor and later matinée idol like Pierre Fresnay. They were thus well equipped for the shifts in mood demanded by the text. But it is Raimu who most spectacularly achieves this duality through his constant recourse to a double register of acting. Like the others, Raimu's performance is pivotal in moving constantly between 'drama' and comedy, but, uniquely, his also shifts from the register of — comic as well as melodramatic — excess, to that of total sobriety. This he achieves through a body language which veers within instants from the exaggeration typical of the burlesque tradition he came from, and the emphatic gestures of the Marseillais (at least according to their accepted representation, a question I will come to later), to the restraint characteristic of modern sound cinema acting — and which is why Raimu was later much admired by Orson Welles. In other words, his two registers correspond to the enunciatory marks of the two forms of the trilogy: theatre and cinema. This capacity to shift instantaneously between the two is particularly effective in such set pieces as the breakfast scene in *Marius*, the reading of Marius' letter in *Fanny*, the conversation with Césariot after he has learnt his true paternity in *César*. Not surprisingly the theatrical mode corresponds to moments when as a character César is in situations of intense representation, usually on a comic register (demonstrating how to make a 'Picon-Grenadine' apéritif in *Marius*, his rendering of the supposed effects of the plague or whooping cough in *Fanny*), and the cinematic mode often to 'serious' moments of intimacy or solitude. In these passages, the gestures acquire a precise and moving sociological weight: sweeping the café, setting the breakfast table, etc. Through the dialectical relation between the two modes, an effect of realism emerges. The naturalistic gestures, the spectacle of realism, are embedded in moments of flaunted theatricality reinforced by the fact that all key locations in the trilogy are themselves public representational spaces: César's Bar de la Marine, Panisse's sailing equipment shop, and Fanny's shellfish stall (it is in the logic of gendered representation that the woman's stall — in the open, in full view of the bar — is itself a spectacle within the spectacle). Finally, the enclosed, U-shaped, Vieux Port is not unlike a stage, while being itself turned towards the spectacle offered by the sea and the ships.

***

In the same way as the trilogy combines different registers of theatre and cinema, it reconciles opposed ideological positions throughout. This mythic structure can be seen, to start with, in the contradictory discourse on Marseilles and the Marseillais proposed by the three films. Legend has it that Pagnol was initially opposed to the filming of *Marius* on the grounds that 'they would not understand it in Lille'. As it turned out, the regional aspect of the trilogy greatly helped its universal success. But Marseilles in the trilogy means more than local colour.

Although in other works, such as *Le Schpountz*, Pagnol shows the dichotomy Provence/France (or to be more precise, Paris) as a basically rural/urban divide, here we are talking of two rival urban cultures. The only French city capable of offering an alternative popular entertainment culture to the Parisian monopoly, Marseilles in the 1930s was a city thriving on the colonial trade and one which had been, since the nineteenth century, characterized by its own rich theatrical and music-hall traditions within which forms such as cabaret and operetta were particularly popular. Concurrently, the early 1930s saw one of the peaks of a fashion for Marseillais — and southern — lore in the rest of France. Clearly linked to the arrival of sound cinema which showcased the southern accent (in addition to the locations already well-documented by silent films), this trend was noticeable in other mechanically reproduced artefacts such as records, printed music sheets, postcards, etc. (see Peyrusse 1986 for a detailed study of Marseillais culture). It is in the midst of this fashion for 'Le midi' that film stars such as Fernandel and singers like Tino Rossi shot to national fame. Most of the trilogy performers — Raimu, Alida Rouffe, Charpin, Orane Demazis, Maupi — hailed from this milieu. But whereas the Marseillais live entertainment was aimed at an indigenous population, in Pagnol's trilogy, as in a spate of other films of the period, the effect is to represent Marseilles to outsiders, and notably Parisian audiences. Though he later claimed it had been originally designed for the Alcazar in Marseilles, Pagnol wrote *Marius* while 'in exile' in Paris, where his career had taken off, and he worked very hard at having it performed on a Parisian stage. Thus Marseilles was already the object of nostalgic longing: 'I did not know I loved Marseilles ... I discovered this after four years of Parisian life' (Pagnol 1981, 145). Some of the best-known Marseillais actors were also well integrated in Parisian society; for instance Raimu who started his career as a *comique troupier* (military comic) in Toulon at the turn of the century, but had by the late 1920s become an established pillar of the smart Champs-Elysées bars, while continuing to base his screen persona on his 'southernness'.

The objectification of Marseilles in the trilogy takes specific linguistic and performance channels: the exaggerated gestures and accent traits, such as Raimu's excessive opening of the vowel 'o' as in 'pôvre' for 'pauvre', become the ostentatious signs of 'Marseillais-ity', though outside France (where the cliché representation of the French is as excitable and gesticulating anyway), they tend to be seen simply as 'French'. Within the French context, this promotion of a regional culture through accent and gestures is a recognition of cultural difference which is not without ideological ambiguities. It is as well to remember that the picturesque southern accent is but a trace of a previous language, *provençal,* obliterated by French hegemonic culture; as Peyrusse (1986) points out, live shows in Marseilles up to the First World War would have been performed in *provençal.* The coming of sound cinema spread southern entertainment as long as it made itself acceptable to the dominant culture.

Alongside dialogues that remain classically theatrical, with an emphasis on well-turned phrases and clear diction,[3] the inflated rhetoric of speech and gestures in the trilogy is itself explicitly shown up as 'theatrical', with many self-conscious references in the lines, and with a constant shifting of the attributes of 'Marseillais-ity' across characters and situations. For example, M. Brun as a Lyonnais stands for the non-Marseillais in his encounters with other characters, including César; but when César himself is with

Escartefigue, it is Escartefigue who becomes the outrageously exaggerated cliché Marseillais, forever boasting and disinclined to work, compared to the then sober César. The Marseillais/rest of the world split covers other divisions too, class in particular. M. Brun as a customs clerk is the most middle-class character — he recites Sully-Prudhomme after Panisse's death, while Panisse himself in *Marius* quotes 'poetry' taken from a tobacconist window. Throughout the trilogy, talking '*pointu*' (with a Parisian/northern accent) equals being educated. But to be an educated Marseillais is to lose one's cultural specificity; to 'make it' as a Marseillais is to leave Marseilles — a paradox evident in the character of Césariot, but equally close to Pagnol's (and Raimu's) own experience. Thus despite the explicit discourse of the film which presents Marseilles as a coherent self-evident norm — against which other cities like Lyons and Paris are comically measured — it is positioned from the start as 'other', as culturally distanced.

While rooted in urban culture, the celebration of Marseilles by the trilogy is also a paean to archaic values. Central to this celebration is the running comparison between two types of knowledge as belonging to different generations. For example, Marius corrects his father's arithmetic in the 'Picon-grenadine' demonstration, and M. Brun corrects several characters' French.[4] Although in each case the correctors are technically right, the Marseillais and the older generation's superiority is constantly re-asserted by the narrative, their knowledge presented as 'natural' as opposed to acquired — folklore rather than culture. César may count four 'thirds' in his Picon-grenadine cocktail, but it is he, not Marius, who runs the bar efficiently. Although signs of modernity are increasingly apparent as the trilogy progresses, the three films cling to these nostalgic values. By the end of the trilogy, 20 years later, Marius himself has graduated to his father's position, and sharply criticizes Césariot's superior scholarly knowledge.

It is indeed the character of Césariot which most acutely shows this split between two types of knowledge, class and culture. As a gifted student at the *Polytechnique* school, Césariot, who wears the uniform of his difference at Panisse's funeral, has reached one of the heights of the French education system, a fact echoed naturally in his (and his friend Dromar's) lack of Marseillais accent. However, Pagnol makes the divide between him and the rest of the family and cast even more radical. André Fouché, as Césariot, has no Marseillais accent (unlike Pierre Fresnay, the only other major trilogy actor not from the south, who, as is well-known, took great pains to acquire a convincing one); his speech pattern is also different from the others, and so are his elocution and type of performance; whereas Robert Vattier as M. Brun, though coded as non-Marseillais, blends in his performance with the rest of the group. An elegant young man with a silk polka-dot dressing-gown and brillantined hair, Césariot seems straight out of a Parisian high society boulevard play or a Sacha Guitry film — even the decor of his bedroom, with

Marius (top) — above left: César (Raimu) and Marius (Pierre Fresnay); above right: Panisse (Charpin).
Fanny (bottom) — below left: Fanny (Orane Demazis) with her mother (Alida Rouffe) and Aunt Claudine (Milly Mathis); below right: César, Marius, and Fanny.

César — Césariot (André Fouché), César, the mechanic (Maupi) and Escartefigue (Paul Dullac); below: Marius and Fanny.

its modish art deco furniture, seems to belong to another film. This jarring effect is itself of course a function of the iconic coherence of the rest of the trilogy, and of Pagnol's work in general. Although traditional film history has retained the radical works of Vigo, early Clair and Renoir, and the populist works of Duvivier, Chenal, and Carné, as the image of French cinema in the 1930s, these filmmakers were in fact a minority who defined their work against the bulk of French films which focused on high society and the *demi-monde* (the double legacy of boulevard theatre and of Hollywood). Pagnol's contribution was to give a local inflexion to the populist iconography of working-class and petit-bourgeois milieux: cafés and shops, 'ordinary' people in everyday clothes: baggy trousers, cloth caps, aprons, rolled-up sleeves; and of course the accent. These attributes were more than merely functional, they established a Pagnol 'genre', metonymically representative of a 'sub'-culture (Marseilles), and metaphorically of a whole (French) culture.

* * *

Powerful as performance and iconographical motifs in Pagnol's work are, they cannot alone account for the lasting popularity of the trilogy. We now have to turn to the type of narrative offered by *Marius, Fanny*, and *César*, and its symbolic and historical significance.

Pagnol's contention that he only wrote about clichés is a useful starting point. The trilogy deals in an apparently candid way with archetypal family relationships and it comes as no surprise that these accord with the dominant patriarchal ideology of the period, a set of values certainly not challenged by Pagnol. However, in its very 'naïvety' and in its explicitness, the discourse on the family proposed by the trilogy comes close, if not exactly to a critique, at least to a laying bare of its own contradictions — in terms of the conflict between generations, of the place of desire within the patriarchal family, and of the figure of the mother. In doing so it allows, crucially, for a variety of normally irreconcilable spectator positions.

Near the final resolution of the trilogy, in *César*, Fanny delivers an angry speech against César's (and her mother's) life-long interference in her affairs. Her heartfelt tirade against *les vieux* (the old ones) is undercut by the narrative, since César at this point is about to reunite her with Marius, but it underlines a basic structure of the three films. In the trilogy power is still firmly in the hands of the older generation. In contrast to the overt justification of building up wealth for the sake of the younger generation, as seen in Panisse's dream of bequeathing his business to his heir, characters who do have children, such as César and Honorine, show absolutely no inclination to relinquish their power to them. There lies one of the crucial narrative determinants of the trilogy — the symbolic, Oedipal blockage from César (who, in *Marius*, repeatedly emphasizes his son's infantile status), and on a lesser register Honorine (who, as a widow, is endowed with phallic power), parallels an economic blockage, and effectively sends Marius on his journey and Fanny into her marriage to Panisse. The thematic configuration of powerful old men, and their marriage to young women, is a staple of French theatre, both comic (Molière's *vieux barbons*) and melodramatic, and is found in a wide range of 1930s French films, as I have developed elsewhere.[5] Its peculiar French predominance has to be seen against the background of the socio-historical structure of 1930s French society. Marriages betwen mature men and much younger women were still widespread among the middle-classes in 1930s France, within a legal system geared towards keeping wealth and property, and hence authority, in the hands of the older generation. Work on contemporary media aimed at women has shown that in the women's magazines of the period discourses aimed at 'preparing' women for such an eventuality coexisted alongside romantic notions of ideal (young) love. These perfectly contradictory positions are exemplified in the trilogy's treatment of the marriage between Fanny and Panisse. An object of mirth when it is first proposed, it is later commented on in terms of its sexual inadequacy despite its economic necessity, a divide succinctly expressed by Honorine ('nightshirts don't have pockets'). What the narrative subsequently and at great length justifies is the desirability of such a marriage in terms of legitimacy.

In the same way as the trilogy contrasts the 'natural' and 'learned' types of knowledge, it opposes two types of inheritance, attached to the two father figures: César and Panisse. Césariot is heir to a 'natural' legacy from César through Marius, and to property from Panisse. This is logical in class terms: the rise of the *petite bourgeoisie* into the elite depends on the money of commerce. In return, the ambitious provincial shopkeeper is stimulated by Parisian-inspired initiative: Panisse modernizes his business for 'the little one'. Though Césariot is the 'true' son of the Bar de la Marine (César and Marius merge into one another on more than one occasion as César explicitly identifies with Marius as lover of Fanny and father of Césariot in Marius' absence), he needs Panisse's money and, even more, his name. For, above all, the point of the marriage is to give Césariot 'a name' — the name of the father, materialized in the letters '& Fils' kept by Panisse in a drawer and triumphantly added to the shop front.

We can see the trilogy, then, as a long declension on the name and nature of the father, a series of variations with, at their core, the character of César enhanced by the star status of Raimu, who understood the centrality of the part of César and turned down the role of Panisse originally intended for him by Pagnol, thus changing the course of the subsequent two works. With the death of Panisse, Marius can return; but more importantly César can be acknowledged as the true ancestor of the child, having occupied all the positions of fatherhood — father, godfather, and grandfather — as well as that of 'father' of the narrative: sending Marius away symbolically in *Marius*, literally in *Fanny*, and bringing him back in *César*, even though this entails a certain amount of 'cheating'. For the law of the father is also shown to be making its own rules as it goes along — a fact comically echoed by the various card games in which César always cheats in order to win. But if the trilogy repeatedly reasserts the power of the father(s), it also explores contradictory, and potentially threatening, forces against this power: the desire of the 'son' on the one hand, and the place of the mother within a patriarchal, Catholic, culture on the other.

Like most classical narratives, the trilogy is the story of a quest by the male hero, on the Oedipus model. Marius' actual and symbolic voyage condenses classical mythology, French popular myths of the 1930s, and Marseillais folklore.[6] Marius and Fanny as Ulysses and Penelope is a clear enough equivalence. Marius' longing for the South Seas, while motivated by the Marseilles location, also corresponds to the obsession with exoticism and sea voyages in 1930s French culture. Clearly, it is traceable, in part, to colonial history, and it is certainly dominant in the cinema of the period in a variety of genres — from Navy melodramas to operettas (including a specifically Marseillais sub-genre) — but best known internationally from 'Poetic-Realist' films. Unlike its expression in Duvivier's *Pépé le Moko* or Carné's *Quai des brumes*, where the Gabin hero's voyage is always blocked, the journey in the trilogy does take place. Its object, however, according to the logic of desire, is shown to be an unattainable illusion. In order for Marius' mythic (and Oedipal) journey to be successful, an object approved by the law — marriage — has to be substituted for his own irrepressible desire for 'elsewhere', while the nature of his desire, threatening the cohesion of the family, is dealt with by his virtual exclusion from *Fanny* and *César*.

In keeping with the patriarchal emphasis, gender roles in the trilogy are unsurprisingly ultra-traditional, not to say archaic, and totally grounded in the family and its rituals. However, as is common in the French cinema of the period, gender divisions within male characters are far more complex than the overt definition of gender roles. Panisse for example occupies both masculine and feminine positions — he gives a name and wealth to the child, but he is also caring and protective; this is the object of the long scene towards the end of *Fanny* in which Panisse's tender nurturing of Césariot is given as justification of his superior claim to fatherhood over Marius' recognized status as biological father. This dual nature of the father is even more explicit in the character of César who is both father and mother to Marius, being, for instance, strongly connected with domesticity while at the same time presented as sexually active (his weekly visits to a mysterious mistress). In this configuration the trilogy is typical of a wide range of 1930s French films, as is the fact that the actual mothers, the older women such as the wives of Panisse and César, are eliminated from the narrative before the films begin. It is true that Fanny's mother, Honorine, is present in all three films, but her narrative function is minimal and her sexuality certainly denied. Though she would seem at first to be the female equivalent of César, the real 'couple' is formed by the latter and Panisse, a couple ultimately consecrated by the name of 'their' child: César(iot) Panisse.

If Honorine is marginalized in the trilogy, her daughter Fanny occupies centre stage as 'the mother'. Within the terms of French and especially

Catholic culture, the place accorded to her is central (as bearer and educator of the child) but concurrently suppresses her as an individual subject in her own right. A good contemporary parallel can be found in Mauriac's *Thérèse Desqueyroux,* published in 1927, in which the pregnant Thérèse is acutely aware that her only value is as a 'container'. Though it is tempting to see the emphasis on motherhood in the trilogy — as in all Pagnol's work — as related to the contemporary concern with low birth rate, it relates more pertinently to generic structures, and in particular those of melodrama in which the classic opposition between the 'good' and the 'bad' woman is really an expression of the conflict between the woman as mother and the woman as individual subject, an antinomy which uncannily evokes Freud's scenario of 'family romances'. Freud's description of the male child's fantasy 'to bring his mother [...] into situations of secret infidelity and into secret love-affairs' (Freud 1977, 223) reads like a blueprint for the scene in *César* where Césariot learns of his true paternity and angrily reproaches Fanny for her love affair with Marius, seeing it as a dereliction of her 'duty', towards her husband Panisse and towards him. Fanny's response is to provoke guilt: she points to the suffering she has endured in order to carry him, give birth to him, and bring him up; such is the mother's revenge under patriarchy.

As is also typical of the maternal melodrama, sacrifice is the only option left to Fanny, one which despite its negativity can be seen at least to validate women's experience, but more fundamentally to point to the fact that this sacrifice is itself also a 'problem';[7] she sacrifices her love for Marius to his greater love for 'the sea' in *Marius,* sacrifices all for her child in *Fanny,* and, arguably, sacrifices her newfound freedom after Panisse's death for the (re)formation of her couple with Marius in *César.* However, despite its masculine bias, the trilogy can be seen to appeal directly to women spectators. As *Fanny* is the film which concentrates most on the female heroine, both as mother and as 'fallen woman' (a combination which is a recurrent thematic thread in Pagnol's work — see for instance *Angèle* and *La Fille du puisatier*), one might speculate on its increased appeal to women. It is telling that, of the three films, *Fanny* enjoyed the highest attendance (Pagnol 1981, 203), and unsurprising that it attracted the strongest critical disapproval. In this respect, Beylie's view is typical of the traditional attitude to melodrama, when he describes *Fanny* as the part of the trilogy where 'male rigorousness' gives way to 'a lacrymose excess a little out of place' (Beylie 1986, 59). Simultaneously offering the image of perfect womanhood and the image of its transgression, the trilogy addresses contradictory impulses and ideological positions in its audience, though of course these contradictory positions are themselves defined by patriarchy. The 'good' and especially the 'bad' aspects of the female heroine are shown as inherent to her 'nature': there are hints of Fanny's own illegitimate birth and there is the often evoked spectre of Fanny's aunt Zoé, a prostitute. At the end of the trilogy César, as always, has the last word. As he is reminded by Marius that Césariot does not bear his (their) name, he retorts:

'This one doesn't, but the other ones will.' Cancelling out the past 20 years (and the last two films of the trilogy), César rewrites Fanny's future as a mother and the perpetuator of his own name.

NOTES

1. For an introduction to the contemporary debates on 'filmed theatre' and reactions to the coming of sound in general, see René Clair (1972) *Cinema Today and Yesterday,* trans. Stanley Applebaum, New York, Dover, and various contributions — including by Clair and Pagnol — in Marcel Lapierre (ed.) (1946) *Anthologie du cinéma*, Paris, La Nouvelle Edition. Beylie (1986) also provides a good overview of the reactions to Pagnol's place in the debate.

2. The Parisian branch of the Paramount studios, located in Joinville, was nicknamed 'Babel-on-Seine' on account of its high production of multi-language versions (including the three versions of *Marius)*, and provoked much commentary and criticism. See Pagnol (1965) in *Cahiers du cinéma* 173, Henri Jeanson 'Cinq semaines à la Paramount, choses vécues', *Le Crapouillot,* special issue, November 1932, and Vincendeau (1988) 'Hollywood-Babel', *Screen*, 29 (2).

3. This is itself a feature of a majority of French films of the 1930s that focused strongly on actors' performances, whether they were based directly on theatrical texts or not. For a close study of dialogue in a Pagnol film, see Marie's contribution (on *Le Schpountz)* to Michel Marie and Francis Vanoye, 'Comment parler la bouche pleine?', *Communications* 38 (1982), special issue 'Enunciation and Cinema'.

4. In a scene from *Marius* (the play) which was not retained in the film, Fanny also corrects her mother's pronunciation of the word 'inventaire' (stall).

5. 'Daddy's girls, Oedipal narratives in 1930s French films', *Iris,* 'Cinema and Narration 2' (2nd semestre, 1988).

6. Within the film's paradigm of sea voyages, the ferry-boat that crosses the Vieux Port functions metonymically, as part of the Marseillais familiar scene. It also works metaphorically, both as sign of a doomed folklore (its existence is threatened by the construction of a new bridge), and as representative of the small-scale, routine existence Marius wants to leave behind by embarking on the glamorous sailing ship.

7. This is a problematic identified notably by Ann Kaplan in relation to Hollywood melodrama. See Kaplan, 'Mothering, Feminism and Representation, The Maternal in Melodrama and the Woman's Film 1910-1987', in Christine Gledhill (ed.) (1987) *Home is Where the Heart Is*, London, British Film Institute.

SELECTED BIBLIOGRAPHY

Audouard, Yvan (1973) *Yvan Audouard raconte Marcel Pagnol,* Paris, Stock.

Bazin, André (1975) 'Le Cas Pagnol', in *Qu'est-ce que le cinéma?,* Paris, Editions du Cerf. This essay is not included in the English translation of Bazin's book.

Bardèche, Maurice and Brasillach, Robert (1948) *Histoire du cinéma*, Paris, André Martel.

Beylie, Claude and Brancourt, Guy (1969) interview with Marcel Pagnol, *Cinéma 69*, 134.

Beylie, Claude (1986) *Marcel Pagnol ou le cinéma en liberté,* Paris, Editions Atlas, Lherminier — an enlarged, up-to-date, edition of Beylie (1974) *Marcel Pagnol*, Paris, Seghers. The best single book on Pagnol, it contains an excellent bibliography and a very complete filmography.

Caldicott, C. E. J. (1977) *Marcel Pagnol*, Boston, Twayne, G. K. Hall.

Castans, Raymond (1978) *Il était une fois Marcel Pagnol*, Paris, Julliard.

Castans, Raymond and Bernard, André (1982) *Les Films de Marcel Pagnol,* Paris, Julliard.

Delahaye, Michel (1969) 'La Saga Pagnol', *Cahiers du cinéma,* 213.
Freud, Sigmund (1977) *The Pelican Freud Library, Vol 7: On Sexuality*, Harmondsworth, Penguin Books.
Gauteur, Claude (1970) 'Marcel Pagnol aujourd'hui', *Avant-Scène Cinéma*, 105/106 (contains excellent bibliography).
Gauteur, Claude (1973) 'Marcel Pagnol inconnu?', *Image et Son*, 275.
IDHEC students' analysis of the trilogy, *Image et Son*, 114, July 1958.
Labarthe, André S. (1965) 'Pagnol entre centre et absence', *Cahiers du cinéma*, 173 followed by an interview with Marcel Pagnol.
Leprohon, Pierre (1976) *Marcel Pagnol, Avant-Scène Cinéma,* supplément d'anthologie, 88.
Pagnol, Marcel (1981) *Confidences,* Paris, Julliard.
Pagnol, Marcel (1933) 'Cinématurgie de Paris', *Les Cahiers du film,* reprinted in Marcel Lapierre (ed.) (1946) *Anthologie du cinéma*, Paris, La Nouvelle Edition.
Peyrusse, Claudette (1986) *Le Cinéma méridional*, Toulouse, Eché.
Roud, Richard (1980) 'Marcel Pagnol', in Richard Roud (ed.), *Cinema, A Critical Dictionary*, Secker & Warburg, London, II.
Sadoul, Georges (1938) article in *Regards,* reprinted (1979) in *Chroniques du cinéma français*, Union Générale d'Editions.
Turim, Maureen (1987) "French Melodrama: Theory of a Specific History', *Theater Journal*, Fall.
Turk, Edward Baron (1980) 'Pagnol's Marseilles Trilogy', *American Film*, VI, I.

SCRIPTS

All three parts of the trilogy have been published in book form and reprinted many times (they are all currently available in the *Livre de poche* collection). The original editions are:

Pagnol, Marcel (1931) *Marius*, Fasquelle.
Pagnol, Marcel (1932) *Fanny*, Fasquelle.
Pagnol, Marcel (1937) *César*, Fasquelle.

APPENDIX

Marcel Pagnol (1895—1974): filmography

(Main films directed or supervised by Marcel Pagnol; for a complete filmography, see Beylie 1986.)

1931 *Marius* (technically directed by Alexander Korda)
1932 *Fanny* (technically directed by Marc Allégret)
1933 *Le Gendre de Monsieur Poirier*
1933 *Jofroi*
1934 *L'Article 330*
1934 *Angèle*
1935 *Merlusse*
1935 *Cigalon*
1936 *César*
1936 *Topaze,* 2nd version — a first version of Pagnol's play was directed in 1932 by Louis Gasnier
1937 *Regain*
1937 *Le Schpountz*
1938 *La Femme du boulanger*
1940 *La Fille du puisatier*
1941 *La Prière aux étoiles*

1943 *Arlette et l' amour* (technically directed by Robert Vernay)
1945 *Naïs* (technically directed by Raymond Leboursier)
1948 *La Belle meunière*
1950 *Topaze*, 3rd version
1952 *Manon des sources*
1953-4 *Les Lettres de mon moulin*
1967 *Le Curé de Cucugnan*

Remakes of the trilogy

a) simultaneous foreign language versions

1931 *Zum Goldenen Anker* (Germany), directed by Alexandre Korda
1931 *Längtan till Havet* (Sweden), directed by John W. Brunius

b) remakes

1933 *Fanny* (Italy), directed by Mario Almirante
1934 *Der Schwarze Walfisch* (Germany), directed by Fritz Wendhausen, with Emil Jannings as César
1938 *Port of Seven Seas* (USA), directed by James Whales, scripted by Preston Sturges, with Wallace Berry as César, Maureen O'Sullivan as Fanny.
1961 *Fanny* (USA), musical directed by Joshua Logan, with Maurice Chevalier as César, Charles Boyer as Panisse, and Leslie Caron as Fanny

Other films cited in the text:

Jean de Florette, Claude Berri (1985)
Manon des sources, Claude Berri (1986)
Le Mot de Cambronne, Sacha Guitry (1936)
Pépé le Moko, Julien Duvivier (1936)
Quai des brumes, Marcel Carné (1938)

MICHELE LAGNY

'*La Bête humaine* is dead': that headline, which appeared in a January 1987 issue of the newspaper *Le Monde,* quoted a remark made by a train driver during one of the most serious strikes in the history of French railways. The report then listed his lengthy complaints about working conditions and, above all, the 'loneliness on the engines; there used to be two of us, and we'd always talk a bit. We've been driving alone for the last three years'.[1] The visual memory of the reader immediately conjures up the opening shot of Renoir's film, where the camera, by tracking back to reveal, behind the gaping mouth of the locomotive, the fireman shovelling in coal and the engine driver at his controls, constructs a centaur with a steel body and a double human bust. At the same time, echoes of old interviews crowd back into the mind — interviews that explicitly recognized the railwaymen's right to dignity in their work which was one of the strikers' demands during the winter of 1986-7: 'The railwayman's job is no joke, it is a grand profession. For some, it's almost a vocation.'[2]

The 'human beast' that persists in our collective memory clearly has nothing to do with Emile Zola's main source of inspiration for his novel: 'The strange case of hereditary criminals who, although not mad, commit murder one day in a morbid fit, driven on by an animal instinct.'[3] That cliché surely harks back to the railway world of the pre-war film, rather than the one portrayed in Zola's late nineteenth-century text. The railway setting, although important, is no more than a backdrop in the opening two chapters of the novel, which are devoted to the murderous jealousy of Roubaud, the deceived husband, and the hereditary *fêlure* (flaw in its twin senses of 'defect' and 'crack') caused by Jacques Lantier's alcoholic antecedents. It is only when the murder sets the story going that Zola begins to emphasize the collective nature of the railwaymen's work and their relationship with their engines: 'Usually the two men got on very well in this long intimacy that took them from one end of the line to the other, shaken together side by side, taciturn, united in the same job with the same dangers'; this remark in fact comes as a secondary one, for it is preceded by a description of the almost sexual relationship Lantier has with his locomotive, which he loves 'with masculine gratitude' (Zola 1977, 156 and 155).

Renoir, on the other hand, devotes his opening sequence to the activity of the locomotive, a powerful beast driven by human toil, and turns what was a sometimes criticized book ('Zola's novel is very bad ... it is an interminable and insipid serial') into a widely admired film: 'It is true cinema, and of the best kind... . All filmmakers have dragged bits of railway engines into their stories, whether relevant or not. This time, the engine is the subject of the film, and it is very thoroughly worked...with the driver handling his controls on one side, and the fireman shovelling in his coal on the other.'[4]

Publicity for the film emphasized the popular imagery of the railwayman right from the moment it was being prepared up until its release, which was aided by a massive press campaign. Reactions were unanimous, from the communist daily, *Ce Soir,* which ran a whole series of interviews with Renoir, to right-wing papers and trade journals. Maurice Bessy (*Cinémonde*) was the most enthusiastic: 'This is the finest film I have seen in 10 years' (Chardère 1962, 265). But even the extreme right-wing critic François Vinneuil (alias Lucien Rebatet) recognized that 'the film is the least fatuous of any based on a Zola novel' (Chardère 1962, 268). It did well at the box office: its first run lasted for four months after a meticulously prepared opening at the cinema La Madeleine just before Christmas 1938; it was later shown at the Venice Biennale and won the Prix Méliès.[5]

The success of *La Bête humaine* has continued ever since: articles and chapters of books devoted to Renoir all pass favourable judgment on the '30 year old masterpiece'.[6] Equally admired are Renoir's faithfulness to the spirit of Zola and the film's value as a documentary on railwaymen's lives or on the atmosphere in France at the end of the Popular Front; 'Renoir assimilates Zola, and surpasses him in analytical insight' (Serceau 1985, 77); 'He is totally in sympathy with the two engine drivers';[7] 'No one could have failed to notice the pessimistic content of the film [...] It buried the hopes of the Popular Front' (Viry-Babel 1986, 109, 111). In the last analysis, the 1987 rail striker was absolutely right: the relevance of *La Bête humaine* remains undimmed.

A three-star film

At the end of 1938, the constellation in question — Zola, Renoir and Gabin — stood out brightly against a rather sombre sky. Both the shooting (in September) and the release (on December 23) of *La Bête humaine* took place at a time when the storm clouds were gathering: not only was the Popular Front in its death throes, but above all there was enormous anxiety about the international crisis, which had been only temporarily eased by Munich.

The organisers of the advertising campaign for *La Bête humaine* must have asked themselves: what does the film offer by way of reassurance and escape? What they decided to bank on were, in the following order:

— 'The fame of Zola, whom everyone has read'
— 'The reputation of Renoir, the wonderful director of *La Grande illusion* '
— 'Gabin's talent'[8]

It would seem, in fact, that it was Gabin who, whether intentionally or not, was the driving force behind the making of the film. He had prepared to play a railwayman in a film which Jean Grémillon had been asked to make by the Hakim brothers; but Grémillon's screenplay, entitled *Train d'enfer*, was not to the producers' liking, so they turned to the celebrated Renoir, who had the idea of adapting the popular Zola novel (Viry-Babel 1986, 107). Whatever their respective importance, there was a strong link between the three partners: Renoir and Zola were old acquaintances (*Nana*, 1926); the Renoir-Gabin connection was more recent but well-established (*Les Bas-fonds*, 1936, *La Grande illusion*, 1937); and Gabin-Zola was an ideal combination: 'I only regret one thing, and that is that Zola can't see Gabin interpret the character. I think he'd be pleased.'[9]

It would be hard to say which of the three stars had the greatest charisma. Zola, 'whom everyone has read', was a staple of middle-class culture: his success was reflected by the many editions of his works and the large number of copies printed.[10] While school anthologies included extracts from his novels[11] the Société Littéraire des Amis de Zola invited Renoir to lecture on his adaptation at the Sorbonne.[12] Renoir in 1938 was not just 'the wonderful director of *La Grande illusion*' (which topped the box office in 1937): unlike most directors at that time, he enjoyed the status of an *auteur*, like a writer. True, not all his films had been outright successes, but the failure of *Toni* and the cool reception given to *Les Bas-fonds* and *La Marseillaise* were compensated for by the critical acclaim accorded to *Le Crime de Monsieur Lange* and the critical and box office triumph of *La Grande illusion*. As for Gabin, 'the only French star' (Vincendeau 1985a, 243-397), he had built up his brand image in ten or so films which, from *La Bandera* to *Quai des brumes*, made him the working-class hero *par excellence* of the French cinema: as late as 1986 a photograph of him wearing a cloth cap in *La Belle équipe* appeared on the cover of Geneviève Guillaume-Grimaud's book on Popular Front cinema. The way Gabin's star image was built up has been so thoroughly analysed elsewhere that there is no point in covering that ground again.[13] As I have already noted, the producers were prompt to seize on that image as the linchpin of the film.

Interestingly, the triple combination of Zola, Renoir and Gabin gives us a clue as to why *La Bête humaine* was such a success: it reflected both the vigour of the French cinema of the 1930s and a society which contemporary nostalgia had transformed into a stable model. 'This most perfect form of Poetic Realism' (Viry-Babel 1986, 108) has been perceived as a model of social documentary, but also as 'a symphony of the railways, of speed, of the engine, of work' (Guillaume-Grimaud 1986, 72), the lyrical expression of a lost world. It was, basically, an excellent 'populist recipe' of the 1930s. The film displayed all the right credentials: it was an adaptation of a text whose literary worth was recognized, and Renoir made it quite clear that he had remained faithful to the spirit of Zola, putting the name of Denise Leblond-Zola on the credit titles, which conclude with Zola's signature and portrait, and

announcing that he had used the novelist's own preparatory notes. Let me list
its basic ingredients:

— *A story of love and fatality*: 'Jean Renoir says: my first love story
for a long time.'[14] Its theme echoed that of 'the great Greek tragedies [...]
Jacques Lantier, the humble railway mechanic, could belong to the family of
the Atridae.'[15]

— *Realism, based on documentary value*: the engine driver was based
on a possible character in real life who had to be described in as accurate a
manner as possible thanks to the research which Renoir says he carried out
(along the lines of Zola's own researches)[16] — he insisted on the contribution
made by the French railways management and of the railwaymen's trade
union, and even more on the efforts made by the actors (Gabin and Carette) to
learn the skills of the characters they were playing. This 'document effect'
justified the making of certain changes to Zola's original: by setting the film in
the 1930s instead of the late nineteenth century and thus rendering an
expensive reconstitution unnecessary, Renoir not only made a vital saving but
avoided the faintly ridiculous quaintness of 1860-1870 rolling stock. The use
of modern engines entailed a change in the characters: in the 1930s 'railway
workers are an elite; they are well educated and very conscious of their
duties.'[17] Better even:

> Transposing the story to a contemporary setting also made me
> change its ending. First of all because modern railway control
> methods are such nowadays as to render the story of this
> runaway train, tearing driverless through the countryside,
> more than improbable. Secondly, the France of today is not that
> of Napoleon III and as it stands with its qualities and its faults, I
> think that it deserves to be defended to the last breath by all its
> citizens. The author of *J'accuse ...!* would probably agree with
> me on that point.[18]

I wonder whether I have quoted Renoir at sufficient length to give the
flavour of his hypocrisy — or the illusions of his period (?) Zola's driverless
train careering through the countryside with its cargo of cannon fodder would
surely not have struck filmgoers in 1938 as an absurd invention.

— *A touch of socio-political commitment* added vital zest to the film.
It was provided by the model of Zola who, 'in situating his heroes in the
working class, in allowing them concerns which, in previous literary works,
seemed to be the preserve of bourgeois and aristocratic characters', acted as a
'great revolutionary'.[19] The authors of the film were regarded as left-wing:
Zola, author of *J'accuse...!*, was the man whose portrait was carried on
Popular Front marches alongside those of Léon Blum and Maurice Thorez
(and whose defence of the crushing of the Commune was occulted); and Renoir

La Bête humaine —'a three-star film' — above: Emile Zola; centre: Jean Renoir; below: Jean Gabin.

was the leader of Ciné-Liberté, who worked for the Communist Party (*La Vie est à nous*) and with the CGT (*La Marseillaise*), before being accused of betraying the working class — precisely in *La Bête humaine*. Political commitment, which is obvious in Zola's original (though he set his novel 20 years before the time at which he wrote it), is less clearcut in Renoir, even if he saw his work as a manifesto against 'ordinary fascism' and even a weapon against Hitler (though these statements were made in interviews given 30 years after he made the film).[20] Lastly, a popular actor was needed to play a working-class figure — no one could have suspected that Gabin would turn into the big landowner of 1962 who was sued by evicted farmers (Vincendeau 1985a, 252).

Built on an intertextual grid which takes us constantly from the film to the novel, from contemporary criticism to historicizing analysis, from authorial discourse to hagiographical excess, Renoir's *La Bête humaine* is an unavoidable monument — hence the cultural reference brought out by the *Le Monde* headline in the article quoted at the beginning of this chapter.

Discordant notes

La Bête humaine has, however, come in for occasional criticism. The attacks on the film on grounds of immorality which, when it was re-released in 1945, resulted in its being banned in various parts of France, were no doubt circumstantial epiphenomena. On the other hand, François Poulle (writing not long after May 1968) demanded that the director stand trial before the Court of History on a charge of betrayal and a 'missed rendez-vous' with the French working class. He criticized Renoir mainly for being unfaithful to Zola, who had 'succeeded in turning the novel into a weapon and a study' for 'a social stocktaking' before a process of reorganization; the director, on the other hand, had not understood a thing about the working class 'whereas *La Bête humaine* could have been the springboard for an authentic French realist school' if only 'Zola's analysis and construction' had been respected 'in the first place' (Poulle 1969, 28, 163).

Most analyses have similarly concentrated on the comparative — in this case social — value of the film and novel. Apart from one analysis of Renoir's cinematic tranposition of the visual qualities displayed by Zola (Gauthier 1968, 29-34), the main subject of debate has been Renoir's departures from the original story line, for example the elision of the socio-political background (resulting from Renoir's drastic slimming down of the role of the investigating magistrate Denizet), the deformation of certain characters (Cabuche in particular, who changes from a quarryman to a kind of drop-out who — as played by Renoir himself — foreshadows Octave in *La Règle du jeu*), the removal of certain spectacular episodes (the snowing up of the locomotive, or the derailment caused by Flore) or the intrusion of new elements such as the 'railwaymen's dance', which is very much in the tradition of the popular merrymaking scenes that run right through the French films of the 1930s.[21]

All these analyses, like the sometimes critical examination of the documentary value of Renoir's reconstitution of the railwaymen's world, regard the film as a vehicle for a series of psycho-sociological representations, but lose sight of its cinematic specificity. This relative indifference to the cinematic text is confirmed by the fact that *La Bête humaine* has been the subject of far fewer articles than *La Grande Illusion* or *La Règle du jeu*.[22] It is almost as if critics were content merely to recognise its intrinsic value while at the same time baulking at an ambiguity in it which is difficult to circumscribe — but which one critic sensed as early as 1939: 'This film, like [Renoir's] others, is a remarkable film. [...] But there is a certain clumsiness in its construction and in the delineation of its characters. At times it is ponderous and slow. One loses sight of a subject one was just about to get interested in. [...] And overall it is a little disappointing... [...] despite some brilliant moments.'[23]

These remarks suggest that it might be worthwhile circumscribing both the way in which an image that is easily identifiable and appropriable by the spectator has been built up, and its possible weaknesses. In order to do so, I shall strive to evaluate structurally the mythical figure of *La Bête humaine* as constructed by intertextual analysis. I shall restrict myself here to two of the factors which encourage spectator involvement: first, the coherence of filmic causality which enables narrative comprehension and secondly, the complex interplay of gazes which facilitates secondary cinematic identification,[24] especially when the spectator is placed in the characters' line of vision. A careful reading of the film from these two angles produces surprising results.

Dislocation of the narrative thread

In order to test filmic continuity and analyse the relationship it sets up between successive diegetic events, I have used the analytical grid proposed by *Générique des années 30* (Lagny, Ropars and Sorlin 1986), which was established on the basis of a corpus of films dating from 1936 to 1939. It makes it possible to break the film down into 23 sequences whose demarcation hinges on punctuations and on the pinpointing of narrative units. To bring out the articulation of those units, I have given priority to the notion of 'implication', i.e. to the type of causality that holds the series of sequences together, whether it is logical-diegetic, chronological or indeterminate ('suspended implication').[25]

SEQUENCE LENGTH	CONTENT	'IMPLICATION'	INTERNAL TEMPORALITY	PLACE
Seq. 1 4'12"	Pecqueux (Carette) and Lantier (Gabin)		Continuity	Railway line

	on locomotive			
		Fade-out, chrono.		
Seq. 2 2'17"	Engine arrives at platform; quarrel between Roubaud (Ledoux) and passenger; engine backs out of station		Continuity	Station
		Cut, chrono.		
Seq. 3 3'1"	Roubaud and Séverine (Simone Simon) decide to go to Paris to see her godfather		Continuity	Flat in Le Havre
		Cut, suspension		
Seq. 4 4'	Evening spent together by driver and fireman		Continuity with ellipses, dissolves	Engine depot
		Fade-out, logical-diegetic		
Seq. 5 2'20"	Lantier at his godmother's		Continuity with ellipses	Gatekeeper's house
		Cut, logical-diegetic		
Seq. 6	Flore and Lantier; his first fit		Continuity	Countryside
		Fade-out, suspension		
Seq. 7 5'3"	Roubauds in Paris; Séverine beaten up and admits relationship with Grandmorin;		Continuity with beginning of alternation	Station; flat, Paris; Hotel Grandmorin; flat
		Fade-out, chrono.		
Seq. 8 5'3"	Train journey; murder of Grandmorin; Lantier and Séverine meet		Alternation	Train platform/ carriage/ corridor
		Fade-out, chrono.		
Seq. 9 5'11"	Discovery of murder; Roubaud, then Lantier, at home		Successive continuities	Station; engine; depot; flat
		Fade-out, suspension, indeterminate chrono.		
Seq. 10 garden 1'55"	Séverine and Lantier meet and talk		Continuity	Public
		Fade-out, suspension, indeterminate chrono.		
Seq. 11	Magistrate's		Alternation	Magistrate's

Sequence / Time	Action	Transition	Technique	Location
4'11"	investigations; arrest of Cabuche (Renoir)			office; corridor
		Fade-out, suspension, indeterminate chrono.		
Seq. 12 6'20"	Lantier at Roubaud's flat; replaces him in Séverine's affections		Continuity, successive scenes	Flat; railway track; flat
		Fade-out, suspension		
Autonomous segment 34"	Driver and fireman on the engine		Continuity	Engine
		Dissolve, suspension		
Seq. 13 2'2"	First nocturnal meeting between Lantier and Séverine		Continuity with ellipses	Engine depot, night
		Fade-out, suspension		
Autonomous segment 27"	Roubaud in the café; loses at cards		Continuity	Café
		Cut, suspension		
Seq. 14 3'22"	Lantier in the engine depot; goes to join Séverine		Continuity with ellipses	Engine depot, night
		Fade-out, suspension		
Seq. 15 2'9"	Roubaud comes home to fetch money; row with Séverine		Continuity	Flat
		Dissolve, suspension		
Seq. 16 5'7"	Lantier and Séverine; she describes Grandmorin's murder		Continuity with ellipses	Flat, Paris
		Fade-out, suspension, indeterminate chrono.		
Seq. 17 3'47"	Lantier cannot kill Roubaud		Continuity	Engine depot, night
		Fade-out, suspension		
Seq. 18 1'13"	Shunting on the engine		Continuity	Engine
		Fade-out, suspension		
Seq. 19 7'23"	Railwaymen's dance; Lantier tries to win back Séverine		Continuity	Dancehall and garden
		Cut, chrono.		
Seq. 20	Lantier joins Séverine		Alternation	Flat;

7'30"	at her flat and kills her			dancehall
		Cut, chrono.		
Seq. 21 1'45"	Lantier in street; Roubaud discovers the dead Séverine		Alternation	Street; flat; railway track
		Dissolve, chrono.		
Seq. 22 3'53"	Just before the train leaves, Lantier tells Pecqueux what he has done		Continuity with ellipses	Engine
		Dissolve, chrono.		
Seq. 23 3'24"	Reverse journey of seq. 1; Lantier's suicide; Pecqueux stops the train		Continuity with ellipses	Engine
		Dissolve, chrono.		
track	Pecqueux closes Lantier's eyes; service resumes		Continuity	Railway
		End		

Up to the moment when Lantier and Séverine get involved with each other, at the time of the murder (which comes more than 30 minutes after the beginning of the film), two narrative threads unfold side by side, each successively interrupting the other: the breakdown of the locomotive, which is hinted at as early as sequence 2, explains why the two drivers stay in the engine depot (seq. 4) and why Lantier goes to see his godmother, who in turn tells him (seq. 5) to join Flore (seq. 6). Meanwhile, Roubaud's visit to his wife (seq. 3) follows, but is not determined by, his altercation with an 'important' passenger (seq. 2); and the decision to visit Séverine's godfather in Paris does not come into effect until sequence 7. The simultaneity of the two narratives is only briefly referred to by the dialogue in sequences 2 and 7. The whole series of sequences is all the more incoherent because this establishing phase comprises powerful punctuation marks which contradict possible continuities: for example, the locomotive's arrival at the station is disrupted because a fade-out and a pause in the music come between an impressionistic shot of an empty and mist-swathed Le Havre station and a close shot showing the engine at the platform.[26]

Detailed analysis of the mode of 'implication' shows the predominance of suspended sequences or sequences with a weak or indeterminate chronological relationship; the rupture effect is further accentuated by the frequency of fade-outs. Two very short segments (of 34 and 27 seconds), one showing Lantier on his engine, the other Roubaud in the café, sandwich the lovers' first nocturnal rendez-vous and appear to be independent of the film's chronological development. Similarly, it is hard to ascertain the temporal relationship which might link sequences 14 and 15: is it the same night that Roubaud loses at cards (segment at the end of seq. 13) and goes home to get some money (seq. 15)? But then how is Séverine, whom we have just seen with Lantier (seq. 14), already there? A chronological thread is firmly established only during the last 25 minutes of the film, reinforced by the use of dissolves: it connects together the dance, the murder while the dance continues, Lantier's flight intercut with Roubaud's discovery of the body, the departure of the train, and Lantier's suicide. But the circularity caused by a repetition in reverse of the train's journey (sequence 23 repeats images from sequence 1) produces a loop and temporal condensation effect. This effect is all the more powerful because no indications of a chronological nature make it possible to measure the relative duration of the story's various episodes. The novel, by contrast, is firmly structured with indications of the date or the time at the beginning of each chapter; these establish precise causality which enables the story to be linearized and not to come to such an abrupt end as it does in the film.

At the same time, there are internal breaks in the sequential continuities — in sequence 2, for example, where Roubaud's altercation with the sugar magnate is sandwiched by two series of shots showing the activity of the men driving the locomotive; or in sequence 7, when the shot of the waiting husband is abruptly interrupted by some shots of Séverine at her godfather's. In both cases, the disruptive effect is accentuated by the editing: the high-angle close shot of the complaining passenger's dog and the façade of the Hôtel Grandmorin, in sharp contrast with the buildings in the popular Saint-Lazare district, reinforce the fragmentation effect which can also be found, in a different way, in the 'episodic' structure of the segment that uses dissolves to link Gabin's and Carette's activities during their evening in the engine depot (seq. 4).

All this could explain the bewilderment of the critic quoted earlier, who said he sometimes lost the thread of the story. For the film to remain legible for the spectator, the latter has to take into account remote narrative clues and above all detect a whole network of repetitions/transformations which, by organising equivalences and substitutions, lend the narrative its compactness and coherence. This network is very dense, and I shall cite only two examples, leaving aside the train motif, which has been very thoroughly discussed elsewhere,[27] and which acts as a veritable 'binding agent' throughout the text.

My first example concerns the formation of the Lantier-Séverine couple, which is alluded to right at the start of the film (two shots of Lantier and Séverine are linked by a dissolve before the title of the film comes up), but which is postponed until sequence 8, more than half an hour into the film. In fact their meeting is already prefigured by the similarity in the way the two characters are shown at the end of sequences 6 and 7. Each sequence closes with a fade-out on a close-up shot of a face with a glazed expression: first

Lantier's, after his row with Flore, then Séverine's, who has just been beaten up by Roubaud; Lantier is shown in a low-angle shot against an almost abstract sky, Séverine in a high-angle shot, but with her eyes looking up. They seem like fellow victims of their *fêlure*, whether it be the hereditary defect referred to explicitly in the quotation from Zola used as an epigraph at the end of the credits and mentioned again in the dialogue with Flore, or the mental block Séverine suffers from because she was raped as a child, which she reiterates later (seq. 12: 'I cannot love'). In this way the conjunction, at once plausible and impossible, of the two characters is heralded.

Two other networks of recurrences organize Roubaud's replacement by Lantier, and Lantier's replacement by Pecqueux. Although all three characters are seen together at the beginning of the film (seq. 2), they are subsequently shown only two at a time. The replacement of the husband by the lover materializes in sequence 12. In it, Roubaud encourages Lantier to come and see Séverine more often, while revealing himself to be fiercely jealous of an insignificant third man. The film plays on shifts in the positions of the characters, but more particularly on the two men's exits and entrances. After Lantier leaves, Séverine refuses to have any sexual relations with her husband, who in turn goes out. A general shot outside the building shows Lantier half cut off on the right of the screen, while Roubaud crosses the railway lines, stops for a moment (has he seen Lantier or not?), then continues on his way. Lantier goes back to Séverine, entering in exactly the same way as the amorous Roubaud did in sequence 3: he comes along the corridor and knocks on the door at the bottom of the stairs, down which a man is coming, just as when Roubaud arrived. This is immediately followed by the two autonomous segments whose chronological dysfunction I mentioned earlier. Finally, in sequence 16, Lantier joins Séverine in the same flat near Saint-Lazare station which was occupied by Roubaud in sequence 7. The two sequences work like exact replicas: the lover is shown waiting for the woman in exactly the same posture and framed in the same way as the husband. He gets up and goes to the door in exactly the same way, after the same ringing of the bell, and he puts the same care into preparing a snack (though it is a classier one, with cake and Malaga replacing pâté and red wine). Finally, and despite different framings, the dramatic content is similar: just as Séverine, when questioned by Roubaud, had admitted her relationship with Grandmorin, she describes, when egged on by Lantier, her feelings while the murder was being committed. Roubaud's threats ('You just wait and see what I'm going to do') are mirrored by Lantier's fantasy ('But we can't kill him'), and sequence 17 (the failed murder of the husband) refers back to sequence 8 (the murder of the ex-lover). Lantier's inability to carry out the act replaces Roubaud's actual violence, but the latter has already been contaminated by it since sequence 12, where he starts going to the café and sinking into apathetic resignation.

Pecqueux on the other hand is constantly represented as the shadow of the engine driver, but it is he who replaces him at the end, and who assumes his ieal power over the train. Lantier's face is replaced, in a dissolve, by his fireman's (the link between seq. 21 and seq. 22). It is he who helps his boss put on his work clothes, and he who stokes up the locomotive he later manages to stop after the driver's suicide. Of the four protagonists that Renoir retained from Zola's novel — 'the husband, his wife, her lover and the railway',[28] the film erases the first three by replacing the ineffectual husband with an equally ineffectual lover, but retains the last protagonist through the replacement of Gabin by Carette.

The circularity of the film's course, its unwillingness to adopt a coherent, linear chronology, and the play of substitutions produce a condensed narrative which is riven with cracks, with *fêlures* that let the tragic flood in, but which also maintains possible openings on to the realm of the social. The very beginning of the film is echoed by its epilogue. The first three shots display a flawless coherence: the editing shows, in succession, the work of the men who feed and drive the engine (shot 1), its direct effect (shot 2: the axles of the driving wheels) and its final result (shot 3: the whole train moving along), and establishes a close link between action and reaction, man and machine. Pecqueux's action after the driver's suicide has the effect of stopping the train, but not rail traffic as a whole: a short epilogue, introduced by a dissolve, marks a pause by way of homage to the dead man, then work starts up again and the film ends with a general shot of the railway tracks. At this point the memory of the 'hereditary flaw' that was supposed to justify the story fades away and is replaced by a positive image of the railways.

The fleeing gaze

Cracks and uncertainties are, however, maintained by the difficulty the spectator has in situating him/herself vis-à-vis the characters portrayed and the world represented. It is not a film in which it is easy to establish a subject of the gaze, as I shall try to suggest by making a few points about the interplay of gazes that takes place in it. I shall not dwell on it at length, partly because of lack of space, but also because it is a theme that has often been touched upon in discussions of *La Bête humaine*,[29] one of whose key scenes hinges on an intense exchange of looks. It comes in sequence 10, where a series of reverse- angle medium close-up shots of Lantier and Séverine enables Renoir to use Zola's sentence: 'Don't look at me like that, you'll wear your eyes out.' — almost an echo of the contemporary *Quai des brumes* in which the hero played also by Jean Gabin pronounces the famous 'you've got beautiful eyes, you know'.

The first sequence of the film highlights the ambiguity of the place assigned to the spectator, despite an overall subjective effect. In the first three shots, the viewpoint remains external, while changing rapidly: the camera is placed, successively, behind the driver and the fireman, at the level of the driving wheels, and below the railway line. Very soon, as tracks, bridges and tunnels race past, we have the feeling we are at the front of the train in the position of the two drivers; this effect is all the stronger because several shots are apparently shown from their viewpoint. Yet we do not see things exactly through their eyes, which are anyway ostensibly masked by protective goggles: in actual fact, the way the shots are linked together does not allow 'internal focalization' to operate.[30] Thus, after the shot of Lantier leaning out of the door of his engine, the track is shown from the very front of the locomotive, and not from the supposed viewpoint of the driver; if that were so, the shot would be more to the side, with a part of the front of the engine in shot. That viewpoint is used several times during the film, but always independently of the driver's gaze; similarly, before the train arrives at the station, a sign marked 'Le Havre' is shown laterally, as if seen through a window. Unlike the novel (where everything is depicted through Lantier's eyes as he stands at the controls), the film both proposes and systematically denies the driver access to the gaze.

More particularly, in the novel, it is from the tunnel, where he has taken refuge, that Lantier sees the couple silhouetted against a window as they commit the murder; Renoir, on the other hand, puts Gabin in the corridor of the carriage where the crime is committed, so that neither he nor the spectator can witness an act which is hidden by blinds that are slammed down inside Grandmorin's private compartment, and which cannot be heard because of the roar of the train in the tunnel. Better even, Gabin gets a bit of smut in his eye, which entitles him to answer in the negative when asked by the police: 'Didn't you see anything?'

A network of recurrences emphasizes the central character's 'flawed gaze' — a series of close-ups of Gabin looking vacantly into the distance, all of which except the first are followed by a fade-out. This series, which begins with the last shot in sequence 5 (when Lantier's godmother has just reminded him of the effect his fits have on his behaviour), ties in with the closing shots of sequences 6 and 12 — first the already mentioned close-up that follows the row with Flore ('I think that women, for me...'), then the one showing that he accepts Séverine's rejection of his advances ('It's much better that way... . So let's just remain good friends...'). The series comes to an end with the last shot of sequence 17, where Gabin, framed from behind, leans his face against the side of a carriage and admits his powerlessness ('I can't do it') after failing to murder Roubaud. In the epilogue, after one last high-angle close-up of the dead Lantier, Pecqueux closes his eyes for good.

The point is that eyes are dangerous, as is shown by the remark of the magistrate Denizet just after arresting Cabuche: 'Did you see his eyes? I always recognise them from their eyes' (end of seq. 11). The reverse-angle shots of the interrogation scene did indeed give the tramp access to 'internal focalization'. On a less tragic plane, the gaze of the two voyeurs who first reveal Flore to us results in one of them being pushed into the water by the wild beauty, who later chides Lantier for looking at her 'like all the others do'. Finally, it is with her eyes that Séverine ensnares Lantier: both at their first meeting, in the carriage where the murder is committed, and at their first rendez-vous, Lantier is caught in the vision that Séverine relays to the spectator. Although the reciprocity of the reverse-angle shots draws the man to his doom, the woman will have to die first. The gaze, when endorsed, is fatal: Cabuche, Séverine and Roubaud have internal focalization, and it earns them prison, death or decrepitude; but avoidance of the gaze, the refusal to see, is no protection. Lantier, when he sees Roubaud, cannot bring himself to strike him, and when he kills Séverine he does so with a knife which he has not looked at but simply snatched in an unconscious movement (a high-angle shot just shows the murder weapon, harshly lit on the white tablecloth, and a hand quickly picking it up). However, after the murder, Lantier passes a mirror and is forced, between a hesitation (a lowered gaze) and a refusal (his eyes turned away), to look at himself at last. It is that reflection which commits him to killing himself.

Here we find Gabin in a role which he often took on — and which I and others have already analysed elsewhere (Lagny, Ropars and Sorlin 1986): that of a scapegoat, constituted as 'the object of the quest for the spectator, who delegates him to the function of subject', so that he dies in his/her place. Not only is that function confirmed in *La Bête humaine*, thus authorizing the reassurance of the spectator, but the film reinforces its effect by exhibiting the interplay of gazes thematically and at the same time undercutting their structural effectiveness, thereby placing the spectator in a position of ubiquity which enables him/her to see without running any of the risks that seeing involves.

* * *

It can be seen, then, that it is the moments of hesitancy in the film's textual system, involving breaks in 'implication' and a denial of the gaze, which take the *fêlure* on board while at the same time papering over it. True, Lantier carries within him a *fêlure* of sociological origin, produced by 'those generations of drinkers', but the brief descriptions of his fits are not very convincing, and it is clear that the main effect of his sacrifice is to destroy the oppressive social organization that turned the petit-bourgeois Roubaud and the pretty Séverine, 'dressed like a princess', into corrupt victims of the grand bourgeois Grandmorin. True, too, the narrative dislocation and the weakness of the subject of the gaze (and many other clues which I have omitted to mention here) could be interpreted as reflecting the uneasy atmosphere of the late 1930s and their uncertainty about what the future held in store. But if Renoir regarded his film as a weapon against Hitler, could it not be because a number of disturbing fantasies are let loose in it? By keeping his spectators in the position of uninvolved voyeurs, but ones that are capable of asking themselves questions, Renoir offers them the shelter which makes a critical position possible.

The effectiveness of this protection answers a question put by Gilles Deleuze in his preface to Zola's novel: 'Why did Renoir shy away from Lantier's vision on the railway track? [...] Why did he replace that scene with one where Lantier comes to the conclusion that the Roubauds are guilty, instead of sensing it instinctively through that vision, which is both certain and indeterminate?'(Deleuze 1977, 20). Reason, which *comes to a conclusion,* no doubt fails to save Lantier, but it is a challenge to what is none other than the death instinct that Deleuze analyses in Zola — not '*just one of many instincts,* but something like the *fêlure* personified, around which all the other instincts seethe' (Deleuze 1977, 14). In the process of *dédoublement* which I have outlined, Lantier's death leaves Roubaud, already corrupted, with (emotional) powerlessness but offers Pecqueux, the proletarian, (social) power. Thus we are brought to the 'vanishing point' which Deleuze again, in another text (Deleuze 1985, 115), regards as characteristic of Renoir, and through which 'something takes shape [...] which will succeed in emerging from the flaw and blossoming freely'. With its epilogue, where railway traffic starts moving again, the film succeeds better than the novel in turning the train into 'an epic symbol [...] which always has a future' (Deleuze 1977, 23), but the train is no longer driverless, and it is Renoir, rather than Zola, who is responsible for that 'socialist optimism ... which implies that, through the *fêlure,* it is the proletariat that wins through' (Deleuze 1977, 23).

Perhaps this is why, in the late 1980s, despite the concerns of the engine driver faced with the new technology which transforms his living and working conditions, and provokes his revolt, *La Bête humaine* lives on after all.

Translated from the French by Peter Graham.

NOTES

1. *Le Monde*, 8 January 1987, 25.
2. Interview in *Ce Soir*, 3 September 1938, in Renoir 1974a, 259.
3. Extract from a synopsis that Zola sent to a publisher, in Mitterand, Henri (1966), 'Etude' on *La Bête humaine*, in *Les Rougon-Macquart* IV, Paris, Gallimard, 1709.
4. Chardère 1962, 266-267. Extract from an article by the right-wing critic Jean Fayard in *Candide*, 28 December 1938.
5. See Faulkner 1979, 113-114. The reason why the film did not feature among the big box-office successes of the end of the 1930s is probably that it was released too late to be included in the 1938 charts and *La Cinématographie Française* figures for 1939 are no longer available.
6. Martin, Marcel, *Les Lettres Françaises*, 19 September 1966.
7. Cournot, Michel, *Le Nouvel Observateur*, 28 September 1966.
8. *La Bête humaine,* cuttings files, Collection Rondel, Bibliothèque de l'Arsenal.
9. Interview with Renoir, *Cinémonde*, 7 December 1938, in Renoir 1974a.
10. Mitterand, Henri (1981), 'Emile Zola en librairie', in *Catalogue général des ouvrages imprimés de la Bibliothèque Nationale, Auteurs*, vol. CCXXXI, Paris, Imprimerie Nationale. In addition to the latest editon of Zola's *Oeuvres complètes* published by Maurice Leblond between 1927 and 1929, various individual editions were available at the time, notably in Fasquelle's 'La Bibliothèque Charpentier' series, but also on the Flammarion list.

Original 1890 printing: 55,000 copies; the 1949 edition carries the indication '179th thousand'.

11. For example: 'Le Passage à niveau' (extract from the derailment episode) in Dumas, L. (1934) *Le Livre unique de français*, 15; 'Le Mécanicien et sa locomotive', in Souché, A. (1936) *La Lecture expressive et le français*, Paris, Nathan, 46-7 (with an illustration); and, with the same title but a different extract (on the relationship between the driver and his locomotive, to which I have already referred, but here in a bowdlerised form: the sentence 'He loved it, then, with masculine gratitude' was excised, in Souché, Dard and Lamaison (1940) *Les Auteurs du nouveau programme*, Paris, Nathan, 1940.

12. Reproduced in *Cinémonde*, 27 December 1938, in Renoir 1974a, 260.

13. See Vincendeau (1985a) 243-397; and 'Community, Nostalgia and the Spectacle of Masculinity: Jean Gabin in Two Films Made During the Period of the Popular Front', *Screen* (1985) 26 (6); Lagny, Ropars and Sorlin (1986).

14. Interview with Renoir, *Ce Soir*, 24 July 1938.

15. *Cinémonde*, 7 December 1938.

16. Renoir made many statements on this subject (e.g. in Renoir 1974a, 260; interview in *Ce Soir*, 4 December 1938), as did his set designer Eugène Lourié, quoted in Viry-Babel 1986, 108.

17. *Cinémonde*, 12 December 1938, in Renoir 1974a, 267.

18. ibid.

19. *Cinémonde*, 4 November 1938, in Renoir 1974a, 262.

20. 1969 interview in Viry-Babel 1986, 108; interview by Michel Ciment, *Positif*, (1975), 173, 15-21.

21. In addition to Poulle 1969, see Gauteur 1980a, 119-130, and Renoir 1974a; Gauthier 1968, 30-2; and Serceau 1981.

22. For an exhaustive list of articles devoted to the film see Faulkner 1979, 112ff.

23. Extract from an article by Pierre Bost in *Les Annales*, 10 January 1939, 111.

24. Metz, Christian (1977) *Le Signifiant imaginaire*, Paris, UGE (10/18), 79.

25. The narrative unit is based on a 'diegetically based entity proposed by the narrative text'. A logical-diegetic 'implication' means that 'the second sequence comes not only after the first, but also because of it', whereas a chronological 'implication' restricts 'intersequential links to the interaction of before and after'. The 'implication' is described as 'suspended' when logical and temporal relationships remain indeterminate, thus producing a certain narrative imprecision. See Lagny, Ropars and Sorlin 1986, 24 and 26.

26. See the shooting script established in Gauthier 1968, 29, which turns the first two sequences into a single one, thus removing the break produced by the fade out.

27. Notably in Gauthier 1968, 32-3, and Guillaume-Grimaud 1986, 72-3.

28. Interview with Jean Renoir in *Ce Soir*, 24 July 1938, reproduced in *Ecran* (1974a), 31.

29. See, for example, Gauthier (1968), 33-4; Guillaume-Grimaud (1986) 75; and Viry-Babel (1986), 108.

30. I have retained the term used in *Générique des années 30*, despite the convincing analysis and concept of 'ocularisation' proposed by François Jost in (1987) *L'Oeil-caméra*, Lyon, PUL, 14-30.

SELECTED BIBLIOGRAPHY

Bazin, André (1971) *Jean Renoir*, ed. by François Truffaut, Paris, Editions Champ Libre. In English: (1974) *Jean Renoir*, trans. W.W. Halscy II and William H. Simon, New York, Dell.

Beylie, Claude (1975) *Jean Renoir*, Cinéma d'aujourd'hui 2, Paris, Film Editions.

Chardère, Bernard (1962) *Jean Renoir*, Lyon, Premier Plan.

Ciment, Michel (1975) 'Interview with Jean Renoir (sur *La Bête humaine*)', *Positif* 173, 15-21.

Deleuze, Gilles (1977) 'Zola et la fêlure', preface to the Folio edition of *La Bête humaine*,

Paris, Gallimard. This text had already appeared in Deleuze (1969) *Logique du sens*, Paris, Editions de Minuit.

Deleuze, Gilles (1985) *Cinéma 2 — L'Image-Temps*, Paris, Editions de Minuit.

Durgnat, Raymond (1974) *Jean Renoir*, Berkeley and Los Angeles, University of California Press.

Faulkner, Christopher (1979) *Jean Renoir, a Guide to References and Resources*, Boston, G. K. Hall.

Faulkner, Christopher (1985) *The Social Cinema of Jean Renoir*, Princeton, Princeton University Press.

Gauteur, Claude (1974) 'Jean Renoir auteur de films (à propos de *La Bête humaine*)', *Ecran*, 31.

Gauteur, Claude (1980a) *Jean Renoir, la double méprise*, Paris, Editeurs Français Réunis.

Gauteur, Claude (1980b) '*La Bête humaine*', *Image et Son, La Revue du Cinéma*, 27.

Gauthier, Guy (1968) '*La Bête humaine*', *Image et Son, La Revue du cinéma*, 227.

Guillaume-Grimaud, Geneviève (1986) *Le Cinéma du Front Populaire*, Paris, Lherminier.

Lagny, Michèle, Ropars, Marie-Claire and Sorlin, Pierre (1986) *Générique des années 30*, Paris, Presses Universitaires de Vincennes.

Poulle, François (1969) *Renoir 1938, ou Jean Renoir pour rien? — Enquête sur un cinéaste*, Paris, Editions du Cerf.

Renoir, Jean (1974a) *Ecrits 1926-1971*, ed. by Claude Gauteur, Paris, Belfond.

Renoir, Jean (1974b) *Ma vie et mes films*, Paris, Flammarion. In English: (1974) *My Life and My Films*, trans. Norman Denny, New York, Atheneum.

Serceau, Daniel (1981), *Jean Renoir, l'insurgé*, Paris, Editions du Sycomore.

Serceau, Daniel (1985) *Jean Renoir*, Paris, Edilig.

Sesonske, Alexandre (1980) *Jean Renoir, the French Films, 1924-1939*, Cambridge, Mass. and London, Harvard University Press.

Vincendeau, Ginette (1985a) *French Cinema in the 1930s: Social Text and Context of a Popular Entertainment Medium*, unpublished thesis, University of East Anglia.

Vincendeau, Ginette (1985b) 'Community, Nostalgia and the Spectacle of Masculinity: Jean Gabin in Two Films Made During the Period of the Popular Front', *Screen*, 26 (6).

Viry-Babel, Roger (1986), *Jean Renoir, la règle et le jeu*, Paris, Denoël.

Zola, Emile (1966) *La Bête humaine*, Paris, Gallimard.

Zola, Emile (1977) *La Bête humaine*, Harmondsworth, Penguin.

APPENDIX

Jean Renoir (1894—1979): filmography

1924 *Catherine (Backbiters)*
1924 *La Fille de l'eau (The Whirlpool of Fate)*
1926 *Nana*
1927 *Sur un air de Charleston (Charleston-Parade)*
1927 *Marquitta*
1928 *La Petite marchande d'allumettes (The Little Match Girl)*
1928 *Tire-au-flanc (The Slacker)*
1929 *Le Tournoi dans la cité*
1929 *Le Bled (The Back of Beyond)*
1931 *On purge bébé*
1931 *La Chienne*
1932 *Boudu sauvé des eaux (Boudu Saved from Drowning)*
1932 *La Nuit du carrefour (Night at the Crossroads)*
1933 *Chotard et Cie*
1934 *Madame Bovary*
1934 *Toni*
1935 *Le Crime de Monsieur Lange (The Crime of Monsieur Lange)*

1936 *Les Bas-fonds* (*The Lower Depths*)
1936 *Une Partie de campagne* (*A Day In the Country*) released 1946
1936 *La Vie est à nous* (*The People of France*) released 1969
1937 *La Grande illusion* (*Grand Illusion*)
1938 *La Bête humaine* (*The Human Beast* [UK]; *Judas was a Woman* [USA])
1938 *La Marseillaise*
1939 *La Règle du jeu* (*The Rules of the Game*)
1940 *La Tosca* (finished by Carl Koch)
1941 *Swamp Water*
1943 *This Land is Mine*
1944 *Salute to France*
1945 *The Southerner*
1946 *The Diary of a Chambermaid*
1947 *The Woman on the Beach*
1951 *The River*
1953 *Le Carrosse d'or* (*The Golden Coach*)
1955 *French CanCan*
1956 *Eléna et les hommes* (*Paris Does Strange Things*)
1959 *Le Déjeuner sur l'herbe* (*Picnic on the Grass*)
1959 *Le Testament du Docteur Cordelier* (*Experiment in Evil*)
1962 *Le Caporal épinglé* (*The Elusive Corporal* [UK]; *The Vanishing
        Corporal* [USA])
1970 *Le Petit théâtre de Jean Renoir* (*The Little Theatre of Jean Renoir*)

Other films cited in the text

La Bandera (*Escape from Yesterday*), Julien Duvivier (1935)
La Belle équipe (*They were Five* [UK]; *A Fine Team* [USA]), Julien Duvivier (1936)
Quai des brumes (*Port of Shadows*), Marcel Carné (1938)

7. Poetic Realism as psychoanalytical and ideological operation: Marcel Carné's *Le Jour se lève* (1939)

MAUREEN TURIM

I. Method of inquiry

Released two years after the demise of the Popular Front and just three months before the entry of France into war with Germany, Marcel Carné's *Le Jour se lève*, from a script by Jacques Viot with dialogues by Jacques Prévert,[1] is a film that more than most suffered from the way contextual factors apparently affected its reception in 1939. It was seen by some critics as a renunciation of the ideals of the Popular Front.[2] Then it was in fact banned by the military censor board as too 'defeatist'.[3] Judging the film from their racist, fascist ideological bias, Bardèche and Brasillach decried the 'judaïzing aesthetic' of *Le Jour se lève* which they compared to the German cinema before 1933.[4] It was not until ten years after its original release that the film's reputation was redeemed (partially due to the efforts of André Bazin),[5] once it could be seen, not necessarily outside of the context of the late 1930s upheavals, but with more distance on the threat its tone implied to diverse groups at that time.

From our position of retrospection, there are many possible readings of the gloomy poetics of a film like *Le Jour se lève*, slightly different from the 1930s critiques, but using the same sort of symbolic approach: as an expression of the mood of despair after the collapse of the Popular Front on the eve of World War II; as the migration into French culture of Nietzschian philosophy; or as Carné and Prévert's personal fascination with and reworking of the US gangster film of the 1930s. All of these have some validity, and the historical thesis is particularly intriguing given the marked difference between the films from the end of the 1930s and those from earlier in the decade. What we will see, however, is that in addition to these readings *Le Jour se lève* prefigures the psychoanalytic narrative economy of the 1940s melodrama and *film noir*[6] in its configuration of a compulsive desire forcing repetitions that can only be stopped with death.

In the discussion that follows, I would like to continue the process of historical re-evaluation initiated by Bazin by proposing an analysis whose method takes into account polysemy, a weave of conflicting meanings, rather than unity of meaning and symbolism. Such a method considers the complexities of intertextuality and ideology in relationship to the multiplicity of meanings a film generates on several levels including psychoanalytical and deconstructive readings. This differs from symptomatic readings in which a given interpretation is said to reflect an assumed prevailing mood.

In the case of *Le Jour se lève*, symptomatic readings tend to emphasize the pessimism and fatalism dominant in the film. Such readings are largely thematic and tend to take these attitudes, as represented in the film, as the meaning of the film itself. If a working-class character or a Frenchman (the two ways of characterizing the hero pertinent to the 1930s critiques mentioned above) is shown to be driven to self-destruction, then the film is somehow seen as not offering the proper inspiration for class struggle or nationalist resistance or nationalist fascist collaboration, as the case may be. However, fictional suicides can also be part of a statement of protest or desperation. Two suicides from the 1930s, that of a friend of the Préverts, the Surrealist Pierre Batcheff in 1931, and that of Socialist Roger Salengro in 1937, Ministre de l'Intérieur under Léon Blum, were in fact seen at the time as just such acts of protest; Salengro's suicide was a major rallying point for the Popular Front, as he was perceived as having been driven to it by his political opponents. Further, if we allow that *Le Jour se lève* is more complex in its use of character than such thematic interpretation admits, the pessimism located within a character or within the trajectory of a character's life need not be taken as the singular 'message' of the film.

Instead, we can see how the film depicts characters whose desires and impulses are positioned as networks of conflicting forces. The tension is not only between characters representing different elements, but within characters, with the protagonist, François (Jean Gabin), providing a central focus of this network. Ginette Vincendeau has analysed how characters played by Jean Gabin figure in the political imagination of the 1930s;[7] François, as one of the late incarnations of a continuing series of like personae, clearly does embody a mythic hero, who while marked as coming from the working class, rarely simply represents a typical constituant of it (his role in *La Grande illusion* is perhaps his most positive and also most typed working-class embodiment). Instead, this hero tends to represent the troubled aspect of a subject whose desires are poetically magnified as outside of control or compromise. The death act then takes a structural place in the narrative as a refusal of suffering and the danger of being further misunderstood or manipulated, as well as presenting psychic volatility as marking the construction of this hero.

As we shall see, this suicidal hero can be seen in relationship to a discourse on memory and the viewing of the past. The hero's focalization of his past serves the film's psychoanalytic unveiling, not merely at the level of psychology of character, but as meta-psychology. The social determination of this character then needs to be construed as an element in relationship to these other operations, symbolically inseparable from them. To retain the weight of an historical context while pursuing a process of reading beyond a symptomatic thematic interpretation into the psychoanalytical narrative economy — that is the goal of what follows.

II. Double time and associative memory objects

In *Le Jour se lève* knowledge of the murder is first given the audience as an intertitle prefacing the frame story, one that was in fact added at the insistence of the producer to clarify the structure for the audience: 'A man has killed. Shut up and besieged in his room, he evokes the circumstances which made of him a murderer.'[6] The frame story then opens with the gunshot we hear, but do not see; the vision of the act of murder itself is withheld until the end of the final flashback. The frame story chronicles the degeneration of the hero's mood through the night towards dawn. The three flashbacks are offered within this frame as the subjective thoughts of this man, described as 'besieged by memories'. The flashbacks are 'causal' segments whose internal temporal structure is a linear progression narrating the jealousy, betrayal and villainous taunting that turns the promise of an ideal romance sour. Like many flashback films, the structure here reverses the cause and effect order, giving us the effect, murder, first, and the cause, an overwhelming psychic tension, following that. In a sense the past is offered to the audience as explanation and justification, though, due to this trope of interior thought, the narrative does not present itself as a courtroom trial, not even indirectly, as does the other famous 1930s French flashback film co-authored by Prévert and directed by Jean Renoir, *Le Crime de M. Lange*. In fact, as the film progresses, the hero rejects the crowd's sympathy for him, misreading it as a perverse fascination, and will not acknowledge his friends who urge him to surrender in order to be given a real trial. Rather than directly appeal to the audience's judgment, *Le Jour se lève* shows us a man who rejects anyone who tries to help or understand him. It problematizes judgment before the inner workings of a psyche, but, paradoxically, it encourages our sympathy by proposing to show us how psychic tension can reach such an explosive level.

This double temporal organization of the film enables fascinating object associations which link the present to the past. These object associations are both an application of a notion of associative memory and a particular inscription of the object symbolism typical of Poetic Realism. The objects that will circulate through other segments, the mirror, the teddy bear and the brooch, are introduced within the first flashback. The scene of their introduction occurs three weeks after the hero's initial meeting with the young florist's assistant, Françoise, with whom he falls in love. He visits her in her room where, in the course of their flirtation, he holds her teddy bear next to his face as he looks in the mirror. This gesture marks his contemplation of Françoise's suggestion that the toy bear and he look alike, both have 'one happy eye and one sad'. The bear becomes a symbol of the ideal of happiness and the melancholy of defeat that coexist in François, and it is this bear that he takes with him upon being sexually rebuffed that evening. The taking of this souvenir, this emblem of himself as consolation, is a way in which the film marks its forces of narrative determination.

In the next return to the present, François repeats the gesture, the look in the mirror while holding a teddy bear, that he made in Françoise's room. The migration of this gesture from flashback to present gives us memory as a repetition of gestures and objects, doubling the sense of over-determination already located in the bear.

The brooch also makes its first appearance in Françoise's room, as one of the objects she puts on before leaving for her mysterious late night rendez-vous. The brooch figures in the complicated psychological torture Valentin devises for François in which he uses Clara's jealousy of Françoise to extract his revenge. Clara explains that the brooch signifies Valentin's sexual conquest of a new woman, that is, Françoise, and she now gives one like it to François as a souvenir of their affair which he has just ended. The brooch then serves as the visual symbol that will bridge the next transition between past and present. The brooch gets thrown by François at the *armoire* in the transitional shot that brings us back to the present.

The brooch inspires an on-going discourse on the relationship between objects and memory that thematizes the associative memory-links the film makes in its flashback structure. This is especially developed in the *double-entendre* in the French word *souvenir* (which means both a memory and a memento), which is developed in the dialogue between François and Clara. This word-play reminds us of how objects become invested with memories, for in Prévert's poetic condensation of *souvenir*, objects and memories are inseparable.

Objects are charged with meanings by the film and their recurrence is a key to the structure of the narrative. This circulation of symbolic objects can also be seen as forming the psychoanalytic narrative economy of the film. The objects provide a metaphorical rendering of imagination and the psyche in relationship to death. The room itself embodies the restriction of freedom through a limitation and closure of space. The response to this restriction is a withdrawal, an interiorization which has as its slogan François' shouts of 'Fous-moi la paix' and 'Fichez-moi la paix' ('leave me alone', but also 'give me some peace'). The window, mirror, door and *armoire* become symbolically rich elements of this architectonic shell. François' barricade against the world is destroyed element by element, first the shattering of the window, then François' breaking of the mirror which fragments his self-image, then the penetration of bullets through the door and then the *armoire* placed in front of it. The final penetration of his space, the ominous explosion of the tear gas occurs in ironic excess of good reason, as it explodes next to his corpse, yet reason enough exists in its imagistic purpose as this 'senseless' explosion, this puff of smoke, fills the space of the dead hero, underscoring the end of the *homme-récit*, the narrative process bound by the course of a fictional life.[9]

Let us take another look at how François' movement in the long take that begins the first return to the present links this shattered window with the mirror, which in turn will be shattered in a later sequence. As window and mirror are both frequent metaphors for cinema itself (for example, Bazin's

Le Jour se lève — above: François (Jean Gabin); below: view of building where François lives.

'window on the world'[10] and the widespread notion of cinema as mirror of society, the psyche or the author) these images gain meta-cinematic, theoretical signification. They place the character in the film as trapped not only by his temporal frame (the frame story) but by his cinematic frame (the image, its architectonics, its means of symbolization). The despair and the fatalism are not only pertaining to the social references, the failure of the Popular Front, they have permeated the language of expression, the controlling metaphors of the cinematic medium.

If these architectural elements become indicators of withdrawal, restriction and annihilation of the self in the present siege of the room, in the flashback past they had been imbued with other meanings. For example, the *armoire* shifts from being a treasure chest whose interior is decorated with photos of Françoise to being François' armor, shielding him from the police. The film plays on the near homonyms, *armoire*, *amour*, *armure* (chest, love, armor) visually and verbally.[11] Consider the dialogue between the commissaire of police and the concierge:

> *Le commissaire*: Dites donc ... Est-ce qu'il y a une armoire dans cette chambre? (Say ... Is there a chest in that room?)
> *Le concierge*: Comment? (What?)
> *Le commissaire*: Je vous demande s'il y a une armoire dans sa chambre? (I'm asking you if there is a chest in his room?)
> *Le concierge:* Naturellement, il y a une armoire. (Naturally, there is a chest.)
> *Le commissaire*: Une grande armoire ... ? (A large chest?)
> *Le concierge*: Une grande armoire? ... j'sais pas, moi! ... Une armoire comme toutes les armoires ... (A large chest? I don't know ... a chest like all the others ...)

This dialogue calls attention to itself through obsessive repetitions, then begs for the substitution of *amour* for *armoire* in the phrase *une grande armoire*, especially when this is further modified by the concierge's answer. In this transposition, François' love, so obsessive as to be self-destructive, is said to be in fact like all other loves; in the transposition with armor, love, which once seemed an escape from an oppressive world, becomes an ineffective shield from a hostile one.

The exchange and contrast between the meanings objects had in the past and the ones they acquire in this new context of the present is so constant as to become an obsessive characteristic of the text. For example, when the bullet causes the door of the *armoire* to swing open, revealing the photos in the present, François slams it shut again, a metaphor for his attempt to not remember, which nonetheless triggers the next flashback. Each of the objects represents in microcosm this difference between two states of being, one in which there are restrictions, but also dreams and hope for change, and one in which hope is lost and death is inevitable. Objects also permit dialogues to be spun around them poetically, and here Prévert displays his similarity to his contemporary, Francis Ponge, in using the object as the basis for an ironic series of philosophical speculations.[12]

The recurrences of these objects also operate abstractly to engage structures of repetition and return. These structures contribute to the fatalism of the film, a film in which the past and the present join on the 'seam' of the murder, and once the murder is regained across this temporal fold, the suicide follows. Are we 'beyond the pleasure principle'? Is this film, structured by deaths, an ode to the death drive?

III. Melodrama: the hero, the villain and the two women

The answer to these questions must be postponed until we take another entrance into *Le Jour se lève*, the consideration of the melodramatic aspects of this narrative. French theatrical melodrama is an important intertextual force throughout the history of French film.[13] This is particularly evident in the collaborative work of Carné and Prévert, including *Jenny*, *Quai des brumes*, and *Les Enfants du paradis* as well as *Le Jour se lève* and Carné's *Hôtel du Nord* from a scenario by Henri Jeanson and Jean Aurenche. *Les Enfants du paradis* even thematizes this melodramatic proclivity on the part of Prévert and Carné by drawing directly on the life of Frédérick Lemaître and the Boulevard du Crime setting.[14] Although several of the films cited above do have novelistic rather than theatrical sources, these novels themselves are marked by the nineteenth-century theatrical melodrama.[15] Like other French films of the 1930s, *Le Jour se lève* concentrates on the male hero as central focus whereas melodramatic films of the 1920s were more likely to make the female central (*Jenny* is one of the exceptions, with its 1930s female focus). If the hero is central through his focalization, the melodrama develops a network of desire and rivalry that contains four principals, which can be diagrammed as follows:

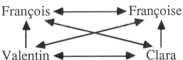

This diagram allows us to see the doubling of the couples and the crossing of the lines of desire. Above we have the hero and heroine, the couple of apparent charmed likeness, François and Françoise, who, except for the 'e', the signifier of sexual difference, share a name, a saint's day, and memories of childhoods as orphans. Below, the couple meet at the point of rupture, the villain and the other woman. As close as it comes in many respects, this is not simply the melodramatic tale of the contamination of pure love by the impure. A look at each of the four characterizations will help show why.

If our hero is complexly drawn, this complexity is an amplification, through traits that construct a character psychology, of the traditional melodramatic hero. He is, on a more basic level, beneath all the elaboration of his subjective vision and his psyche, the romantic lead in a tale of morality, attempting to secure for himself and his love object an ideal life together. Valentin is a pure melodramatic villain, a cruel ringmaster who treats others in the melodrama like the dogs he trains for his *café-concert* act.

If the hero and villain follow the generic pattern of melodrama, the two women are harder to categorize. Françoise 'should' be the ideal innocent heroine and Clara, the other, fallen, woman, but here is where the film performs some of its most interesting play with character. The first flashback introduces both women, placing them in parallel roles in the working-class and marginal *café-concert* milieu of the film. The contrasts that melodrama might impose between them (a good/bad woman split) are mediated in a number of ways.

First, the opposition between the heroine and the other woman is modified by Françoise being far more worldly and far less innocent (in her attraction to Valentin) than she initially appears to François when he is interrupted at work by her confused attempt to deliver her flowers. Her chance appearance at his factory bearing azaleas on their mutual saint's day which begins his infatuation is painted as an array of symbols. In the protective suit of a sandblaster, François takes on the almost surreal appearance of the modern industrialized man, while Françoise appears as an ideal vision, innocence bedecked with flowers. The ideal image is destroyed soon thereafter, when François follows Françoise on her late night sortie to a *café-concert* where he discovers that she is enraptured by a rival, Valentin. François judges Valentin by watching the act, as does the audience; Jules Berry's exaggerated performative gestures as Valentin present him as self-aggrandizing and belittling others (Clara and the dogs who are presented by him as puppets rather than as intelligent performers).

The triangle (hero—innocent—villain) is doubled when François begins talking with Clara (Arletty), Valentin's co-performer and mistress who has just walked out on him. Clara's saucy rejection of Valentin, her refusal to continue to perform with/for him, given first as a flippant gesture, the purposeful missing of her cue to catch his top hat, aligns her with François' sensibilities, his distaste for Valentin's pseudo-elegance. François and Clara demonstrate from their initial meeting onward that indeed they speak the same language, a language without pretences at being anything other than what they are. The flashback ends with a confrontation between Valentin and François, not over Françoise, but over Clara. This uneasy substitution of Clara for Françoise continues throughout the next flashback.

If Clara's substitution for Françoise is a temporary compromise on François' part within the diegesis, it accrues a different reaction from most spectators. Arletty is so dynamic a performer in the role of Clara, and so winning not only in her independence, but also once she softens to admit her love of François, that it is actually difficult to accept emotionally the logic of the narrative by which François must break off with her to return to his doomed idealization, his infatuation with Françoise. We can analyse this intuitive discomfort not only in terms of a casting imbalance (the comparative weakness of Jacqueline Laurent's performance) that undercuts narrative determinations, but also as a longing, ultimately suppressed by the film, to step outside the overdetermination of the death drive as guarantor of narrative closure. The initial encounter between Clara and François at the bar of the *café-concert* is characterized by a revitalization of the romantic exchange of glances as a female-initiated, sardonic volley. For example, in response to François' assertion that with all her make-up he cannot know if she is pretty, Clara, non-plussed, replies 'Make-up? I always take it off before I go to bed'. The film flirts with allowing a proletarian couple to evade the frame of pessimism of late 1930s French melodrama and reconstitute their lives on terms that offer a class-conscious, if personalized, alternative.

The glimmer of such an alternative is often suggested in the film, in ways that the dominant readings often ignore. We can understand this in terms of the affinities established between the two women that efface their opposition. Both women are presented as workers; though Clara is a performer, her job in the act is parallel to Françoise's role as service assistant to the florist. Discussions of representations of the working class in 1930s films tend to ignore such representations of the female work force, focusing exclusively on the male factory worker.[16] Yet it is significant that, despite the romantic rivalry that will make them opponents, a solidarity between them, at least on Clara's part, will ultimately surface in the narrative. This occurs in the scenes surrounding the final flashback, when, in the present, Françoise shows up on the street below François' room in a state of hysterical delirium. It is Clara who takes Françoise away to comfort her, bringing Françoise to her room, and listens sympathetically while she rants of her love for François and, ironically, the insignificance of his tryst with Clara.

Clara and Françoise are also linked to the male workers, the comrades of François who form a kind of Greek chorus commenting on the action from their position beneath François' window. Unlike the bourgeoisie who assume a criminal or insane identity for François because he has committed a murder, the working-class representatives imagine that he must have had good reasons, that the killing was justifiable, something that Clara and Françoise know first-hand. Here the film joins the logic of *Le Crime de M. Lange*, where the collective knows Lange's murder of Batala (also played by Berry) to be justifiable, and Lange's woman friend is able to communicate this to a group of strangers, also proletarians, whose sympathetic understanding and collaboration is attained at the film's end. If Prévert retells his *Le Crime de M. Lange* in far less optimistic terms in *Le Jour se lève*, the traces of the earlier film's class awareness remain in this retelling.

Indeed, *Le Jour se lève* goes further than *Le Crime de M. Lange* in its effort to depart from moral absolutes and either a happy or a retributive resolution. It is not just a more pessimistic film, but one less certain that the moral oppositions of early melodrama can serve a leftist ideological framework for narrative. Instead, the elements of melodramatic form are inscribed with considerable tension and reworking. If the villain remains a consummate villain, the hero, due to the complexities of his psyche, cannot simply defeat the villain without defeating himself, while the heroine and the other woman overlap rather than forming a neat opposition. The lines between self and other, so fixed in melodrama's character types, are here more ambiguous. The reason for this ambiguity is not just a greater political scepticism at the end of the 1930s, although that certainly plays a role, but a more subjective and intersubjective view of narrative.

The questions about the death drive with which the second section of this essay ended can now be reframed by this conclusion. We can see that the film's concern with subjectivity and intersubjectivity, especially as articulated through the depiction of memory, lends itself to this tendency towards a romance of the death drive. Pleasure, imagined as a bicycle ride to pick lilac by François or as a stay on the Côte d'Azur among the mimosas by Françoise, is always deferred and unattainable; identifying with bourgeois dreams will certainly not bring happiness, but neither, apparently, will acceptance of one's proletarian being.[17] The self contains its own debilitating contradictions, and romance with a proletarian existence is dissipated by a harsh look at what François' working conditions mean. The unhealthiness of the sand, the slow death it means to the blasters, the psychological toll the job extracts from François, are motifs introduced in the factory scene (a graphic image of work in a factory rare in this period of French film) and repeated throughout the film.

The murder and suicide which bring together the two temporalities at the end of the film join the other ironies developed earlier. For ultimately, when the final flashback unfolds, we learn, despite the film's seeming to present us with causes, that there is no reason for François to kill Valentin; Françoise has already pledged her love to François, and it is only through Valentin's goading François into shooting him that the young couple's future is foreclosed. François explodes irrationally in what amounts to a nervous breakdown. This is not just Gabin's famous short tempered scene of anger that is replayed from film to film, although it does culminate the development of that image.[18] François is a character who has unraveled.

The dual temporality of the film can be seen as the piecing together across past and present of this unraveled psyche we come to inevitably in the end. Francois' psyche is not just the subject of this interlacing of past and present, but is defined by the weave of retrospective linkages evoked in the film's imagery. Psychic functioning is presented primarily through external elements weighted with symbolic heuristic value. If the working-class hero destroys himself in the end, the film constructs not so much the causes of his behavior but the forces associated with objects and people which rage in a milieu and have no outlet, no place to simply dissipate. Valentin resurfaces to accomplish, through his provoked murder, the foreclosure of the promise of and nostalgia for peace and happiness in quite the same manner in which the brooch reappears. The torment of the inherently evil recurring object is a figuration of psychic temporality itself, non-linear and repetitious, a circulation of forces.[19]

IV. Realism, poetry and memory

In his article on *Le Jour se lève*, Bazin speaks of the realism of Alexander Trauner's sets, all built for studio production, crediting the great designer with the detailed touches that make the images of this film seem, in Bazin's view, like such an accurate 'social documentary'.[20] Yet Bazin also notes how Trauner has composed this little square in a working-class suburb 'as a painter would his canvas', and remarks continually on the dramatic role of the decor in the film, comparing it with Fritz Lang's *M*, while contrasting it with other works of German Expressionism.[21] If an element of contradiction appears to open up here in Bazin's insistence on social documentary on one hand, and poetic function on the other, this leads to his direct theoretical assessment of Poetic Realism. He argues that Trauner and Carné have infused this reality with poetry, and he praises Poetic Realism for founding its metaphors and symbolism, what he terms its 'metaphysical' signification, in the accurate depiction of a milieu.

We might well ask, however, if the textual strategy of Poetic Realism can any longer simply be seen in such terms. Recent work on the theory of realism in painting, literature and film demands a greater critical distance on the apparently real created through a weave of metonymic detail. We can recast Bazin's argument by acknowledging how the film's sets use metonymic elements as devices in which the codes of realism and analogy serve the codes of metaphor and the self-consciously poetic. Such incredulity before the real is all the more appropriate when looking at a film that renders the world as composed of metaphors. Poetics of the sort pursued by this film formulate a rhetoric that is quite different from a controlled documentation of the social. While Trauner (and the Carné/Prévert team in general), may have set out to recreate in the space of the studio a corner of a working-class suburb, such descriptive mimesis immediately becomes appropriated by the symbolic structuration and interior vision of this film. We should not let our desire to know the interior of a factory or a *café-concert* in 1939 let us substitute the image given to us in this film for that reality.

By extension, we should not allow our desire to know the interior life of a working-class man to permit us to substitute this film's treatment of memory and interiority for that which escapes our gaze. The images of the past the film gives us as François' memory are less like memory processes than the images of memories in the silent 1920s films of Louis Delluc, Germaine Dulac and Abel Gance. Here the only imagistic trope of memory is associative recall, the seeing of an object triggering the recall of a memory associated with that object. Even this device is presented less as part of a mimesis of memory *per se* than as part of the network of object symbolism and circulation discussed earlier. Perhaps unconsciously, the film marks in its treatment of memory its lack of concern with documenting the memory process; memory appears to be of interest as a dramatic trope, subjected to the discipline of the film's poetics rather than truly constructing the text.

In Poetic Realism, then, the accent is on poesis, on the trope deployed strategically, framed in a manner that sparkles with a simultaneous sense of design and imaginative play of thought and language. To move ever further into such poetics when the political climate chills in the way it did in 1939 is finally a quite comprehensible response on the part of artists who cared deeply about the working class their fictions represented. It is a response that sees fiction and the reality that is its context as complexly interactive. François' outrage and self-destruction are perhaps a displacement on to the working class of the self-portrait of the poets themselves.

NOTES

1. The question of authorship of this film (who is responsible for what) is not really my focus here. We know the film to be a collective effort, benefiting from the combined talents of a group who worked together repeatedly. While many discussions of the film assign a certain quality of the contribution to Viot, Carné, Prévert, Trauner, Maurice Jaubert, the actors and actresses, they tend to do so without any historical documentation of the process involved. For my purposes here, I am quite willing to accept that the work is a group project in which each of these strong personalities and talents interacted. At the end of the article, when I speak of 'the poets' I am referring to this collectivity.
2. Geneviève Guillaume-Grimaud (1986) *Le Cinéma du Front Populaire*, Paris, Lherminier.
3. Gérard Guillot (1966), *Les Prévert*, Paris, Seghers. The same source also says that later 'Vichy authorities held *Quai des brumes* accountable for the defeat of France before the Nazi regime.'
4. Maurice Bardèche and Robert Brasillach (1948), *Histoire du cinéma*, Paris, Martel, as quoted in *Avant-Scène Cinéma*, 53, 1965. The anti-Semitism here seems aimed at Jacques Prévert.
5. André Bazin (1963), 'Fiche du *Jour se lève*', originally distributed as a leaflet at ciné-club presentations of the film, published in Jacques Chevallier (ed.) *Regards neufs sur le cinéma*, Paris, Seuil. Reprinted as part of the chapter 'Marcel Carné' in André Bazin (1983) *Le Cinéma français de la Libération à la Nouvelle Vague (1945-1958)*, Paris, Editions de L'Etoile, 53-69. John Mathews' (1970) English translation of extracts of Bazin's article appears in the 'Classic Film Scripts' translation of the script of *Le Jour se lève*, New York, Simon and Schuster, 5-12.
6. The pessimistic atmosphere, which has structural determinants in the film, is a strong prefiguration of the structure and tone of the American *film noir* flashback. *Le Jour se lève* did open in New York, under the title *Daybreak*, but to less than completely enthusiastic reviews. A remake, *The Long Night*, Litvak, 1947, starring Henry Fonda, Barbara Bel Geddes, Ann Dvorak and Vincent Price, attests to the interest in *Le Jour se lève* by an emigré director known for *film noir* at the beginning of the peak period of production of this genre of film. Taken together these facts suggest that the film was perhaps historically influential in the development of American *film noir*. Even if this were not the case, however, a comparison of structure between *Le Jour se lève* and the *noir* genre would still prove intriguing.

7. Ginette Vincendeau (1985), 'Community, nostalgia and the spectacle of masculinity: Jean Gabin in two films made during the period of the Popular Front', *Screen* 26 (6).

8. This and all other dialogue citations are taken from the script published in *Avant-Scène Cinéma*, 53, 1965.

9. Tzvetan Todorov (1971) *Poétique de la prose*, Paris, Seuil, 78-91.

10. André Bazin (1971) *What is Cinema?* trans. Hugh Grey, Berkeley, Los Angeles and London: University of California Press, 111. It is also worth noting in the context of this analysis of *Le Jour se lève* that Bazin's use of the metaphor is in the context of a contrast drawn between theater and film: '... we see that the basic aesthetic problem of filmed theater is indeed that of decor. The trump card that the director must hold is the reconversion in a window on to the world of a space oriented toward an interior dimension only, namely the closed and conventional area of the theatrical play.' Bazin's article on *Le Jour se lève* praises the film's use of windows and mirrors which I develop more thoroughly here.

11. Admittedly, the treatment of plays on words and objects that I analyse here moves slightly beyond what is actually given in the text; it constitutes a reading between lines and images. I believe, however, that Prévert's work with wordplay and object symbolism in his poetry and film scripts (most notably for the poetry, *Paroles*, and for the films, *Un Oiseau rare* [1934], in which a parrot devises advertising slogans) justifies this play on my part, which at any rate in the context of the contemporary critical methods of Jacques Derrida or Jacques Lacan does not necessarily require such historical and intertextual evidence.

12. Francis Ponge (1942) *Le Parti pris des choses*, Paris, N.R.F.

13. See my discussion of this intertextuality in silent French cinema in Turim (1987) 'French Melodrama: A Theory of a Specific History', *Theater Journal*, Fall.

14. See discussion of the melodramatic heritage of this film in Marcel Oms (1979) '*Les Enfants du paradis* ou la mutation cinématographique du mélodrame', *Cahiers de la cinémathèque*, 28, 141-148.

15. A point Peter Brooks (1976) makes in generalizing about the nineteenth-century French novel in his *The Melodramatic Imagination*, New Haven and London, Yale University Press.

16. As does François Garçon (1984) in his section 'Images de l'ouvrier à l'écran', *De Blum à Pétain*, Paris, Editions du Cerf, 53-57.

17. Ginette Vincendeau has brought to my attention that this desire to identify with bourgeois dreams is a theme in French popular songs of the 1930s as in *Tout change dans la vie*, sung by Fréhel, where visions of the Côte d'Azur are opposed (albeit ironically) to the dreariness of everyday life on the *zone*. Similarly, flowers, and in particular lilacs, are a recurrent motif of the working-class version of the pastoral offered by popular songs, as in *Entre Saint-Ouen et Clignancourt*, an early Piaf song.

18. Bazin (1963) 70.

19. Let me suggest that this analysis differs markedly from that offered by Gilles Deleuze (1985) in *L'Image-Temps*, Paris, Les Editions de Minuit, 67, in which he argues that the flashback structure in *Le Jour se lève* does nothing more than assure a linear progression. His dismissal is dependent on a reading of the film, derived from Bazin, as using its flashbacks to merely represent the causes of François' behavior.

20. 1963, 63.

21. 1963, 63.

SELECTED BIBLIOGRAPHY

For a selected bibliography on Marcel Carné see chapter 8, on *Les Enfants du paradis*.

SCRIPT

Carné, Marcel and Prévert, Jacques (1965) *Le Jour se lève*, *Avant-Scène Cinéma*, 53.

APPENDIX

Marcel Carné (1909—): filmography

1929 *Nogent, Eldorado du dimanche* (short)
1936 *Jenny*
1937 *Drôle de drame (Bizarre Bizarre)*
1938 *Hôtel du Nord*
1938 *Quai des brumes (Port of Shadows)*
1939 *Le Jour se lève (Daybreak)*
1942 *Les Visiteurs du soir (The Devil's Envoys)*
1943-5 *Les Enfants du paradis (Children of Paradise)*
1946 *Les Portes de la nuit (Gates of the Night)*
1950 *La Marie du port*
1951 *Juliette ou la clef des songes*
1953 *Thérèse Raquin (The Adulteress)*
1954 *L'Air de Paris*
1956 *Le Pays d'où je viens*
1958 *Les Tricheurs (The Cheaters)*
1960 *Terrain vague*
1963 *Du mouron pour les petits oiseaux*
1965 *Trois chambres à Manhattan*
1968 *Les Jeunes loups (The Young Wolves)*
1970 *La Force et le droit*
1971 *Les Assassins de l'ordre*
1974 *La Merveilleuse visite*
1976 *La Bible*

Other films cited in the text

Le Crime de M. Lange (The Crime of M. Lange), Jean Renoir (1935)
La Grande illusion (Grand Illusion), Jean Renoir (1938)
M, Fritz Lang (1931)

8. Beneath the despair, the show goes on: Marcel Carné's *Les Enfants du paradis* (1943-1945)

JEAN-PIERRE JEANCOLAS

The cinema which historians have definitively labelled Poetic Realism was, between 1935 and 1939, a cinema conjugated in the present tense. Jean Renoir, Julien Duvivier and Marcel Carné, Charles Spaak and Jacques Prévert, made their heroes dance to the music of their time: René Lefèvre, Jean Gabin, Charles Vanel and Jules Berry were contemporaries, even next of kin, of the viewers who were living the excitement of the emerging Popular Front in *Le Crime de Monsieur Lange*, its uncertainties in *La Belle équipe* or the bitterness of its disintegration in *La Bête humaine* or *Le Jour se lève*. The occupation of France in 1940, the control — direct or indirect — of its cinema by the German forces, condemned this use of the present tense. Fiction films were allowed, at best, to portray a kind of 'vague present day', a period which had the appearance of the present, but not its singular hardships: the cars or the costumes are of 1943, but the French are depicted in lighthearted romantic entanglements, stories that never show the daily problems of finding food, or the presence of Nazi uniforms. Even the rare 'realist' films of these bleak years, those of Jean Grémillon, or Clouzot's *Le Corbeau*, avoid any too obvious references to the hard times: the throb of civilian planes in *Le Ciel est à vous* has nothing to do with occupied France.

The type of realism associated with Carné and Prévert, in the era of *Le Quai des brumes* and *Le Jour se lève*, had less to do with a 'reality effect' than with the creative spirit of an exceptionally homogeneous team of artists: a designer who could reconstruct, in the Joinville studios, a street in Le Havre or a hotel on the outskirts of town so that street and building were quintessentially real, but at the same time planned with a view to lighting effects and camera angles; a director of photography, trained in the *noir* style of the Berlin studios, who knew how to juxtapose light and dark with a sense of drama that owed not a little to Expressionism; a scriptwriter-poet whose highly literate dialogues escaped sounding like sententious aphorisms thanks to the talent and rigorous professionalism of the actors — Jean Gabin, Michel Simon, Jules Berry or Arletty; actors both popular and familiar to audiences who recognized Jean Gabin before they identified the deserter or the killer of the blackmailer ... Carné's 'realism', more than Renoir's in the same pre-war period, was in fact the orchestration of a myriad of artifices controlled with exceptional talent by the director.

The realism which for half a century has been so lauded by devotees of Carné, by writers and historians, rests on a convention, a tacit agreement between the artist and his audience. Of course this is the case with all realism, but more so with Carné than with Renoir or the post-war filmmakers who gave greater scope to, among other things, outdoor shooting and natural daylight. Renoir, in some of his silent films, as well as in *Toni* or *Une Partie de campagne*, purposely sets the camera at the water's edge, and accepts the rustic authenticity of occasional non-actors, and even the awkwardness (which we find endearing) of his own acting in *Une Partie de campagne*, *La Bête humaine* and *La Règle du jeu*.

However, they all avoid, not to say banish, the 'reality effect' that occurred fortuitously in the films of Feuillade and Antoine. When Feuillade filmed a car chase through the streets of Paris, he aimed his camera, mounted on top of a car hurtling along at top speed, at the convertible in which Inspector Juve was hot on the trail of the saloon which everyone knew held Fantômas. He filmed two cars, but he also caught the street, the pavements, the Paris façades racing past, the carriages and the occasional horse droppings. He captured the passers-by and the idle strollers, and it is not unusual to see one of these chance extras gazing with interest at what he has realized is the shooting of a film. When Antoine, in *Le Coupable*, places his main characters in one of the river buses that travelled along the banks of the Seine in 1917, he captures extraordinary documentary footage of wartime Paris, both of the real-life crowd and of the billboards that extol the true Frenchness of such-and-such a brand of soup. The screen fiction was loaded with a mass of information that had little to do with the original script. This practice, although not accidental (neither Feuillade nor Antoine were so naïve), brought an extra dimension to the filming. When Carné films the street in Le Havre where Michel Simon keeps shop, or the square in front of the hotel where Jean Gabin dies, he checks everything that appears on the screen: the cobbles, the railings, the Dubonnet advertisements, the lighting and the human beings, whether actors or extras directed by assistants under his orders. In the studio, nothing is left to chance: if a raised cobblestone catches the light from a streetlamp, it is because Trauner wanted the cobblestone and Schüfftan aimed a spotlight at it. Carné's cinema does not reproduce reality, it produces its own reality, by consensus.

Later, and elsewhere, the filmmakers of the New Wave were to rediscover the Feuillade effect (Godard's hidden camera in the Champs Elysées sequence of *A bout de souffle*) but without the innocence of the father of *Fantômas*. The creators of *cinéma-vérité*, the 'cinéastes du réel' — in France Jean Rouch or, even more so, the Chris Marker of *Le Joli mai* — would no longer see it as an effect, but as the very nature of filmmaking. For them, the function of the camera became to seek out the 'reality effect', in the locations, the people, the words and the sound. Spontaneity of action counted for more than perfection of lighting.

The 'realists' of 1939, as embodied by Carné and Prévert, were the architects and builders of a fictional universe which they synchronized with the times, with real life. But they were better equipped than others to transpose their work into a temporal 'elsewhere', when the constraints of the Occupation required them to do so.

* * *

After an abortive attempt at a futuristic film (it was not yet called science fiction) in 1941, *Les Evadés de l'an 4000*, Carné rejoined Prévert who offered him the script of a film in the past historic mode, *Les Visiteurs du soir*. The film they made of it, produced by André Paulvé, was released in December 1942, to the acclaim we now know. Carné had regained a position in the profession which allowed him to propose a more ambitious and perhaps more personal project. This was to be, after a certain amount of trial and error, *Les Enfants du paradis*.

The French cinema of the Occupation is in every respect a singular one. The catastrophe of 1940 had left deep wounds. Many were absent: some had been killed, like Maurice Jaubert, the musician of the great pre-war films; many were prisoners in Germany; some left of their own accord (Jean Renoir, René Clair, Julien Duvivier went to Hollywood, as did Jean Gabin and Michèle Morgan); and others were outlawed under the anti-Semitic laws imposed in October 1940 by the Vichy government. Alexandre Trauner and Joseph Kosma, both Jews of Hungarian origin, were severely affected by these restrictions: they went into hiding in the south of France where the Italian occupation, more lax than the heavy German one in Paris, was more inclined to turn a blind eye to the presence of numerous Jewish refugees, particularly if they were associated with the cinema.

The cinema of the war years was hemmed in by a network of professional regulations, sometimes laboriously worked out by the last governments of the Third Republic before its defeat, and hastily instituted by Vichy at the end of 1940. The government of occupied France, an unstable mixture of clerical conservatism and technocratic modernism, created the COIC (Committee for the Organisation of the Cinematographic Industries) which had the ultimate authority over the profession, and which ruled it within the confines tolerated by the Germans.

These were years which paradoxically combined prosperity and poverty. French cinema was healthy: it was producing films, even big budget films after a time, and they sold well. The market was dominated by national products: English-speaking films were prohibited because of the war, American films in particular becoming inaccessible. Italian films were rare, German films disdained by a proportion of the public. Yet these were years when the public queued at the box-office. The cinema was cheap entertainment at a time when entertainment was sparse, its was also a safe place until the end of 1943. It provided the illusion and escape which were the necessary antidotes to daily misery — the difficulty of finding food, the queues in shops, the cold. Cinemas were heated, and you could also hide there ... . The demand for films was pressing. The studios were active in 1942 and 1943. Producers were doing good business.

At the same time, film production (and especially for a weighty film like *Les Enfants du paradis*) came up against innumerable obstacles: finding wood and nails to build sets, fabrics for costumes, food to feed a troupe of famished technicians, actors and extras for weeks, electricity and, above all, film stock. Classified as a strategic commodity, film stock was only granted with the consent of the COIC and the German authorities. Production companies paid employees to besiege the offices that handed out the indispensable supply coupons or the 'goods coupons' which allowed them to buy all the necessary materials. Pathé even paid a worker to reclaim and straighten nails from disused sets.

So the adventure of *Les Enfants du paradis* was played out in a context of extreme tension (of which the finished film gives little hint). French cinema in 1943 had two capitals, Paris and Nice. André Paulvé, the producer of *Les Visiteurs du soir*, was quartered in Nice. Jacques Prévert and Alexandre Trauner lived a few miles away, at Tourettes sur Loup, Trauner in semi-hiding protected by sollicitous friends. Carné joined them there. With Prévert, he was looking for the subject of their next film, which Paulvé had contracted to produce with a big budget. A chance encounter with Jean-Louis Barrault, on a café terrace on the Promenade des Anglais, was a turning-point: he told them a series of anecdotes revolving around the mime Debureau and the Boulevard du Crime at the time of the Restoration (1814-1830). Carné returned to Paris to gather material, and came back with a sheaf of reproductions which he tossed on the table of Le Prieuré, the house at Tourettes which served as base camp for the entire team. There was enough there for several films, the more so as Prévert wanted to introduce and develop, within the story, the character of Lacenaire, the romantic murderer whose *Mémoires* and legendary exploits had fascinated generations of free thinkers since his execution in 1836.

Paulvé, when consulted, actually suggested making two films. According to Trauner, Prévert even envisaged a triptych, with the third section of the story devoted to the trial of Lacenaire: all Paris would have rushed to see it, as if to some rare spectacle, especially to hear the voice of Debureau in the witness box ... . The script was written in the spring of 1943. Faced with the magnitude of the project, Paulvé took on as associate producer the Italian firm Scalera, with whom he had already produced L'Herbier's *La Vie de bohême*. The film would therefore be a co-production. The roles were assigned: Jean-Louis Barrault would obviously be Debureau, with Arletty as Garance, Marcel Herrand as Lacenaire, Pierre Brasseur as Frédérick Lemaître, Louis Salou as the Comte de Montray. Maria Casarès, making her film début, would play Nathalie, and Le Vigan would play Jéricho, the rag-and-bone man. It was agreed that Léon Barsacq would be in charge of building the big sets in the studios at La Victorine in Nice, from sketches which Trauner would send to him; and that Joseph Kosma, also a refugee in the area and banned from working, would write part of the music, the rest to come from Maurice Thiriet. Some of the interior scenes would be shot in Paris, where the editing and sound synchronization would later be done.

Les Enfants du paradis — above: the 'Gods' (*paradis*, upper gallery) of the theatre; below: Frédérick Lemaître (Pierre Brasseur), Garance (Arletty) and Baptiste (Jean-Louis Barrault).

Shooting began in Nice in August. The big Boulevard du Crime set was not yet finished, so Carné started with the scenes at the Grand Relais, the boarding house where Baptiste and Frédérick Lemaître live. They had hardly started shooting on the Boulevard set when the war upset the production schedule: the Allies had landed in Sicily, Mussolini was overthrown. The order came from Paris to suspend filming. Scalera backed out of the contract that linked them with Paulvé. The entire company — apart from Trauner and Kosma, naturally — had to withdraw to Paris. Then another crisis occurred: Paulvé found himself banned by the Germans from producing films. Three months went by in attempts to save the film. Through the intervention of Louis-Emile Galey, head of COIC, Pathé was persuaded to take it on. Filming could start again. But without Le Vigan: too compromised by his active collaboration (an anti-Semite who denounced Jews, he sided with the writer Louis-Ferdinand Céline, with whom he would follow the defeated German armies), he abandoned the part of Jéricho, for which it seems he had done little more than a screen test. Carné replaced him with Pierre Renoir. In February 1944 authorization was granted to film again in Nice. Trauner's big set had been damaged by the winter and had to be restored, and the Germans refused to have it lit at night. Several scenes had to be cut, eventually to be replaced by cutaways and linking material shot in the studio in Paris.

The film was still not finished by the spring of 1944. Carné tells how, when he heard the news of the Allied landings in Normandy, he purposefully slowed down the post-production operations. He was marking time so as to release his film in a France at peace. He had, however, one more battle to fight, against the distributor, Gaumont. He wanted them to agree to screen the two parts of the film, *Le Boulevard du Crime* and *L'Homme blanc*, as a single programme lasting just over three hours. He got his way. On 9 March 1945, in an almost totally liberated France, *Les Enfants du paradis* was premiered at a gala evening at the Palais de Chaillot. A few days later, it was released in two first-run cinemas, and was received enthusiastically by both the critics and the public.

The film exists. Broad, complex, with a wealth of characters swept along by the action like the extras in the carnival scene on the Boulevard du Crime, *Les Enfants du paradis* marks a rare dimension in French cinema. Like some great novels, it is both dense and heterogeneous, fragmented into a plethora of heroes who reconcile history (Debureau, Lacenaire, Frédérick Lemaître) with the historical imaginary (the rag-and-bone man is a stock character from popular theatre) and with the contemporary imaginary of its creators: Garance is a creation of the Carné-Prévert duo.

Like many French films in the years between 1935 and 1950, *Les Enfants du paradis* is first and foremost a superb piece of scriptwriting. There has been much debate over the respective roles of Prévert and Carné in the writing of the films they made together. For *Les Enfants du paradis*, all accounts, including those of the two interested parties, are in agreement. The long task of developing the script, once Jean-Louis Barrault's initial idea had been adopted, evolved at Le Prieuré in an atmosphere of mutual agreement and collaboration. Prévert built on his own ideas, on those of Carné, on the documentation Carné had collected at the Musée Carnavalet in Paris, on the suggestions of Trauner. The isolation, amounting almost to sequestration, which the hard times imposed on them, helped the collective effort.

The script is Prévert backed by his small team. The dialogue, however, is Prévert alone, supreme master of his language, already close to many of the actors for whom he had etched superb lines in other Carné films, and his Frédérick Lemaître for Brasseur is also an extension of the already Shakespearean melodramatic actor created a year earlier in Grémillon's *Lumière d'été*. Jacques Prévert wrote to measure, for Brasseur, for Arletty, and especially for Marcel Herrand. Alexandre Trauner quotes his reply to Jean-Louis Barrault who insisted that the character of Debureau be mute: 'I understand. You don't want to talk! Never mind, I'll put someone else in who talks enough for two. That will restore the balance.'[1]

The script is divided into large blocks, which are closer to the chapters of a novel than to the normal sequence of a French film, the exceptional length of the film allowing it to develop in depth. The work of Carné and the director of photography, Roger Hubert, on Prévert's material, has remarkable clarity. Anyone seeing the film and not knowing the vicissitudes surrounding its shooting, would never suspect the problems, the interruptions, the changes in lighting, the improvised linking material which the director had to contend with. Carné was at the height of his powers.

In his masterpieces of 1938 and 1939, Carné's vision was definitely in the *noir* mode. He depicted the end of a civilized world, the sordid, suicidal despair of a degenerating society. His heroes were crushed: Jean Gabin died on screen, betrayed by the vile cunning of the ultimate *salauds* (Pierre Brasseur, Michel Simon, Jules Berry) whose actions were inexcusable, and one could imagine the sad and solitary fate awaiting the hero's companion, whether Michèle Morgan or Jacqueline Laurent. It was irredeemably a dog's life. The sky was leaden, the streets slippery, society repulsive. These films bore the mark (the shadow) of the refugee German cameramen who had lit them. *Les Enfants du paradis* is less sombre. The 1943 film distills, sums up and surpasses French-style 'realism'. The characters imagined by the poet, Prévert, come alive, they are no longer 'acted upon' by an inhuman fate. All of them, even the minor characters and extras, have rare depth and complexity. With the exception of Jéricho, the rag-and-bone man who derives from the past and brings only misfortune, they are both manipulators and manipulated, at the same time or alternately; they have their reasons for what they do, and among these reasons there are some good ones. Even Lacenaire, the cold-blooded killer, is also a romantic rebel whom Marcel Herrand endows with a charm more sarcastic than perverse.

Les Enfants du paradis is also (again) a film about despair, about the impossibility of love, about living a dog's life. Its heroes are unhappy, their love affairs go wrong. But it doesn't leave that impression of the world coming to a sordid end that oppressed the films of 1938. There are moments of fulfilment in *Les Enfants du paradis* which in a way compensate for the fate of the protagonists. Beneath the despair, the show goes on.

And *Les Enfants du paradis* is a film about spectacle. It is the cinema in all its glory paying homage to the theatre. The curtain that rises on the Boulevard du Crime is a device reminiscent of Renoir. Carné and Prévert borrow it for the duration of one film to heighten the sense of illusion that makes reality bearable. In *Le Jour se lève* the spectacle was dire: Valentin humiliated his performing dogs in a degrading masquerade. In *Les Enfants du paradis* the actors are supreme, beautiful and strong — strong enough and clever enough in the practice of their art to turn a grotesque play to their advantage: *L'Auberge des Adrets* is no doubt a worthless drama, but Frédérick uses it as a springboard to release his creative energy, and he holds the delighted audience in the palm of his hand. It is surely not by chance that Carné's film shows us the whole sprectrum of what the theatre can do: from the opening farcical pantomime of the Funambules — with Frédérick trussed up in a lion's skin — to the poetic mime of Baptiste, 'Chand' d'habits'; from the serial melodrama of *L'Auberge des Adrets* to the inspiration of *Othello*. The cinema is paying homage to the theatre, to a theatre which is like its mirror: silent theatre, like silent film, loses nothing to the spoken word, even when the word is Shakespeare's. It is, among other things, a homage to the 'primitives' of theatre and of film.

The story of the theatre is also the story of the feverish activity backstage, the crush and the impatience. It is also the audience, whether in the stalls or the 'gods', the demanding, cheeky, public that makes the careers of Baptiste and Frédérick. It is even Paris, the most beautiful stage in the world, an idealized Paris, gilded by the nostalgic imagination of Parisians exiled in the countryside around Nice. Life is not much fun, especially in 1943. But for one moment, one evening, one night of love, life is redeemed.

Les Enfants du paradis occupies a unique place in French cinema. It is one of the rare films to have been genuinely popular — because of its subject, its roots and its history. It is a film which has become greater with the passage of time. Prévert and Carné together created, all of a piece, a world peopled by a half-dozen protagonists who, with their common, deep bond with a basic French culture, rank with the tremendous characters created by Victor Hugo and Emile Zola. The Jean Valjean of *Les Misérables* has had several screen versions; the adaptations of the best known of Hugo's novels by Henri Fescourt or Raymond Bernard are great films, both of which manipulate epic imagery. But that imagery pre-dated the cinema. The first viewers of *Les Misérables* on the screen compared the Jean Valjean interpreted by Gabriel Gabrio or Harry Baur with the original in the novel. Garance was created by the cinema. Imagined by Prévert, moulded by Carné, she is an original — a complex, astonishing and definitive heroine — which the seventh art has lodged in the collective imaginary for at least two generations. For the past 20 years, there has rarely been a week when *Les Enfants du paradis* has not been shown in some small Paris cinema,[2] and it is frequently broadcast on the (too small) television screen.

Like the great archetypal novels of the nineteenth century, *Les Enfants du paradis* is always alive to an audience that does not age. On 14 December 1984, an elegant cinema was opened in the Pompidou centre in Paris. It is called the 'Salle Garance'.

Translated from the French by Marianne Johnson.

NOTES

1. Alexandre Trauner, unpublished interview collected by Nicolas Bourdais and Véronique Guyot, 1987.
2. Likewise, *Les Enfants du paradis* is regularly screened in French film seasons in the UK and the USA, and ranks among top favourites (eds).

SELECTED BIBLIOGRAPHY

Affron, Mirella Jona (1978) '*Les Enfants du paradis*: Play of Genres', *Cinema Journal*, 18 (1).
A la rencontre de Jacques Prévert (1987) Fondation Maeght.
Barsacq, Léon (1976) *Caligari's Cabinet and Other Grand Illusions: A History of Film Design*, Boston, Little, Brown & Co.
Cahiers de la cinémathèque 5 (1972) special Carné issue.
Ciné-Club (1949) nouvelle série: special Carné issue.
Carné, Marcel (1975) *La Vie à belles dents*, Paris, Ollivier.
Chazal, Robert (1965) *Marcel Carné*, Paris, Seghers.
Jacob, Guy *et al.* (1960) *Jacques Prévert*, Lyon, Premier Plan, 14.
Freadman, Anne (1986) 'Reading the Visual', *Framework*, 30/31.
Guillot, Gérard (1966) *Les Prévert*, Paris, Seghers.
Oms, Marcel (1979) 'Les Enfants du paradis ou la mutation cinématographique du mélodrame', *Cahiers de la cinémathèque*, 28.
Perez, Michel (1986) *Les Films de Carné*, Paris, Ramsay.
Queval, Jean (1952) *Marcel Carné*, Paris, Editions du Cerf.
Rachline, Michel (1981) *Jacques Prévert: drôle de vie*, Paris, Ramsay.
Turk, Edward Baron (1979) 'The Birth of Children of Paradise', *American Film*, 4 (9).

SCRIPTS

Carné, Marcel and Prévert, Jacques (1967) *Les Enfants du paradis*, Paris, *Avant-Scène Cinéma*, 72-3.
Carné, Marcel and Prévert, Jacques (1968) *Les Enfants du paradis*, trans. by Dinah Brooke, London, Lorrimer.
Carné, Marcel and Prévert, Jacques (1974) *Les Enfants du Paradis, album photo*, Paris, Balland (an illustrated book of the film).

APPENDIX

Marcel Carné (1909—): filmography

See Chapter 7, on *Le Jour se lève*, for a full filmography

Films cited in the text

A bout de souffle (*Breathless*), Jean-Luc Godard (1959)
La Belle équipe (*They were Five* [UK]; *A Fine Team* [USA]), Julien Duvivier (1936)
La Bête humaine (*The Human Beast*), Jean Renoir (1938)
Le Ciel est à vous (*The Sky is Yours*), Jean Grémillon (1944)
Le Corbeau (*The Raven*), Henri-Georges Clouzot (1943)
Le Coupable, André Antoine (1917)
Le Crime de M. Lange (*The Crime of M. Lange*), Jean Renoir (1935)
Les Enfants du paradis (*Children of Paradise*), Marcel Carné (1943-5)
Fantômas, Louis Feuillade (1913-14)
Le Joli mai, Chris Marker (1963)
Le Jour se lève (*Daybreak*), Marcel Carné (1939)
Lumière d'été, Jean Grémillon (1943)
Les Misérables, Raymond Bernard (1933)
Les Misérables, Henri Fescourt (1925-6)
Une Partie de campagne (*A Day in the Country*), Jean Renoir (1936)
Le Quai des brumes, Marcel Carné (1938)
La Règle du jeu (*Rules of the Game*), Jean Renoir (1939)
Toni, Jean Renoir (1934)
La Vie de bohême, Marcel L'Herbier (1943)
Les Visiteurs du soir (*The Devil's Envoys*), Marcel Carné (1942)

9. Gender politics — Cocteau's Belle is not that Bête: Jean Cocteau's *La Belle et la Bête* (1946)

SUSAN HAYWARD

In June 1952 Cocteau wrote in his diary : 'the legend of Psyche is word for *word* that of Beauty and the Beast.'[1] It is also, by his admission,[2] a reinscription of Madame Leprince de Beaumont's eighteenth-century moral fable which is in itself a rewriting of the story of Cupid and Psyche in *The Golden Ass* — the eleventh book of Apuleius' *Metamorphoses* (written in AD 2). Apuleius' text derives from Alexandrian literature and the Grecian myth of Eros and these in turn draw from the even earlier Indian myth of the Vedic Aspara, Urvasi. Already so many texts — and doubtless more traces could be found. However, a cursory glance at the transformations exercised within these particular rewritings of this 'same' myth will throw an interesting light on the most modern — technologically — of these reinscriptions; that is to say, Cocteau's film *La Belle et la Bête*.

Two essential motifs, fidelity to a pledge on the one hand and marriage on the other, link these time-wise disparate texts. The myths of Psyche and Urvasi hinge on the crucial pact to withhold the gaze upon the male body in exchange for nuptial favours. To look at the loved one (as is the case for Psyche) or to be made visible to the loved one (as occurs for Urvasi) will mean to forfeit the object of one's desire. In both instances, it is jealousy — either of relatives (Psyche's two sisters) or friends (Urvasi's companions the Ghandharvas) — which forces the invisible male into visibility and subsequently causes the disappearance of the loved one. In the case of these two myths the pledge coincides with the conferment of sexual favours. With regard to the two more recent versions, the pledge is a promise on Beauty's part to return to the Beast. The pledge is sealed by the conferment upon Beauty of one of the Beast's magical treasures. In each case the object is a direct/clear metaphor for the impending undoing of female virginal sexuality. In Mme Leprince's tale, the Beast gives Beauty a ring; Cocteau's Beast endows her with a key — and it is no ordinary key for it will open up Diana's temple and give Beauty access to all of the Beast's wealth. Failure to honour the pledge will mean death for the Beast. This pact then becomes similarly centred around sex and absence. And once again it is jealousy — this time of Beauty's two sisters — which jeopardizes the union.

In the earlier myths, the male lovers are not beasts but remain unseen. Urvasi forbids her husband to ever show her his naked body, Eros forbids Psyche to gaze upon his face. A first distinction, then, occurs between these two myths as to which gender insists on a suspension of the gaze; in the first instance it is the female who imposes the taboo, in the second the male. However, a remnant of the earlier, clearly matriarchal myth, resides in the

Orphic descriptions of Eros which portray him as 'double-sexed' [3] — that is to say, Eros' ambisexuality embodies the conflation of the eastern and western myths. The order to withhold the gaze disappears in Mme Leprince's fairy tale only to resurface with fierce intensity in the mouth of Cocteau's La Bête. But, then again, Mme Leprince's tale is socio-moral in purpose and its main pretext is to demonstrate the need for the preservation of the patrimony which only a marriage of reason can guarantee. The daughter is the symbolic object through whom the father will pass on his powers to the husband. The patriarch is renewed. Leprince's text addresses the issue of patriarchal possession rather than the issue of sexual difference, hence the absence of the taboo and, similarly, any possible reference to ambisexuality.

Such, however, is not the case for Cocteau. I do not wish to dwell too much on the straightforward Freudian analysis — already competently discussed by Jean Decock (1973), i.e. that the tale narrates the transference of sexual desire by Belle from a fixation with the father to one with her husband. For I also perceive that there is a greater number *still* of sexual contexts in play here and that the gaze, whilst certainly unidirectional, shifts in its understanding of 'otherness'.

The object of the gaze is La Bête, the very one who must not be looked upon. The look being forbidden does not however preclude the ability to narrate the object, to re-represent it. Thus the original object becomes specified in language — a secondary order of signs. La Bête is resignified four times: once by the father and in terms of 'her' strength ('La puissance de cette bête est si grande'); twice by Belle and in terms of 'his'/'her' goodness; and finally by Avenant in terms of 'her'/'his' hold over Belle. Belle's narrations are particularly significant, firstly, because they represent her longest contributions within the script and, secondly, because her ascription of gender to La Bête varies according to that supplied by her interlocutors. In her first narration which is with her father, La Bête is renamed — by the father — 'le monstre' and throughout that dialogue Belle refers to La Bête as 'il'. In her second narration, it is once again the male — this time in the form of Ludovic and Avenant — who imposes the choice of gender and La Bête becomes 'elle'. At one point Belle refers to La Bête as 'il' — significantly when she is relating how 'he' has confided the key to his treasures to her — but she is very quickly made, by Avenant, to resume the use of the female gender. In Avenant's own narration of La Bête, he is persuaded that 'she' has cast a spell over Belle and then goes on to try and persuade Belle that 'he' has forgotten all about her and cannot possibly be suffering as much as he (Avenant) is. In other words: as a 'she', La Bête is a witch; as a 'he', the monster becomes a rival.

Thus La Bête's sexuality is re-represented according to others' desired perceptions, according to the particular mirror they wish to hold up. And in this respect it is largely a homo-erotic 'text' (La Bête as text because here she/he is the object of narration and not of the gaze) that is being constructed. In the presence of Belle's earthly aspirant — Avenant — she is required throughout her descriptions of her daily dealings with La Bête to refer to her as female; in the presence of her father the opposite occurs. Two genders are being constructed. Why? And in what way can we talk of a predominantly homo-erotic 'text'? To elucidate this particular point, it is appropriate now to introduce the significance of the mirror within the film.

The father, Belle and subsequently La Bête all appear in the magic mirror. This mirror is Belle's and is the agent of her reflection: 'I am your mirror, Beauty. Reflect for me. I will reflect for you.' In Cocteau's mythology, the mirror is the metaphor *par excellence* for the unconscious (Decock, 1973, 10). In Lacanian theory, the mirror stage is the perception of 'otherness' and also of similitude. The first reflection which Belle gazes upon is that of the father. In Lacanian theory, this first reflection — that of the father — is the moment when the girl child recognizes her 'otherness'; simultaneously, it is the moment when the father's phallus is proclaimed taboo: presence is made absence. 'Otherness' and absence (that which cannot be made present and thereby possessed) conflate at this moment of recognition of *différence*. It is at this juncture that the child recognizes her similitude with the mother. Now, the second reflection for Belle in her mirror is significant in that it comes in three stages; the first is a framing of her as she lies down to gaze into it, the second is an image of La Bête, the third — coming a few shots later — is an image of the mirror shattering itself. This is the crucial moment of awakening from the infantile homo-erotic love of the 'mother' to that of adult masculine sexuality. Hence Belle's despair when she cannot find the key (the symbol of the potential sexual awakening) given to her by La Bête. Her last cries — also desperate — for 'Ma Bête!' signify an ultimate recognition of the locus of that earlier love (for the 'mother') and too of the impossibility of retaining that love. It is at this point that the film moves, awakens from its homo-eroticism and appears to place a conventional ending on this unconventionally told fairy story.

Cocteau did not like the ending of his film. However, he chose not to close it with the death of La Bête, a possibility he had considered.[4] There are nonetheless two ambiguities to the ending which should have given him heart and I shall return to them in a little while. For now, there is more to be said about the double-genderizing and the homo-erotic text.

As I mentioned above, when in the presence of her father or suitor (Avenant), Belle's gender ascription to La Bête is controlled by their male discourses. To the father, the masculine 'monstre' is threatening and dreadful, to Avenant a rival who must be overcome. The feminine La Bête, according to the father, has such powers that she cannot be overcome. As for Avenant, he will — he declares on several occasions — overcome her and kill her. In both gender instances what is being focused upon — though not spoken — is the sexuality of the Beast. The word makes the referent absent, the subject becomes object. La Bête is fetishized, through retelling the story, as fierce and indomitable on the one hand and as an object of revilement to be removed on the other. But what remains is the unspoken, unvisual presence. Sex is never mentioned but is always present because never present, never spoken. Thus, central to their requests that Belle describe La Bête is their fascination with his/her sexuality. Central to their reactions is the threat that that sexuality poses. 'Beauty, I've seen him. He has a dreadful face', says the father; 'You love her?', shouts Avenant.[5]

The homo-erotic nature of the representation of La Bête is not however the exclusive domain of Belle and her male entourage at her father's house. La Bête also constructs her/himself. And, in the first instance, her ambisexuality is symbolically represented through her clothing. Whilst doublet, shirt and breeches may well concur with male Flemish fashion of the sixteenth century, the collar most assuredly does not. Noble-men of that time wore a ruff and not the very high, rigid lace collar which surrounds La Bête's fiercesome face. In paintings of that period, it was noble-women who wore such adorned collars. Equally, the lace around the boots is a finishing touch not without its sexually ambiguous irony.

In the second instance, at one point in the film La Bête sets up a mirror image of her/his self for Belle and, by inference, her/himself to look upon. This gaze at one remove for Belle prevents the fatal gaze into the eyes which makes La Bête burn (with desire one assumes). But this image construction (because she/he can also gaze upon the self) is at the same time homo-erotic. In this series of shots, the meaning construction reveals a self-regarding narcissism and simultaneous erotico-voyeurism. La Bête arrives late to meet Belle for their usual evening tête-à-tête. The first shot of him is a reflection caught in the mirror suspended above a burning log fire. This shot is inserted between two of Belle looking up to — but not framed with — the mirror. The symbolism of auto-eroticism is clear enough (Narcissus fired by his own reflection); and with La Bête thus absorbed (the self being reflected), Belle can safely be voyeur to the image. This process recalls a description provided by Cocteau in his imputed *Le Livre blanc* — a treatise on homosexual love/eroticism written in 1929 — where a young man presses his fully naked body against (unknown to him) a two-way mirror; Cocteau goes on: 'Invisible as a Greek god, I pressed my lips against his and imitated his gestures. He never knew that the mirror, instead of reflecting, was participating, that it was alive and loved him' (1969, 53). As with Cocteau's narrative, the mirror in the film becomes the metaphor for desire. The question is whose desire and desire of whom? And it is the homo-erotic nature of these different representations of La Bête which causes all this disquieting ambiguity. Which gender and which sexuality is being held up to the consciousness? It is as if the linguistic conditions which govern recognition and identity have been removed. And misrecognition occurs through the shifting of the representations of La Bête's 'otherness'.

It is my contention, however, that misrecognition only appears to occur because the assumption underlying this fairy tale is that heterosexual marriage will be the eventual outcome: Belle will relinquish her fascination with the father and the mother and marry the husband intended for her. It is also my contention that Belle is a much more forceful and important character than

La Belle et la Bête — above: La Bête (Jean Marais); below: La Bête and Belle (Josette Day).

earlier analyses might have perceived and that her role is not necessarily to adjust to adult masculine sexuality but rather to act as the one who investigates by scrutiny the 'otherness' of La Bête. In other words, the film is less about Belle's coming to terms with her 'otherness', less about structures which construct woman as 'other' in a patriarchal society, but more, far more, about a female construction of masculinity.

Cocteau's Belle is not the passive young woman encountered in Mme Leprince's tale — at least not when in La Bête's castle. There, she actively adopts the role of voyeur, spying on La Bête. She scrutinizes La Bête's bodily movements and functions, searching for the self-evident symbol for sexual difference: the phallus (Belle is bound to do this since La Bête keeps proposing marriage). Thus Belle examines La Bête in an endeavour to see if her earlier experience of difference (with the father and Avenant) is the same here. In other words, Belle's scrutiny raises the following questions about gender-identity and its organization. Is the Beast La Bête-as-phallus? And if *she* is, is La Bête-as-phallus symbolically organizing the subjective (sexual difference)? Or, is all organized according to phallic discourses? Is Belle merely alterity? And does the whole ideological representation of difference, which is guaranteed by 'the way things are', prevail? [6]

A comparison between the representation of gender roles in both 'worlds' provides an answer. In the world of her father, Belle is the servant perpetually preoccupied with the cleanliness of the house and the bed linen (and most specifically the sheets!). She is the object which can be grabbed at any moment by her suitor Avenant (he does it three times) and ordered (not asked) to marry him; she is also, incidentally, the object Avenant wishes to awaken from 'this nightmare' as he calls her inability to abandon either La Bête or her father. In the world of La Bête she is master, La Bête kneels before her and takes Belle's orders. It is Belle who orders La Bête to clean herself up, Belle who takes possession of La Bête when she cries out 'Ma Bête!' And it is Belle alone who can awaken La Bête from her state. Conversely, La Bête can only come each evening and put the same question to Belle: 'Belle, will you be my wife?' And finally, when Belle asks to return to her father for a week, La Bête confers upon her all the powers she possesses — in other words, the father does not pass on possession to the younger man, quite the opposite in fact.

Whilst in the form of La Bête, then, La Bête is not constructed as male in the sense that she does not represent the phallus as mark of the symbolic construction of subjectivity — quite unlike the patriarchal norm represented by Avenant and the father in relation to Belle. In this respect the film *La Belle et la Bête* demonstrates that the phallic norm is not necessarily natural. Both male and female homo-erotic representations are equally part of the symbolic construction of subjectivity. And in this case subjectivity comes to mean, simultaneously, recognition and love of sexual sameness.

And this brings us back to the conclusion Cocteau provided for the film. Before taking a closer look, let us quote from Cocteau — it is an explanation as to why he did not change the ending — 'My goal was to make the Beast so human, so likeable, so superior to man, that her transformation into Prince Charming would be, for Belle, a terrible disappointment and would oblige her in a way to accept a marriage of reason' (1973a, 111). Maybe, but there are two imagistic occurrences whose meaning construction undermines any complete acceptance of the phallic construct — and these are beyond Belle's very clear distress at the disappearance of La Bête. First, there is Avenant's transformation into La Bête — he is shot in the back by Diane, she who is the goddess of hunting, virginity and childbirth. And all who would try to rape Diane were turned into stags. The brutality of Avenant reaps its deadly reward at the hand of femaleness personified. This is not a phallic construct since Diane turns against the potential rapist the very weapon, the arrow, which had been identified with him from the beginning of the film (remember also that Avenant had tried to entrap Belle with his arrow). Thus the phallic object is turned against the phallus-as-mark of the symbolic construction of subjectivity.

But there is a second meaning construction to these sets of images. For whilst Avenant dies, La Bête is transformed into a Prince Charming. In the Leprince version and in the words of the Prince, La Bête had to be looked upon with the look of love in order to be changed into a man. In Cocteau's version, the look of love does not seem to have been enough since the death of another man — Avenant — is necessary to complete the transformation. The ambiguity surrounding the transformation does in some respects put into question the notion of desire, of the look of love being able to release that which is beautiful in the object of one's gaze. It could be argued that only upon Avenant's death could La Bête be released and accept the gaze which before burned her so. Viewed in such a light, this emergence of the Prince could be seen as a faintly grotesque exercise in necrophiliac substitution; however, this emergence could also be read in a manner more consistent with the homo-erotic interpretation argued for earlier — i.e. as a release into beauty and love of one man by another man. This homo-erotic reading gains credence when one considers that one man — Jean Marais — plays all three roles. Thus, at the point of transformation all three personages meld into one. The moment is not one of pure narcissism because reflection can no longer occur. It is, however, the moment of participation in desire of which Cocteau speaks in *Le Livre blanc*.

The second imagistic occurrence is less replete with intellectualism but is certainly there as a Cocteau joke. The very closing shot of the Prince and Beauty wafting up into the sky cannot but recall Poussin's *Le Ravissement de Saint Paul* (1644?). The analogy is deliberate and so too is the ambiguity of the intertexts. In the painting it is the angels who spirit Saint Paul away. However, 'ravissement' means more than to spirit away, it means to transport, to ravish. Therefore, what are the angels doing to Saint Paul? And in the film the question becomes who is ravishing whom? Only Belle knows that answer. In all this uncertainty, 'La Belle n'est pas si Bête'.

Cocteau's film was not liked by critics when it first appeared in 1946.[7] They accused it of being cold (including Bazin), painterly and — worst of all — picturesque. The Picturesque was a genre loathed by Cocteau and which he hated to see applied to his own work. Some reasons have been supplied for this critical distaste for *La Belle et la Bête*. At the time of its appearance, critics were much enamoured with the socio-realism *à l'italienne*. The Neo-Realist school was applauded as the cinema of relevance. It is hard though not to read a hidden agenda behind these plaudits because it became clear that critics of the 1940s saw in this new cinema which they valued so highly many of the hallmarks of France's former quality cinema of the 1930s. Poetic Realism had reached its end with *Les Enfants du paradis* and fairy tales were not going to shape the new cinematographic ontology. Numerous critics further accused Cocteau's film of being expressionistic and even of verging on academicism. However, it is when they come to accuse the film of possessing Germanic aesthetics,[8] and criticize certain images for displaying the affected simperings of an old queen[9] that one can begin to perceive what perturbs them so much about this film. It is indeed a film made by a man who never denied his homosexuality. Not all homosexuals who make films make gay films, of course, though certainly their homosexuality affects how they will make their films. The aim of my analysis has been to show that Cocteau's *La Belle et la Bête* is about homo-erotic love; it is also about attempting to discover a different, non-phallic, perception of human relationships, and, furthermore, to ground the process of signification in a language where the phallus is not the mark of the symbolic construction of subjectivity. And in this respect, it is interesting to note that one contemporary critic accused Belle and La Bête of having unsexed voices which sounded alike and the film of being one where there was little talk.[10] Silence, unlike eloquence, is not the rhetoric of the irreversible — rather, it is the very sound of subversion.

NOTES

1. Cocteau (1983), 175, Cocteau's stress.
2. Cocteau (1973a), 106.
3. Graves (1982), 1, 30.
4. Sensing that the public preferred La Bête to the Prince (as indeed does Belle), Cocteau wished that he had ended the film with La Bête's death and left Belle in mourning for La Bête (Cocteau [1973b], 52).
5. Naturally, the English translation of the subtitles and the English script (Hammond 1970) do not convey this distinction in the use of personal pronouns — which is a pity.
6. In this part of my analysis, I am indebted to Dugald Williamson's very elucidating article on Lacanian theory, 'Language and sexual difference' in *Screen*, 1987, 28 (1), 10-25.
7. In the Balland edition (Cocteau 1975) of the script of *La Belle et la Bête*, there is a dossier of press cuttings taken from newspapers which reviewed the film upon its release. Reaction on the whole was fairly negative, spiteful even in some cases, especially when attacking Cocteau's person rather than reviewing the film — see Jacques Potier's comments (210), Jean Fayard's (211) and Michel de Saint-Pierre's (220).
8. In the Balland edition (Cocteau 1975), Armand de Johannès speaks of the film's expressionism (222), Michel de Saint-Pierre of its disconcerting Germanic flavour (220).

9. Again, Michel de Saint-Pierre's comments are the most vicious in their contempt (speaking of La Bête's movements, he says: 'these mincings of an old queen, similar to those I have witnessed by Mr. Jean Cocteau when he recites his poems in public', Cocteau 1975, 220), but Jacques Potier is incapable of hiding his distaste for Cocteau's sexuality ('the unsavoury character which emanates from his person', 210).

10. This time it is the very right-wing Jean Fayard who unwittingly puts his finger on what is so subversive about this film (in Cocteau 1975, 212).

SELECTED BIBLIOGRAPHY

Beylie, Claude (1966) 'Cocteau', in *Anthologie du cinéma*, 12, 57-112.
Cahiers du cinéma, 1959, 100, special issue on Cocteau.
Cocteau, Jean (1946) *La Belle et la Bête: Journal d'un film*, Paris, Janin (re-edited by Editions du Rocher, 1958). This edition may be difficult to find; however, Cocteau (1970) in Hammond's version includes substantial excerpts from this diary.
Cocteau, Jean (1951) *Entretiens autour du cinématographe*, recueillis par André Fraigneau, Paris, Editions André Bonne.
Cocteau, Jean (1969) *Le Livre blanc* (translated by Margaret Crosland), London, Peter Owen.
Cocteau, Jean (1973a) *Du cinématographe,* Paris, Pierre Belfond.
Cocteau, Jean (1973b) *Avant-Scène Cinéma*, 138/139, 51-53.
Cocteau, Jean (1983) *Past Tense*, London, Hamish Hamilton.
Crosland, Margaret (1955) *Jean Cocteau*, London, Peter Nevill Ltd.
Decock, Jean (1973) 'Surréalisme et symbolisme', *Avant-Scène Cinéma*, 138/139, 8-11.
Graves, Robert (1982) *The Greek Myths*, Harmondsworth, Penguin.
Image et son (1972) 262, special issue on Cocteau: interviews, reviews, quotations from his own writings on film.
Prédal, René (1983) 'Jean Cocteau et son temps', *Cinéma 83,* supplement to 293, 4-53.

SCRIPTS

There are two very useful scripts of *La Belle et la Bête*. The first is a bilingual version edited by Robert M. Hammond (1970). The second, which is the publisher Balland's (Cocteau 1975) version already referred to, is a photo-script and includes the press response at the time of its release. This version is a collaborative work under the direction of Gérard Vaugeois. The references are as follows:

Cocteau, Jean (1970) *La Belle et la Bête*, in R. M. Hammond (ed.), New York, New York University Press.
Cocteau, Jean (1973) *La Belle et la Bête*, in *Avant-Scène Cinéma*, 138/139.
Cocteau, Jean (1975) *La Belle et la Bête*, in G. Vaugeois (ed.), Nantes, Balland.

APPENDIX

Jean Cocteau (1889—1963): filmography (as director)

1930 *Le Sang d'un poète (The Blood of the Poet)*
1946 *La Belle et La Bête (Beauty and the Beast)*
1948 *L'Aigle à deux têtes (Eagle with Two Heads)*
1948 *Les Parents terribles (The Storm Within)*
1949 *Orphée (Orpheus)*
1950 *Corolian* (short)
1951 *La Villa Santo-Sospir*
1959 *Le Testament d'Orphée (The Testament of Orpheus)*

Other films cited in text

Les Enfants du paradis (*Children of Paradise*), Marcel Carné (1943-5)

10. The sacrament of writing: Robert Bresson's *Le Journal d'un curé de campagne* (1951)

KEITH A. READER

> '... these categories of salvation
> or loss or grace derive their
> strength only from this sense of
> the real, and not vice versa.'
> (Arnaud 1986, 20)

Scarcely any other 'adaptation' of a major literary work for the cinema has had the impact of Robert Bresson's filming of Georges Bernanos's *Le Journal d'un curé de campagne*. The inverted commas are there to emphasize how little Bresson's film owes to canonical concepts of filmic adaptation, which it did much to challenge but which are still overwhelmingly dominant in the world of television and largely so in that of the cinema. (An interesting recent example is the international impact of Volker Schlöndorff's *Un Amour de Swann* compared with the smaller-scale television and art-house success of Percy Adlon's *Céleste*, another 'Proust film' which in its use of silences and image/sound dialectic has much in common with the work of Bresson.) The paring-away of many elements of Bernanos's text, the scrupulous — religious — fidelity to what remains, the austerity of the filming and the avoidance of star actors, even of actors *tout court* — these have been commented upon by virtually every writer on the film, and in the French cinematic world of 1951 their contrast with what had gone before was particularly striking.

For *Le Journal d'un curé de campagne*, in the history of its making as well as in its textuality, marked a radical break with the 'film de qualité' characteristic of much post-Occupation cinema, and of its literary adaptations in particular. Jean Aurenche and Paul Bost were the screenwriting team that established virtual rights of ownership over this area, notably through their scripts for Jean Delannoy's *La Symphonie pastorale* and Claude Autant-Lara's *Le Diable au corps*. The Aurenche and Bost 'recipe' involved the use of well-known actresses and actors (Michèle Morgan, Gérard Philippe), carefully constructed period atmosphere, and often also the introduction of one or two elements extraneous or marginal to the literary text, as if to append their authorial signature in between that of Gide or Radiguet and that of the director. (One example is the much greater stress given to the Armistice Day celebrations in the film of *Le Diable au corps*.)

Bresson's film is so clearly the antithesis of all this that it comes as a surprise to learn that the first adaptation of *Le Journal d'un curé de campagne* for the screen was by Jean Aurenche, in 1947. This was rejected by Bernanos himself, for reasons eloquently summarized by Michel Estève:

> ... the disappearance of characters essential to transcribing Bernanos's vision of the world (Torcy, Delbende, Olivier), the replacement of inner revolt by spectacular blasphemy (Chantal's spitting out of the host), and of 'everything is grace' by 'everything is death', were obvious betrayals of the spirit of Bernanos's novel. (Estève 1983, 26)

An attempt by the Dominican Father Bruckberger, which apparently translated the action into the Resistance period, was likewise rejected. Bresson's adaptation in its turn was rejected by the initial producer, and it was not until 1950, with finance from the Union Générale Cinématographique, that he was able to begin filming. The result led André Bazin, in his fundamental essay '*Le Journal d'un curé de campagne* and the stylistics of Robert Bresson', to say: 'After Bresson, Aurenche and Bost are but the Viollet-le-Duc of cinematographic adaptation'(Bazin 1967, I, 143).

Viollet-le-Duc was best known for his architectural restorations of medieval monuments (such as the walled city of Carcassonne) in an idiom often a long way removed from the original, and characterized by anachronistic or superfluous flourishes. Bazin's remark is thus a direct thrust at the Aurenche-Bost conception of stylistic authenticity, which *Journal* (as it will hereinafter be referred to for brevity) did more to eradicate than any other film, except maybe Jean-Pierre Melville's *Le Silence de la mer*. Jean Lacroix, writing in *Le Monde* of 15 May 1954, distils well the specific quality of Bresson's fidelity to the text, a fidelity which is grounded in ascesis:

> The astonishing success of Bresson's film [...] is that it corresponds perfectly to Bernanos's text, not by being slavishly literal, but through a recreation that rigorously eliminates the psychological and the social alike, to centre everything on the spiritual drama. (in Estève 1983, 30)

Bernanos's novel abounds in sensory and social detail, excized or minimized in Bresson's film. Bresson shot, but eliminated in the editing, a number of scenes showing the priest in relationships with his parishioners (for instance, saying Mass), and the novel's descriptions of the village of Ambricourt, along with the touches of Flemish regional colour that are an important part of the character of the Curé de Torcy, all but disappear from the film.

This is not to say, however, that the film's ascesis makes of it a rarefied or dematerialized work. On the contrary; the sound of the gardener's rake gathering up the leaves, of the priest's pen as it moves across the page, of the bottle of wine as it falls to the ground has an impact as great as that of any visual image, and we are put in mind of Bresson's maxim: 'When a sound can replace an image, cut the image or neutralize it. The ear goes more towards the within, the eye towards the outer' (Bresson 1977, 28).

The sounds are 'realistic'(their place in the diegesis is clear, they do not come laden with pre-digested psychological or symbolic significance), yet that realism is precisely what bestows upon them, or reveals within them, a mystical or supernatural quality. In this respect the film itself can be seen as a *sacrament* — the outward sign of an inward grace, neither perceptible except with and through the other. Here there is an important analogy with post-Saussurean developments of the relationship between signified and signifier, seen (at least since Lacan) no longer as dissociable entities, but as indissolubly welded in their very difference from each other. If sacraments are linguistic, language is also sacramental.

The doubling-up of narrative in the diary scenes, where the text is pronounced by the priest's voice as we see his hand writing it, is the most striking instance of this sacramental view of language, at once Way of the Cross and way of salvation. *Journal* is not, however, a logocentric film, and the opening sentence of St John's Gospel would be a quite inappropriate epigraph to it; for the diary scenes make it impossible to decide which comes first, speech or writing, or indeed whether such a question is even meaningful. The first sentence that we hear and see ('I don't think I am doing wrong in jotting down, day by day, without hiding anything, the very simple trivial secrets of a very ordinary kind of life' [Bernanos 1956, 10]) is, precisely, language reflecting on itself — the voice destroying the myth of its own origin and authorship not only through what it says, but also through the trace of the writing hand across the paper. The sacrament of writing does not, for Bresson as for Derrida, give access to a metaphysics of presence.

This is most graphically illustrated by the film's final image — the (empty) Cross filling the screen as the priest's friend Dufréty recounts his final moments and dying words: 'Tout est grâce.' The last diary scene, immediately before, has shown the priest writing with great difficulty and without a voice-over, as though to figure the imminent disappearance of his body. Just as the social body of Ambricourt and of the Church has disappeared from the film, so the priest's body and that of Christ disappear, or are not present, at the film's climax. This needs to be borne in mind as an important corrective to Dudley Andrew's statement that 'his rigorous instrument of self-knowledge — his writing — has brought him into focus with his image and, therefore, has made him one with Christ' (Andrew 1984, 130). The oneness with Christ, suggested in a host of ways throughout the film (as when Séraphita, Veronica-like, wipes the priest's exhausted face with her kerchief), can achieve its apotheosis only through absence, and in this way the film seems to me closer than the novel to the notion of Godhead as kenosis or emptying-out — as renunciation, that is to say, rather than as plenitude.

Related to this is Bresson's almost legendary antipathy to the use of 'actors' on the one hand and to any taint of psychology on the other. 'The thing that matters is not what they show me but what they hide from me and, above all, what they do not suspect is in them' (Bresson 1977, 2); Bresson's remark shows how alien to his concerns any view of actors 'understanding' their part is. The weeding-out of all non-believers before Claude Laydu was cast as the priest, Laydu's spending time fasting and meditating in Normandy before filming started, Bresson's use of real live coals in the fire from which the priest plucks the Countess's medallion — these are superficially akin to the tricks and techniques of Stanislavsky or the Actors' Studio, but Bresson's 'method' is quite other. Psychology, for him, intrudes between surface and soul, between matter and spirit, seeking to explain what can only be shown. Here again we find echoes of Lacanian psychoanalysis, in the resolute antipathy to rationalization and the stress on engaging with language as material process. Lacan, in *The Four Fundamental Concepts of Psychoanalysis*, speaks of sacraments as operative (much as for J.-L. Austin in *How to Do Things with Words* they would be examples of performative speech-acts) and as 'struck by a kind of oblivion'(Lacan 1977, 265). The 'oblivion' in question is — for Bresson at least — *inter alia* that of the world of ego-psychology and of understanding, whether rational or intuitive. Lacan's definition of desire in/of analysis as 'a desire to obtain absolute difference' (Lacan 1977, 276) presents analogies with Bresson's attitude towards his models (he refuses the term 'actors'), and the oneness of which Andrew speaks is achieved in the end only through — is perhaps paradoxically the 'same' as? — the absolute difference figured by the absences — of voice-over, of bodies, of Body, almost of image — in which *Journal* culminates.

Jean Sémolué, in his monograph *Bresson*, sees the film as following the overall pattern of the novel in its division into three unequal parts, each organized around three fundamental themes relating to the priest's solitude — sickness (the 'solitude of the body'), sacerdotal or spiritual solitude, and social solitude (his alienation from his parishioners). The film's opening sequences — the first writing of the diary, the priest mopping his brow, the glimpse through the château gates of the Count and his mistress Louise embracing furtively, the priest entering the presbytery — give us these three forms of solitude in a way that immediately suggests a world without wholeness or totality. Ambricourt is nowhere presented as a community, and the priest's speaking of 'my parish, my first parish' is thus a poignant, almost nostalgic utterance — an aspiration towards a transcendental unity that will be achieved only with his death. The priest's end, like the film's, is implicit in its/their beginning.

It very quickly becomes impossible to view the priest's ill-health in purely medical terms. When we not only see, but hear his voice describing the 'meals' of stale bread dipped in wine that are his sole sustenance, the sacramental dimension could hardly be plainer. Paul Schrader, author of a major essay on Bresson but better-known as the scriptwriter of the Scorsese films *Taxi Driver* and *Raging Bull*, both strongly Bresson-influenced, alludes to this when he has taxi-driver Travis Bickle — a tormented 'priest' of a quite different kind — feed himself on bread and apricot brandy. To persist in drinking the cheapest of *gros rouge* when subject to agonizing stomach pains runs counter to any conceivable verisimilitude, and thereby warns us from an early stage not to read the film too referentially or 'realistically'. When a bottle of wine falls from the table and breaks, much later in the film, the dark rivulets across the floor inevitably remind us of blood — the blood the priest will cough up more and more as his agony reaches its end... The important

Le Journal d'un curé de campagne — above: the priest (Claude Laydu); below: the priest and Séraphita (Martine Lemaire).

point is that this is done without pathos, that the wine and the blood signify the priest's sufferings rather than inviting some impossible empathy with them. The sacramental quality of the text is once more plain beyond the comparatively obvious level of its subject-matter.

* * *

The priest's social solitude — needless to say not given any 'psychological' justification — is plainest in his relationship with the Curé of Torcy. The Curé — played by Armand Guibert, a psychoanalyst acquaintance of Bresson's — represents a robust, combative type of priesthood seemingly at odds with the country priest's, but in fact its necessary complement. The Church Suffering requires the Church Militant that it may become the Church Triumphant, just as neither the active nor the contemplative life is conceivable without its counterpart. The Curé of Torcy's understanding of his colleague is thus of a spiritual rather than a psychological kind, and — by stressing the two priests' reciprocal otherness — paradoxically reinforces the very loneliness it might appear to alleviate.

Psychological incomprehension and spiritual understanding (however shadowy) characterize the attitudes of many of the other inhabitants of Ambricourt towards the priest. Séraphita Dumouchel, his brightest catechism pupil, says that she listens to him only because 'he has very beautiful eyes', yet she will be there when he faints at the climax of his agony in Ambricourt. Chantal, the daughter of the Count and Countess, pours forth her hatred — of her father and his mistress, but also of herself and (thus) of God — in tones that cruelly mock any exhortations to love, yet when the priest divines her deeper intentions and asks her to hand over the suicide note he realizes she is carrying, she does so with a whispered: 'Are you then the Devil?' This may put us in mind of Bernanos's *Sous le soleil de Satan* (recently filmed by Maurice Pialat with Gérard Depardieu), in which Satan is invoked to raise a child from the dead. Good and evil, and often in both Bernanos and Bresson, exist as complements rather than opposites — as so to speak allotropic variants of one spiritual state — in a way distinctly Catholic rather than just 'Christian' (Chabrol, Graham Greene, Hitchcock, Mauriac, Scorsese all display a similar tendency in their work). If the major 'epistemological break' between Catholicism and Protestantism was that between justification by works and justification by faith, it needs to be added that the works by which, in a Catholic perspective, we are justified may 'belong' to us only in a seemingly arbitrary, even random, manner. This evokes the disturbing rhetoric of grace constantly present in Bresson, and distilled in the memorable *pensée* of one of his major pre-texts, Pascal: 'Be comforted; it is not from yourself that you must expect it, but on the contrary you must expect it by expecting nothing from yourself'(Pascal 1966, 95).

It also presents striking parallels with the Freudian psyche, most significant precisely where it escapes the subject's control — for Lacan, 'là où ça parle', where 'it' but also the id (*ça* in French) speaks, in the text of the unconscious.

That unconscious, structured like a language, thereby returns us again to the materiality of the linguistic — thus also sacramental — sign. This is most strikingly apparent in the film's — literal and spiritual — centre, the long dialogue between the priest and the Countess. It is here that the dialectic between psychological and spiritual affinity is given its fullest development, reinforced in its insistent materiality by the sound of the gardener's rake gathering up the leaves — an echo of the priest's pen moving across the diary pages, a suggestion that what is going on inside the château, on the screen, is some kind of raking bare or gathering up of souls, the rhythmic *archiécriture* of grace? ... Bazin describes the dialogue as 'the opposite side of the coin, if one dare to say so, of the Divine Countenance' (Bazin 1967, I, 137). This formulation will obviously pose problems for non-believers, or at any rate for those to whom the soul is a concept at best nebulous, at worst obscurantist. One way of dealing with this is to view the soul not as some primary essence, whose very antecedence makes it necessarily unsayable, but rather as that which remains as a signifying absence after 'everything else' — the bodily, the psychological, the gestural — has been stripped away. (There are parallels here with Lacan's notion of the necessary-but-unsayable 'real'.) If, that is to say, the soul is viewed differentially rather than as the apogee of a metaphysics of presence, the dialogue can be seen as leading into the final conversation with Chantal, immediately before the priest leaves for Lille, in which he counters her defiant threats of evil-doing with the phrase: 'I answer for you, soul for soul.' This transposes the Pascalian wager on the existence of God on to the plane of difference and exchange; what is important is not the plenitude of the two souls but their interchangeability, in accord with the Catholic notion of transferability of grace and redemption. The ascetic quality of the film is thus spiritually as well as aesthetically significant, reaching even to that ineffable innermost essence that is for orthodox Christianity the soul.

It is immediately before this dialogue that the film introduces a diegetic ambiguity absent from the novel, and one whose theological implications seem to me so fundamental that I am surprised that no writer on the film known to me has commented on them. The priest, on his rounds to far-flung parishioners, walks, or stumbles, with great difficulty, eventually to faint and be discovered by Séraphita Dumouchel. The Bernanos text describes what is clearly, depending on one's faith or lack of it, a mystical vision or the hallucination of one very close to death: 'I feared, in opening them [my eyes] to look upon the face before which all must kneel. Yet I saw it. And it was the face of a child, too — or a very young girl — only without the spark of youth' (Bernanos 1956, 184).

This is followed, after he has picked himself up and walked a little further, by his second fainting and the intervention of Séraphita. What Bresson does — and of all the myriad ways in which he stresses the insistence of the spiritual in the material this is perhaps the most remarkable — is to conflate the two losses of consciousness. The screen goes dark (though emphatically not empty) as the voice-over recounts the priest's vision, and this runs into a close-up of Séraphita wiping his face. In the novel, the vision of the face of God precedes the encounter with Séraphita; in the film, it seems to me that we are invited to identify the two, that the 'face before which all must kneel' is quite literally Séraphita's. The divine permeates and is permeated by the human, rather than being transcendentally set against it. Paul Schrader speaks of a hypothetical 'irate viewer' antagonized by the film's refusal to allow her or him place for intellectual or emotional judgement. For Schrader, 'he [sic] has mistaken the everyday for transcendental style and has only seen a fraction of the film' (Schrader 1972, 70). I would qualify this, at least for certain key points in the film, by saying that there is a sense in which the transcendental re-immanentizes itself — most notably in the diary-writing, but most audaciously perhaps in the episode to which I have just referred.

The process of ascesis and stripping away that is the aesthetic and spiritual dynamic of the film reaches its climax, as I have suggested, at the end, beginning when the voice-over disappears from the final diary-writing sequence. This does more than suggest the priest's terminal exhaustion; it also focuses our desire as spectators upon the trace of the written characters. Jacques Derrida's contention in *Of Grammatology*, that the traditional primacy of speech over writing rests upon a delusive metaphysics of presence has by now acceded to the rank of a post-structuralist commonplace. Here, in a film whose concluding words, and their theological context, would seem to point towards just such a metaphysics, the disappearance of speech at such a key moment acts to undercut such a presupposition. Presence is always-already impregnated with absence, in the filmic text far more than in the novel, as though Bresson's weaving of doublings-up, ellipses, and silences added even as it appears to take away.

We are reminded too of Lacan's stress on the importance of the scopic drive — the desire to look. It may appear difficult to transpose this into the world of Bresson's film, apparently as desexualized as any text-to-be-looked-at ever can be; but if we at the same time return to the notion of writing as sacrament, and think of the successive holding-up of the host and the chalice in the Catholic Mass as they are consecrated, the difficulty will become less. Writers as different as Georges Bataille (in *Histoire de l'œil*) and Annie Leclerc (in *Hommes et femmes*) have spoken of the erotic charge carried by the sacrament of Communion; we may think too of the work of Buñuel, the 'Beggars' banquet' parody of the Last Supper in *Viridiana* and the mysterious First Communion photograph of Séverine in *Belle de jour*. The holding aloft — *erect* — of the chalice, so evident a vaginal symbol, by a celibate male to a congregation that will not partake of its contents (Catholics receiving only the Host at Communion) is a striking example of the Roman Church's *nonpareil* choreography of desire and denial. E. M. Forster, being a humanist, could ground an ethics that was also an aesthetics in the phrase 'Only connect'; Bernanos, and after him Bresson, knew that for Catholic mysticism and the post-Freudian psyche 'Only cathect' would be nearer the mark.

The Cross that fills the screen at the end takes the dialectic of presence to its furthest conceivable point. The absence of the body (of the priest from the screen, of Christ from the crucifix as from the tomb on the third day) is a conventional theological signifier of an eternal, because no longer material, presence. Yet that presence is dissipated and disseminated by the words that accompany the visual image: 'Tout est grâce.' Claude Laydu did not realize until he had watched the final version of the film that he had been playing a saint. Sanctity and grace, Laydu's experience and the final shot alike suggest, are process not telos, their presence diffused and deferred throughout the film and its ultimate recognition (as process), as Harold Bloom would say (Bloom 1975 and 1982), belated. That which hostile critics of the film singled out as its most profoundly uncinematic aspect turns out to be a supreme meditation, not merely on film as textuality, but on the whole dialectic of presence and absence in which theodicy is grounded. It is virtually a commonplace nowadays that filmmakers such as Eisenstein or Godard were able to write political essays in film; Bresson, with *Journal d'un curé de campagne*, produced not merely a qualitatively new type of literary adaptation, but probably the first theological essay to be written in the film medium.

N.B. Where readily available published translations of the original French texts exist, I have used these. All other translations from the French are my own.

SELECTED BIBLIOGRAPHY

This is necessarily brief and selective, concentrating on major or widely available texts, mostly in book form.

Andrew, Dudley (1984) *Film in the Aura of Art*, Princeton, New Jersey, Princeton University Press.
Arnaud, Philippe (1986) *Robert Bresson*, Paris, Cahiers du cinéma, Paris, Editions de l'Etoile.
Bazin, André (1967) *What is Cinema?*, trans. Hugh Gray, Berkeley, Los Angeles, London, University of California Press.
Bernanos, Georges (1956) *Journal d'un curé de campagne*, trans. Pamela Norris, and London, Collins/Fontana.
Bloom, Harold (1975) *A Map of Misreading*, New York, Oxford University Press.
Bloom, Harold (1982) *Agon: Towards a Theory of Revisionism*, New York, Oxford University Press.
Bresson, Robert (1977) *Notes on Cinematography*, trans. Jonathan Griffin, New York, Urizen Books, London, Pluto Press. Reprinted, London, Quartet Books, 1986.
Durgnat, Raymond (1969), 'Le Journal d'un curé de campagne', in Cameron (ed.) (1969) *The Films of Robert Bresson*, London, Studio Vista, 42-50.
Estève, Michel (1983) *Robert Bresson — la passion du cinématographe*, Paris, Editions Albatros.
Lacan, Jacques (1977) *The Four Fundamental Concepts of Psychoanalysis*, trans. Alan Sheridan, London, Hogarth Press.
Pascal, Blaise (1966) *Pensées*, trans. A.J. Krailsheimer, London, Penguin Books.
Reader, Keith (1986) ' "D'où cela vient-il?" ': notes on three fims by Robert Bresson', *French Studies*, XI, 4, 427-442.
Schrader, Paul (1972) *Transcendental Style in Film: Ozu, Bresson, Dreyer*, Berkeley, Los Angeles, and London, University of California Press.
Sémolué, Jean (1959) *Bresson*, Paris, Editions Universitaires.

Sloan, Jane (1983) *Robert Bresson, a Guide to References and Resources*, Boston, Mass., G.K. Hall.
Sontag, Susan (1966) *Against Interpretation*, New York, Farrar, Straus and Giroux.

APPENDIX

Robert Bresson (1907—): filmography

1934 *Les Affaires publiques* (short), co-director, Pierre Charbonnier
1943 *Les Anges du péché (Angels of the Street)*
1945 *Les Dames du Bois de Boulogne (Ladies of the Park)*
1951 *Le Journal d'un curé de campagne (Diary of a Country Priest)*
1956 *Un Condamné à mort s'est échappé (A Man Escaped)*
1959 *Pickpocket*
1962 *Le Procès de Jeanne D'Arc (The Trial of Joan of Arc)*
1966 *Au hazard Balthazar (Balthazar)*
1967 *Mouchette*
1969 *Une Femme douce (A Gentle Creature)*
1971 *Quatre nuits d'un rêveur (Four Nights of a Dreamer)*
1974 *Lancelot du lac (Lancelot of the Lake)*
1977 *Le Diable probablement*
1983 *L'Argent*

Other films cited in the text

Un Amour de Swann (Swann in Love), Volker Schlöndorff (1982)
Belle de jour, Luis Buñuel (1967)
Céleste, Percy Aldon (1983)
Le Diable au corps (Devil in the Flesh), Claude Autant-Lara (1947)
Raging Bull, Martin Scorsese (1979)
Le Silence de la mer, Jean-Pierre Melville (1949)
Sous le soleil de Satan (Under Satan's Sun), Maurice Pialat (1987)
La Symphonie pastorale, Jean Delannoy (1946)
Taxi Driver, Martin Scorsese (1976)
Viridiana, Luis Buñuel (1961)

11. A breath of sea air: Jacques Tati's
Les Vacances de M. Hulot (1952)

PIERRE SORLIN

Les Vacances de M. Hulot turned out to be a success the very first week of its release. Not a *big* hit: the 300,000 seats sold in Paris put it in seventh position in the 1953 box-office. Hollywood had lost its predominance, and the winners of the year were French-Italian coproductions — *Le Retour de Don Camillo* and *Le Salaire de la peur*, two expensive, cleverly made, well photographed pictures. An American movie as lavish as the former, *The Greatest Show on Earth* came third. As for the other three films the difference with *Hulot* was small: Tati could easily have been in fourth place. At least, his was the first French film on the 1953 list (Centre Nationale de la Cinématographie, 1954).

The picture was poorly advertised. The cast was not impressive: outside the director (and screenwriter) Jacques Tati, who plays the part of Hulot, it was made up of little-known stage-actors, most of whom would never make a brilliant career. Among the technicians, only the chief-editor was highly experienced,[1] and the producer had only made two other movies. Notwithstanding these shortcomings, the film was praised by all critics and movie-buffs and met with a good response. The unexpected had happened four years before when *Jour de fête*, a hastily completed movie with almost no dialogue and an ill-defined plot, made a great deal of money and was awarded significant national and international prizes.[2] *Jour de fête* was something totally new in French cinema. *Hulot*, which made another step in the same direction, is more famous. This may be due to the fact that *Jour de fête* is a picture of the post-war Reconstruction era and manifests typical features of the period. Postman François, the main character, is greatly excited by the projection of an American picture, one of those naïve propaganda works which introduced Europe to the 'superiority' of American management. François tries to adapt American methods to his deliveries. The setting of the film is a village at a time when many French movies emphasized the importance of the rural tradition and of the revival of the countryside in post-war France. *Hulot* is (seemingly) exempt from these connections with the spirit of the times. It is a blast of fresh air, a pleasurable moment outside the ponderous conventions of current production, a floating story with shaky characters and a humour distinct from the wordy theatrical comedies or the clumsy slapsticks which were usually offered on French screens.

Hulot is still a highly enjoyable piece of cinema, but film studies cannot be content with simply expressing appreciative statements. There is always something in films which escapes easy evaluation, but we must continue to analyse pictures in so far as they are structured combinations of perceptible data.

Narrative categories become ineffective where *Hulot* is concerned: there is no coherent, logically organized plot. We are in a French seaside resort on the Channel. Tourists arrive at the beginning of the summer vacation at the outset of the picture. They leave at the end. There are scenes on the beach, in a hotel and a boarding-house, on a tennis-court and in a small harbour. Is it then a documentary? Not in the least, since we lack certain necessary information: the precise location of the resort, a description of the surroundings, etc. The movie-camera seems to have been placed at random in more or less convenient corners. Consider the first shots on the beach. People merely pass by. Then there are several short scenes: a man who has just lain down is called and has to scramble up quickly. A woman is cross because she has not brought the right things. A boy burns the strings of a tent with a sun-lens. Another unfastens a boat which is swept away by the waves. Funny though they are, these snapshots are hardly likely to make viewers cry with laughter. Spectators enter a different, bizarre atmosphere; jokes raise only distant smiles and actions are not tied together, not even by Hulot, who is personally unaware of what is happening around him.

This very lack of coordination gives the picture part of its charm: we are sometimes left in ignorance of where the scene is taking place, we are in no hurry and do not anticipate the unexpected or the sensational. But the ostensible looseness is a trick: the film is in fact carefully, deliberately constructed. There are no sequences, in the common meaning of the word, but rather 'moments', identified less by incidents (of which there are few) than by the time of the day, the location, or meeting with people. The film may be summarized as follows:

1) A railway station; moving trains on a summer day;
2) Cars driving towards the sea;
3) Martine's arrival at her boarding-house;[3]
4) Hulot's arrival at his hotel;
5) Evening meal at the hotel;
6) The beach; Hulot takes a walk among the bathers;
7) Lunch at the hotel;
8) Arrival of Martine's aunt;
9) Evening at the hotel;
10) The beach; Hulot hits a bather (Smith) and hides in a dinghy;
11) Hulot dripping wet re-enters the hotel at lunch time;
12) Hulot in a cemetery;
13) Hulot plays tennis;
14) Evening at the hotel;
15) Hulot's abortive attempt to ride a horse;
16) Fancy-dress ball;
17) Jaunt in the countryside;
18) During the night Hulot accidentally sets fire to the fireworks;
19) End of the holiday.

This summary allows us to see how well-crafted the film is. 'Moments' 1 to 4 introduce the situation (holiday) and the characters — or at least the people who will recurrently be seen on the screen. An opposition outside/inside is then used in 5 to 12 and interplays with an alternation of meals and leisure. From 13 to 16 the same contrast operates, but the relationship is reversed. The seven last 'moments' expand upon possibilities opened in 6 to 12, in other words amusements offered to tourists on a beach. 'Moments' 5 to 12 could also be understood as: the first evening, the first day, the second day; but they might also just as well be every morning, every lunch, every afternoon, etc.

Most viewers miss this extremely cohesive, almost exaggerated regularity and see the picture as a free variation on the theme of vacations. They are not wrong in that: every 'moment' is made up of a collection of small, unrelated details which could be inserted in another part of the filmic concatenation. A man wants to photograph his family but he is called to the telephone, and the others have to wait for him. The scene opens 'moment' 8 but would not be out of place in 6 or 10. The structure, rigid on paper, is constantly blurred on the screen by many of the moments' fungibility. The boundaries between moments dissolve with the intrusion of images taken from another filmic space. At the end of 6, Hulot is in the street; at the beginning of 7, he enters the dining-room: outdoors/indoors. But it is hard to decide when 7 ends: some shots are taken outside, while the soundtrack still conveys the unmistakable noises of the dining-room. Subsequent shots show the street as seen from the hotel, or picture the candy-seller, whom Hulot looks at at the end of 6, at lunch (the meal is a staple theme). The candy-seller is one of the many people, possibly inhabitants of the village, foreign to the cast, who intervene fleetingly as if they were going to become characters in the fiction and then vanish forever. By mixing up space and by focusing short scenes around different people, the film never stops undermining its own ability to follow a well-defined order.

From a formal point of view, the film is to be read as a conflict between necessity and chance. Yet the clash neither disconcerts the audience nor gives it the impression it is being offered an 'absence of film'. Antagonistic elements are of different nature and strength. While necessity is deeply rooted in a systematic use of conventions with which filmgoers are familiar, chance is limited to an erratic depiction of settings or a temporary fading of characters. All the night-time 'moments' are enclosed by a fade — probably the tritest of all cinematic devices. 'Moments' 1 and 2 are firmly linked by an identity of motion inside the frame: 1 closes with a train arriving from the left background and turning towards the left foreground; 2 begins with a car driving in the same direction. 'Moment' 2 is devoted to the road but its last shot, by panning on to a beach from a car-window, ties up 2 (cars) to 3 (the seaside resort). What is more, the film obeys the rule of coherent structure by creating its own references so that the audience can interpret the relationship between people and surroundings. *Hulot* 'arrows' the spectators' itinerary throughout the film with recurring images which reintroduce already known, therefore reassuring places. Although there is no delineation of the whole village, the audience is rapidly acquainted with a few locations. Provided the guide-marks are noticed, the cyclical disappearance of characters presents no difficulty for the audience.

The above might be taken to mean that Tati is not innovating in the field of cinematic expression. If a film is considered as a system in which signs are articulated by certain rules of combination, the assumption is correct, since *Hulot* operates according to well-established patterns. Certainly, the editing is perfectly classical, there are no brutal transitions or 'cheat cuts' between images, the shots are assembled in relation to the framing, lighting and tonality of the whole 'moment', and the advance from image to image is visually linear. On the other hand, in most films formal arrangement is utilized to guarantee the progression of the story. As there is neither story nor narrative progression in *Hulot*, viewers meet with routine stylistic figures but do not have to use them to make sense of a missing plot. In that lack lies one of the film's original features.

Instead of providing its audience with uninterrupted information, the film creates blanks. None of the characters is 'the hero', and it is hard to develop a story-line without one or two people who focus the attention. Yet the sophisticated deployment of the characters unveils another of Tati's originalities. Nearly all the characters in *Hulot* are stereotypes: *the Commandant*, a retired officer who never stops recounting his deeds and giving orders, *the* small, black-haired, touchy South-American, *the* chattering, bustling English spinster, *the* fat English businessman, unpleasant with everybody and quick to peep through the holes of the women's beach huts. Being nameless (the businessman has a name which is a non-name: Smith) and caricatural as social identities they can change neither themselves nor the fictional world of the film. They are a mere background against which the film builds up Hulot and Martine. Unlike the rest, the latter have proper names but cannot be assigned social positions: where they come from and where they will go after their vacation are equally a mystery. In contrast with the rest of the characters, they do not speak. When he enters the hotel, Hulot introduces himself to the landlord: 'Hulot, Monsieur Hulot.' These are the only words he utters. Martine's few words are unintelligible. Their case is puzzling, and there is deep ambiguity in the highly calculated cleverness (or perversity) with which Tati simultaneously suggests that they are different and prevents his audience from identifying them as 'heroes'.

Take Martine first. She gets out of the coach and enters the boarding-house, where there are three nice shots, classically edited, of her discovery of her room. She arrives in a leisurely fashion. We think we are looking at her through the window from the right, but when she moves from the left we understand that the supposed window was a mirror-wardrobe (an

Les Vacances de M. Hulot — above: M. Hulot (Jacques Tati); below: M. Hulot's car

extremely trite cinematic trick which has no specific purpose in the circumstance); she laboriously opens drawers and arranges her belongings. Finally, she opens the window. There is something reassuring in these shots. We believe we are grasping elements of a portrait to be, but we shall never be granted another scene of the same length. Later we see her talking with three young men and we wonder whether she is a flirt. At another time we witness her putting a record on a record-player: is she fond of music? Needless to say, there is no answer.

There is more consistency on the side of Hulot. He is remarkably tall, awkward, and gangling. He is forever clumsily greeting people. He tries to be helpful by carrying a boy's rucksack or giving a lift to a man who has missed the coach. Is he then 'a nice guy' or a fool who intervenes at the wrong moment? He looks polite and friendly; but on the other hand he never addresses his tablemate and does not hesitate to disturb the man in an extremely irritating manner. When he sees Smith peeping through a hole in the side of a cabin, he kicks him in the backside before running away and spending a long time trying to hide. However, if he wanted to protect someone's privacy, surely it is Smith who should be ashamed; perhaps Hulot himself was tempted by an attractive bottom? The question is of course meaningless. It is vain to try and put together aspects of Hulot's personality, every episode being developed for itself with no reference to the others. Hulot sees a new arrival greeting her hosts. He picks up the suitcase, which is too heavy for him. Its weight carries him into the house, drags him across the ground floor, and out into the courtyard where he collapses. The guest, of course, believes that her suitcase has been stolen. The scene is built around the gag of the space traversed and of the false robbery. It would thus be futile to interpret the details as psychological hints of Hulot's character.

Are Hulot and Martine then empty forms, moving images deprived of any fictional personality? Partially, but not entirely. Imprecise clues give Martine some sort of relief. She goes in for tennis and horse-riding, she dances, she can laugh: there is nothing precise, only fragments of a sketch. She has her own musical theme, however, since she is connected with the leitmotif of the film, a slow, quite unexpressive melody which is first heard when she arrives at the boarding-house and is afterwards mostly associated with her.[4] More importantly she is 'Martine'. This relates more to the context than to the text. Although not exceptional, the name Martine was not in current use after the War. In 1953, whenever it was pronounced in the world of movies it referred to the only undisputed female star of the moment, Martine Carol. There was no other actress whom popular or movie magazines called simply: 'Martine'. *Hulot*'s Martine is not meant to look like Carol. Yet she is blonde, slim, pretty, easy-going like her famous counterpart, quite unlike the smaller, sexier, whimsical star-to-be Brigitte Bardot. Even the least-informed spectator could hardly miss the reference to *the* cinematic female name — and hence make the assumption of Martine's 'star' status in the film.

Hulot is best defined by the tremendous noise of his old rattletrap and the outlandishness of everything associated with him — his car, his outdated bathing-costume, and strange, baggy clothes. By playing the part himself, Tati accentuates these characteristics. Unknown before 1948, the director-actor sprang to fame in *Jour de fête*. Miming rather than acting, he took advantage of his six feet and more to establish a clumsy, touching figure, a gigantic silhouette. In *Hulot*, his hat seems to bob above most heads, and he moves with a curiously mechanical, bent-backed gait, geometrically across the surface of the screen. His awkardness reaches its apotheosis in the legendary tennis scene. Hulot buys a racket. Having (presumably) never played before, he improvises: racket horizontal, elbow backwards, wrist forward, bang! Even experienced players give up as Hulot repeats his absurd gesture again and again. Hulot's blunders point to a general inadequacy. He is forever nowhere or somewhere else — at any rate never where the others are. This is not a positive description so much as a definition by absence.

In so far as fictional characters are collections of peculiarities which spectators more or less organize into a 'personality', Martine and Hulot are not characters. Subjective glances exist in *Hulot*, but they are attributed to secondary or even unknown characters. Hulot is deprived of his own viewpoint; we never watch what he watches.[5] Analysis of narration also defines characters as producers of events. In this respect, Hulot and Martine are different. Martine is passive while Hulot takes decisions or triggers events. Yet his actions have no long-term effects. Unlike orthodox characters, Hulot does not tie motifs together throughout the film.

Although the film lacks plot and characters, most spectators credit it with a meaning or a message. Recent research puts the emphasis on the function of the spectator in making sense of a film: thanks to her or his previous awareness of fictional convention and the clues given by the text, the viewer organizes the internal relationships into a narrative. Although Tati was probably completely unaware of this theory, he applied it to perfection. Many people perceive a love-affair in the film and bewail Hulot's loneliness.

Are there elements of a love-story? Love can be suggested by words, looks, or attitudes, and we have seen that the former are missing. As for attitudes, Hulot and Martine are only twice in close proximity — once for a short talk in the street, secondly when they dance at the fancy-dress ball.[6] Their hypothetical interaction is inferred from the fact that they are a man and a woman, i.e. the unavoidable constituents of romance in most films. A close analysis shows that in some 'moments' shots of Martine and shots of Hulot alternate; if there is no meeting in the actual shot, the spectator is quick to bind together independent images and to interpret them in classical narrative terms. Hulot never complains. His impassive face does not allow us to decide whether he feels lonely. It is the strong contrast between him and the others, the permanent cumbersomeness of his behaviour which make us feel sorry for him. The unaccountable seductiveness of *Hulot* derives significantly from the intensive work performed by the viewer himself. Neither love-affair nor loneliness are unambiguously indicated in the film. But it is impossible to say that audiences are wrong if they apply their fictional experience to create them in the film.

Hulot is a wonderful combination of the ordinary and the unexpected. Although elements of its material are borrowed from classical cinema, it firmly rejects established patterns. Its bizarre humour, quite unlike that of contemporary comedies, is nevertheless well-rooted in tradition. A streak of macabre humour, linked to the absurd, has always existed in French films and was revived in the 1950s with works such as *Jeux interdits* which gain their effect by ridiculing death or mourning. In *Jeux interdits*, for example, while the Germans are overrunning France (in 1940), two families fight for the control of a grave in a churchyard. That farcical vision of burials appealed to Tati. An important moment of his film takes place in a cemetery where Hulot is trying to mend a flat tyre. The crowd is more interested in his efforts than in the graveside liturgy. The inner-tube is mistaken for a wreath and put on the grave where it goes merrily flat. People mistake Hulot for a relative. Some start crying, more begin laughing, and presently Hulot's rattletrap joyously delivers back home a few of the mourners. Tati prefers understatement to outrage and, unlike in *Jeux interdits*, the joke is not taken to extremes; but the inspiration is identical.

Tati's adherence to previous models, especially to comics of the silent era, has often been noted, and it would be all too easy to list the gags adapted from a pre-existing stock — such as the banging door in the restaurant which gets in the way of the waiters. Familiar jests from old movies are generally performed quickly and in succession. Tati innovates by repeating the best jokes as if to get more out of them: Hulot is twice dragged down by heavy luggage, he comes back twice to his hotel dripping wet trying to escape the waiters, etc.

Whether borrowed or invented, all the jokes are screened with the same avoidance of haste. As we follow Hulot's drive towards the beach, the camera momentarily leaves him and films a village street where a dog lies down in the road. We know that Hulot will arrive, stop, and spend a long time before the lazy beast moves; and indeed he does exactly as expected. Later the old car starts popping. We conjecture it will break down. Not yet. It climbs the hill, making more and more noise. Now it has reached the top. Pop pop again. We insist: it must have engine trouble. At last, here we are, the roar dies away, the gag happens, as a reward for our long anticipation.

Spectators are challenged in various ways, and their deep involvement runs at curious odds with the limited commitment of the film: the audience tends to find more in it than is offered. By preventing the full development of actions or effects, *Hulot* creates a sense of the hiatus and inconsequentiality of holiday time, a period of leisure and ephemeral encounters. Hulot has gone on vacation and, as he is not a real protagonist, we can freely enjoy the flavour of vacant days.

Hulot is neither the first nor the only picture about summer holidays, but its relationship to the social context is peculiar; it in part accounts for the film's popularity at the time of its first release. Here again Tati succeeded in addressing his audience and making it compare the actual situation to the behaviour of the characters. In the France of 1953, July and August were not the months of ritual holiday exodus that they later became. Wage-earners had only two weeks annual holiday (the third was not granted until 1956), and most of them spent it at home. Two years old, the *Club Méditerranée* offered its cheapest package at 25,000 francs, the monthly salary of an unskilled worker, or half the price of a fridge. Hotels were few and expensive. Travelling was not particularly easy. One Frenchman in twenty-five had a car, the same proportion as in 1939; the production of vehicles was drastically limited and, if Hulot's banger was an oddity, the old cars depicted in the movie are typical of the period. It is true that the country was on the verge of a revolution: Citroën announced his *2 C.V.* in 1953, but buyers were warned that the first cars would not be available before 1955. An advertisement (in fact the only one which dealt with vacations in the summer of 1953) read: 'They are really happy because they chose a motorbike for their holidays.' Popular though motorbikes were they hardly allowed a family trip to the sea. Rather than dream of beach holidays and seaside resorts for themselves, the French welcomed foreign tourists, businessmen, and bachelors like Hulot. Hence the strangeness of the people in the film: they are exceptions and yet, even at the time, they already belong to a bygone age, the era of individual holidays.

Nowadays the decline of the old customs described in the picture is probably more perceptible than it was in 1953. But *Hulot*'s fascination has always been found less in its consonance with the period than in its contradiction between strong structure and absence of overt message. Unlike avant-garde films, *Hulot* does not distort cinematic forms to tell viewers they are looking at a movie. It is classically built, but spectators find less in it than what they bring — hence their enjoyment.

NOTES

1. Tati formed his crew from young people he knew well and with whom he had already worked. *Jour de fête* and *Hulot* are 'films de copains' made at low cost and with profit-sharing.
2. Cady-films, which had only made shorts previously, associated with Fred Orain, a noted producer, for *Jour de fête*. The film was sixth at the box-office with 260,000 tickets sold in Paris: the result was about the same for *Hulot* which suggests that the same people saw both films. Cady-films financed *Hulot* with the returns of *Jour de fête*.
3. She does not get her name before 'moment' 8, but in this short abstract it is simpler to call her Martine from the beginning.
4. The melody became a hit in the mid-1950s with the title of 'What's the weather like in Paris?'.
5. Martine is conceded a 'subjective vision' when she is presented in 'moment' 3, but her temporary capacity to 'see' results in nothing.
6. In an early version of the film, before the final view of the empty beach, Martine and her aunt are filmed in a train. The aunt alludes to Hulot, and Martine answers scathingly: 'Oh, M. Hulot...' Her scorn means that she has an opinion. In the final version the shot has been dropped, so that we do not know whether Martine has ever taken notice of Hulot.

SELECTED BIBLIOGRAPHY

Agel, Geneviève (1955) *Hulot parmi nous*, Paris, Editions du Cerf (a moralistic, sentimental book, which illustrates the response of the first spectators of the film).

Carrière, Jean-Claude (1958) *Les Vacances de M. Hulot d'après le film de Jacques Tati*, Paris, Robert Laffont.

Cauliez, Armand-Jean (1962) *Jacques Tati*, Paris, Seghers (documents well Tati's early films and the genesis of *Hulot*).

Gilliat, Penelope (1976) *Jacques Tati*, London, Woburn Press (the most reliable biography of Tati).

Thompson, Kristin (1977) 'Parameters of the Open Film: Les Vacances de M. Hulot', *Wide Angle*, 1 (4). (This excellent paper has exempted me from attempting a structural analysis and has led me to look more at the feelings and reactions of the film's contemporaries).

APPENDIX

Jacques Tati (1908—1982): filmography

1947 *L'Ecole des acteurs* (short)
1948 *Jour de fête*
1952 *Les Vacances de M. Hulot. (Mr. Hulot's Holiday)*
1953 *Mon oncle (My Uncle)*
1968 *Playtime*
1971 *Trafic (Traffic)*
1974 *Parade*

Other films cited in the text

The Greatest Show on Earth, Cecil B. De Mille (1952)
Jeux interdits (Forbidden Games), René Clément (1952)
Le Retour de Don Camillo (The Return of Don Camille), Julien Duvivier (1952)
Le Salaire de la peur (Wages of Fear), Henri-Georges Clouzot (1952)

12. *Casque d'or, casquettes,* a cask of aging wine: Jacques Becker's *Casque d'or* (1952)

DUDLEY ANDREW

> There's the sentimental [*fleur bleue*] side to yourself. You think of your youth [the further you get from it the more you think back] with a limitless tenderness, so much so that tears can well up in your eyes at nearly any moment. (Jacques Becker, interview in *Cahiers du cinéma*, 1954, 32)

The sheer surface appeal of *Casque d'or* necessarily increases every year; not as compound interest on the capital of its signification, but through the slight chemical agitation that thickens the texture across and through which such signification must be realized with each viewing. The wine (a Bourgueil) that Leca peddles to the owner of L'Ange Gabriel deepens in color and fragrance for us. It already attracted the film's first viewers in 1952 with its cool musk, preserved in crafted wooden barrels. The 35 years since the film's première doubly ages the wine, redoubling the appeal of the film.

Let us name this appeal: professionalism, forthrightness, sincerity; and to these let us append nostalgia. Jacques Becker surely traded on nostalgia in imagining the decor, the gestures and the codes of the *belle époque*. In France's post-war crisis of values where 'ambiguity' clouded personal and political motives and acts, the apparently limpid moral codes of 1900 must have felt like a tonic, a restorative rebuke. No qualms qualify Leca's duplicity or the police commissioner's routine corruption. No speeches motivate their venery; no anguished self-doubt crosses their confident worldly faces. Such villains belong on screen next to Simone Signoret with her flushed cheeks and Serge Reggiani with his deep, unblinking eyes. This was an era that knew what it wanted out of life, and pressed unapologetically to attain it. The sureness of Manda's strokes as he planes fine boards in the cabinet shop defines both his ability and his determination; they define the competence of an era for a later, degenerate era at the brink of losing its skill in carpentry and in living.

Becker kept before himself a representation of that way of life: Auguste Renoir's *Le Déjeuner des canotiers* (1880-1).[1] Early on he provides us this painting as a tableau vivant, staging at the airy *guinguette* the buoyant dancing, drinking, and fighting that Renoir's shimmering colors and mobile composition suggest. If he felt capable of mimicking the unselfconscious integrity of Renoir's lusty yet social painting, it was because he had imbibed that spirit from Jean Renoir during the flourishing cinema of the Popular Front.

And so Becker's is an earned nostalgia, neither vague nor sentimental. He displayed for his generation exactly what the modern world and modern art lack: professionalism, forthrightness, and sincerity. We now experience this lack at a double remove, for Becker's own era, as troubled as it was, seems incomparably more professional and sincere than our own. Hence the aroma of the images is more luxuriant for us.

The difficulty of actually seeing this film today promotes its aura as a classic. At the moment of my writing, no print can be obtained in the USA. My analysis is prepared from memory of many viewings a decade ago, from the *Avant-Scène* script, and from a VHS tape lent me from England where the film is evidently more easily available. The commercials that interrupt the narrative every twenty minutes set off the film's sincerity through absolute contrast, for they promote high tech products that were part neither of Jacques Becker's nor of Auguste Renoir's world. Their computer-edge style is facile beside the painstaking human care evident in the production of Becker's images. This care one can sense even on tape. I imagine the 16mm copy; I dream of a re-release in 35mm. Thus the conditions of its modern viewing amplify the nostalgia the film calls up, ratifying the aura within which it brings to life the era of Auguste Renoir.

This is not the solemn aura of high art disposed of by Walter Benjamin, but the tobacco flavour of a bygone populism where solid artisanship stands above fine art.

*   *   *

Pride in artisanship returns us to the 1930s, to Jean Renoir's vision of filmmaking, to the subjects of films like *La Belle équipe*. *Casque d'or* in fact was first envisaged in this period. Renoir purportedly looked at Henri Jeanson's scenario of the subject in 1939 and Julien Duvivier was in pre-production for producer Robert Hakim when World War II opened. Hakim then tried to mount the film in Hollywood with Jean Gabin as Manda. As a project, *Casque d'or* comes through the Occupation and Liberation preserving the Poetic Realist sensibility.

The tale, taken from lurid newspaper accounts of the lives and deaths of romantic *apaches* at the turn of the century, is related most closely to the swan song of Poetic Realism, *Les Enfants du paradis*. Itself a romanticized evocation of the nineteenth-century Parisian *demi-monde*, *Les Enfants* stages a multilayered Oedipal struggle at the center of which is the mysterious Garance, flower of the underworld, whose welcoming glance at the mime Baptiste precipitates the longing, the intrigues, and the disasters that carry the film across its marvellous three hours. Those intrigues involve the misanthropic poet and assassin Lacenaire, whose vendetta against society

makes him the most perverse avatar of Oedipus in the film. A healthier
Oedipus, Frédérick Lemaître directs his limitless ambition so as to rise atop
the world of theater. Unscrupulous, talented, and truant, he finally and
literally rewrites a drama during its performance, outraging its authors to the
point of precipitating a sunrise duel. Meanwhile Baptiste displaces his hatred
of his father and the prison of his domestic life on to his mute masterpieces that
mesmerize immense popular audiences at the Théâtre des funambules, the little
child-theater set opposite the magnificent house where the garrulous Lemaître
plays before the dandies of society.

Jacques Becker began to work on *Casque d'or* in 1946, the year following
the triumph of *Les Enfants du paradis*. It would take him five years to find his
Arletty in Simone Signoret, five years to reshape a scenario that had been, like
that of *Les Enfants*, packed with subplots, thrillingly contorted coincidences,
and flowery language. Becker mercilessly slashed scenes, characters, and
dialogue but only so as to stage more purely and directly the film's mythic
theme. In their lengthiest, most ebullient love scene, a promenade in the forest
covered in ten shots, Marie utters two brief sentences, Manda utters none. The
film as a whole, like Baptiste and like Manda, is modest, reticent, yet full of
romantic longing. In 96 minutes of screen time, Serge Reggiani recites a total
of only 78 sentences, more than the '60 words' Becker was fond of bragging,
but fewer than any other hero in the history of French sound cinema
(Couturier 1957, 10; Truffaut and Rivette 1954, 13). Language is the privilege
of fathers, of the eloquent Lacenaire, the strident Frédérick Lemaître and, in
Becker's film, the dandy Leca. Language seduces and lies. The mime Baptiste,
the taciturn Manda distrust it. The film's directness and sincerity cut through
the overwrought, loquacious 'cinema of quality' whose frothy costumes and
sets, whose romanticized plots and flowery language, filled French screens in a
vain attempt to replicate the Carné-Prévert masterpiece. Indeed, Carné and
Prévert were the first victims of this decadent post-war aesthetic in their much
reviled *Les Portes de la nuit*. In the history of French cinema, then, the
production of *Casque d'or* is itself the drama of Oedipus, Becker wrestling the
cinema of quality to the ground in his desire to attain whatever the cinema is
capable of. Golden Marie, like Garance, is that very cinematic treasure figured
directly within the cinema. A goddess who rows up to the napping man and
bestows herself upon him, she is both the ideal of beauty French cinema has
flirted with all century long, and the fickle public for whose favors, for whose
attention and gaze, filmmakers have betrayed one another. She is the mythical
destiny of popular romance, over whom father and son will lose their lives.
Becker was devoted to her.

There is something legendary in this film's title, in its production, and in
the tale it tells. It inspired the *enfant terrible*, that self-declared Oedipus,
François Truffaut, to set it off against that 'tendency' of French cinema he
mercilessly excoriated as 'le cinéma de Papa' (Truffaut 1954). And its star,
Simone Signoret, likewise saw it as a rebuke to the established order. The film
submitted to its poor reception, she suggests, 'murdered by the critics and at

the box office', as though this were the law of the father, just as a law beyond even Leca's power commands Manda's ultimate castration at the guillotine. Despite the cold response it received from those who ruled French cinema, Signoret would call it a production graced by good fortune, by good will, and by the supreme effort of all concerned. It was, she declared, her greatest role, as the British would have to prove to the French (Signoret 1978, 107-110).[2]

It is certainly her most mythic role. She is introduced immediately as the golden treasure of Leca's band, rowing her snivelling boyfriend to the shore. He is never anything more than an errand boy, escorting and amusing Marie in the absence of Leca. They are all Leca's boys, fanning out in Belleville to find her and bring her to him. 'Pauvre mec', Marie sighs in the film's first scene. 'Pauvre Roland', Manda follows in the next scene. Confined to the ante-chamber, Roland truly is pathetic as he listens to his boss proposition Marie, then send him packing when he complains. Thinking to win Marie by imitating the 'father', Roland thereby renounces the Oedipal drama and dies for it, sent as the father's substitute out into the cul-de-sac behind L'Ange Gabriel, there to do battle with the real son, the rebel Manda who has shown up to carry off Marie.

Serge Reggiani's character is truly Oedipal. An orphan in the original script, an ex-convict for Becker, his identity is immediately at stake when Raymond recognizes him at the *guinguette*. For Raymond's old cellmate, 'Jo', has re-emerged baptised 'Manda', an apprentice to the Belleville carpenter played by Gaston Modot. The action at the picturesque *guinguette* is a quaint miniature of the deadly drama that will unfold. Manda leaves his *patron*, lured by the welcoming gaze of Marie, 'Casque d'or'. Set off from the rowdy band in medium shot, they are all seated as Raymond makes the introductions. Each member has an epithet, each a girl (ignored in the introductions). Manda instead has his *patron* and his work. 'Monsieur travaille', Raymond quips, offering him a mug of beer. And it's true. Manda, sweaty from constructing the music platform, was amused to watch these boys waltz each other, amused till he saw Marie dance with Roland. Now she asks him to dance, 'Ils savent danser, les charpentiers?' How simple it is to displace Roland, outdancing, then outboxing this poor pretender. The worker's conquest has been too swift; a greater rival will have to be met, Leca, under whose authority and at whose pleasure this band and this woman strut the streets of Belleville.

The historical Manda broke off with Leca to lead a splinter gang, precipitating the violent jealousy over a beautiful woman. Becker's Manda, at ease in the underworld, nevertheless presents himself as a worker. He proudly wears the casquette that Leca's middle-class pretension scorns. How close Becker has come to the most classic of Poetic Realist films, *Le Jour se lève*, where the worker François, likewise an orphan, stands up to, then cuts down the corrupt dandy, Valentin, both 'father' and lover to the beautiful Françoise. Jean Gabin, like Serge Reggiani, refuses to flee, dying in the sight of a great public among whom is the girl at the core of the drama. In a complex but nevertheless clear echo, Reggiani is guillotined in the street, while Marie looks

Casque d'or — above: Manda (Serge Reggiani) and Casque d'or (i.e. Marie, played by Simone Signoret); below: Casque d'or with group of men including Leca (Claude Dauphin).

on from a top-floor room in what could be Gabin's fleabag hotel. Recall that Gabin lost his life in the top floor, while a crowd looked on from the street. Becker seals the citation when he matches Carné's famous camera angle looking down flights of concentric railings as Marie ascends.

As in Poetic Realism, the romantic purity of characters and motives in *Casque d'or* is tempered by modesty and stylistic rectitude. Manda is no knight errant in search of adventure. His silent integrity he inherits from Gabin. Manda belongs to the 1930s. He belongs with the solid carpenter Danard and with his old buddy Raymond, for whom he is ready to die. Serge Reggiani even belongs with Gaston Modot and Raymond Bussières, the two veteran actors Becker chose to take on these characters. They carry the 1930s in their blood, having worked with the surrealist Buñuel, with Prévert, and above all with Renoir. These actors carry forward the virtues of the workers' theater tradition.[3]

We might say that the drama of *Casque d'or* pits this older world against modern life. When Manda leaves his *patron*'s care to seek Marie at L'Ange Gabriel, he abandons his patrimony, both the little shop and the plain, long-suffering daughter he is in line to possess. Marie makes him take on the modern world, the one that has grown up while he was in prison, just as Becker must confront the cinema of dandyism that flourished during the Occupation and that replaced the Poetic Realism it nevertheless claimed to have inherited. But Becker is the true inheritor; and the real 'casque d'or' is the little *casquette* Becker placed on Manda's head. It is a challenge thrown quietly but directly at the pretensions of post-war cinema, a challenge that comes from the cinema of the pre-war days when films were made like good cabinets. Becker and Manda walk right into the gangsters' den to walk off with what they alone know how to love, the golden beauty of L'Ange Gabriel.

* * *

An exquisite period piece, suspended in the warmth of the Popular Front atmosphere for a dozen years, what sort of relation can *Casque d'or* maintain with its age and its audience? Becker always declared himself a 'social *cinéaste*' (Truffaut and Rivette 1954, 8); he has been likened to Renoir and through Renoir to Zola and Maupassant (Sadoul 1952a). His previous six films had zeroed in on various classes and locales in French life, specifically avoiding the *recherché*. *Rendez-vous de juillet* was hailed as a first-class inquiry into the Saint Germain youth culture during the existentialist days after the war. *Edouard et Caroline* used the lightness of comedy to batter the *grand monde*. And now suddenly Becker's most meticulous and expensive production throws us into a world of *apaches* at the turn of the century. What has happened?

To what shall we lay the difficulty we have in linking the film to the social issues of the day? Shall we fault Becker? Georges Sadoul, a great supporter of Becker whom he put alongside Renoir and Clair, complained that Manda's love affair betrayed the mission of every working man (Sadoul

1952b) The film he found to be well-crafted but its subject was insignificant, disappointing all those who had invested their hopes in Becker. He even refused *Casque d'or* entry on the list of the key films of 1952. Only three films out of 100 merit his favor that year: Christian-Jacque's *Fanfan la tulipe*, Clément's *Jeux interdits*, and naturally André Cayatte's *Nous sommes tous des assassins* (Sadoul 1962, 266). But Becker, it appeared in the early 1950s, had shucked off the social temperament and aptitude that marked him in some quarters as France's answer to Neo-Realism. Beginning with *Casque d'or*, he 'oriented himself toward "entertainment cinema" toward which nearly all the major French cinéastes have rallied in reaction against the *film noir* of the past few years and also against the "problem film"' (Leprohon 1957, 387).

If in the 1950s French cinema as a whole turns toward mere entertainment, as Pierre Leprohon believed, *Casque d'or* becomes a brilliant emblem of a weak age. Not in every era do the arts touch the pulse of a nation. Compare Italian Neo-Realism, so often in touch with the sensibility, if not the issues, of the day, with that of the French cinema of the Occupation which understandably produced films whose cool distance provided a place of refuge for a beaten audience. *Casque d'or* struck critics in 1952 as a film cut off from social life and even, on account of its deliberate rhythm, cut off from the sensibility of what was becoming the jazz age.[4]

But what artworks responded directly or adequately to the 1950s in France? Cynicism ruled the theater, probably the form that drew most attention to itself. Beckett's *En attendant Godot* was staged in 1950, Ionesco's *La Cantatrice chauve* in 1951 and *Les Chaises* in 1952 (Tint 1970, 187-189). Critics read these plays as hardened rejections of the optimism that greeted the Liberation. Sartre's call for a new humanism, for an extension of anti-fascist solidarity into socialist communality had been dashed by the Cold War, by Indochina, by Korea, and by the return to political power of the moneyed class. Although the cinema of the late 1940s had tried to foster solidarity (one would have to mention Becker here, but also Clément, Grémillon, Le Chanois, Daquin), by 1950 films like *L'Ecole buissonnière* or *Le Point du jour* must have seemed naïve.

One might go further and suggest that the nationalist enthusiasm attending the Liberation was, from the first, tainted with self-interest. In the sector of the cinema, the term 'quality', employed in the very first issue of *Le Film français*, was a term rife with business sense. Quality films aimed to recapture the authenticity of Poetic Realism which had won over an international audience; instead they exhibited only good taste and advanced moral values in a paternalistic fashion. The populism of *Les Portes de la nuit*, *Les Amants de Vérone*, *Au-delà des grilles,* and even *Le Diable au corps* was visibly calculated, just as Yves Allegret's dark *Dédée d'Anvers* and *Une Si jolie petite plage* appear disingenuous and forced against the more natural pessimism of *La Bête humaine* or *Le Jour se lève* a decade earlier.

Casque d'or, scheduled for production in 1946, based on a romantic pre-war script, was a post-war project in the quality image. Yet the finished film assiduously avoids association with that school of filmmaking. A costume drama it was, but one in which Mayo's understated costumes were worn, not strutted, and where the sparse dialogue is never edifying but serves instead as an index to each character's style. Truffaut (1954) was right to mention *Casque d'or* as a film incomprehensible to those raised on the anodyne 'psychological realism' of the tradition of quality. *Casque d'or* strips cinema down to its purest, seeking to distill emotions and codes of behavior that the loquacious, pretentious, paternalistic, and flamboyant post-war culture has sold off.

And so one might say of *Casque d'or*, as one says of the Theater of the Absurd of the times, that its refusal of political and social relevance shouts out a political and social message. *Casque d'or*'s contribution to the politics of the culture that surrounds it, then, is as discreet as its style. One looks in vain for an allegory of the Fourth Republic or of the Cold War. The broadcast of the film, like that of most films of the day, reaches no further than the sphere of the cinematic. The film does not speak to the literary concerns of the day, nor to those of the theater. It is a filmmaker's film, one Truffaut thought must be seen, because of its great candor, as an indictment of reigning approaches to period pieces, indeed as an indictment of the reigning 'tendency' in the industry altogether. *Casque d'or* concludes with an image of two lovers dancing alone into a future that has already been cut short. It offers neither program nor project, merely an unforgettable emblem, a 'legend' (in the strongest sense) of real love that we, who are fated to live in this era of compromises, must never forget.

* * *

And Becker makes certain we cannot forget it. He has his title character row the film directly to us. In the first scene she deposits a worthless companion, exchanging him in dance for Manda. The film's second act begins when the boat she rows alone floats gently to the same shore, and to Manda sleeping in the grass. A halo floods around her head which eclipses the sun as she descends from heaven to wake him with a kiss. A dissolve to them naked in bed, her hair unhinged, figures their wordless union and our blind acceptance of a cinematic love. Other dissolves use the buffer of our mind to interlace the fragments of disjointed drama. When Manda leaves Danard, the godfather — who has watched over his life of calm routine — fades and is reshaped into Mère Eugène, the peasant godmother, guardian of the dreamy rural hideaway. These kindly, legendary oldfolk divide the world into country and city, a symbolic opposition of values that is utterly undisguised. When Manda and Marie lie down in the soft grass, the camera tilts up to mime their passion. At its height the sky imperceptibly changes and the subsequent tilt back finds us in front of L'Ange Gabriel in Paris. Such punctuation of sequences insists on the clarity of values alive in the world of the *apaches*. Likewise Becker's *mise-en-scène* compels us to register the similarity of the cul-de-sac where

Manda kills Roland and the one where, mercilessly, he guns down the terrified Leca.

Compositions are often boxed tightly as in cartoons. The lovers happen upon a country wedding, which they can scarcely glimpse from the back of the church. Yet Becker frames the comic organist and choir close up and straight on. Then comes a solemn portrait shot of the stiff couple getting married that carries with it simultaneously the tint of old photographs and an air of mockery. The gendarmes who show up so often yet so ineffectually in the film seem likewise to have stepped from the pages of a comic book or, better, from the old serials of Louis Feuillade that captivated Becker as a youth (Sadoul 1962, 117). Even the gang, when first introduced to Manda, affect attitudes as caricatural as the epithets by which they know one another. When Leca approaches to slap Fredo for palming 300 francs, the frightened toughguy sticks out his forearm rigidly to protect his face. The gesture is a pose from a lost repertoire we are asked to bring to mind. In scenes like these Becker achieves his wish to avoid the painterly and arrive instead at a look straight out of those magazines of his youth such as *Le Petit journal illustré* (Sadoul 1952a). Once, gratuitously, Becker tracks away from a scene to fade out on a nearby poster, an art nouveau girl advertising *Triple Sec*.

Becker's search for clarity of presentation is less defensible when we catch him helping us with the plot. Do we really need the newspapers that inform us of Raymond's incarceration? Worse, do we need the photo of Anatole brought out at L'Ange Gabriel to help us identify the waiter rubbed out as a police informer? In case we still had trouble understanding that his 'accident' had been pre-arranged, Leca whispers between his teeth to one of his henchmen. 'Did it go OK?' 'A piece of cake' is the reply, as they all make contributions for Anatole's grandmother.

But while playing up to his audience, Becker finds one occasion to rebuke us and make us rethink our role. We first enter L'Ange Gabriel with a party of bourgeois carousers who, after a fine dinner no doubt, have dared to cross the tracks to sample the atmosphere at one of Belleville's most notorious *boîtes*. The regulars recognize this contrast of life-styles, and they recognize it as condescending. First they stage a thrill to mock these voyeurs, when Roland presses one to dance with him, then pulls her roughly around the floor in a gesture of rude eroticism. The thrill is soon multiplied when the police invade the place and Roland's body is carried out past them.

If we are to be voyeurs, it will not be the sort that safely sit on the outside. Instead Becker makes us track forward with Manda in his desperate search for Marie. We push Fredo aside and climb the stairs to Leca's apartment. With him we lean down to find Marie's slippers beneath Leca's fine sheets. Becker forces this primal scene upon us, fastening us to Manda's side till we wind up with him in the cul-de-sac of the gendarmerie, Leca's corpse at our feet. Without missing a note, the music carries us through a fade out/fade in to Marie's silhouette in a carriage. It's the dead of night as she pulls up to the cheap hotel beside the guillotine. This transference from the spent energy of

Manda to the vigil Marie keeps for him struck François Truffaut (1964) as one of the most brilliant strategies of scriptwriting he had ever encountered. Not only do we flow with the music from the internal perspective of one character to that of another (his lover), we are carried by this movement past the vengeance we have desired to its immediate consequence, the guillotine. The quaint set-ups taken from *Le Petit journal illustré* have given way to a mode of viewing which is utterly tied to the characters, indeed which their love permits to be passed between them. Marie has brought us this film, has rowed it to us from the lovely waters of the Marne. We now watch with her. As the big knife falls, her own head nods forward. We track in to an enormous closeup of that head and of its magnificent hair. As the music comes up, the film's final image wells up as though within Marie's mind: the couple whirling eternally in love. Is this her final vision? Or is it his last thought (for he had promised her in bed, 'I never stop thinking of you, Marie'). Or is it our vision, we who carry this legend on?

The merging together of Manda and Marie in total identification lures us to merge into them and into the film as well. The beams of reflected light fall to us from the screen, as we lie daydreaming; the film presses up to our eyes and lips, and asks us to embrace it. But something restrains us and interrupts this ageless dream of fusion. The pictorialism of the style, its search for a lost means of popular representation, is something to appreciate rather than merge with. *Casque d'or* tempts us with its alluring purity but continually asserts its temporal distance from us, its pastness. Hence its calculated and clever nostalgia.

The tone Becker achieves can be better appreciated by setting the film alongside another major work of 1952, Max Ophuls' *Le Plaisir*. Similarities between the films immediately arise.[5] The sets of both were designed by Jean D'Eaubonne who sought to bring alive a world like that of Maupassant. But the nostalgia Becker tenders a modern audience is explicitly mocked by Ophuls, or rather by his chosen narrator, Peter Ustinov, who wryly introduces each of the three episodes that comprise the film. Ophuls' usual cynicism makes his vision of the past truly sophisticated in its artifice. We moderns can indeed laugh but only if we are prepared to laugh at ourselves. In the final episode of *Le Plaisir* ('La Maison Tellier') the camera creeps up the wall of Madame Tellier's notorious house. It moves from window to window, framing vignettes of the members of the human species at their pleasures. The distance of viewer and viewed is spatial. We are blocked from the image by its frame, by the window, and by the screen Ustinov repeatedly reminds us of.

On the other hand, the distance of viewer from viewed in *Casque d'or* is temporal. We are encouraged to enter the image but are made to realize that it fades as we watch. In the final shot, the couple dances away from us, then evaporates to leave us alone with a sad song, *Le Temps des cerises*. Becker's nostalgia is a rebuke to a present that has failed to live up to the image he casts of the past. The past looks *different* from the present, and this difference keeps us, despite our boundless admiration, from complete identification with it.

Raymond's role is a figure of this difference, a third term prizing us away from uncritical immersion in the lovers and in love. While Raymond brings Manda to Marie, first at the *guinguette*, then later, through his handwritten message, to the tryst at Mère Eugène's, allegiance to Raymond is what pulls Manda from his embrace with Marie, and back to the city, to arrest, and to decapitation.

Although he mocked Manda's staid and virtuous life in the carpenter's shop, Raymond maintains this same old fashioned virtue even within the gang. 'Don't touch Manda', he tells Leca threateningly, 'I can count on him and that doesn't happen very often.' Clearly he cannot count on the band he has joined, for all of them are Leca's tools, morally unformed little boys. Thus the film upholds the strength of the natural and the heterosexual. You can see the health of it on Marie's face. Manda is worthy of her, having passed beyond the adolescence that binds the other boys to Leca.

Another Prévert film now rises to view, *Quai des brumes,* where the moral strength of the deserter, Jean Gabin, shatters the puerile bravado of Pierre Brasseur and his gang of thugs. The apparently respectable but depraved Michel Simon controls this gang from his basement where he also tries to rape his 'daughter', Michèle Morgan, before Gabin bashes his head in. Prévert and Becker lean on the popular psychological account of the fascist sensibility as being one of arrested adolescence and displaced homosexuality. The fascist leader, on the other hand, has no excuse and is pictured as unregenerate, cruel, and duplicitous. When caught stealing from the gang, Fredo not only whimpers as he takes his punishment, he then meekly goes to buy his boss some cigars. Instead of rebelling, Fredo completely introjects this 'father'; he abjures all interest in women, and bullies his mates. Leca recognizes a miniature of himself in Fredo, making him his right-hand man.

Ultimately Leca's strength, like that of Fredo and Roland, is shown to be pure bravado, a façade that crumbles as he pleads, 'Don't shoot, Manda. Don't shoot.' Manda not only shoots; he empties his gun into Leca. But even before this, we learned that Leca's power rests on that of the commissioner of police, who in turn jokingly claims to take orders from his wife, a woman Leca buys off with gifts of port wine. In this world of slaps and favors, no one is at the top. To belong to the system is to kneel before another man, weakly, childishly, in hopes of replicating within oneself the power that disciplines.

Raymond refuses the narcissism of this economy, insisting on the difference of a kind of friendship that 'doesn't happen very often'. In his undemanding affection for Manda, Raymond offers an alternative to the film's presentation of the oblivious union of heterosexual passion and the pathological infantilism of homosexual dependency. This difference is that of a chosen brotherhood, established in, and as, history.

With such sentiments in mind, Raymond returns us once more to the era of the Popular Front, the 'temps des cerises' of the title song. This famous song recapitulates in its lyrics and its history the complications followed out by the allegory of the plot. Composed in 1866 by Jean-Baptiste Clément, this romantic ditty expresses the sentiments of passion and regrets that at first blush carry the film (Buchsbaum 1983, 289). Yet immediately there accrued to it direct revolutionary overtones when Clément published it along with other songs in his *Chansons révolutionnaires* in 1868. He became a member of the Paris Commune (Belleville district) and was exiled to England and Belgium for a decade after that. A celebrated Socialist, he stands alongside Eugène Pottier who wrote the *Internationale* at just this time.[6] It was in Belgium that Clément re-published his little masterpiece, belatedly dedicating the song to a female ambulance driver of the Commune (Noel 1971, 75; Brunschwig, Calvet, and Klein 1981, 361). After his death, but in harmony with his life, this tune would sport radical new lyrics and a small but radical shift in title, *Le Temps des crises* (Berbier 1959, 80). Overtaking France during the end of the *belle époque*, performed by Montéhus, the great 'anarchist crooner of the world of the *apaches*' (Brunschwig, Calvet and Klein 1981, 74), this now utterly political anthem would persist into the 1930s when it was sung along with the *Internationale* as an antidote to *La Marseillaise* which tended to be appropriated by the Right.

The political intent behind the use of this song as the major leitmotif in *Casque d'or* , is ratified by a powerful 'coincidence'. In 1937, as Jean Renoir was seeking to wrest *La Marseillaise* from its adoption as theme-song by the Right, his co-director at Ciné-Liberté, Jean-Paul Le Chanois, was busy making a Communist feature film the title of which was indeed *Le Temps des cerises*. Becker had worked with Le Chanois the year before on Renoir's *La Vie est à nous,* a film edited by *Casque d'or*'s editor Marguerite Renoir. As in *Casque d'or*, the action of *Le Temps des cerises* begins at the very end of the nineteenth century. Like *Casque d'or* it features Gaston Modot playing a carpenter who grows old in the course of the film.

The song's simultaneous expression of joy and regret is given a political referent in Le Chanois' film, which hailed a lost past (the Paris Commune of 1871) while pointing to a utopia where social injustice and economic privation will have vanished. Thus the mixture of tones that Truffaut (1964) found so exhilarating in *Casque d'or* (and which later he specifically imitated in *Tirez sur le pianiste,* especially in the back alley fight scene) is embedded in the film's theme, in its theme-song, and in the history of both. Nor has that history run its course. In 1975 one of the politically enlightened heroes of Alain Tanner's *Jonas qui aura 25 ans en l'an 2000* takes a job caring for the aged. He leads them in a reprise of *Le Temps des cerises*, whose theme Tanner, like Becker, continues to employ to underscore a lost political utopia. The fact that a now aged Raymond Bussières takes a major role in Tanner's film links it even more closely to *Casque d'or* and through it to the Popular Front. Indeed Bussières continues to proclaim to the disillusioned veterans of 1968 who populate Tanner's movie, that life was better in 1936.

And so it must have been for Jacques Becker who once exclaimed, 'I have a horror of my own generation' (Queval 1962, 46). *Casque d'or* looks back to its version of a better time and finds it precisely in the era of the Popular

Front, which in its turn had looked back to the Commune in search of political direction. The difference this time is that *Casque d'or* displays no hope of a better future. The 'temps des cerises' was but a brief moment of fraternity and love in a world dedicated to smashing both. If the film strikes us as delicate and vaguely otherworldly in its feeling and design, then Becker has delivered the film he had in mind, one which, because of the discouraging impasse of the post-war years, must be read as both social and tragic in its ineluctible confrontation of the possible and the impossible. We are further than ever from establishing a world where human work and love prevail, and so this is a film whose delicacy grows rarer each day. *Casque d'or* has become an image for us of a better era, or at least a better cinema, one based on solid craft and direct sentiment, a real 'temps des cerises'. The genius of the film is that it predicted, understood, and thematized this inevitable process of decay and nostalgia. It made of it a legend.

NOTES

1. The opening of *Casque d'or* in fact recalls a half dozen Renoir canvases, including *Bal du Moulin de la Galette* (1876), *La Seine à Asnières* (1879), *Déjeuner au bord de la rivière* (1879), *La Dance à la campagne* (1883), *Le Bal à Bougival* (1883). Rowboats, dancers, drinking boatsmen, trellised dance-floors, and a riverside setting certify the reference to the great painter.
2. André Bazin confessed that he should have known better and that it was Lindsay Anderson who had pointed to the film's brilliance (Bazin 1971, 91).
3. Raymond Bussières has pursued this vocation from the 1920s into our own era, appearing most recently in another film evoking the Popular Front ethos, Alain Tanner's *Jonas qui aura 25 ans en l'an 2000*, a film we shall have occasion to return to in this essay.
4. Although Sadoul in his already cited review mentions *Bicycle Thieves* as a precursor for the tight dramatic logic and the lack of fatalism in *Casque d'or*, Queval and Bazin both point to the effect of destiny produced by 'the encounter of the possible with the impossible' (Queval 1962, Bazin 1955)
5. The link between Becker and Ophuls would be sealed five years later when, upon the latter's death, Becker completed *Montparnasse 19*, another film of *belle époque* Paris.
6. Clément and Pottier are often linked. In 1924 their songs were published together in a German translation, *Französische Revolutionslieder* (Berlin, Malik Verlag).

SELECTED BIBLIOGRAPHY

Bazin, André (1955) 'Autocritique', *Cahiers du cinéma*, 35.
Bazin, André (1971) *What is Cinema? II*, Berkeley, University of California Press.
Berbier, M. (1959) 'Vers la belle époque', *Histoire de France par les chansons*, 3, Paris, Gallimard.
Brunschwig, C., Calvet, L.-J. and Klein J.-C. (1981) *Cent ans de chanson française*, Paris, Editions du Seuil.
Buchsbaum, Jonathan (1983) 'Left Political Filmmaking in France in the 1930s', Doctoral dissertation, New York University.
Couturier, Jean (1957) *Fiche filmographique*, 113.
Leprohon, Pierre (1957) *Présences contemporaines: Cinéma*, Paris, Debresse.
Noel, B. (1971) *Dictionnaire de la Commune*, Paris, F. Hazan.
Queval, Jean (1962) *Jacques Becker*, Paris, Seghers.
Sadoul, Georges (1952a) 'Interview with Jacques Becker', *Les Lettres françaises* (10 April).

Sadoul, Georges (1952b) 'Puissance de la Sobriété' (review of *Casque d'or*), *Les Lettres françaises* (17 April), reprinted in Sadoul (1979) *Chroniques du cinéma français*, Paris, Union Générale d'Éditions, 120-124.
Sadoul, Georges (1962) *Le Film français*, Paris, Flammarion.
Signoret, Simone (1978) *Nostalgia Isn't What it Used to Be*, New York, Harper and Row.
Tint, Robert (1970) *France Since 1918*, New York, Harper and Row.
Truffaut, François (1954) 'Une Certaine tendance du cinéma français', *Cahiers du cinéma*, 31.
Truffaut, François (1964) 'De vraies moustaches' *Avant-Scène Cinéma*, 43.
Truffaut, François and Rivette, Jacques (1954) 'Entretien avec Jacques Becker', *Cahiers du cinéma*, 32.

SCRIPT

Becker, Jacques (1964) *Casque d'or*, in *Avant-Scène Cinéma*, 43.

APPENDIX

Jacques Becker (1906—1960): filmography

1935 *Le Commissaire est bon enfant* (short)
1935 *Le gendarme est sans pitié* (short)
1935 *Tête de Turc* (short)
1942 *Dernier atout*
1943 *Goupi mains-rouges* (*It Happened at the Inn*)
1945 *Falbalas* (*Paris Frills*)
1947 *Antoine et Antoinette* (*Antoine and Antoinette*)
1949 *Rendez-vous de juillet*
1951 *Edouard et Caroline* (*Edward and Caroline*)
1952 *Casque d'or* (*Golden Marie*)
1953 *Rue de l'estrapade*
1954 *Ali Baba et les quarante voleurs* (*Ali Baba*)
1954 *Touchez pas au grisbi* (*Grisbi*)
1957 *Les Aventures d'Arsène Lupin* (*The Adventures of Arsène Lupin*)
1958 *Montparnasse 19* (*Modigliani of Montparnasse*)
1960 *Le Trou* (*The Night Watch*)

Other films cited in text

Les Amants de Vérone (*The Lovers of Verona*), André Cayatte (1948)
Au-delà des grilles (*The Walls of Malapaga*), René Clément (1948)
La Belle équipe (*There Were Five* [UK]; *A Fine Team* [USA]), Julien Duvivier (1936)
La Bête humaine (*The Human Beast*), Jean Renoir (1938)
Dédée d'Anvers (*Dédée*), Yves Allégret (1947)
Le Diable au corps (*Devil in the Flesh*), Claude Autant-Lara (1947)
L'Ecole buissonnière (*Passion for Life*), Jean-Paul Le Chanois (1949)
Les Enfants du paradis (*Children of Paradise*), Marcel Carné (1943-5)
Fanfan la tulipe, Christian-Jacques (1952)
Jeux interdits (*Forbidden Games*), René Clément (1952)
Jonas qui aura 25 ans en l'an 2000, Alain Tanner (1975)
Le Jour se lève (*Daybreak*), Marcel Carné (1939)
La Marseillaise, Jean Renoir (1927)
Nous sommes tous des assassins (*We Are All Murderers*), André Cayatte (1952)
Le Plaisir, Max Ophuls (1952)
Le Point du jour, Louis Daquin (1948)

Les Portes de la nuit (*Gates of the Night*), Marcel Carné (1946)
Quai des brumes, Marcel Carné (1938)
Une Si jolie plage (*Riptide*), Yves Allegret (1949)
Le Temps des cerises, Jean-Paul Le Chanois (1937)
Tirez sur le pianiste (*Shoot the Pianist*), François Truffaut (1960)
La Vie est à nous, Jean Renoir (1936)

13. How history begets meaning: Alain Resnais' *Hiroshima mon amour* (1959)

MARIE-CLAIRE ROPARS-WUILLEUMIER

For the spectator of 1959 who saw it when it first came out, seeing *Hiroshima mon amour* anew in the 1980s could jeopardize the memory of a film whose shock waves provoked more than one to refuse for some 20 years to see it again. Viewed from this later perspective, however, it is impossible not to perceive the film's modernity displayed through its very obsolescence: the theme of memory everywhere present in the action has become a commonplace convention; the anti-heroes whom we saw as free from psychological stereotypes have become the prototypes of the rising intellectual bourgeoisie; even the narrative, with its pauses and its ellipses, its vagaries and its open ending, declared the coming of a new narrative convention which would project the subjectivity of the characters through the representation of objects and places. *Hiroshima*'s legacy is substantial; yet the film, unmakable and never remade, remains without an heir, and in that respect it is unique in so far as it defies that very law of succession which it created. At the precise moment when the lines of meaning converge they disappear, or disperse laterally: a thematic is enounced, but no theme can be isolated, no phrase separated from the voice which utters it; characters appear clearly constructed but they divide into two interweaving networks; the remorseless diffraction of the editing breaches the film open to an audial and visual space which the action cannot saturate. It is here that we can locate the 'nocturnal clarity' of *Hiroshima*, which simultaneously tells an easily understandable story and interposes between that story and its perception a screen of multiple signs resistant to narrativity. This double movement now makes clear today the film's interest: *Hiroshima* precipitates a rupture of codes, through a forceful cinematographic *écriture* it dismantles the conventional order of cinema — hence the shock felt in 1959; but at the same time, the film makes readable what is at stake in its aesthetic of modernity by exposing, with its own particular force of rupture, the mechanisms of integration which that aesthetic puts into play.

It is this readability that escaped people in 1959: the rupture was understood but the reasons for it were not clear. If a controversy was started up it was on ambiguous lines because it began, on the one hand, with the marginalization of the film — it was turned down as the French selection for the Cannes Festival for reasons of political opportunism (not to upset the Americans) — and ended, on the other hand, with the commercial success of the film, thanks partly to a counter-attacking publicity campaign which stressed the erotic audacity of the subject matter (the raging passion between a Japanese man and a French woman). Unconditionally supported by the intellectuals and the young directors of the time, who saw themselves in this different language and identified with a distanced way of belonging to the world, the film did not remain confined within this avant-garde framework: outside, it caused running battles in the press and public enquiries, both of which served to create further confusion by ultimately allowing the scandal to be recuperated. Whilst the work itself broke with the accepted repartition of categories and values in the establishment, the debates surrounding it marked out carefully partitioned areas of investigation: the aesthetic which tended either to promote the invention of an opera-film or, on the contrary, to denounce a failure which was, moreover, imputed to the literary pretentiousness or mental confusion of Duras alone; the political, which either stressed its absence (since when is Hiroshima apolitical?) or deplored its presence (but this is Hiroshima and a love-story!); the sociological, which insisted on the advent of the figure of the free woman and warned against ideological debate which could obscure the novelty of the tone and mores espoused by the film. This co-optation, whether positive or negative, operates in fact contrary to the impact of the film, whose modernity comes, first, from its refusal to separate the political and the aesthetic, the private from the public, the world-wide cataclysm and the individual trauma. The old territorial distinctions collapse, doubtless dissimulating the advance of new partitions. But acclaim, be it critical, intellectual or cinephilic, lags behind the discursive event this film represents. A beacon-film for a whole generation, *Hiroshima mon amour* crystallizes a certain number of theoretical and conceptual mutations, whose readability implies, beyond renouncing fascination, recourse to a textual approach already anticipated by the form of the film.

Breaking out of the cinematographic field, the 'Hiroshimanian' transgression can be read first in the context of the production modes it brought about. There has been a lot of critical comment on the collaboration between Resnais and Duras, without always taking into consideration the complexities of such an encounter which simultaneously opened up two divergent routes into the cinema that followed, and which, simultaneously, dominated the making of the film — thus problematizing the question of shared authorship. *Hiroshima mon amour* was Alain Resnais' first full-length feature film (to date he has made 11), but it also represented Marguerite Duras' first cinematographic intervention (since then she has put her name, as director, to 16 full-feature or short films). Henceforth their trajectories have never ceased to diverge: from *Hiroshima* to *Mélo* which leads Resnais to a theatre simulacrum, or from *Hiroshima* to *Dialogue de Rome* which leads Duras to the dialogic exacerbation of a faceless voice. On the one hand, a game of substitution and remakes, which reveals in what way shots and words become hackneyed; on the other, a verbal doubling-up, which inscribes the absence of the being within the presence of the word. However, there is little doubt that *Hiroshima* is the link that ties these two chains together, in so far as the film provokes a contamination between literature and cinema which profoundly disturbs the generic specificities, thus putting an end to the innocence of cinema and, also, to the complacency of literature.

Duras' heritage is the novel, Resnais' that of the documentary short film. But when Resnais, in response to a Japanese request for a film on the atomic devastation, decided not to confine himself to the documentary-style testimony of *Nuit et brouillard*, it was neither a film script nor a proper novel that he commissioned from the novelist but rather a fictional apparatus which would structure the film and which he would create with her. Certainly, the text published by Duras in 1960 carries the title 'script and dialogues'. However it is unusual in that it contains, apart from a description of the film made, elements of another film, one that would have been different but did not get made. This 'subterranean continuity', needed by Resnais to establish the characters, seems obliterated by the actual film, which allows no direct mention to surface. By taking charge of the *romanesque* left-overs, this 'subterranean continuity' frees the filmic continuity from any explanatory impediment, and thus makes possible the functioning of an internal discontinuity; but at the same time this 'subterranean continuity' increases the fragmentation of the Durassian *opus* whose extreme literariness goes hand in hand with an unrealizable homogeneity: one part becomes the libretto of an organized film, whilst the other harnesses the temptation of realism and breaks it into pieces.[1]

Such is the peculiarity of this commission that the filmmaker makes the author write by forcing her to re-write, and only generates the writing to turn it to the sole advantage of the film. According to Resnais, the purpose was to create at the cinema the equivalent of the reading process. This fertile paradox arises from the fact that when this reading occurs it will no longer rely on an already written text. To the appeal of the literary, which primed the cinema at that time, Bresson's response was to transcribe and Godard to quote; Resnais, for his part, would always refuse adaptation, only *Mélo* feigns an exception to this rule; and the reading that *Hiroshima mon amour* brings into play, because it is a reading and a writing, inscribes into the film a reminder of the missing book, the existence of which the film both prevents and presupposes. This is already to define the alteration entailed by a filmic conception of writing which includes linguistic signs but simultaneously absorbs them into a style of editing with multiple entry-points, vocal and figurative. But it is also to invite us to shift the relationship between reading and the work read: to read, therefore, would mean to write, but only by turning writing (via the short-circuit of the cinema) into the point of disjunction of the bookish mode. It is Duras who pursued this paradoxical route, which leads to writing in order to film and to filming in order to destroy both text and film, whose respective identities in turn are shattered through an inability to define themselves exclusively. But Resnais, in multiplying his literary collaborations, never ceased to reiterate the act of exaction inaugurated with *Hiroshima*. On both accounts, *Hiroshima mon amour* represents the entry into the cinematographic world of the notion of film-text: the film becomes text, not because it includes a text (even were it blown up to the lyrical dimensions of a cataclysm), but rather because it incorporates a textual apparatus which deprives the written text of its autonomy, its specificity even, and at the same time lays the film open to the invasion of an off-screen space, by definition hidden.

Borne on the necessities of fiction (which sealed the Duras-Resnais pact) and discernible only today, a second sectorial disruption arose. The taste for stories, either cheap novelettes or melodrama, is common to both authors, but in neither instance do they come back to the historical evidence. What Resnais appears to retain from *Moderato cantabile* (published in 1958) is the manner in which Duras starts a story by throwing into it the fragmented memory of another story: he then asked the author for a fictional construction based on two tempos, the structure of which is not dissimilar, on the scale of a full-feature film, to the temporal distanciation experienced in *Nuit et brouillard*. Duras grafted on to the Hiroshima love story, the plot of which is supposed to respond to the Japanese commission, the memory of a German love affair, which carries, in the film, the name and the place Nevers, thus satisfying the Franco-Japanese nature of the production. But the invention of Nevers draws from sources other than the fiction of Hiroshima, as the recent publication of *La douleur* testifies — this is a diary which seems to have been written in April 1945, although Duras is quite adamant that she does not remember when she wrote it.[2] Through the multiplication of the referential signs which link the text to the end of the war, by focusing it on the reception given to the first deportees to return from the concentration camps, the reader discovers, in the form of disconnected traces, the generic image of the German adventure (a young German soldier agonizing on the quai des Arts), the 'cry' incessantly repeated, coming from she ('I', 'Marguerite L.', 'M. Leroy') who hopes for the return of her deported husband, the obsessive fantasy of a corpse 'in the black ditch', on which is based the love for the absent one. And, when the return of the dying deportee occurs, the reader notices that the diary has changed into a story in order to relate, after the event, the lengthy task of rehabilitation, followed by the narrator's pronouncement of her decision to leave the one she has brought back to life: a pronouncement which coincides, approximately, with the press reports of the 'A' bomb explosion in Hiroshima.

I will return later to the structural implications of such a confluence whereby the tone, sometimes the rhythm, and above all the underlying structure of *La douleur* seem to have slipped into the story of Nevers. But the echo effect, which associates fragmentarily these two texts, leads one inevitably and immediately to stress to what extent fiction, in Duras' work, contaminates the real. Certainly, the German story — pure outgrowth of an image glimpsed at and suppressed — is in no way autobiographical; but the tonal resemblance between *Hiroshima* and *La douleur* invalidates, for the latter text too, any illusion that it might be autobiographical. If the diary in *La douleur* undoubtedly transcribes elements of Duras' life, the style of this diary leads one to suppose that it is in fact a 'false' diary, whose writing-up, spread apparently over two epochs, could have coincided with that of *Hiroshima*.

Hiroshima mon amour — above: *La mémoire* (memory); below: ... *des signes* (of the signs)

A single gesture with Duras — the act of *écriture* — designates and destroys the real. *La Vie est un roman* (life is a novel), says Resnais, thereby generating a film which plays on convention in its purest state. Literature is the real, Duras might say, whose recent intervention in a legal matter, where she decided all on her own between what was true and false, thus substituting the logic of fiction for that of the event, is well known.[3] This awareness of pretence causes, between Duras and Resnais, a bringing into question of the function of the documentary: for contradictory reasons, a shared suspicion prevails over the issue of representation, whether fictitious or discursive, whose narrative source has been exposed. However, even narration itself risks teetering when it is anchored in the double play of a memory given as a condition of entry into the event, and where, paradoxically, it erases that which it inscribes. As an abstract and not a psychological notion, the 'Hiroshimanian' memory does not belong to the subjective reality of the recollection, but to the complexity of the rapport which the movement of resurfacing mobilizes when it is conceived of as a movement of divergence/a divergent movement. Here, once again, the Resnais-Duras encounter leads to divergence depending on whether the stress is placed on the conceptual machine which attaches memory to the whole space of time — this is the memory-world or brain which Deleuze imputes to Resnais — or, on the contrary, whether one insists on the theoretical mechanism of a memory-oblivion which seals the secret relationship between Duras and Blanchot, by opening the text to an infinite repetition of signs. Nonetheless, via these two different meanings, which lead either to *Mon oncle d'Amérique* or to *Aurélia Steiner*, a similar problematics of the trace articulates, in *Hiroshima mon amour*, the perspective of memory and the editing work: remembrances, sounds and images become traces, not so much because they refer back to an exterior reality which they would confirm, but because they indicate, at every point of actual perception, the potential absence of that point always drawn, by the attraction of the relationship to the other, out of the perceptible sphere of presence.

Caught in this paradoxical logic, it is the very remembrance of the bomb at Hiroshima or of the death at Nevers that will activate the decoupling editing style whereby the syntax of *Hiroshima* pushes back the memory that the sign wishes to approach. But between the evocation of Hiroshima and that of Nevers a rupture occurs, reflected in the structural heterogeneity of a film divided into the prologue and the rest of the film: the trace, the substitute for representation, can lead to a narrative-line or stay with the explosive violence of an *écriture* with no narrative outcome. Crossing the cinema-literature frontier, conflating the reality-fiction distinction, *Hiroshima mon amour* points, more obliquely, to the new division which has opened up in the field of representation between the referring of the real to the writerly urge and the reduction of the real to a referentializable narrative. The fact that the event at Hiroshima is at the centre of this division gives the film its specifically historical dimension, whereby history recognizes itself as tributary to a discourse whose narrative growth is no longer self-evident .

Amongst the various disjunctions that this film activates, the most extraordinary one surely has to do with the unclassifiable nature of the opening sequence or prologue whose discontinuous montage, horizontal and vertical, cancels out the narrativity that the credit titles seemed to announce.[4] The irregular alternation between embracing bodies and burning bodies, the recitative of two unlocatable voices off-screen, the uninterrupted tension of image and voice — such is this opening sequence. This disruption appears even more provoking since this inaugural passage, which lasts 15 minutes[5], represents the sole reconstruction that the film provides of the atomic explosion. The violence of the relationship established between extreme pain and extreme pleasure — the horror of destruction and the erotic disaster — has attracted all the attention; but the disorder introduced into our scale of values runs the risk of obscuring the aesthetic daring of a sequence constructed on a principle of general dislocation, according to which the profusion of verbal, visual and musical themes defies reduction to a stabilized structure. There is no doubt that this opening sequence, in refusing to document the effects of the bomb, infused the editing itself with the force of radiation linked to atomic disintegration.[6] If Resnais exorcizes the documentary illusion and refers it back to the 'film on Peace' which he refuses to make, he retains from his experience in short films an ability to transpose on to filmic *écriture* the apparatus that generates the object to be conjured up.

To film Hiroshima, then, means to show in what way the event exceeds the possibility of fixing it within filmic representations. The monstrous debris in the museum and the mutilated survivors in the hospitals, the photos, newsreels, reconstructions — all the figurative signs like all the verbal details — point to the impotence of sight and knowledge to organize the readability of an event which can only be acknowledged through the mimicry of a fragmented editing style constructed on the model of the atomic explosion. Resnais' experience in short films allows him to fissure the full-length feature film and to achieve, around the unrepresentable, the exchange of the event for an inscription of that event. But a second operation, less immediately interpretable, negotiates another exchange that is active underground as early as the prologue: the one which will allow the transference, later on in the film, of the 'unrepresentable' of Hiroshima on to the 'narratable' of Nevers. Contributing to the tearing of the filmic fabric, the editing which links the lovers' bodies with those of the victims serves simultaneously to discharge on the erotic encounter the disjunctive energy emitted by the explosion; once narrativized — and that constitutes the rest of the film, during which time is measured and mental pertubations become embedded subjectively — the couple's liaison will re-route the rupture contained in the prologue, and make it enounciable by displacing it on to another narrative delivered in the stead of and in the locus of the narrative which was impossible. How to change an event into writing *and* writing into history? this is the purpose of a transference from desiring pulsion to desired object, the actualization of which is prepared by the prologue of *Hiroshima* — meantime indicating, by the disproportion of the parts, the incommensurable nature of the two operations.

A deformed hand, a destroyed eye, hair torn out, a distraught woman breaking out of a cavernous dwelling, a twisted bicycle, legs of passers-by, river, anger, stone — long is the list of materials which the narrative of Nevers drags out of Hiroshima's museum and reconstructs into appeased, if not acceptable, forms. The germ of the story takes the lovers' bed as the source of a narration which will intertwine, in a weak echo of the prologue, the close views of the bodies and the distant ones of the Loire; and the story itself only comes to the film in dislocated pieces, alternating with the duration of an encounter and doubling up its trajectory. But as distinct from the prologue — hence the purpose of the transference — the fragmentation does not remain fragmentary: organized and controlled, the discontinuity serves henceforth to manipulate, with the story of the German past, the work of narrative production which authorizes the reconstruction of facts.

What does telling a story mean? If we believe the story of Nevers, it means to transform one isolated, brutal, incomprehensible image — the first mental visualization of the dying German — into a coherent and continuous whole whose verbalization guarantees, moreover, its interpretation. All that is needed is less a chronological line — the story remains disorganized, progressing in either concentric or successive waves — than a beginning and an end, a transmitter and a receiver. This story, initiated by an unclear image of death, will not end until it has tied the chain of cause and consequence around this death. In answer to a death shot which remains undeciphered (shot 273) comes — through the relentless play of questions and answers — a later reprise of an almost identical shot with this difference that it is now linked, by two internal panoramic shots, to the logical diachronic sequence of the 'before' and 'after' (shot 313): the shot begins with a quick glance of the young woman as she appears at the top of the bridge, and then turns to a high-angle shot of the dying body; the shot ends with another simulation of the glance, looking up to a balcony already seen in an earlier flashback (shot 237) whose signification is now understood because it is the place from which the fatal bullet was fired. Thus, one single shot serves to articulate the fact (the death) and its origin (the murder); at the same time, and within the same visual continuity, the shot reveals the action of discovering the fact whereby the subject accedes to knowledge; the shot even inverts the ordering of elements since the subjective comprehension precedes the reprise of the event, thus permitting a return to the cause which has now become enounciable.

Telling a story, then, means making an event readable by inserting it into a logical continuity. The execution of this operation cannot happen without a lengthy investigation — signified in this instance by dual elaboration of the couple's dialogue: it is the receiver — the Japanese man — who through his repeated questions extracts from the holder of the secret — the French woman — an evocation of the past whose exposure must be organized. Obviously, the scene simulates the psychotherapeutic process of voluntary memory —

anamnesis — whereby the analyser transforms a fantasy into a story and transfers the obsessional charge on to the analyst who is, in turn, capable of involving himself in the story obtained: this is what the Japanese man will do in identifying with the German. But the psychoanalytical simulacrum, so frequent in Duras' work which always tries to outsmart Lacan, is less important here than the act of transference which it clearly designates: through the elaboration of Nevers, it is the appropriation of Hiroshima which *Hiroshima mon amour* relates, the spectator is invited to transfer on to this simple story that has become transparent, the opaque memory of an event whose importance cannot be formulated — hence the verbal conflation (upon the last shot of the Nevers story) between the finally understood death of the German and the discovery of Hiroshima in the Parisian newspapers (shot 323). With all the links established, and the disparate series of events articulated one to another, a dating becomes possible ('14 years have passed', shot 324); and the uncontrollable explosion of Hiroshima, which seemed relegated since the end of the film's prologue, can at last open on to a familiar chronology, a formulated reference — in short a historicity, where the mediation of Nevers has shown the essential role that narrativization plays.

To historicize Hiroshima, by giving it a place in time and space (in our western time and space), such appears to have been the oblique function of the long detour undertaken in the Nevers story. The modernity of the film transpires from its actualization of this transference by dismantling, through cinematic means, the mechanism of the process: making history is making a story, by diverting indescribable sights towards a discursive continuity they become seizable for the subject and can, therefore, be channeled: 'I have told our story. You see, it was, after all, tellable.' That betrayal has occurred here, such is the inference to be drawn from the structure of *La douleur* which once again we see in operation here: the donation of story-telling goes hand in hand with the abandonment of that which was narrated; and the narration, in separating life from death, completes the mourning work by severing the link between Eros and Thanatos.[7] Once the story has been told, all there remains for Nevers is the cantata of oblivion, where the subject — created by the act of her narration and exclusive possessor of the off-screen voice — expels the Nevers memory and exchanges it for views of modern Hiroshima. That is the ultimate goal of the transference. Such as it is generated by the prologue, the explosion at Hiroshima eludes both the subject and the object, both the word and direct figuration, only a trace remains. Projected on to the streets of Nevers, and linked to a narration which takes its place, the scar of Hiroshima enters in turn into the domain of oblivion whose exclusive memorableness the film guarantees. The process of obliteration is double-edged, and the itinerary which inscribes Hiroshima into a story remains reversible: although circumscribed, the fragmentation of the editing can always let filter through, under the known and named present, the resurgence of the unnamable that the writing has focused on the name Hiroshima, and where the film is dispersed. This, then, is the final paradox, whereby the writing completes its task of an ordering into signs or, in other words, its double task of signification and obliteration.

In asserting, at the end of the film, the substitution of names for persons and things, *Hiroshima mon amour* designates the progress of a modernity which refers History's transparence back to the opacity of signs which history both lays down and deciphers. There lies the ambiguity of the trace — indisputable but unclaimable: in order to read it, it must be written, and in order to write it, it must be modified. The strength of the film is in its ability to show how the endlessly open system, from one trace to another — in other words writing — can be transformed into a closed narrative, without the sign, now readable, ever completely obliterating the process of writing and its burden of unreadability. The name Nevers is transparent in French, that of Hiroshima simultaneously conveys the weight of a historicizable referent and the potential for linguistic and figurative dislocation which its hieroglyphic form symbolizes.[8] Impelled by this name, the editing of *Hiroshima mon amour* manages to make the 'Hiroshimanian' trace into a floating fragment, capable of furnishing material to historical signification and, too, to keep open, by the very language of the film, the gap between history and a trace which remains unassignable. The story-line may well change our vision, however. The film obliges us to acknowledge the mechanism of an exchange in which we participate. In making the spectators take on, within the filmic perception, the burden of the transference and the modulation of remembrance-oblivion,[9] *Hiroshima mon amour* demands that we realize, in every meaning of the word, the ambiguity of a historicization which the textual mediation renders necessarily indirect and thus uncertain. Unless it is inscribed in bodies, History leads to the museum; the trace is at once an aid to readability and a sign of the unfamiliar; and if the reading still remains to be done, the writing-reading reminds us, by its surplus and its overflowing, of the loss of substance that the acquisition of meaning costs.

It is no longer possible today to cheat with the implications of a mutation that was formerly glossed over by false debate. If an emerging generation recognized itself in *Hiroshima*, it is because the film proposed, and at the same time legitimated, on the aesthetic and political fronts, a 'dubious' representation not of morality — as Riva declares, who doubts of the morality of others — but most certainly of historicity. Despite the mnemonic kinship, *Hiroshima mon amour* does not remake *Nuit et brouillard*: the latter underscored the distance in time between the film's gaze and the reality of Auschwitz, but confirmed, in a few shots, the unmasking of an inescapable horror; the horror of Hiroshima is not eclipsed, but it becomes the object of a secret reflection upon the terms of both enunciation and expulsion of the historical event. Filmed during the Algerian war, *Hiroshima* cannot and will not refer to it: only *Muriel* speaks of it, but not until the Evian agreements have been signed and even then with an extreme form of distanciation which renders inaccessible, except in the shape of a verbal narration embedded into a fiction, the representation of acts of war. Coming between *Nuit et brouillard* and *Muriel, Hiroshima* marks the moment when, in the aesthetic world, that consciousness of an irreducible gap between facts and their formulation emerged. If, with the Resnais-Duras encounter, writing comes to the cinema, it is through the discovery that language is a screen: caught in the trap of having to testify, sight exhausts itself in the process of self-affirmation; to state the act of seeing is already to see no longer, and to condemn oneself to seeing again: the strategy of the film consists in playing this gap-screen dynamic by problematizing it within the apparatus of a divided fiction which both distances the event and gets closer to it in a most oblique but nonetheless critical manner. In order to integrate Hiroshima into our history, we must go through the betrayal of Nevers, the love affair of Nevers. Seeing *Hiroshima mon amour* again means taking on, simultaneously, the genesis and the rejection of all historical revisionism.

Translated from the French by Susan Hayward.

NOTES

1.   The fragmented nature of these explanatory passages is reinforced by a splintered style which seems contaminated by the editing of the film: an accumulation of brief notes, corrections, additions and shifts, as if the enunciator was grabbing at straws in the wind. Dismantled and repetitive, the explanation becomes hackneyed. The erosive effect is all the more active since a discursive subject ('I') often gets mixed up with the object of the commentary ('she', 'Riva'), thus rendering problematic the status of the narration. The future of another text slips into this memory of a film that is other.
2.   Marguerite Duras (1985) *La Douleur*, Paris, POL. The book contains, beyond the diary entitled *La douleur*, four unpublished 'stories', sometimes described as 'true', at others as 'invented'. The subject matter concerns the war period, but the writing, sometimes rewritten, escapes dating. There is also a re-edition of *Aurélia-Paris*.
3.   The case referred to is the Gregory affair. A small child was murdered and his mother was duly charged with his murder. Duras aserted her opinion that the mother was innocent (eds).
4.   Organized along the lines of the most classical model possible of the French cinema of the 1930s. The only clash is the image which acts as a background for the letters: a trace in the shape of an irregular scar, which the film will not pick up again, except once, in the prologue.
5.   And with 133 shots. According to the shooting script published in *Tu n'as rien vu à Hiroshima* (1962) the whole film, which lasts one and a half hours, is made up of 423 shots; this then represents a particularly fast montage for such a long opening sequence. In the rest of my analysis, I shall adopt the numbering used in this edition — the transcription is reasonably trustworthy.
6.   On this point, see Ropars-Wuilleumier (1983).
7.   As for Duras, she never ceases to return to this love of the dead which she will eventually name *La Maladie de la mort*. Resnais, for his part, will favour *L'Amour à mort,* surviving beyond death. Once again, this encounter causes two inverted paths to cross. The complexity of *Hiroshima* comes also from the multiplicity of divergences which feed the film.
8.   The insistence on the part of the dialogue to stress the insignificance of Nevers is a game of trompe-l'oeil: 'négation' (ne) and 'naissance' ('née'), 'novation' ('neuve') and 'errance' ('erre'), the name Nevers accumulates semantic indicators the most important of which is undoubtedly the designation of 'verre' (glass), which comes into play in a number of filmic forms all of which rely on the transparence of the material. The name Hiroshima,

also stressed by the dialogue, is the subject represented in hieroglyphics and duplicated in English words (see shot 91).

9. As privileged operators of this transaction, we retain the musical thematization: the musical themes are established as soon as the opening sequence, but their semantic identification is particularly random, because they will not become attached, during the rest of the film, to any particular figuration. When a theme returns, the spectators acknowledge having heard it, but do not recognize the musical image which they thought they had heard: the trace brings with it alteration, and memory gains access to oblivion. The so-called musical theme of oblivion is precisely the one of the credit titles and the closing shot.

SELECTED BIBLIOGRAPHY

Avant-Scène Cinéma (1966) 61-62, special issue on Resnais.
Armes, Roy (1968) *The Cinema of Alain Resnais*, London, Zwemmer.
Benayoun, Robert (1980) *Alain Resnais, arpenteur de l'imaginaire*, Paris, Stock.
Bounoure, Gaston (1962) *Alain Resnais*, re-edited in 1968 and 1974. French bibliography up-dated in 1968.
Cahiers du cinéma (1959) 97.
Cinéma 59 (1959) 35 and 38.
Colpi, Henri (1960) 'Musique Hiroshima', *Cahiers du cinéma*, 103.
Esprit (1960) special number on French Cinema, Paris, Seuil. See also their October 1959 issue which presents a debate on the film.
Etudes cinématographiques (1960) 3-4.
Image et Son (1959) 128, Fiche UFOLEIS.
Monaco, James (1978) *Alain Resnais, the Role of Imagination*, London, Secker & Warburg, New York, Oxford University Press.
Pingaud, Bernard (1959) in *Positif*, 31, Paris, Le Terrain vague.
Pingaud, Bernard (1960) in *Positif*, 35, Paris, Le Terrain vague.
Pingaud, Bernard (ed.) (1967) *Alain Resnais ou la création au cinéma*, in *L'Arc*, 31. Contains an excellent interview with Resnais.
Premier Plan (1959) 4, Lyon, Serdoc.
Premier Plan (1961) 18, Lyon, Serdoc. Contains French and overseas bibliography.
Ropars-Wuilleumier, Marie-Claire (1983) 'Le Film lecteur du texte', *Hors Cadre*, 1, Paris, P.U.V.
Ward, John (1968) *Alain Resnais or the Theme of Time*, London, Cinema One.

SCRIPTS

Duras, Marguerite (1960) *Hiroshima mon amour*, Paris, Gallimard.
Duras, Marguerite (1961) *Hiroshima mon amour*, New York, Grove Press.
Tu n'as rien vu à Hiroshima (1962) Séminaire du Film et du Cinéma, Institut de Sociologie de l'Université libre de Bruxelles. Photo-script of film.

APPENDIX

Alain Resnais (1922—): filmography

1948 *Van Gogh* (short)
1950 *Gauguin* (short)
1950 *Guernica* (short)
1955 *Nuit et brouillard* (short)
1956 *Toute la mémoire du monde* (short)
1957 *Le Mystère de l'atelier* (short)
1958 *Le Chant du styrène* (short)

1959 *Hiroshima mon amour*
1961 *L'Année dernière à Marienbad*
1963 *Muriel*
1966 *La Guerre est finie*
1967 *Loin du Vietnam* (sketch in this collective work)
1968 *Je t'aime, je t'aime*
1974 *Stavisky*
1976 *Providence*
1980 *Mon oncle d'Amérique*
1983 *La Vie est un roman*
1984 *L'Amour à mort*
1986 *Mélo*

Other films cited in the text

Dialogue de Rome, Marguerite Duras (1982)

14. The script of delinquency: François Truffaut's *Les 400 coups* (1959)

ANNE GILLAIN

Throughout his career, François Truffaut often expressed some degree of displeasure when critics labeled his work autobiographical. His ambivalence on this record is apparent as early as 1959 when his first film, *Les 400 coups*, was released to world-wide acclaim. His interviews at the time reveal two types of contradictory statements. He first adamantly claimed that nothing in the film was an exaggeration and that he had experienced as a child all the hardships endured by Antoine Doinel in the film. He also flatly denied that *Les 400 coups* was his biography (Truffaut 1959). For this there were of course reasons of a personal nature. The film was after all a violent indictment of his parents, particularly of his mother. Both were alive when the film came out and Truffaut had been trying to establish a normal relationship with them during his years as a film critic for *Cahiers du cinéma*. But, more importantly, this denial was prompted by reasons pertaining to aesthetics.

Autobiographies, even the least sophisticated, involve elements of stylization. By turning experience into language, autobiographical narration injects it with meaning. The need to understand oneself better, the desire to establish one's unique identity or the urge to interpret one's life — all these motives account for the autobiographical impulse. In order to treat the self as a narrative object, the author must select the facts that he or she recalls to reconstruct the unity of his or her life. The author must also impose an order on its individual events and bestow upon them narrative coherence, as well as achieve the creation of an imaginary self. These constraints explain Sartre's remark in *Les Mots* (Brooks 1984, 114) that autobiographical narration is obituary in its nature. Such narration entails the creation of a space between the narrating and the narrated selves in order to allow for the former to objectify and look back on the latter. In Truffaut's case this distancing is made particularly complex and fascinating by the fact that his autobiography is not enclosed within one given film but spread over 21 full-length features, each of them attacking the problems of genre, narrativity, authority and closure from a fresh perspective. While each picture is entirely self-contained, it can also be read as a piece of a puzzle to be inserted within the wider image formed by the whole body of his works. The open-ended nature of this process seems infinite and there is no doubt that, had he lived another 30 years, Truffaut could have extracted many more films from his life experience. In this creation *Les 400 coups* evidently occupies an exceptional place, not only because it is the most universally admired of his films but because it unleashes, in a literal way, Truffaut's imaginary world, with a passion, a vigor and a mastery which set the model for all his future works.

In his interviews Truffaut described *Les 400 coups* as the chronicle of the 13th year, the most difficult since it marks the passage from childhood to adolescence. Born in 1932, Truffaut reached that age in 1945 during the turmoil of the Liberation of Paris after four years of German occupation. In the picture, the time period is transposed to 1958 when the actual filming took place. This temporal distortion is counter-balanced by the documentary exactitude of the spatial background of the film. Most of the exterior shots were set in the exact neighborhood where Truffaut grew up, chiefly rue des Martyrs, a lively popular street that runs down from Montmartre towards the grands boulevards. The Doinels' cramped apartment was certainly reminiscent of Truffaut's modest lodging in rue Navarin. His young parents had met at the French Alpine Club and were both fervent mountaineers. They would often leave their son alone on weekends to go rock-climbing in the Fontainebleau forest. In the film, this sporting activity is replaced by the passion of Antoine's stepfather for automobile rallies. Truffaut's mother worked as a secretary for a magazine and does not seem to have ever displayed much interest in a child she had never wished to have. Neglected at home, the young Truffaut soon retaliated by skipping school and running away from home. Cinema and his friend Robert Lachenay (René in the film) were his only companions. From 1942 on, the situation progressively worsened until in 1947 Truffaut was arrested at his father's request, not for stealing a typewriter as in the film, but for running the cine-club he had created with stolen funds. After two nights in the central jail, the boy was sent to a center for delinquent minors at Villejuif which was part insane asylum, part *maison de correction* (reform school) (Walz 1982, 3). Truffaut's legendary friendship with André Bazin saved him from this tragic situation. The adolescent had met the film critic when he had opened his cine-club and had much impressed Bazin with his encyclopedic knowledge of films and his fervor for cinema. Bazin would rescue him a second time from jail in 1951, when Truffaut went AWOL after enlisting in the French army to fight in Indochina. Bazin and his wife sheltered the young man in their home, where he wrote his first articles as a journalist. By 1954 he had become the most famous film critic of his generation and by 1958 he had joined the ranks of the New Wave filmmakers. Sadly enough, Bazin died on the first day of shooting of *Les 400 coups*. Truffaut dedicated the film to his memory.

This brief outline confirms Truffaut's declaration that his first film reflects the bare facts of his own existence as a child. It also shows how close to destruction the experience of delinquency brought his life in his formative years. This experience has, in my opinion, been underplayed in the analysis of his work as a filmmaker. Incarcerated twice, Truffaut was to remain profoundly marked by a sense of exclusion from society, which accounts for his sympathy for outcasts. Most of his heroes will be misfits. My contention is that, not only *Les 400 coups*, but all of Truffaut's films offer a complex variation on the same hidden and repressed scenario of childhood, or what I will call 'the script of delinquency'. 'A man is formed between seven and sixteen', Truffaut once remarked, 'later he will relive all his life what he has acquired between these two ages' (Sand 1968, 13). This comment can be applied to the films, but to understand Truffaut's use of autobiography, one must discard the facile notion of a direct transposition from life to films. If the director's youth informs his stories, it is as an atemporal matrix structure which each film replays in a different vein, on a different tone. The constant quality of the script of delinquency relies on affects not on events. In this light, *Vivement dimanche* is as autobiographical as *Les 400 coups*. This script generates a phantasmatic matrix which gives form and content to the relations of desire played out in the films. In *Les 400 coups*, this script unravels for the first time the figural and narrative patterns for the films to come.

Essential to the script of delinquency is first a peculiar quality of space. Visually *Les 400 coups* is built on an elegant binary opposition which is maintained throughout the film. Inside, at home or at school, the narration is dominated by static shots and close-ups, while outside, long and mobile shots prevail. These alternations give the film its powerful rhythm of tension and release. A prisoner indoors, Antoine becomes in the streets a child free to roam, play and explore. The examples of this dual regime are numerous but one of its most effective uses occurs after Antoine's first attempt to run away from home, following his encounter with his mother and her lover in the street. When his mother has brought Antoine back to the apartment, she gives him a bath and undertakes to win back his affection, and probably to buy his silence, by reminiscing about her own youth. She also proposes a contract to him: if he writes a good essay, she will reward him with money. This tense exchange is filmed in a shot/reverse shot pattern, reflecting each character's guarded position. The next image abruptly presents an exterior scene where the gym teacher leads the column of schoolchildren through the streets. All of them will progressively scatter and disappear in the course of this exercise. First shot at eye level from a standard angle, this vignette suddenly switches to a bird-like point of view where the dynamics of the group appear to be watched by a distant and ironic observer. This striking visual effect, in sharp contrast with the preceding scene, injects this episode with mythic significance and makes it one of the most memorable moments of the film. A tribute to a similar scene in Vigo's *Zéro de conduite*, it captures the boundless energy of childhood and becomes an allegory of its dispersion within the currents of life. In the same vein, the credits of *L'Argent de poche* present a crowd of schoolchildren cascading down the narrow streets of a village as a free, joyful and irrepressible flow. In *Les 400 coups* this scene also programs Antoine's final escape from the columns of young delinquents in an attempt to assert his own separate and unique identity.

Another important characteristic of the street scenes lies in the scarcity of their information content. In fact, an episode such as the gym lesson could be placed anywhere in the narrative. It is not linked by any cause-effect relationship to what precedes or follows. It appears as a pure interlude when all the constraints of the plot are suspended. In the streets, Antoine benefits from an amnesty which relieves him from the steady flow of disaster besieging him at home or at school. An obvious example of this occurs when Antoine accidentally meets his mother and her lover. This momentous encounter will have surprisingly few effects on the plane of reality. The spatial alternations coincide in effect with a dual temporal regime: a cyclical time, built on the repetition of the same, and devoid of information, is opposed to a linear time that nourishes the plot with events and carries forward the story. These two temporalities are typical of Truffaut's films, where the narrative process often seems to be a struggle to delay the revelation of some dismal truth.

This spatial and temporal freeze/flow effect is reinforced by another set of oppositions in the film between the photographs and the rotor in the funfair. The image of the pin-up will start Antoine's ordeal, the picture of Balzac will set the house on fire and Antoine's face will be brutally entrapped in the mug shots at the police station. Photographs are always for Truffaut pieces of evidence, pointing to some inaccessible secret. They are the indicators of time marking the path towards death. The enigmatic value of the famous last shot of the film carries the weight of these associations. In contrast, the rotor, one of the most commented-upon figures in *Les 400 coups*, has long been associated with cinema by the critics. Its circular and playful space is also clearly a maternal one where the child curls back in a fetal position while time is suspended. Cinema as a place of affective compensation for parental neglect played such a role in Truffaut's own experience.

In order to understand fully the connection between these spatio-temporal structures and the script of delinquency, it is helpful to invoke D. W. Winnicott's theories on anti-social behaviors and, in particular, his concept of the transitional space. Briefly stated, the transitional space is the area which allows the child to approach external reality in the first years of his/her life and to adjust successfully to it. By creating a world subjected to the infant's desire, the mother gives him or her the necessary trust to discover the outer reality and to explore its boundaries: 'The mother's adaptation to the infant's needs, when good enough, gives the child the illusion that there is an external reality that corresponds to the infant's own capacity to create' (Winnicott 1975, 22). His or her first creation will be what Winnicott calls the transitional object, a favorite toy which embodies all the positive values of the transitional space and allows him or her to tolerate the threat of separation. The paradox of this object is that in order to be *created*, it has first to be *found* in the external world. It is both a subjective and objective phenomenon and bridges the gap between outer and inner reality. Later on, the transitional space will become the area for playing and creativity, and the transitional object will be replaced by cultural experiences. But if the child is deprived for too long of maternal care in his or her youth, he or she will lose his or her ability to relate to the external world and suffer what Winnicott calls an 'unspeakable agony'. A sense of danger will replace trust. The transitional space will fill with persecutive elements and change into a carceral space. Delinquency is one of the less damaging outcomes to this predicament, which

Les 400 coups — above left: Antoine Doinel (Jean-Pierre Léaud) at his mother's dressing table; above right: Mme Doinel (Claire Maurier), M. Doinel (Albert Rémy) and Antoine in their car; below left: Mme Doinel, M. Doinel and Antoine; below right: Antoine stealing a bottle of milk.

can also lead to autism — as *L'Enfant sauvage* shows. *Les 400 coups*, like most of Truffaut's films, focuses on this critical situation and presents the hero's attempts to recapture, after the breakdown of his environment, the transitional space of communication, creativity and shared experience. An analysis of the first two sequences of *Les 400 coups* will demonstrate how Winnicott's views help to enlighten the interconnection of the themes developed in the narrative.

By setting his opening scene in a classroom, Truffaut immediately denounces the failure of an institution designed to facilitate the child's adaptation to social reality. He also makes clear that Antoine is an exceptionally creative youth. The fatal pin-up picture will quietly circulate among his schoolmates until he decides to draw a moustache on it. Punished and isolated in a corner, which is the first representation of a carceral space, he will not remain passive but will compose a poem on the wall. In the decline and fall of Antoine throughout the film, writing evidently plays the role of the original sin. Whenever writing is involved, disaster will strike. In this vein, the absurd choice made by Antoine to steal a typewriter makes perfect sense. There is no point insisting on the overwhelming importance of language in Truffaut's films. Within the sphere of the transitional activities, verbal expression is one of the most effective ways to reach and master the external world or, to use Lacanian terminology, language represents the passage from the Imaginary to the Symbolic, from past to present, from a dual relationship dominated by the mother, to a reality mediated by the paternal law. In *Les 400 coups*, this primordial activity is shown from the start to be hopelessly hampered.

While Antoine is writing his fateful poem, two inserts show the other children playing in the schoolyard. This filmic construction points to the similarities between these two forms of expression. If writing is doomed to failure throughout the film, playing will assert in contrast the indomitable spirit of childhood. Antoine will share many games with René and will even play at the *centre d'observation* (the center for delinquent minors). The redeeming nature of this activity is made particularly clear by one scene. When Antoine spends his first night at the police station, a long silent sequence reveals the nocturnal routine in this carceral space. Two pan shots (the second of which is filmed from Antoine's point of view) show a couple of policemen absorbed in a silly child's game played with plastic horses and dice.[1] This sequence, which constitutes the most desolate episode of Antoine's exclusion from society, is much lightened by the insertion of these images where a transitional activity injects a note of hope within the carceral space.

Antoine's resilience in the face of adversity is made obvious by a third activity: stealing. It is first mentioned when René and Antoine leave school in the first scene and ask the sinister Mauricet where he stole the money to buy the goggles he is proudly wearing. Stealing is, in *Les 400 coups*, as in most of Truffaut's films, indeed a pervasive habit. Antoine and René will devote to it most of their energies, and both their mothers will prove adept in this art. A thug in the streets, a child in the school corridors, will also try their hand at it.

In his study of anti social behaviors, Winnicott (1957, 159-73; 1971, 279-304; 1975, 119) characterizes stealing as a gesture of hope on the part of a child who feels he or she has been deprived of the care and love to which he or she was inalienably entitled. The young robber is not looking for objects but trying to re-establish contact with a maternal figure who failed to recognize his or her needs. In this sense, stealing and delinquency represent positive behaviors endowed with healing powers. Instead of renunciation, the youth demands reparation. Stealing constitutes an attempt to avoid withdrawal from reality and to recapture the transitional space. An elliptic and beautiful scene illustrates this process in the film, when Antoine and René make the momentous decision to steal the typewriter during a puppet show in the Luxembourg gardens. This conversation is framed by numerous shots of young children enthralled by the spectacle. This odd association suggests an analogy between both activities. Stealing, in this context, appears as a desire to claim back, in a forceful and destructive way, the passionate involvement with reality generated by transitional experiences. Finally, it is characteristic that, in the film, the only person to be robbed is Antoine's stepfather who keeps lamenting the loss of his Michelin Guide. This points to the obvious failure of his authority and of the law he should represent.

After this magisterial opening where all the symptoms of Antoine's inner conflicts are revealed, the second sequence will unveil the source of his discontent. The first three actions he performs in the Doinels' deserted apartment are gestures of anger and destruction: opening the stove, he lets high flames surge in the room; wiping his dirty hands on the curtains he soils them, a tribute to Renoir's *Boudu sauvé des eaux*, and he then proceeds to steal some money.

In contrast with this display of violence, the bedroom scene that follows expresses an elegiac nostalgia for an absent mother. Antoine smells her perfumes and toys with the strange contraptions designed to enhance her beauty. Three mirrors capture his lonely figure and reflect the painful fragmentation of his self in search of an identity. Commenting on Lacan's 'stade du miroir', Winnicott (1975, 153) simply observes that 'the precursor of the mirror is the mother's face'. The child staring at his image tries to catch back in his reflection his mother's glance. Antoine is a youth who longs to be seen, to be acknowledged and, within the visual dynamics of the narrative, looks will play an essential role. They will always, however, be hostile and bring him reprimands, slaps, denunciations. Antoine will only manage to attract the icy stare of the law. When Madame Doinel arrives home, she will not even glance at her son but will display, with a stark contempt for his young sexual awareness, her silky legs. This shot is seminal in Truffaut's films, and legs will remain for ever linked to maternal exhibitionism and sexual appeal. In *Baisers volés*, the 'magic' Fabienne Tabard will first meet Antoine when she is trying on a pair of shoes. In *L'Argent de poche*, Madame Riffle will be painting her toes when an enamoured Patrick brings her red roses. The examples are too numerous to all be reviewed. These legs frighten the child as much as they seduce him. Directing his glance towards the 'mystery' of female sexuality, they generate anxieties which account for the systematic fragmentation of the woman's image in Truffaut's films. *L'Homme qui aimait les femmes* presents a deep and lucid account of the pathological structures which develop from this early fixation on the maternal body. In this film, an eloquent scene shows the young hero, Bertrand Morane, reading a book while his mother walks around in an elegant négligé indifferently exhibiting her legs. The unmediated fixation of the adolescent's desire on her body will result in his future inability to resolve his Oedipal crisis. In his adult life, women's legs and books (both strongly connected in his early experience with the maternal body) will function as fetishes allowing him to maintain a regressive and painful situation of pre-Oedipal fulfilment.[2] The position of a maternal figure is central to the script of delinquency, and each film will offer a solution to the conflict-relationship between mother and son.

Madame Doinel is, throughout the narrative, the principal generator of textual energies. Whether he sees her with her lover, declares her dead, or sets the house on fire, Antoine's actions are always determined by his Oedipal pulsions towards her. It is important that his most significant attempt at creativity is directly linked to maternal attention. As mentioned earlier, after his first flight from home, Madame Doinel proposes a contract to her son. This scene is followed by an evening at the movies which represents the only joyful evocation of family life in the film. But Antoine fails to fulfil his part of the contract by involuntarily plagiarizing a text by Balzac. The narrative makes plain that Balzac is in fact a transitional object for the young hero (Antoine organizes a sort of cult around the novelist's image) and his problem arises from a confusion between finding and creating, outer and inner worlds. Misunderstood in his attempt to reach external reality, he will end up a delinquent.

But *Les 400 coups* would not have retained its relevance over the years if it were simply a story of deviance and despair. It is essential to see that behind the realistic plot linked to linear time, lies a second scenario. The script of delinquency involves a powerful phantasmatic component which, in all the films, relies chiefly on what the psychoanalysts Laplanche and Pontalis have defined as 'primal phantasies', i.e. on phantasies which are inherent in the development and maturation of any human being. In *Les 400 coups*, the underlying plot expresses a passionate desire for fusion with a maternal figure. This desire is not presented as real, for Madame Doinel will never fulfil it, but as the expression of a haunting nostalgia.

Nostalgia runs high in Truffaut's films and always represents the precarious hold an individual can have on the inner representation of a lost object. Nostalgia points to an archaic past, and Antoine, like many of Truffaut's heroes, seeks the realization of his desires in the reproduction of indestructible signs of infantile satisfaction. The yearning to fuse with a maternal figure is expressed by images of a mythic nature for the first time in the introduction and then again in the conclusion of the film. The credits unroll

on shots evoking an impatient attempt by the camera to be reunited with the
Eiffel Tower. Similarly at the end the child will be followed by a long tracking
shot until he reaches the exact point where the waves touch the sand. Freud is
barely needed here to validate connotations of birth. Poets have said long
before him that the shore is the mother's body where the child is born: 'On the
seashore of endless worlds, children play.'[3] Truffaut freezes this last image,
blending the evocation of birth with a threat of death. This brilliant synthesis is
typical of the ambivalence of his imaginary world. But within the film itself,
the wish for fusion is expressed by Antoine's love affair with Paris. The city is
a maternal space which shelters the child, protects his games, hides and feeds
him. The moving episode of the night in Paris shows Antoine stealing a milk
bottle and stealthily drinking it in the deserted streets. The only time he
displays grief and cries is when he is separated from this symbolic maternal
body.

At the center for delinquent minors, a powerful scene will actualize these
nostalgic images of reunion with a maternal figure when Antoine, facing the
camera, engages in a free and lively conversation with the psychologist. In this
scene, it is essential to note, first, that the psychologist is a woman, and second,
that this woman is represented as a disembodied voice.[4] As a woman, the
psychologist clearly evokes a positive maternal figure (contrary to Madame
Doinel, a sexual taboo is cast on to her body: another young delinquent warns
Antoine not to look at her legs), and Antoine trustfully converses with her. He
looks relaxed, playful and happy. This exchange where the child is allowed for
the first time to formulate a lucid account of his problems, attests to his inner
resilience and to his capacity for analysing his predicament. In this scene, a
successful communication is established with a maternal substitute. However,
the absence of the psychologist from the filmic space and her representation as
a disembodied voice points to the limits of this communication. The maternal
body for which Antoine yearns, which both fascinates and frightens him,
remains absent and seemingly inaccessible. Antoine is in fact addressing the
spectator through the indirect mediation of the filmic apparatus. Cinema, as
the ultimate representation of transitional activities in Truffaut's own personal
development, will compensate for parental neglect and allow for an approach
of external reality.

In contrast to these evocations of the child's yearning for a reunion with a
maternal figure, the film also imposes on the viewer a complementary
phantasmatic reading focusing on Antoine's profound ambivalence towards his
actual mother. Truffaut achieves this effect by cultivating an elliptic and
disconnected mode of narration. Certain scenes, as it was observed earlier,
seem not to bear any relationship to the main plot and to slow down the story.
A close analysis reveals, however, that they are designed to feed the
phantasmatic vein and that they form a closely knitted network within the
narrative. Two examples of these subterranean signifying chains will
demonstrate their common concern with a definition of Madame Doinel.

In the first scene at school, an ironic vignette shows a little boy struggling to copy down a poem. He will end up lost in an ocean of ink and crumpled paper. This episode metonymically refers to Antoine's own difficulties with writing. But it also metaphorically introduces in the film the important theme of trash, dirt and mess. Antoine soils the curtains and seems for ever unable to wash. He is also officially in charge of the garbage at home. A scene describes his trip down the stairway and his disgusted handling of a pestilential looking trashcan. Stairs, a prevalent figure in Truffaut's work, are often associated with women's legs. Monsieur Doinel will invite his son to admire his mother's legs when they climb the stairway after the movies. Interestingly enough, Truffaut cut a scene from the US commercial version of the film (it is present in the UK version) which casts some light on these associations. Situated in the second sequence of the film, it shows Antoine arriving at a store to buy flour for his mother. There, he is seen overhearing a conversation which centers around the description of a difficult and bloody birth and ultimate hysterectomy. He almost vomits. Truffaut may have removed this scene because it pointed too clearly to the phantasmatic content of the film. To be effective, the content of the phantasy must remain latent and not trigger on the spectator's part a possible reaction of censorship. In this process of indirect revelation, repetition under the form of displacement and condensation represents a major operative factor. The repetitive network linking trash, women's legs and stairways discloses the deep anxiety the feminine body inspires in Antoine. This body constitutes for him a frightening mystery generating visions of chaos, dirt and blood.

Melanie Klein (1980, 279-83) in her analysis of epistemological disorder in adolescents observes that learning disabilities spring from an inability on the child's part to form an image of the interior of the woman's body and in particular to understand its special functions such as conception, pregnancy and birth. In the film, the associative network we have examined evokes these sexual fears and their consequences, but in an indirect way, through a system of displacement and condensation which does not threaten the spectator's psychic apparatus with crude images of violence. During his night in Paris, Antoine will throw the milk bottle into a sewer. A similar scene will be found both in *L'Argent de poche* and in *L'Homme qui aimait les femmes*. This odd gesture points to an attempt to probe the bowels of the city. In *Baisers volés*, the famous episode describing the trajectory of a letter through the *pneumatiques*, an underground mail system (now discontinued), displays the same curiosity and concern. There again, we find metaphoric expressions of the constant fascination with the mother's body which all of Truffaut's films reflect. Spatial representations in his work often reproduce an intricate maze of corridors, stairways, trapdoors and caves. All of these allude to the labyrinth the female body constitutes for the child's imagination. *Le Dernier métro* is, in this respect, exemplary.

The second example involves one of the most enigmatic scenes in the film. Set at the center for delinquent minors, it presents three little girls being locked up in a cage. To account for this fragment, two complementary scenes must be invoked. In the first one, Madame Doinel comes back home late one night. The noise of the car that brings her back wakes up Antoine in his bed. His stepfather will angrily accuse his wife of sleeping with her boss. At the police station, Antoine will also be awakened by a car. This time, it is a van bringing in three prostitutes to be locked up behind bars. In an interview (Gillain 1981, 33), Truffaut declared that, in this segment, he had deliberately adopted the style of a fairy tale, the three prostitutes speaking in turn as do fairies in children's stories. The three little girls in their cage are obvious references to them. Antoine's ambivalence towards his mother is all inscribed within this signifying chain. The noise of the engine suggests that she is a whore; the three prostitutes say that she is a fairy; the shot of the little girls adds that she is, like her son, an imprisoned child who longs to roam the streets of Paris with her lover.

The script of delinquency is a useful model to account for the common features all of Truffaut's films share. Applied to *Les 400 coups*, it serves to illuminate the deep and complex work of stylization to which the director subjected his life experience. Among his films, it is certainly the most directly autobiographical. Its beauty, however, springs from Truffaut's ability to create a system of representation which transmutes the private data of an individual destiny into a universal language. Truffaut's goal was never to reveal anything about his own life but rather to make his life narratable by structuring his personal memories into a construction of mythic significance.

NOTES

1. In several other films by Truffaut, we see grown men engaged in professional activities which resemble children's games. For instance, in *Domicile conjugal* or *L'Homme qui aimait les femmes*, Antoine Doinel and Bertrand Morane work with miniature boats. This obsession with toys and regressive behaviors points, in a humorous vein, to Truffaut's male characters' inability to adjust to social (and sexual) maturity. The only adult activity available to them will be creative expression: both Antoine and Bertrand write a novel. This makes evident once more the link between transitional activities and artistic realizations.

2. For a more extensive discussion of transitional phenomena and fetishism in Truffaut's films, see Gillain 1985, 114.

3. R. Tagore quoted by Winnicott 1975, 132.

4. It is worth mentioning that for this role, Truffaut (Wilderstein 1959) had chosen a young actress, Annette Wademant, who happened to be absent from Paris when the scene was filmed. Truffaut decided to take the shots with Jean-Pierre Léaud and intended to add at a later time the reverse shots with the psychologist. Jean-Pierre Léaud was given only a few vague indications as to what the questions would be and invited to improvise the answers. There was no written script. The result of the rushes was so striking that Truffaut and his operator, Henri Decae, gave up the project of filming the reverse shots with Annette Wademant and simply added her voice to the images.

SELECTED BIBLIOGRAPHY

Allen, Don (1974) *Truffaut*, New York, Viking.
Allen, Don (1985) *Finally Truffaut*, revised and updated edition of *Truffaut*, London, Secker

and Warburg.

Baby, Yvonne (1959) 'Les Quatre Cents Coups: Une chronique de l'adolescence nous dit François Truffaut ' (interview), *Le Monde*, 21 April, 12.

Billard, Pierre (1959) '*Les 400 coups* du père François' (interview), *Cinéma 59*, 37, 136-137.

Bonnafons, Elizabeth (1981) *François Truffaut*, Lausanne, l'Age d'Homme.

Brooks, Peter (1984) *Reading for the Plot*, New York, Vintage.

Capdenac, Michel (1967) 'Tour d'horizon avec François Truffaut: Des *400 coups* à *La Mariée était en noir*', *Les Lettres françaises*, 1179, 18.

Collet, Jean (1977) *Le Cinéma de François Truffaut*, Paris, Lherminier.

Collet, Jean (1985) *François Truffaut*, Paris, Lherminier.

Crisp, V.G. (1972) *François Truffaut*, New York, Praeger, London, November Books.

Crowther, B. (1977) '*The 400 Blows*', in *Vintage Films*, New York, G. P. Putnam's Sons, 175-178.

Dalmais, H. (1987) *Truffaut*, Paris, Rivages/Cinéma.

Desjardins, Aline (1973) *Aline Desjardins s'entretient avec François Truffaut*, Ottawa, Leméac.

Doniol-Valcroze, Jacques (1959) '*Les 400 coups*', *Cahiers du cinéma* 16, 96.

Dupont, C. (1974) 'François Truffaut et l'enfance' (interview), *Ciné jeunes*, 78, 1-7.

Durgnat, Raymond (1963) *Nouvelle Vague: The First Decade*, Loughton, Essex, Motion Publications.

Fanne, D. (1972) *L'Univers de François Truffaut*, Paris, Editions du Cerf.

Fieschi, Jacques (1975) 'L'Enfance', *Cinématographe*, 15, 10-13.

Gillain, Anne (1981) 'Reconciling Irreconcilables: An Interview with François Truffaut', *Wide Angle*, 4 (4).

Gillain, Anne (1985) 'The Little Robber Boy as Master Narrator', *Wide Angle*, 7 (1 and 2).

Insdorf, Annette (1978) *François Truffaut*, Boston, Twayne, G.K. Hall.

Kinder, M. and Houston, B. (1972) 'François Truffaut', in *Close up: A Critical Perspective on Film*, New York, Harcourt Brace Jovanovich, 183-197.

Klein, Melanie (1980) *Essais de psychanalyse*, Paris, Payot.

Lopez, A. (1985) 'An Elegant Spiral: Truffaut's *The 400 Blows*', *Wide Angle*, 7 (1 and 2).

Maillet, D. (1984) 'François Truffaut' (interview), *Cinématographe*, 105.

Maraval, P. (1975) 'Antoine Doinel', *Cinématographe*, 15, 14-17.

Mardore, Michel (1962) 'Les Aveux de Jekyll Truffaut' (interview), *Les Lettres françaises*, 911, 25-31.

Monaco, James (1976) 'Truffaut', in *The New Wave*, Oxford and New York, Oxford University Press, 13-97.

Murray, E. (1978) '*The 400 Blows* 1959', in *Ten Film Classics*, New York, Frederick Ungar, 121-133.

Nelson, J.R. (1985) 'The Rotor: Elements of Paradigmatic Structure in Truffaut's *The 400 Blows*', *Wide Angle*, 7 (1 and 2), 137-143.

Parinaud, A. (1959) 'Truffaut: Le Jeune cinéma n'existe pas' (interview), *Arts*, 1, 9.

Petrie, Graham (1970) *The Cinema of François Truffaut*, New York, Barnes, London, A. Zwemmer.

Prédal, René (1976) 'Images de l'adolescent dans le cinéma français', *Cinéma 76*, 214, 19-28.

Rabourdin, D. (1985) *Truffaut par Truffaut*, Paris, Editions du Chêne.

Rhode, Eric (1961) '*The 400 Blows*', *Sight and Sound* 29 (2), 89-90.

Sadoul, Georges (1959) 'Je crois à l'improvisation' (interview), *Les Lettres françaises*, 775, 1, 6.

Salachas, G. (1959) '*Les 400 coups*', *Télé-Ciné*, 83, 1-11.

Sand, L. (1968) (interview), *Jeune cinéma*, 31, 10-15.

Thiher, Allen (1979) *The Cinematic Muse: Critical Studies in the History of French Cinema*, Columbia, University of Missouri Press, 143-164.

Truffaut, François (1959) 'Je n'ai pas écrit ma biographie en *400 coups*', *Arts*, 715, 1-5.

Walz, E.P. (1982) *François Truffaut: A Guide to References and Resources*, Boston, G. K. Hall.

Wilderstein, P. (1959) 'Conversation avec François Truffaut' (interview), *Télé-Ciné*, 83, 2-8.
Winnicott, D.W. (1957) *L'Enfant et le monde extérieur*, Paris, Payot.
Winnicott, D.W. (1971) *La Consultation thérapeutique et l'enfant*, Paris, Gallimard.
Winnicott, D.W. (1975) *Jeu et réalité*, Paris, Gallimard.

SCRIPTS

Moussy, M. and Truffaut, F. (1959) *Les 400 coups, récit d'après le film de François Truffaut*, Paris, Gallimard.
Truffaut, F. (1969) *The 400 Blows*, in Denby, D. (ed.), trans. D. Denby, New York, Grove Press.
Truffaut, F. (1971) *The Adventures of Antoine Doinel: Four Autobiographical Screenplays*, trans. H. G. Scott, New York, Simon and Schuster.

APPENDIX

François Truffaut (1932—1984): filmography

1954 *Une Visite* (short)
1957 *Les Mistons* (short)
1958 *Histoire d'eau* (short)
1959 *Les 400 coups (The 400 Blows)*
1960 *Tirez sur le pianiste (Shoot the Pianist)*
1961 *Jules et Jim (Jules and Jim)*
1962 *Antoine et Colette (sketch in L'Amour à vingt ans)*
1964 *La Peau douce (Silken Skin)*
1966 *Farenheit 451*
1967 *La Mariée était en noir (The Bride Wore Black)*
1968 *Baisers volés (Stolen Kisses)*
1969 *La Sirène du Mississipi.*
1970 *Domicile conjugale (Bed and Board)*
1970 *L'Enfant sauvage (The Wild Child)*
1971 *Les Deux Anglaises et le continent*
1972 *Une Belle fille comme moi*
1973 *La Nuit américaine (Day for Night)*
1975 *L'Histoire d'Adèle H.*
1976 *L'Argent de poche (Small Change)*
1977 *L'Homme qui aimait les femmes (The Man who Loved Women)*
1978 *La Chambre verte (The Green Room)*
1978 *L'Amour en fuite (Love on the Run)*
1980 *Le Dernier métro (The Last Métro)*
1981 *La Femme d'à côté*
1983 *Vivement dimanche (Finally Sunday! [UK]; Confidentially Yours [USA])*

Other films cited in the text

Boudu sauvé des eaux (Boudu Saved from Drowning), Jean Renoir (1932)
Zéro de conduite (Zero for conduct), Jean Vigo (1933)

15. 'It really makes you sick!': Jean-Luc Godard's *A bout de souffle* (1959)

MICHEL MARIE

Jean Luc Godard shot *A bout de souffle* (*Breathless*) in four weeks, from 17 August to 15 September 1959, on location in Marseilles and on the 'Nationale 7' highway, but principally in various parts of Paris. His modest budget was only 40 million francs at 1959 value (50 million according to *Le Film français*), half the average budget for the period (Godard 1980, 26).

By 1959, Godard had made five shorts, the first in 1954, *Opération béton*, which he produced himself, the second in 1955 in 16mm, *Une Femme coquette*. Pierre Braunberger produced the three 35mm shorts he made for Pléiade films: *Tous les garçons s'appellent Patrick*, *Charlotte et son Jules*, and *Une Histoire d'eau*. But by August 1959, Godard had become one of the last of the *Cahiers du cinéma* critics to embark on a feature-length film. Shortly before, Rohmer had begun shooting *Le Signe du lion* (July-August 1959), produced by Claude Chabrol for AJYM Films. As for Chabrol himself, he had just made his third feature, *A double tour*, which was to be released on 4 December 1959. In it, Jean-Paul Belmondo plays a friend of the son of the family, a young sponger called Lazlo Kovacs. *Le Beau Serge* and *Les Cousins* had come out on release in February and March 1959. *Les 400 coups*, François Truffaut's first feature, which had been selected for the Cannes Festival where it was awarded the prize for *mise-en-scène*, came out on 3 June 1959, followed by *Hiroshima mon amour* by Alain Resnais on 10 June. And Jacques Rivette had begun filming *Paris nous appartient* in 1958, to be finished in 1961. Godard knew that Sergei Eisenstein and Orson Welles had made their first films at the age of 26; he had just turned 29 and desperately needed to get into the swim and, like his hero Michel Poiccard at the beginning of the film, forge ahead: 'After all, I'm an idiot. After all, yes, I must. I must!' This convergence between the director's position and that of the central character was to be a determining factor in the film's rhythm. It was absolutely essential that this first attempt should prove to be the work of a master. 'Afterwards I felt nothing but terror, the terror of not being able to make another film, like not being able to get food' (Godard 1985, 16). Truffaut wrote later, 'While he was making *A bout de souffle*, Godard didn't have enough money in his pocket to buy a metro ticket, he was as destitute as the character he was filming — more so, really' (Godard 1985, 28).

A bout de souffle was produced by Georges de Beauregard. Born in 1920 in Marseilles, he was not yet 40 and already had five features to his credit. A former journalist, Beauregard specialized in the overseas distribution of French films, especially in Spain, which had led him to produce two of Juan-Antonio Bardem's best-known features, *Muerte de un Ciclista* and *Calle*

Mayor. He then produced *La Passe du diable*, co-directed by Jacques Dupont and Pierre Schoendoerffer, then two Pierre Loti adaptations directed by Schoendoerffer (*Ramuntcho* and *Pêcheurs d'Islande*). At this juncture, Godard was editing documentaries for Pierre Braunberger and travel films for the publisher Arthaud, and he also wrote dialogues for Edouard Molinaro and Jean-Pierre Mocky, for two films that were never made. In 1958 he worked on the dialogue for *Pêcheurs d'Islande* and was present at the beginning of the shooting. His experience in editing and dialogue was to be decisive for *A bout de souffle*. Pierre Schoendoerffer had been a cameraman in the armed forces film unit, then a war correspondent in Indochina. Schoendoerffer's cameraman on his three features had also himself been a cameraman for the armed forces in Indochina, then a great reporter, and Beauregard insisted that Godard should use him for his film: it was of course Raoul Coutard.

The script for *A bout de souffle* was written by François Truffaut:

> [...] a month after the premiere of *Les 400 coups*, he asked me to lend him the scenario of *A bout de souffle* so he could give it to Beauregard to read. It was a story I had written several years earlier. I had been following an incident that took place over one weekend and made a deep impression on me. (Truffaut, in Collet 1963, 171)

Beauregard had turned down an earlier proposal from Godard: *Une Femme est une femme*; although, in fact, Godard had published the original script of this film in August 1959 in *Cahiers du cinéma* (98), a few weeks before making *A bout de souffle*. And that same year Philippe de Broca made *Les Jeux de l'amour* based on a script developed by Godard (from an idea by Geneviève Cluny). *A bout de souffle*, as directed by Godard, is reasonably faithful to the way the narrative develops in the script by Truffaut (Truffaut, in Godard 1968, 47-49). The opening quotation from Stendhal, 'We are going to speak of dreadful things' is replaced by a dedication to Monogram Pictures, a small American company specializing in low budget Westerns and horror films, and crime series like *Gun Crazy*. Truffaut's Stendhalian 'Lucien' was rechristened Michel, the name of the friend at the Inter-Americana Agency in Truffaut's version, who was renamed Tolmatchoff in the film. But most significantly, Godard took complete responsibility for the dialogue and reworked many details of the script. The most fundamental change was the development of the very long sequence in the hotel room (more than 25 minutes) which was only ten lines in Truffaut's script; similarly, the second long sequence in the Swedish woman's flat was scarcely hinted at in the original text. The last change was the ending, which was much less tragic in Truffaut's version where Lucien was allowed to escape, calling Patricia names:

> Lucien is furious. But he has to get away. He starts up the car

which Berruti has driven over in. From the car-door, he hurls insults at Patricia. The last shot shows Patricia watching him drive off, not understanding a word because her French is still not good enough. (Truffaut, in Godard 1968, 49)

According to Truffaut,

Jean-Luc chose a violent end because he was by nature sadder than I. He was in the depths of despair when he made that film. He needed to film death, and he had need of that particular ending. I asked him to cut only one phrase which was absolutely horrible. At the end, when the police are shooting at him one of them said to his companion: "Quick, in the spine!" I told him, "You can't leave that in." I was very vehement about it. He deleted the phrase. (in Collet 1963, 174)

Michel Poiccard is played by Jean-Paul Belmondo. In 1959 the actor was twenty-six. From 1953 to 1956 he had been a student at the Conservatoire d'Art Dramatique in Paris. He then joined a little theatre company with Annie Girardot and Michel Galabru. In 1955 he had a part in a film about *Molière* (by Norbert Tildian) and began to appear in comedies: *Sois belle et tais-toi, A pied, à cheval et en voiture*. He made an impression as one of the gang in *Les Tricheurs*, but Laurent Terzieff was the star of the film. In a review of *Un Drôle de dimanche*, Godard was highly critical of both screenplay and actors:

The script is lamentable, so are the actors. [...] but you can't save much of a Serge de Boissac script with Bourvil, nor Jean Marsan dialogue with Cathia Caro. With Jean-Paul Belmondo you just might, since he is the Michel Simon and Jules Berry of tomorrow; even so this brilliant actor would have to be used differently and elsewhere. (Godard, in Milne 1972, 99)

This is what Godard did himself by giving the actor the central role in his short film *Charlotte et son Jules*, dubbing it with his own voice:

For Jean-Luc's friends, there is something particularly precious in this film, in that Belmondo, who was doing his military service, was dubbed in by Jean-Luc. Jean-Luc's intonations make this little film more moving, less relaxed than it would have been had Belmondo dubbed himself. (Truffaut, in Collet 1963, 170)

The theme of this little sketch is well-known. Charlotte returns briefly to the home of her old boyfriend (her 'Jules'), who proceeds to bombard her with words, in turn scornful, moralizing, protective, loving, begging, not allowing Charlotte to open her mouth, until the final moment when she confesses that she has come back to fetch her toothbrush. This film, dedicated to Jean Cocteau, and a real homage to the filmmaker Guitry, prefigures in more than one way the manner in which words function in *A bout de souffle*, especially Michel and Patricia's two long parallel monologues; and it was fortunate that Godard was able to use Belmondo again for his first feature rather than Jean-Claude Brialy, the eponymous hero of *Tous les garçons s'appellent Patrick*, who was considered briefly for the role of Poiccard (Salachas 1960, 8).

Jean Seberg, twice Otto Preminger's leading lady, in *Saint-Joan* and *Bonjour tristesse*, was the only possible choice for Patricia. Godard declared on many an occasion,

> For some shots I referred to scenes I remembered from Preminger, Cukor, etc. And the character played by Jean Seberg was a continuation of her role in *Bonjour tristesse*. I could have taken the last shot of Preminger's film and started after dissolving to a title, "Three Years Later". (Godard, in Milne 1972, 173)

There is a certain physical resemblance between Jean Seberg and Anne Colette, the heroine of Godard's two previous shorts who was dressed like Patricia in a T-shirt with horizontal stripes, and had ultra-short blonde hair and a rounded figure. In a letter to Pierre Braunberger written during the shooting of *A bout de souffle*, Godard wrote,

> I would like to be the only person to like this film, I'd like everyone [except Melville and Anne Colette] to detest it. [...] Even the film stock, you'll see, will be breathless. Seberg is panicking and wishes she hadn't agreed to do the film. I start shooting with her tomorrow. I'll say goodbye because I must work out what to film tomorrow. (in Braunberger 1987, 184)

The atmosphere of the shooting was fairly tense. Seberg was at her wits' end and Jean-Paul Belmondo felt as if he was working on an amateur silent film. The technical crew were not very enthusiastic either.

> At the rushes, the entire crew, including the cameraman, thought the photography was revolting. Personally I like it. What's important is not that things should be filmed in any particular way, but simply that they should be filmed and be

A bout de souffle — above: Michel Poiccard (Jean-Paul Belmondo); below: Michel and Patricia (Jean Seberg).

properly in focus. My main job is keeping the crew away from where we're shooting. [...] On Wednesday we shot a scene in full sunlight using Geva 36 film stock. They all think it stinks. My view is that it's fairly amazing. It's the first time that the maximum has been expected from film stock by making it do something it was never intended for. It's as if it was suffering from being pushed to the limit of its possibilities. (in Braunberger 1987, 183-184)

Raoul Coutard has given a lengthy explanation of Godard's technical requirements involving the use of Ilford H.P.S. film stock which he usually used for photographic journalism in natural light (Coutard quoted by Courtade 1978, 277). Godard refused artificial light; he also refused the machinery of the studio. 'If we used a hand-held camera, it was simply for speed. I couldn't afford to use the usual equipment, which would have added three weeks to the schedule' (Godard, in Milne 1972, 173). But why all these technical innovations, why this intransigence towards the dominant practices of French cinema in 1959, to the point of using a type of film stock hitherto used only in photography and which had to be spliced end to end in rolls of 17.5 metres? It was because Godard, filming after Chabrol, Truffaut and Resnais, wanted to make *A bout de souffle* the standard-bearer of a new aesthetics, that of the French New Wave of 1959. His film was to explore a hitherto unknown continent in the aesthetics of cinema, smash the boundaries of the conventionally 'filmable' and start again from scratch:

A bout de souffle was the sort of film where anything goes: that was what it was all about. Anything people did could be integrated in the film. As a matter of fact, this was my starting-point. I said to myself: we have already had Bresson, we have just had *Hiroshima*, a certain kind of cinema has just drawn to a close, maybe ended, so let's add the finishing touch, let's show that anything goes. What I wanted was to take a conventional story and remake, but differently, everything the cinema had done. I also wanted to give the feeling that the techniques of filmmaking had just been discovered or experienced for the first time. The iris-in showed that one could return to the cinema's sources; the dissolve appeared, just once, as though it had just been invented. (Godard, in Milne 1972, 173)

In this sense, *A bout de souffle* set out to secure a position in the history of the cinema analogous to that of the monumental *Citizen Kane*, a megalomaniac 26-year-old director's first feature and another manifesto issued some twenty years earlier in defiance of the cinema industry. The similarity between the two title sequences, or rather the absence of a title sequence in both films, confirms the wish for an explicit reference. After the dedication to Monogram, two vigorous notes of music by Martial Solal accompany the title, which is displayed full frame in white letters on a black background, foreshadowing as in *Kane* the later inserts of newspaper headlines. Welles' film begins with the death of the eminent citizen whose biography is then reconstructed bit by bit through newsreel, eye-witness accounts and press headlines. At the start of *A bout de souffle*, Poiccard is a man living on borrowed time, whose tragic progress is punctuated first by the editions of *France-Soir* and then by the neon lights flashing, 'The net is closing in around Michel Poiccard', then 'Michel Poiccard, arrest imminent', just as neon lights had announced to the world the death of the American press magnate.

First of all, everything was possible technically. The signifying potential of editing was to be pushed to the limits, in the manner of *Citizen Kane*. Godard thus did not hesitate to follow a very high angle establishing shot with a big close-up (Patricia runs to give Michel a kiss at the end of their first meeting; the next shot is an insert of a poster saying 'Live dangerously till the end', while Michel crosses the frame in medium close-up); nor did he hesitate to alternate hyper-fragmentation of the image and rapid montage (the series of shots of Patricia's face in profile in the car as Michel declares 'I love a girl who has a pretty neck, pretty breasts, a pretty voice, etc.') with a long continuous take (when Michel finds Tolmatchoff at the Inter-Americana Agency, the camera tracks back in front of them all the time they're walking, the first metaphor of the labyrinth and of the trap in which the tragic hero is caught).

Right from the beginning of the film, the 'Nationale 7' sequence ruthlessly violates the moribund codes of spatial and graphic continuity editing which were so scrupulously observed by professional editors in 1959. It cuts in quick succession between a number of rapid panning shots from side to side of the road, close-ups of the driver framed from the passenger seat or the back seat, intercut shots of the road flashing by, inserts of headlights or of the central white line which the driver transgressively crosses, up to the famous sequence in extreme close-up detailing the cylinder and barrel of the colt, with a cutaway in the opposite direction to the motorcycle cop collapsing. Godard could not have found a more devastating way of reviving the dynamics of Eisensteinian montage and the deconstruction of the revolutionary machine-guns in *October*.

At the other end of the scale, when Michel finds Patricia in the Champs-Elysées the camera tracks the couple as they walk up and down, refusing the classic shot/reverse shot alternation in order to avoid any ambivalent identification with the characters and to underline the parallel progression of the two monologues, or rather of the soliloquy which Michel began in the opening sequence, and which Patricia's replies merely bounce off, without any real communication ever being established. The motif of the labyrinth, where two parallel paths never meet, is taken up again when Michel and Patricia find themselves in the Swedish woman's flat, the final trap: the camera follows first Michel, then Patricia, as they pace up and down the room. Michel says, 'Whenever we talked, I talked about myself, and you talked about yourself. [...] But you should have talked about me, and me about you.'

This dynamic conception of editing first and foremost has a rhythmic function. As we have seen, Poiccard, like Godard, sets the ball rolling by throwing himself behind the wheel of his 1950 Oldsmobile. The diabolical rhythm of his race to the finish must not lose its hold on the spectator, and the moments of respite based on continuous takes are as breathtaking in their movement as the bursts of shots in discontinuous sequences. The important thing is to keep the pace up and not stop until the very last breath, the last grimace, when all the spectator sees of Patricia is the nape of her neck, hiding her soul, as Bruno Forrestier, the little soldier (in *Le Petit soldat*), and Nana, the prostitute (in *Vivre sa vie*), were to say.

As Michel and Patricia kiss to get their breath back, in the darkness of a cinema auditorium two voices, one male, one female, call them to order amid the pandemonium of a Western shoot-out. The man (Godard's voice) says,

> Méfie-toi Jessica.
> Au biseau des baisers — les ans passent trop vite —
> Evite, évite, évite — les souvenirs brisés.
>
> Beware, Jessica.
> With the sharp cut of kisses — the years pass too quickly —
> keep away, away, away — from shattered memories.

— an extract from a poem by Aragon, the alliteration of which, in French, echoes the title of the film, as Marie-Claire Ropars has indicated (1982, 59-81). The woman rejoins:

> Vous faites erreur, Shériff ...,
> notre histoire est noble et tragique comme le masque d'un
> tyran.
> Aucun détail indifférent ne rend notre amour pathétique.
>
> You are making a mistake, sheriff ...,
> our story is as noble and tragic as a tyrant's mask.
> No insignificant detail brings pathos to our love.[1]

(extract from the poem *Cors de chasse* by Apollinaire in the collection *Alcools*).

The most fundamental innovation of *A bout de souffle* is the dialogue, which constitutes the most revolutionary use of language since the coming of sound. We know that the film was made entirely without sound. Godard edited a first, post-synchronized, version which was an hour too long. Then he decided to make cuts in the middle of sequences, eliminating particular fragments (shots of Van Doude telling a story about going to bed with some girl) or series of shots (countershots of Michel accompanying the views of Patricia, framed in profile in the car while he is enumerating her charms). This deliberate opting for visual discontinuity goes hand in hand with the general autonomy of the soundtrack, which has its own time, regardless of its links with the image. Thus, at the beginning of the film, while Michel is talking to himself at the wheel of his American car, the image track cuts between fragmented images of his journey with very obvious spatial ellipses, while the language, however nonsensical, operates in a relatively continuous way.

> La, la la, la (he hums). Buenas noches, mi amor, ... If he thinks he's going to get past me in that bloody car... Pa, Pa, Patricia! Patricia! So, I'll get the money, I'll ask Patricia for a yes or a no... and then. Buenas noches, mi amor... Milano! Genova! Roma!

Michel Poiccard is the one who is cursed, the one who brings bad luck ('la poisse'). According to the *Littré* dictionary, from the beginning of the seventeenth century, 'poissard' (Poiccard) was the name given to the slang of the lower classes. Despite the distinctive language used by Henri Jeanson and his disciples, Poiccard was the first film character to violate the refined sound conventions of 1959 French cinema by using popular slang and the most trivial spoken French. The 'Nationale 7' sequence, in itself a demonstration of what the film as a whole sets out to do, piles up sweeping examples of spoken French, of contemporary slang which was to be heard even within the intellectual microcosms of the Champs-Elysées and Saint-Germain des Prés, and of a language reminiscent of Céline, which scriptwriters in French cinema had never before rendered on screen except via the conventions of *série noire* slang. To come back a moment to the opening monologue quoted briefly above, it offers: the humming of an onomatopoeic tune, the chorus of a popular song ('Buenas noches, mi amor'), a fixed slang expression ('sa frégate à la con'/ 'his bloody car'), provocative pseudo-sentences and gratuitous aphorisms of an ideological nature ('Women at the wheel are the epitome of cowardice'), made-up quotations ('And as old Bugatti said, cars are made to go, not to stop'), and frequent spontaneous interjections of slang ('Yes, shit, roadworks, shit, the fuzz'). There is no point in giving more examples, the whole linguistic texture of the film is shot through with a wealth of popular and slang terms and expressions.

Through his use of language Godard was clearly showing what he had learnt from the central character of *Moi, un noir*, filmed and recorded by the ethnologist Jean Rouch at Treichville in the suburbs of Abidjan (made in 1958, winner of the Prix Louis Delluc in 1959 and released on 12 March 1960, a week before *A bout de souffle*). He wrote two very appreciative articles on Rouch's film in *Cahiers du cinéma* in March and April 1959. Jean Rouch's film portrays an unemployed youth from Abidjan nicknamed 'Lemmy Caution' and his friends 'Eddie Constantine' and 'Dorothy Lamour'; Rouch used a handheld camera to follow the half-improvised adventures of the characters. Even more remarkably, the actor Oumarou Ganda (who plays 'Edward G. Robinson') dubbed himself, improvising a monologue as he viewed the edited version of the image track. At one point in the film when 'Eddie Constantine' meets 'Dorothy Lamour' in the street, the voices are those of the two actors who improvised *a posteriori* a converstion which is very approximately synchronous with the image. Later on in the film, 'Robinson', both narrator and character, mixes simultaneous dialogue with subjective comments added later.

> One must take it at its word when it comes from the mouth of Lemmy Caution, American federal agent and unemployed of Treichville, as he waits for girls at the church door, or tells Petit Jules why France lost the match in Indo-China in a speech which is part-Céline, part-Audiberti, part nothing at all ultimately, because the conversation of Rouch and his characters (whose resemblance to persons living or dead is absolutely not coincidental) is as new and as pure as Botticelli's Venus, as the black rising from the waves in *Les Statues meurent aussi*. (Godard, in Milne 1972, 129)

> And when Eddie Constantine, American federal agent, is arguing with P'tit Jules in a staggering flow of words along the lines of *Bagatelles pour un massacre*, and Rouch, kneeling beside them with the camera on his shoulder, suddenly straightens up slowly and lifts *à la* Anthony Mann, his knees serving as the crane, to frame Abidjan, O! Abidjan of the lagoons, on the other side of the river, I love it. (ibid., 134)

A bout de souffle even contains a direct reference to a brief moment in *Moi, un noir* which illuminates Poiccard's offhand manner when, having seen the body of the pedestrian knocked over by the Renault 4CV, he merely crosses himself and continues on his way, reading his paper. At the beginning of *Moi, un noir*, 'Robinson' is wandering through the streets of Treichville when he sees a crowd of people idly staring at a motorcyclist who has been knocked down. He merely remarks in a detached voice, 'Oh! Another accident! There are such a lot of accidents in Treichville! Cars here last two months at the most ... . That's why it's such a shambles.'

There can be no doubt that 'Robinson's' long monologue at the beginning of the film had a direct influence on Poiccard's soliloquy at the wheel of his car. Similarly, the constant film references in *A bout de souffle* which everyone has commented on, and which have since been detailed by Dudley Andrew (1986, 11-21), the reworking of American B movie *film noir* (the homage to Bogart, the posters of *The Harder They Fall*, the quotation from *The Enforcer* when Poiccard knocks out the customer in the toilets, the sound-track and photos from *Whirlpool*, etc.) originated in the fanciful imagination of Rouch's young Africans who identified with American *film noir* actors and their parodic French imitations to such an extent that they only had assumed names: 'Eddie Constantine', 'Edward G. Robinson' and 'Dorothy Lamour' never use any other name, whereas when Poiccard finds himself face to face with the picture of Bogart, he murmurs the actor's nickname (Bogie) but retains his own identity.

In *A bout de souffle*, Godard was exploring every facet of verbal language. So far, the opening monologue and the false dialogue which characterizes the confrontations between Michel and Patricia have been discussed. These examples alone do not do justice to the wealth and diversity of the verbal material used in the film. First there are the innumerable literary, cinematographic, pictorial and musical quotations exchanged by Michel and Patricia; then there are the little stories that Michel recounts, like the one which Van Doude also tells about the bus conductor who had stolen five million francs to seduce a girl, obviously a *mise-en-abyme* of the film ('I'd known this girl for two years', etc.). There is a play on the variety of different languages: the international Americanese that Michel uses ('As you like it baby'), the odd words of Italian ('ciao', 'buon giorno') and Spanish ('amigo', 'buenas noches'); stereotyped plays on words ('Maintenant, je fonce, Alphonse!'), alternation between the formal and the familiar words for you ('tu' and 'vous'), the use of ambiguity and misunderstanding ('qu'est-ce que c'est dingue?' 'qu'est-ce que c'est dégueulasse?'). To sum up, *A bout de souffle* is a tragedy of language and of the impossibility of communication.

This allows us to tackle the question of the subject which Godard talks about in relation to the film:

> *A bout de souffle* is a story, not a theme. A theme is something simple and vast which can be summed up in twenty seconds: vengeance, pleasure. A story takes twenty minutes to sum up. *Le Petit soldat* has a theme: a young man is mixed up, realizes this, and tries to find clarity. In *Une Femme est une femme*, a girl wants a baby right away. In *A bout de souffle* I was looking for the theme right through the shooting, and finally became interested in Belmondo. I saw him as a sort of block to be filmed to discover what lay inside. Seberg, on the other hand, was an actress whom I wanted to see doing little things which amused me [...].
> (Godard, in Milne 1972, 177)

However, it is easy to sum up the 'subject' of *A bout de souffle* in the way that director did for *Une Femme est une femme*. A young small-time hoodlum and car thief goes up to Paris to find the young American girl he is in love with, cash a fat cheque and leave with her for Italy. But this synopsis merely reduces the subject to the initial situation of the story, the hero's 'project'. When Poiccard hot-wires the car to get it started in the first few seconds of the film, he sets in motion an infernal machine. The goal of his quest is his desire to sleep with Patricia again. As soon as he finds her, he says quite clearly, 'Are you coming to Rome with me? Yes, it's stupid, but I love you ...' and later, 'Are we sleeping together tonight?' Before that, he refuses the more or less direct advances of several dark-haired young women: the girl on Marseilles' Vieux Port who asks him to take her away with him, his former mistress whom he wakes up at seven o'clock in the morning. Just as he makes the observation that the two girl hitch-hikers are not fanciable enough, he finds the colt in the car glove compartment, after switching on the radio for a few moments to let us hear Brassens' famous song 'Il n'y a pas d'amour heureux'/'there is no such thing as happy love'. Immediately afterwards, Michel defies destiny by shooting at the sun, and this playful act evokes both the revolver shot fired at the sun by the German engineer at the end of the first part of *Le Tigre du Bengale* by Fritz Lang (released in France on 22 July 1959) and Meursault getting blinded by the sun on the Algerian beach at the beginning of Camus' *L'Etranger*. Indeed, quite unconsciously Poiccard is defying the gods and performing an absurd act, since it is destiny which pulls the trigger at the end of the cutaway travelling shot framing the barrel of the colt.

Michel's stations of the cross are marked by the signs of destiny. When Patricia offers him the *New York Herald Tribune*, he refuses it because it does not have a horoscope; throughout the film, once he has left Marseilles, he keeps asking the time, making telephone call after telephone call, buying the paper, then lighting up cigarette after cigarette, like the hero of *Le Jour se lève*, imprisoned in his hotel room and also destined to die in a hail of police bullets. Patricia, the object of his desire, a little girl with a handbag and a teddybear (another obvious reference to Carné's film) is the agent of destiny. The caricature of her in the opening shot (the 'pin-up' on the issue of *Paris-Flirt* that Michel is reading) indicates as much right from the start: Michel '*must*' go on until death. When she goes to ring the police at the end of the film, she in her turn buys *France-Soir* and goes past a kiosk with a woman selling lottery tickets who calls out, 'Your lucky day! Try your luck, buy a ticket!' As for Michel, he commits act after act of provocation as if they were gratuitous acts proving that he was free to exercise his freedom; but 'between sorrow and nothingness' he knows that he has chosen nothingness. He knows that destiny is waiting for him at the end of the road (rue Campagne Première) just as Godard knew that he had to get to the end of the film, to keep going come what may. Poiccard's death, despite the concession made to Truffaut, is still agonizing: the camera follows Michel's crazy attempt to run down the street until he collapses on the pedestrian crossing, murmuring with his last breath and with a last grimace, 'C'est vraiment dégueulasse'/'It really makes you sick'. Here Godard is making a direct reference to the spectacular death-scene of a character in *Man of the West* which he had just reviewed, under the title 'Super Mann', in *Cahiers du cinéma* (1959, 92). It's the death-scene of a dumb man, a member of the gang led by a megalomaniac old bandit played by Lee J. Cobb, who makes his way down a seemingly endless street in the middle of a deserted village with a bullet in his back, as Poiccard was to do, until he finally collapses, uttering his first cry and drawing his last breath as he does so.

A bout de souffle was to be Godard's first cry, the only one in his long early career to be heard by a fairly large public: almost 260,000 people saw the film in seven weeks of its first run in Paris from 16 March 1960. Poiccard knew that he was playing double or quits, as Patricia says. He also observes near the end, 'I'm fed up, I'm tired, I want to sleep'. As for Godard, he was to move on immediately to an even more personal second film, *Le Petit soldat*, and despite the fact that the film was completely banned by the censor until 1963, in 1961 he was able to direct the film he had first proposed to Georges de Beauregard, *Une Femme est une femme*. Since then he has never stopped making films, even in the 1970s when he decided to adapt the technical conditions of his projects (16mm films, video) to the nature of his discourse. He's still not breathless.

Translated from the French by Carrie Tarr

NOTES

1.   This is an extract from the poem *Cors de chasse* by Apollinaire in the collection *Alcools*.

SELECTED BIBLIOGRAPHY

Andrew, Dudley (1986) 'Au début du souffle: le culte et la culture d'*A bout de souffle*', *Revue belge du cinéma*, 16 (special Godard issue).
Braunberger, Pierre (1987) *Cinémamémoire*, Paris, Centre Georges Pompidou, Centre National de la Cinématographie (CNC).
Brown, Royal S. (1972) *Focus on Godard*, Englewood Cliffs, New Jersey, Prentice-Hall.
Collet, Jean (1963) *Jean-Luc Godard*, Paris, Seghers.
Collet, Jean (1970) *Jean-Luc Godard*, trans. Ciba Vaughan, New York, Crown Publishers.
Collet, Jean and Fangien, Jean-Paul (1974) *Jean-Luc Godard*, Paris, Seghers.
Courtade, Francis (1978) *Les Malédictions du cinéma fançais*, Paris, Alain Moreau.
Goldmann, Annie (1971) *Cinéma et société moderne: le cinéma de 1958 à 1968*, Paris, Editions Anthropos.
Godard, Jean-Luc (1980) *Introduction à une véritable histoire du cinéma*, Paris, Albatros.
Godard, Jean-Luc (1985) *Jean-Luc Godard par Jean-Luc Godard*, Paris, Cahiers du cinéma, Editions de l'Etoile.
Lesage, Julia (1979) *Jean-Luc Godard: A Guide to References and Resources*, Boston, G. K. Hall.
Milne, Tom (ed.) (1972) *Godard on Godard*, London, Secker & Warburg.
Milne, Tom and Narboni, Jean (eds) (1986) *Godard on Godard*, New York, Da Capo (revised edition of Milne [1972], with preface by Annette Michaelson).
Monaco, James (1976) *The New Wave*, New York, Oxford University Press.

Ropars, Marie-Claire (1982) 'L'Instance graphique dans l'écriture du film', *Littérature*, 46, Paris, Larousse, 'Graphies'.
Salachas, Gilbert (1960) '*A Bout de souffle*', fiche filmographique 36, *Télé-ciné*, 89.

SCRIPTS

Godard, Jean-Luc (1968) '*A bout de souffle*', *Avant-Scène Cinéma*, 79 (contains Truffaut's original script).
Godard, Jean-Luc (1974) *A bout de souffle*, Paris, Balland, 'Bibliothèque des classiques du cinéma' (illustrated book of the film).

For other works on Godard, see bibliographies in chapters 16 on *Le Mépris* and 18 on *Sauve qui peut (la vie)*.

APPENDIX

Jean-Luc Godard (1930—): filmography

1954 *Opération béton* (short)
1955 *Une Femme coquette* (short)
1957 *Une Histoire d'eau* (short)
1957 *Tous les garçons s'appellent Patrick (All Boys are Called Patrick)* (short)
1958 *Charlotte et son Jules* (short)
1959 *A bout de souffle (Breathless)*
1960 *Le Petit soldat (The Little Soldier)*
1961 *Une Femme est une femme (A Woman is a Woman)*
1961 *La Paresse* (sketch)
1962 *Le Nouveau monde* (sketch)
1962 *Vivre sa vie (It's My Life* [UK]; *My Life to Live* [USA])
1962-3 *Les Carabiniers (The Soldiers* [UK]; *The Riflemen* [USA])
1963 *Le Grand escroc* (sketch)
1963 *Montparnasse-Levallois* (sketch)
1963 *Le Mépris (Contempt)*
1964 *Bande à part (Band of Outsiders* [UK]; *The Outsiders* [USA])
1964 *Une Femme mariée (A Married Woman* [UK]; *The Married Woman* [USA])
1965 *Alphaville*
1965 *Pierrot le fou*
1966 *Anticipation* (sketch)
1966 *Deux ou trois choses que je sais d'elle (Two or Three Things I Know About Her)*
1966 *Made in USA*
1966 *Masculin-féminin (Masculine-Feminine)*
1967 *L'Amour* (sketch)
1967 *Caméra-oeil* (episode in *Loin du Vietnam*)
1967 *La Chinoise*
1967 *Weekend (Week-End)*
1968 *Un Film comme les autres (A Movie Like the Others)*
1968 *Le Gai savoir*
1968 *One Plus One (Sympathy for the Devil)*
1968-9 *One American Movie 1 A.M.*
1969 *British Sounds*
1969 *Pravda*
1970 *Jusqu'à la victoire (Till Victory)* (short, unfinished)
1970 *Luttes en Italie (Struggle in Italy)*

1970 *Vent d'est (East Wind)*
1970 *Vladimir et Rosa*
1972 *Letter to Jane*
1972 *Tout va bien*
1974 *Ici et ailleurs*
1975 *Numéro deux*
1976 *Comment ça va*
1976 *Six fois deux*
1978 *France/tout/détour/deux/enfants*
1980 *Sauve qui peut (la vie) (Slow Motion* [UK]*; Every Man for Himself* [USA]
1981 *Passion*
1982 *Scénario du film Passion*
1982 *Lettre à Freddy Buache*
1982 *Prénom Carmen*
1983 *Je vous salue Marie*
1984 *Detective*
1987 *Soigne ta droite*

Other films cited in the text

Le Beau Serge, Claude Chabrol (1958)
Bonjour tristesse, Otto Preminger (1957)
Calle Mayor (The Lovemaker), Juan-Antonio Bardem (1956)
Citizen Kane, Orson Welles (1941)
Les Cousins, Claude Chabrol (1959)
Un Drôle de dimanche, Marc Allégret (1958)
The Enforcer, Raoul Walsh and Bretaigne Windust (1951)
Gun Crazy, J. H. Lewis (1949)
The Harder they Fall, Mark Robson (1956)
Hiroshima mon amour, Alain Resnais (1959)
Les Jeux de l'amour, Philippe de Broca (1959)
Le Jour se lève (Daybreak), Marcel Carné (1939)
Man of the West, Anthony Mann (1958)
Moi, un noir, Jean Rouch (1959)
Muerte de un Ciclista (Death of a Cyclist), Juan-Antonio Bardem (1955)
October, Sergei Eisenstein (1927)
Paris nous appartient, Jacques Rivette (1958)
La Passe du diable, Jacques Dupont and Pierre Schoendoerffer (1956)
Pêcheurs d'Islande, Pierre Schoendoerffer (1959)
A pied, à cheval et en voiture, Michel Delbez (1958)
Les 400 coups, François Truffaut (1959)
Ramuntcho, Pierre Schoendoerffer (1958)
Saint-Joan, Otto Preminger (1956)
Le Signe du lion, Claude Chabrol (1959)
Sois belle et tais-toi, Marc Allégret (1957)
Les Statues meurent aussi (short), Alain Resnais (1953)
Le Tigre du Bengale (Tiger of Bengal), Fritz Lang (1959)
Les Tricheurs (The Cheaters), Marcel Carné (1958)
Whirlpool, Otto Preminger (1949)

16. The fall of the gods: Jean-Luc Godard's *Le Mépris* (1963)

JACQUES AUMONT

Thirty three is, quite literally, a crucial age for any western male, the age of crucifixions and triumphs. The 33-year-old Jean-Luc Godard who made *Le Mépris* was no beginner since he had already directed five features, five shorts, and three episodes for 'omnibus' films, and long since put behind him the period of his masterly first attempts. But in the course of a career that had consisted solely of climaxes, each more powerful than the last, 1963 was the year in which he made not only *Les Carabiniers*, his most resounding flop and most provocative movie, but also *Le Mépris*, the film that came closest to the prevailing models of the time, from both an aesthetic and an industrial point of view.

Let me immediately remove any possible ambiguity: although *Le Mépris* was a more 'normal' production than Godard's previous films (big budget, international co-production, cast of stars) it is above all, in retrospect, the prototype of a configuration that often recurred subsequently in his career — the wholesale destruction of an apparently traditional screenplay, the misuse (or abuse, or non-use) of stars, a stylistic impertinence. This is a configuration that can be found, to varying degrees, in *Pierrot le fou*/Belmondo, *Sauve qui peut (la vie)*/Dutronc/Baye, and *Détective*/Halliday. It has become a commonplace to say, but it is nonetheless true, that Godard was extraordinarily successful in integrating himself into the film industry, but in a totally idiosyncratic manner (involving, very early on, the crediting of his own name as filmmaker *on an equal footing* with any other name or body).

Itself a big-budget movie, *Le Mépris* can thus be regarded — and today should be regarded — as a commentary, at once ironic and nostalgic, on the big-budget movie. Of all the French films made in 1963, it was one of the most costly,[1] both thanks to and because of Bardot's presence: 'It was the only time I had the feeling I was going to be able to make a big film with a big budget. In fact it was a small budget for the film, as all the money went to Brigitte Bardot, Fritz Lang and Jack Palance' (Godard 1980, 73). But of all 'Bardot's' films it was the one which made the least money, along with Louis Malle's *Vie privée*. It is impossible not to be reminded, while making all due allowances, of another 1963 movie, Joseph Mankiewicz's *Cleopatra*, a bottomless pit that swallowed up so many millions of dollars it hastened the demise of the studio system. Godard was certainly not responsible for any such disaster, and one of the admirable qualities of *Le Mépris* is that, first, it forewarns us of that demise, and then poeticizes, *ante factum*, its infinite sadness. If one excepts the first two shots in the film (the sequence against which the credits are spoken, and the celebrated shots of the naked Bardot, which were imposed by the producer), the movie opens with views of Cinecittà and Francesca's remark: 'The Italian cinema's doing very badly.' Now Francesca, the 'go-between', as Marie so rightly calls her (1986, 35), is played by Georgia Moll, an actress who made a career in Italian *peplum*[2] films, but who was also noticed in Mankiewicz' *The Quiet American* — and who is thus in an ideal position to remark on the demise of Cinecittà and, at the same time, to prophesy that of Hollywood.

If *Le Mépris* is a film which lays itself open, almost too easily, to feverish intercultural interpretation, it is chiefly because it is a kind of melancholia for the cinema, a lucid *mise-en-abyme* of the 'death' of the cinema that was marked once and for all by the end of Hollywoodian classicism. Indeed, from that angle the film can be interpreted in many ways: as a *'politique des auteurs* in the flesh' (Marie 1986, 29), but flesh doomed, alas, to the frailty of old age — or, correlatively, as a veritable lampoon against blind and deaf producers, a kind of *'J'accuse ...!'* which portrays them as dealers of death. That Jeremiah Prokosch is a satirical character could not be more obvious; Godard's choice of Palance to play the part leaves no room for ambiguity, and the man with the sardonic grin, the sadistic black-gloved killer of *Shane*, does not inject any superfluous subtlety into his portrayal of the man who 'draws his chequebook' whenever he hears the word culture, the producer who makes up for his semi-culture and semi-competence by repeatedly 'humiliating and offending his employees or friends' (Godard 1985, 243). He is the only character in the film (except perhaps for the character played by Godard himself) who is treated as a puppet, and above all as someone who has an extremely naïve view of the cinema: when three naked young women swimmers appear on the viewing theatre screen, he has the same besottedly lecherous, adolescent leer as Michel-Ange in *Les Carabiniers* before he tries to leap into the bath-tub projected on the screen.

Not all that many films portray the movie world. In that respect, *Le Mépris* lies somewhere between Minelli's, *The Bad and the Beautiful* and Truffaut's *La Nuit américaine* — between totally mythical self-congratulation, with a central character (a producer) wracked by a desire for Art, and the family film that affectionately recounts the harmless intrigues of people in the movie world (under the stewardship of a benign director). In Godard's film, the basic idea is simpler: the director, Fritz Lang, is a conscience and a victim, while the producer's ambition (which is worthy of Kirk Douglas in the Minnelli movie) degenerates into sadistic madness. What is certain is that the film is a somewhat embittered discourse on the film *industry*, unlike another film, *8 1/2*, also made in 1963, where the anxiety of creation seems in the end to shake off all material constraints. That is surely no coincidence: by siding with poor Lang against the villainous Prokosch, Godard takes revenge a hundred times over for the humiliation he suffered at the hands of Carlo Ponti and Joseph Levine[3] — and, more generally, gives vent to his customary feelings about producers, which could hardly be described as overflowing with the milk of human kindness.[4] Godard clearly cannot bear the idea that, in the

the conflict which always pits the producer against the director, he should fail to get the upper hand, or at least have the last word. The famous second shot of *Le Mépris* is a fine example of the art of how to have the last word: at the insistence of Levine, who thought the film did not show enough of Bardot as Bardot (i.e. 'sexy'), Godard added a long take of the naked star, but what might have been a fetishistic reification of a body in box-office terms is instead an affectionate, almost awestruck moment of contemplation (even *Positif*, which loathes Godard, admired the shot). What is more, Godard somehow manages to make that last-minute addition tie in with the rest of the film — with that other, briefer shot of the lower part of B.B.'s body against a background of red velvet (a strident, fleeting allusion to Marilyn Monroe's celebrated calendar), and, of course, with an already mentioned scene, where Prokosch smirks at the sight of the naked young women he has clearly forced Lang to include in the film. Godard, obviously, is a past master at falling on his feet.

By the time *Le Mépris* was released, there was already an image — and an already stereotyped image — of Godard and his style. Critics harped on two or three aspects of that style: its jerky rhythm, its 'crossings-out', its frequent quotations, and above all the casual way such quotations are introduced. *Le Mépris* is no exception really, and any list of the quotations it contains would be lengthy; what makes them different, perhaps, from the excessively ludic quotations in *Les Carabiniers* and *Une Femme est une femme*, is that they both accompany and are based on the 'materialist' discourse on the art of film which I have already mentioned. *Le Mépris* quotes *both* the film industry *and* the history of the cinema, which is why it is, among other things, a sort of compendium of classical cinema (cinema of the kind which was loved, defended and dreamt of by the young *Cahiers du cinéma* critics). The film's interweaving of references and filiations has often been noted, not least by Godard himself. Jack Palance, Georgia Moll and Fritz Lang are vehicles, in the flesh, of part of the past, of history. They are living quotations and, already, survivors of a vanished world (one is reminded of the book-people in *Fahrenheit 451*): through them, Godard quite consciously evokes not only his own immediate past as a *cinéphile* —*The Barefoot Contessa, The Quiet American* — but a more distant, already heroized and mythicized past (Lang's legendary meeting with Goebbels). But this wealth of direct quotation is complemented in the film by a dense nexus of indirect quotations, not all of them equally profound. Sometimes Godard simply raises his hat to favourite movies like *Some Came Running*[5] (which is itself, up to a point, a tragedy of cowardice and contempt) or *Hatari!*, which Godard rated 'the best film of 1962', and a poster of which, curiously, is stuck up on the Cinecittà set (it is perhaps worth mentioning that it appears just before Camille first feels contempt for Paul; 'hatari', incidentally, means 'danger'). More essentially, there is the subterranean but powerful presence of another reference, a reference to Europe, to Italy, and more particularly to one film, Roberto Rossellini's *Viaggio in Italia*.

It can never be emphasized too much that Rossellini was the filmmaker who had the most direct influence on the *Cahiers* group, at least as much because he met them regularly and urged them amiably, but insistently, to make films themselves, as because of his 'Bazinian' mantle of glory as the inventor of Neo-Realism. Shooting *Le Mépris* in Italy, Godard could hardly have failed to think of Rossellini, but there was nothing to suggest that his film would take its cue as directly as it did from Rossellini's. In fact the subject is the same: how misunderstanding (*méprise*) can lead to contempt (*mépris*), cross-purposes to cross exchanges. The story-line is the same: a couple of foreigners, who have married almost by chance and come to Italy, quarrel fiercely and realize they have already grown apart and will have to separate — there is even the same final intervention of chance (the miracle in one film, the fatal accident in the other). Lastly, both films give the same feeling of an almost physical presence of the gods, and not just because Godard films his plaster reproductions with the same majesty as Rossellini does the statues in the Naples Archaeological Museum.

So *Le Mépris* bristles with references, and insistent ones at that; again and again acts of homage are paid, and models hinted at. This is hardly surprising, as Godard has always been, ever since he wrote for *Cahiers*, the recognized master of the quotational genre (only recently he was preening himself on the fact that not a single line of the dialogue in *Détective* or in *Soigne ta droite* was written by him). However that may be, the striking thing about *Le Mépris* is the way such references are concentrated on the cinema, its history and its philosophy, whereas in Godard's earliest films, still typically those of the young *cinéphile*, it is commoner to find literature rubbing shoulders with *film noir*, or painting, and drama with comedy. *Le Mépris* is one of the rare films by Godard where we never glimpse the familiar, and in a sense reassuring, figures of Klee, Matisse, Renoir or Picasso. It is also one of the few where literary quotation is used, precisely, as a quotation — i.e. spoken, in quotes, by one character to another, instead of being an integral part of the movie like, for example, the quotation from Poe's *The Oval Portrait* in *Vivre sa vie*. (Surely the absence of Godard's customary references must be regarded as one of the most visible aspects of Rossellini's influence? If Moravia's *Il Disprezzo*, on which *Le Mépris* is based, is, as Godard generously put it, a *roman de gare* — the kind of cheap novel you buy at a station bookstall — then *Viaggio in Italia* is a *roman-photo* entirely improvised by Rossellini from stock situations; in *Le Mépris*, Godard relies much less on improvisation than in any of his other films, and exploits stereotypes as well as psychological and dramatic conventions to an unaccustomed degree.)

* * *

What of it? Doubtless, as I pointed out at the start, Godard's aim with *Le Mépris* was to take his bearings *vis-à-vis* history, to accentuate a sense of history as an escape, a loss, to intensify a delectable anxiety about the end of

Le Mépris — above left: Jeremy Prokosh (Jack Palance), Camille (Brigitte Bardot) and Paul (Michel Piccoli); above right: Camille and Paul; below: Michel Piccoli, Jack Palance, Fritz Lang and Jean-Luc Godard.

history. That concern was shared by the whole generation of the New Wave, and more particularly the *Cahiers* group, and centred on the important notion that filmmaking was but an extension of the critic's or aesthetician's activity, and that each individual film would therefore be a re-reading, a re-writing, of the entire history of the cinema (a very particular kind of history, of course, polarized by strongly voiced likes and dislikes). In that respect, Godard was very typical of his generation, and he does not really go much further than, on occasion, Truffaut, who prided himself on *Jules et Jim's* 40-odd quotations and acts of homage. Godard was simply more systematic, and above all more persistent, gradually elaborating, from film to film, something that came to be seen by the end of the 1960s as an aesthetics of the fragment (people at the time were less interested in the actual insistence of Godard's use of quotation than in the almost detachable nature of the quotations themselves and, correlatively, in his masterly use of collage and the cut-up technique).

It was precisely Godard's persistence and systematic obstinacy that lent him an affinity, not found in any other New Wave director (with the possible exception of Rivette, but on a completely different register), with what can only be termed the literary 'avant-gardes' of the 1950s and 1960s. The use of the second degree, self-reflexivity, specularity and other 'defamiliarizing' techniques was characteristic of what came to be known as the *Nouveau Roman* group, which was just as loosely structured as the New Wave. Much sarcasm was directed at such 'novelties' (they were even accused of conforming too closely to the 'modernizing' ideology and phraseology of the Gaullist Fifth Republic). The sarcasm turned to scorn when, taking the practical premises of Butor's *La Modification*, Ollier's *La Mise-en-scène* and Robbe-Grillet's *Les Gommes* to their logical conclusion, Barthes and the Tel Quel group erected them into a theory. To be quite accurate, this intellectual terrain was not, directly or at first hand, that of Godard himself (who was more familiar with such precursors of the *Nouveau Roman* as Joyce, Faulkner and Céline). All I am attempting to do here is, if you like, to point to a cultural coincidence. But it is well known that as far as culture goes no coincidence is the fruit of pure chance: in this particular case, Godard (and some members of the New Wave), the *Nouveau Roman* (and those sometimes linked with it like Le Clézio, whom Godard met in 1966)[6] and, more generally, a large section of the French intelligentsia of the 1960s did at least share one basic notion: that any work worthy of the name must contain its own keys. Their complicity was not only formal, but ideological: modernity, this 'novelty' so often foolishly derided and violently denigrated, also resides in a rejection of naïvety, a wish to show that one knows what one is doing (a wish which, towards the end of the decade, and more particularly in Godard's case, naturally took on a directly political form).

Thus, to return to *Le Mépris*, it contains other references, which are given a varying degree of prominence, and through each of which the film seems to be looking back on itself. The painted eyes of the statues supposedly filmed by Lang call to mind other painted eyes, those of Cocteau, a poet whom

Godard admired, and another first-person filmmaker, who constantly explored and pointed up the powers of the cinema. The way Godard films the Villa Malaparte in Capri, and the very idea of using its rectilinear architecture, outdo Antonioni at his own game — which is of some relevance in a film which Godard wanted to be 'a successful Antonioni, in other words filmed by Hawks'. In short, *Le Mépris* is a movie in which the filmmaker's 'authorial' self-awareness is never far below the surface and a deliberate reflexivity constantly asserts itself.

That reflexivity was something that 'art' films of the 1960s seized upon with relish, particularly through the specific stylistic figure — also found in *Le Mépris* — of the 'film within the film'. By about the middle of the decade, any movie with ambitions would systematically, but not always very subtly, exhibit the whole paraphernalia of its own shooting, e.g. *Persona*, and *La Chinoise*, or at least refer to itself as a film, for instance *L'Amour fou*, and *Belle de jour*. The presence of the film equipment, technicians and actors in *Le Mépris* remains, as in its Hollywoodian predecessors, unobtrusively confined to the diegesis, and thus does not possess the disruptive impact of the appearance of the camera and clapperboard in *La Chinoise*. Even so, the existence of the film within the film does tend to have an effect of disruption, of tearing the fabric of the narrative. In this respect the credit-title sequence of *Le Mépris* works to perfection, as it combines the principal modes of 'distancing' and of interpellation of the spectator (voice-over, film equipment shown on the screen, the camera pointing at 'us') with what is already the beginning of a narrative: in that first shot of the film, Georgia Moll — or should she already be referred to as Francesca Vanini — is tracked by the camera as she walks down a studio-built street in Cinecittà which, in the third shot, she walks up in the opposite direction, now accompanied by Paul Javal/Piccoli as well as the camera (on the same rails).

This credit-title sequence is remarkably striking, as well as being famous — at least in France, where it was long used for the credits of a now defunct television programme on the cinema. It is also, as Jean-Louis Leutrat has shown (1986, 68), totally representative of a film in which 'the characters are affected' by a certain 'indecision'. I myself would even go so far as to contend that not only the characters but the whole story and the whole diegesis are affected by that indecision. What is basically at issue here is Godard's conception of the cinema, which attempts to combine and to embrace both the classical heritage (the conception of the open, transparent window) and something which can now clearly be seen to be modernity (distancing, the play on shifters). It is of course no coincidence that Godard here quotes from André Bazin, the champion of Neo-Realism and Rossellini, and defender of the kind of cinema which respects 'the ambiguity inherent in reality'. But the Bazin quotation is itself not unambiguous, first because it comes at the precise moment when the camera lens (the monstrously large CinemaScope lens) tilts down towards us, and we cannot clearly see, at that point, what 'replaces our look', unless it is the look at another look that is looking at us, and secondly because Godard has here somewhat shortened the quotation: Bazin's words, as heard on the record in *Une Femme est une femme*, are 'the cinema replaces our look in order to offer a world which matches our desires' (Godard 1985, 211), whereas the credit-title sequence of *Le Mépris* tells us that 'the cinema replaces our look with a world which matches our desires'. To say that the cinema replaces our look is to pinpoint its essentially *documentary* nature, whereas if it does propose to replace our look with anything it is with an intellectual, *imaginary* construction. This may be only a minor point, but it is anyway symptomatic of the film's key position — its intermediary position (which is paradoxical, like any intermediary) between a belief in documentary revelation and an unavoidable knowledge of the imaginary nature of film ('Just an image', as Godard was to theorize in 1970).

This duplicity is, moreover, evident in the very style of the film. The long scene in the apartment consists mostly of an almost didactic demonstration of the 'ambiguity inherent in reality', since it involves turning the space, which is explored from every angle, into a place where 'the misunderstanding that gives rise to contempt will occur' (Faux 1986, 105): the scene is a translation, in the film, of the characters' curious opacity (as if they really existed in their own right) which comes across in the '*Scénario*' published by Godard (1985, 241). On the other hand, Godard, the great inventor of forms, has left traces of his intervention throughout the film. Taken at random, they include: violent ellipses (the accident at the end), rhythmical editing (the to-ing and fro-ing around the lamp), 'the longest tracking shots in the history of the cinema' (the credit-title sequence, but also the tracking shot of the naked Bardot), sound editing effects (e.g. the arbitrary cutting off of the song during the variety turn, so the dialogue is heard against a background of total silence), and even — though less characteristic of Godard's style — two or three quick montages of subjective flashes.

* * *

How are we, then, some 25 years later, to determine the place which this film, and the paradoxical conception of the cinema it points up and puts into practice, should occupy in the history of film? On this point as on others, I am loath to give the impression of seeing too much significance in the coincidence of dates. But the following brief chronology is surely eloquent enough: on the death of Bazin, at the end of 1958, Eric Rohmer took over as editor of *Cahiers* and gave it the rather extreme orientation that might have been expected from his earlier theoretical articles (a somewhat rigid and doctrinaire defence of a cinema of 'pure' *mise-en-scène*). His aesthetic extremism, which was accompanied, on occasions, by a similar political extremism, resulted in Rohmer being ousted by Jacques Rivette and Jacques Doniol-Valcroze in 1962. The *Cahiers* line then became more hesitant, but under the influence of Jean Douchet and newcomers brought in by him (Jean-Louis Comolli, Jean Narboni) it gradually began to call into question the *politique des auteurs* and to show a very keen interest in the 'new cinema' and 'young *auteurs*'. In the articles he wrote in the 1950s, in particular 'Le Celluloïd et le marbre', Rohmer the aesthetician placed the cinema on a higher plane than the other arts, because the latter had already entered their period of decadence whereas the cinema, paradoxically taking advantage of its innate backwardness, had yet to experience its 'classical' age. What happened instead, with the sudden emergence of new Czech, Brazilian, Canadian and British directors in the mid-1960s, was an explosion of the baroque, almost as if — and that was rather the feeling one had at the time — the classical age in question were already over and done with.

In a sense, the rapidity of that process has no parallel in the history of the arts, and there is some significance in the fact that *Le Mépris* was made when the upheaval was at its height. By 1963 Godard had already parted company with Rohmer (who influenced him considerably when he started out as a critic), because he no longer — or no longer solely — espoused the credo of *mise-en-scène*; and most of his subsequent movies up to *Weekend* (1967) marked a gradual shift towards another kind of *écriture*, one based on greater prominence being given to editing. Godard's situation in general, and more particularly in *Le Mépris*, was highly original: he was constantly tempted by classicism, but also, to an equal degree, by another, very different desire for mastery — a kind of mastery which, precisely, can be engendered only by a reflection on classicism. Indeed, that originality, that duplicity of the position of *écriture* in *Le Mépris*, now seems to go without saying, but this is largely because of the subsequent evolution of a movement which Godard initiated.

What has undoubtedly changed in the perception critics may now have of this kind of position as filmmaker are the references they attribute to it and the parallels they draw. They would certainly feel happier using the word 'mannerism' rather than *écriture*, because everyone nowadays likes to compare the cinema to painting, and also because a movie like *Le Mépris* invites such a comparison, since it illustrates one of the principles of stylistic duplicity — 'making a hole in the wall' while at the same time indicating its surface — which lay at the roots of pictorial mannerism (the film also displays equally mannerist secondary tactics, such as the off-centred presence of the filmmaker in his own work, which acts as a signature). And although crude historical parallels between painting and the cinema are always highly suspicious (their respective histories do not interlock sufficiently), the fact remains that over the last ten years or so Godard has built up an image of 'painter/filmmaker' which undoubtedly prompts a re-examination of his 'first manner' from a plastic — and, if the word needs to be used, pictorial — viewpoint. So here goes.

Le Mépris is in Technicolor. This must come as a surprise to anyone who remembers the flamboyant Technicolor of the Kalmus[7] era, during the 1940s and 1950s. While the charm of early Technicolor now seems to reside in its very flashiness, in the brilliance, even garishness, of its colours, the colour of *Le Mépris* appears on the whole much more pastel-like, much more 'moderate', much more 'natural' (it is in *Une Femme est une femme, Pierrot le fou, Made in USA* and other films Godard shot in Eastmancolor that violent colours are to be found in abundance, and increasingly so as his taste for flat-tints became more pronounced — viz *La Chinoise*). Colour is not absent from *Le Mépris*, but, put simply, it could be said that it seems to have been used not as a purely plastic material, but almost always for its emotional or symbolic impact. The strongest impression left by the shots of the trees, rocks and sea around Capri is one of light — the dazzling, relentless light of the Midi (of 'midi le juste', as Paul Valéry puts it in *Le Cimetière marin*; and, as in that poem, what the light accompanies and signifies is the presentation of a tragic world under the constant gaze of the gods). In the other parts of the film, it is the colour red that plays the most important role: it is initially associated with contempt, through the red Alfa-Romeo, because it is when she is forced to get into that car that Camille first feels contempt for Paul, but also because its facile and vulgar phallic symbolism embodies the contemptuous attitude the film shows towards the producer, himself a vulgar and macho character. The colour red seeps from the car into other scenes, and it is, for instance, when she rolls up and unrolls her red bath towel, in the apartment scene, that Camille comes to realize her mounting contempt for Paul. (The end of the film, of course, sees the return of the most basic signification of red — blood and death.) There is unfortunately no space here to discuss the blue stains on the statues (a pre-echo of Belmondo's face at the end of *Pierrot le fou*), or the saffron-yellow of Camille's and Francesca's bathrobes in the last scene in the villa.

Side by side with this work on colour, the other main plastic constituent, the frame, is similarly employed in two different ways — as a *cadre-fenêtre* (the frame as a window on the world) and as a *cadre-limite* (everything composed within the frame). Examples of the first mode include the film's (few) landscapes (the sea, the countryside around Rome), the extraordinarily flexible way the camera explores the space of the apartment, and the virtuosity of the tracking shots. But, in contrast to that, there are elements which obstruct the straightforward and natural functioning of the 'window' and tend, for example, towards the 'compositional', towards the frame as a plastic boundary. First of all there is the format of the picture itself, CinemaScope, which as everyone knows — whatever Bazin may have thought of it, and despite the rather naïve notion that more surface means more reality — is the most unrealistic format there is. As Fritz Lang rightly says to Paul Javal, it is a format that is no good for anything except, at a pinch, filming snakes and funerals (a quip which, oddly enough, cites one of the examples — the snake — given by Eisenstein in his argument in favour of changing the format from shot to shot). So Godard repeatedly uses CinemaScope here in such a way that it becomes a caricature of itself, as in the celebrated scene around the lamp, or, more obviously, in the scenes 'from *The Odyssey*' (I am thinking in particular of the shot where two statues are banished to the far left and right of the screen). But Godard exploits the frame in other ways as well. Mention must at least he made, because it recurs more than once, of the way he films viewing theatres from the proscenium, so as to show the spectators looking (or not looking) towards the screen, in a reversal of the 'normal' point of view — a 'defamiliarizing' mode of filming, and one of the manifestations of a Griffith-like archaism in Godard, where excessive transparency destroys transparency.

My last few remarks need enlarging upon, but there is no space to do so here. What I have tried to suggest is that there may be an extension, in the actual way the visible material is exploited, of the fundamental stylistic characteristic of *Le Mépris*, which is duplicity. Something finally should be said about one of the essential features of the film — the fact that it is an adaptation. In this respect as in many others, the film occupies a special position in Godard's *oeuvre*, since it is the only one of all his 'adaptations' where the plot, the characters, the situations and even some dialogue from the original novel have been retained (Godard's casual approach to the 'adaptation' of literary works is an integral part of his brand image as an iconoclast). It is in fact the only one of his films where the novel is treated as it would have been by a Hollywood director. It is consequently of some interest that the story of the film within the film itself centres almost exclusively on problems of adaptation (of *The Odyssey*): Paul Javal is hired by Prokosch to rework that adaptation, and, more importantly, most of the discussions between Lang, Prokosch and Javal are about the meaning that should be given to a modern reading of *The Odyssey*. Lang's professional and moral principles prevent him from seeing it as the story of a 'modern neurotic', while Javal, partly out of eagerness to please and partly from sincerity, ends up believing not only that this is a possible interpretation, but that he is himself a kind of unhappy Ulysses, despised by the impenetrable Penelope/Camille. But the most remarkable thing is that *Le Mépris* does not come down in favour of either of these two points of view (the third, held by the producer Prokosch, is discounted); it maintains both of them. It is as if the film accepted, pragmatically, the possibility of two or more interpretations not only of Homer's work, but of the cultural heritage in general, depending on the interpretative approach — and always supposing that it is coherent. Lang distances himself (through quotations from both Dante and Hölderlin) from any 'archaeologizing' approach to the story of Ulysses, because for him the gods are dead; but there is nothing to prevent Javal from projecting himself into a dramatic situation which, with a few minor adjustments, seems tailor-made for him — perhaps because, as Godard says, he is 'an anguished dreamer who is searching for an identity, without wishing to admit as much' (1985, 242).

The Odyssey is an epic, but also a tragedy, in the sense that it shows how the fate of mankind is sealed in advance by superior forces. *Le Mépris*, too, is a tragedy, even if the forces that grip Camille and Paul are not divine, but all too human (or socio-psychological, to use the terminology of the period). In the movement from one of these tragedies to the other, the task of the filmmaker is one of rewriting — in a way that respects the original, instead of a massacre *à la* Prokosch. It is a simple, ambitious task, which must get across the notion that even if our culture is nothing but a gigantic and interminable process of rewriting we shall always have to go back to our sources — that even after their twilight, we must still speak of the gods.

Translated from the French by Peter Graham

NOTES

1. About 500 million francs. I obtained this information from the best article so far published on *Le Mépris*, by Michel Marie (1986).
2. A popular Italian genre of the 1950s and 1960s, consisting of costume epics set in Antiquity (eds).
3. Even Leonard Maltin noticed: 'Producer Joseph E. Levine didn't seem to understand that Godard, who appears here as Lang's assistant, held *him* in contempt, making the film a highly amusing "in" joke' (1987, 186) — though to me the joke seems acerbic rather than funny. 'Before May 1968, Godard used to send telegrams addressed to "Mussolini Ponti" and "King Kong Levine" ' (Piccoli 1970, 91).
4. See, for example, his letters to such an understanding and agreeable producer as Pierre Braunberger, which, although friendly in tone, show Godard maintaining a certain directorial aloofness (Braunberger 1987, 180-189).
5. Paul's celebrated hat, too, comes straight out of *Le Doulos* (J.-P. Melville, 1962), in which Piccoli got his first really major film part; Godard was friends with Melville at the time — 'doulos' is a slang word for 'hat'.
6. *L'Express*, 9 May 1966 (reproduced in Godard 1985, 286-291).
7. Herbert T. Kalmus was a pioneer in colour technology and the founder of the Technicolor Company. Here, however, 'Kalmus' refers principally to Nathalie Kalmus (his former wife), a formidable character most dreaded by directors of photography, who, as 'technical advisor for color', made her mark on *all* Technicolour films from the 1930s to the 1950s.

SELECTED BIBLIOGRAPHY

Aumont, Jacques (1986) 'Godard peintre', *Revue belge du cinéma*, 16, 41-46.
Braunberger, Pierre (1987) *Cinémamémoire*, Centre Georges Pompidou, Centre National de la Cinématographie.
Eisenstein, Sergei (1930) 'Le Carré dynamique', French trans. *Au-delà des étoiles*, Paris, UGE, 1974, 209-223.
Faux, Anne-Marie (1986) 'Quelque chose à entendre et à regarder', *Revue belge du cinéma*, 16.
Godard, Jean-Luc (1980) *Introduction à une véritable histoire du cinéma*, Paris, Albatros.
Godard, Jean-Luc (1985) *Jean-Luc Godard par Jean-Luc Godard*, Paris, Editions de l'Etoile, 241-248.
Leutrat, Jean-Louis (1986) 'Il était trois fois', *Revue belge du cinéma*, 16.
Maltin, Leonard (1987) *TV Movies and Video Guide*, New York, New American Library.
Marie, Michel (1986) 'Un monde qui s'accorde à nos désirs', *Revue belge du cinéma*, 16.
Piccoli, Michel (1970) 'Rencontre avec Michel Piccoli', *Cinéma 70*, 147.

For additional Godard bibliography, see Chapter 15, on *A bout de souffle*.

APPENDIX

Jean-Luc Godard (1930—): filmography

See Chapter 15, on *A bout de souffle*, for full filmography.

Films cited in the text

L'Amour fou, Jacques Rivette (1968)
The Bad and the Beautiful, Vincente Minnelli (1952)
The Barefoot Contessa, Joseph Mankiewicz (1954)
Belle de jour, Luis Buñuel (1967)
Les Carabiniers (The Soldiers [UK version]; *The Riflemen* [USA version], Jean-Luc Godard (1963)
La Chinoise, Jean-Luc Godard (1967)
Détective (Detective), Jean-Luc Godard (1985)
Le Doulos (Doulos the Finger Man), Jean-Pierre Melville (1962)
Fahrenheit 451, François Truffaut (1966)
Une Femme est une femme (A Woman Is a Woman), Jean-Luc Godard (1961)
Jules et Jim (Jules and Jim), François Truffaut (1961)
Made in USA, Jean-Luc Godard (1966)
Le Mépris (Contempt), Jean-Luc Godard (1963)
La Nuit américaine (Day for Night), François Truffaut (1973)
8 1/2 (Otto e Mezzo), Frederico Fellini (1963)
Persona, Ingmar Bergman (1966)
Pierrot le fou, Jean-Luc Godard (1965)
The Quiet American, Joseph Mankiewicz (1957)
Sauve qui peut (la vie) (Slow Motion [UK]; *Every Man for Himself* [USA]), Jean-Luc Godard (1980)
Shane, George Stevens (1953)
Soigne ta droite, Jean-Luc Godard (1987)
Viaggio in Italia (Voyage to Italy [UK]; *Strangers*[USA]), Roberto Rossellini (1953)
Vie privée (A Very Private Affair), Louis Malle (1962)
Vivre sa vie (It's My Life [UK]; *My Life to Live* [USA]), Jean-Luc Godard (1962)
Weekend (WeekEnd), Jean-Luc Godard (1968)

17. Eye for *Irony:* Eric Rohmer's *Ma nuit chez Maud* (1969)

NORMAN KING

> 'You can say that my work is closer
> to the novel — to a certain classic
> style of novel which the cinema is
> now taking— than to other forms
> of entertainment, like the theatre.
> And that, for me, is significant.
> (Eric Rohmer 1971)

How faithless filmmakers, critics and audiences can be. In May 1969, the first anniversary of certain celebrated events, the French entry at Cannes was *Ma nuit chez Maud* which, after a highly favourable reception there, was quickly released in Paris, instantly drawing big houses both on the Right Bank and in the Latin Quarter. It was as if May '68 had not existed, or at least as though audiences could simply overlook it in a nostalgic glance back towards less troublesome times. That, to a great extent, was the secret of *Maud'*s success. It was not mindless, but it made you think in a comfortable way. Whether God was in his Heaven or not, all was not irredeemably wrong with the western world's traditional views on politics and morality. *Maud* was a film which happened on the cinematic scene at the right moment. It turned over an old leaf.

For once the critics were almost unanimous.[1] Here was a film that went against the grain but which was intelligent, admirably subtle, psychologically rich and captivating. It was actual in that it was in tune with 'the true morality and the true sensibility of the France of today'.[2] Yet it was also a continuation of great literary traditions: the psychological novel in its analysis of states of mind, its rigour and its economy; the realist novel in its attention to time and place, to the influence of environment on behaviour. Critics writing in conservative or progressive papers cite different examples but their standpoint is basically the same.

What is at stake, though, in this rehabilitation of the traditional is not just a hearty appeal to well-tried values after an upheaval which could still not be properly understood. It was not only the abortive revolution of May 1968 that was being effaced, but great swathes of political, moral and aesthetic history. When Henry Chapier, reviewing *Maud* in *Combat* (a radical daily) compares Rohmer to Flaubert, it is as if everything back to Zola and the Paris Commune is taken out of play. And when Jean-Louis Bory, film critic of the *Nouvel Observateur*, sees *Maud* as a brilliant dialogue within which Diderot occasionally hands over to Marivaux, it is almost as though 1789 had not happened either. Indeed, if *Maud* had appeared in 1790, 1871, or 1888 (the year after the violent split between naturalists and psychological realists), the critics would possibly have used similar arguments, more abrasively perhaps, but no less complacently. One critic does extend the literary analogy to a musical one, but only to compare *Maud* to a Mozartian cadence, a small clear note breaking through the cacophony which surrounds it. Having already described it as the opposite of a revolutionary cry and praised its classical virtues, he is like Jean de Baroncelli, valuing the film because it sets aside the troubles and obsessions of the present.[3]

Rohmer, hitherto so unfashionable, was now in favour because he made it possible to forget about so much, so many frustrating disturbances and drastic upheavals. *Maud*'s immediacy was that it offered a return to pre-revolutionary situations, to humanist values and pre-modernist aesthetics.

In one of his many interviews, Rohmer claims to be apolitical, quickly adding that whether or not he is a right-winger, he is certainly not a man of the left.[4] That is exactly how *Maud*'s spectator appears to be constructed, as intelligent abstentionist who can take discreet pleasure in the charms of bourgeois democracy, in discussions about good and bad faith, and how to make tea.

The point is not, of course, to berate Rohmer, *Ma nuit chez Maud*, its reviewers or its audiences, but to begin to understand its historical inscription, what made *Maud* so appealing to audiences in the France of 1969 and in the western world of the early 1970s. And why, in spite of Rohmer's attentiveness to the cinematic, the film has continued to be discussed in terms derived from literary debates. The reference to the past with its assurance of the permanence of value systems involves not just the denial of the actual. It evacuates in one blow the politically controversial and the blatantly commercial. It also improvises a direct line between immediate desires and the literary concerns of a hundred, two hundred or three hundred years ago.

Maud seems then to belong to a category of reactionary films which seek to efface the impingement of more urgent debates. It proposes a world of continuity rather than of radical change. While the characters talk about the actuality of Pascal, the critics refer to Diderot, Marivaux and to Flaubert, as if they could be assimilated into one great unified tradition. Yet the equation of reaction and tradition is too neat. *Maud* cannot be explained away quite so easily.

In 1966-7, when Rohmer claims the screenplay was written, *Maud* would have been set alongside *Deux ou trois choses que je sais d'elle*, and perhaps found wanting both in terms of the study of environment and of cinematic language. But in 1968-9, while Godard was struggling with *Vent d'est*, it was time to return to something safer, to the sweetness and light of *L'Enfant sauvage* and the melodramatic *La Femme infidèle*. In that context *Maud* may not seem quite so reactionary. Its challenges may appear to be gentle — but appearances in Rohmer's films are deceptive. There is always more at stake than we can initially guess. And the tradition the reviewers refer back to may not be so barren in that it does at least escape the sentimentalism of Truffaut and the self-indulgence of Chabrol. Rohmer's literariness may in fact signal a way ahead in the development of the cinematic, in the shifting of spectator position, in the construction of a cinema which does indeed feed upon tradition, arguing from the inside while gnawing away at the structures it apparently supports. In short, a cinema of irony.

There are of course other reasons for considering Rohmer's films as deriving from the literary, not least the choice of 'Moral Tales' as generic title for the series which includes *Maud*, plus the insistent references to written texts as well as the process of writing: Aurora as novelist in *Le Genou de Claire*, Bougainville as lure in *L'Amour l'après-midi*, Rousseau and Pascal as centres of debate in *La Collectionneuse* and *Ma nuit chez Maud*. Yet these are all traps in which we are invited not to be caught. Whether they hark back to early written projects formulated before Rohmer's involvement with cinema or are merely convenient structuring devices demonstrating how the characters fictionalize (or mythologize) their day-to-day existence, they are only pre-texts. It does not much matter either that Rohmer, in his own idiosyncratic way, subsequently published the Moral Tales as a series of short and not very interesting novels, or that his shooting scripts gave him the impression that he was re-working pre-existent material. What does matter is a process of conversion which draws on the literary as source for the transformation of the cinematic, redefining it and expanding its language. Or rather its signifying system, since the late 1960s were also a crucial moment in the development of a semiotics of cinema. By exploring the ironic within what had been considered a literal medium, Rohmer was, however derivatively, staking out a claim for new territory, making a film which undercut all the discourses it contained and, to an extent, its own. That, after all is what irony is about. While arguing for changes, it does not usually tell us how we can make them happen.

The literary analogies are thus more relevant than they might seem. In spite of their apparent contradictions, the examples quoted are nearly always the same ones: the psychological novel, or rather the 'roman d'analyse', since its exponents argue that it is a specifically French genre (even though its exemplar, Benjamin Constant's *Adolphe* was written by a Swiss protestant); and the 'roman réaliste', typified by Flaubert's *L'Education sentimentale*.

The two genres appear at first to share few characteristics. *Adolphe* is a short first-person narrative with few characters and virtually no description. *L'Education sentimentale* is on the other hand as concerned with environment and the meticulous study of historical events as with the behaviour of the numerous characters. But both, like most of their counterparts, are novels of misapprehension. Adolphe as narrator may seek to criticize and to justify his behaviour as protagonist, but the reader, distanced by ironic strategies, can fully accept neither the criticisms nor the justifications. In *L'Education sentimentale* the characters seek always to control their social and political environment but are unknowingly motivated and manipulated by it. Their thoughts and actions are always undercut by narrative strategies such as Flaubert's celebrated free indirect style. A double irony, then, in both instances: one which we could think of as appertaining to the intrigue, and one which is integral to a narrative discourse. We could add a third one, an irony which undermines the position of the reader, leaving him/her in a state of uncertainty, trying to resolve the enigma but unable to do so, being sent back to the beginning to try again.

Maud is also a tale of misapprehension and its strategies of irony closely resemble those of the literary genres which *Adolphe* and *L'Education sentimentale* have come to represent. Both the novels and the film foreground speech rather than action: the protagonists spend much of their time talking about, and trying to explain their actions in terms which are never quite convincing. The attempt to control via language is always illusory. The unsaid 'speaks' more clearly, undermining all certainty, except one that can be found only outside the fiction in a changed apprehension of the real.

This does not mean that we can simply assimilate *Maud* into a tradition which has such impeccable credentials, nor that we can integrate the literary analogy by shifting its terms of reference. It does not in that sense matter whether Rohmer had read Constant and Flaubert, or Diderot and Marivaux … or Jane Austen and Henry James. The literary, as subject matter, tradition or analogy, provides a lead rather than a source. It can suggest different ways of analysing irony and perhaps reflect back on the way the literary is often discussed. In other words, *Maud* as example of a cinematic irony may impose a redefinition of how it functions in written texts, diverting attention away from its classification as rhetoric towards the study of a practice, towards a notion of irony as being as historically inscribed as any other mode of discourse.

Since irony has a habit of cropping up in the most likely circumstances, signalling a disjuncture, a displacement of problems which cannot be resolved, it might be defined as pervasive discrepancy. It is less a set of rhetorical devices than a discourse which articulates the presence/absence of power, which attempts to impose power from an apparently powerless position and ultimately undercuts the illusory control of the reader/spectator. The positioning process, in filmic terms, creates a distance between the protagonist's 'I' and the viewer's eye, while providing the ambivalent pleasure of challenge, of the unresolved, and insoluble. Irony is recognition of a lack and its transferral.

Maud's narrator claims to have a hold on his life, to be in control of his luck, but from the outset he is, like Adolphe, misplaced. Returning from Valparaiso (or is it Canada?) to the Michelin tyre factory, to Clermont-Ferrand, catholicism, Pascal, Chanturgues, and a rented house in Ceyrat, he has no 'territory'. He does not even have a name. That might be called the first level or irony, a situational one. However much our narrator may seem to be the organizer of his life, events do not occur quite like that. If he does find himself in the right place at the right time, it is apparently by chance and like Flaubert's Frédéric Moreau, he attributes this to his good fortune or, more precisely, to the imperatives of the laws of fortune.

That is why the plot is so obviously contrived. If it were not, there would be no story to speak of, for when our No Name (N for short) sets off in search

Ma nuit chez Maud — above left: Maud (Françoise Fabian) and Jean-Louis Trintignant; above right: Françoise Fabian and Antoine Vitez; below: Françoise Fabian and Jean-Louis Trintignant.

of something — or someone — he encounters something or someone else, an edition of Pascal, Vidal or Maud. Françoise is seen by chance in Clermont cathedral, N's attempts to meet up with her fail, and it is only by the most outrageous of coincidences that they bump into each other, twice in the same day, after visits to Maud.

Although fundamental to the plot, this structuring irony, or irony of circumstance, is not, taken on its own, especially remarkable. Its impact derives from a combination with a second ironic level. The shooting script and the novelistic version of *Ma nuit chez Maud* are both written in the first person. Although there is a shift from the future tense at the beginning ('Je ne dirai pas tout dans cette histoire') to the past historic at the end ('Je la pris par la main et courus vers les vagues') the narrative is almost all in the present tense. More importantly, the narrator's intentions are spelt out, cutting out almost entirely the distance between the two 'I's in *Adolphe* and the use of free indirect style in Flaubert's novels. In the film the first-person, present-tense narrative has almost entirely disappeared and is replaced by an image which is discrepant. N's persistent attempt to control the event is undercut by what we see. Thus many of his seemingly haphazardous encounters are in fact motivated by unavowed intentions. N, we increasingly realize, is in the right place at the wrong time, looking for what he does not find. That is why he spends so much time exploring the centre of Clermont-Ferrand after work. He is, without admitting it, looking for Françoise. Hence his visit to the bookshop where he rediscovers Pascal, his entering a bar frequented by students only to chance upon Vidal, his acceptance of Vidal's invitation to Léonide Kogan's concert where instead of listening to the music — Mozart of course — he spends his time scanning the audience, looking to see if Françoise is there. At Midnight Mass he does the same, while Vidal, a committed Marxist, seems as genuinely interested in the ritual and the homily as he was in the sonata.

In literary terms this second level might be called the distance between engagement and estrangement, the slippage between first and third person. Its importance for cinema is that it presents a filmic equivalent of free indirect style. It is an irony which privileges the attentive spectator who is cast in a position of intelligence, whose understanding surpasses that of the characters. It establishes a complicity between the spectator and the image at the expense of the protagonists.

But irony also operates against the spectator. During the long sequence in Maud's apartment, after Christmas has been celebrated a second time and Vidal has left, Maud talks about her life, her estranged husband and her lover who died in a car crash. It is one of the few really emotional moments in the film. There is a pause, a shadow passes across the lamp and we assume, correctly, that N has changed places. But our desire, mobilized by Maud's confusion and our look at her, is that N has got up from his armchair to comfort and embrace her. In the film there is an abrupt cut. Suddenly N is standing at the window, looking at the weather conditions to see if he can go home instead of participating in Maud's distress. Along with Maud, but in a different way, we have been caught out. We already knew that the characters were not what they seemed. Now we find that the image cannot be relied upon either. In the novelistic version there is just a gap. Perhaps that shadow was not even intended to be interpreted that way. But irony is not necessarily intentional, as readers of Daisy Ashford's *The Young Visiters* (sic) will know.

There is the epilogue too, with its voice-over, again in the past historic, closing off the narrative in a way we cannot accept. Once again the audience has been taken in. We could have guessed that Françoise's lover was Maud's husband and, indeed, as in *Adolphe*, *L'Education sentimentale* and a myriad of detective stories, we are sent back to look for clues we missed or misinterpreted — and have in consequence to reflect on what has been happening to us, on how we have been misled by the layering of ironies (fortune, *mauvaise foi*, manipulation). Unlike detective stories, however, the problem is not neatly resolved by an imagined re-reading. N, as we already know, lied to Françoise in order to gain her confidence. Now he compounds that lie, putting himself in the wrong in a doubly ironic way, sinning in his own catholic terms against the Holy Spirit while she repeats her sin of omission by not at last taking the opportunity to recount that vital episode in her past life. The rest is a silence founded on an illusory confidence, on untruths which undermine all that we have just seen and everything we have witnessed previously. There is no place here for complacency, just for discrepancy, in time as well as action. Everyone is deceived, including ourselves.

When, after all, is this epilogue taking place? The main action of the film looks for all the world as if it is set in Clermont-Ferrand in December 1968 (even though there are no references to current events, no apparent attempts are made in the location shooting to put us back a few years in time). Yet the epilogue takes place several years later (five in the novelistic version and the shooting script), and Rohmer's meticulously realist signalling of days of the week and dates cannot, according to the calendar, correspond to 1968. They could be 1964 but in that case the epilogue has to be situated after the film has been completed, and after its release. That is its final irony, as text which gives us no secure place from which to start or finish. It is like Flaubert's 'Vers le début de cet hiver' in the final chapter of *L'Education sentimentale* (is it *this* or *that* winter? — 1869 or 1867 — probably the former, the one which implicates the reader).

This third level is both pernicious and crucial as an ultimate undermining of the spectator's confidence, whether we realize it or not. Without it, the other levels would hardly be worth analysing except as rhetorical devices. With it, it becomes possible to begin to sketch out a politics of irony and of its historical incidence which could, in the examples quoted here, be considered as displacement of the political to the moral and of the moral to the aesthetic.

Constant, by setting the main strand of his narrative in late eighteenth-century Germany and Poland, completely effaces the political as actuality. Instead he transfers the terms of the debate to morality, even suppressing the sections of his preface which did indeed link the moral to the political. In the end he resorts to the aesthetic as the only possibility of change. Flaubert described *L'Education sentimentale* as the moral history of a generation which, living in a world of misapprehension, had no hold on its time. Like N, the characters never quite get their act together, blaming fate for good or bad luck without realizing that there are other factors at work. Flaubert does not efface the political, as Constant and Rohmer do. On the contrary, he upfronts it, but only to subject it to his heaviest ironies, unmasking it as the determinant of a suspect morality (there are no moral politicians and those who believe there might be are deluded). Only the artist can speak the unpalatable truth.

Both novels thus foreground the moral as yet another trap. It provides no answers whereas the political should and the aesthetic could, if only in the Imaginary. The displacement is in effect a sabotaging of the moral, using it as a passage from one instance to another. It is an attempt to reassert power.

Constant sketched out *Adolphe* during the First Empire but completed it only during the Restoration. In both instances he was marginalized, unable to pursue the political career he valued more than literature. Flaubert in his insistence on art was even more out of sympathy with his time. If the moral was a pretext, the aesthetic was a refuge from the political. Irony in both cases is a specific response to a historical moment. It is political because it can only respond in an aesthetic way. It asserts a power which it does not really have.

That punctuality of irony, always there when there is nothing else to be done, is what makes *Maud* distinctive. The world we are confronted with is patently provincial France of the late 1960s. It looks and it sounds tremendously convincing. Yet the political, that unavoidable issue in 1960s France, has apparently been evacuated and the moral centred. But yet again the moral is undermined. The aesthetic reigns not as content or form but as a discourse founded upon traditions which are both upheld and challenged. The film's ironies are only a feigned absence of power, giving the momentary impression that the protagonist, the environment or the reader might possibly be in control of meaning. Its object is to construct the author-in-the-text as sole incidence of true knowledge.

Irony also negates that attempt to impose a discourse of control. In one of his many interviews Rohmer expressed a desire to create a cinema in which the camera would be absolutely invisible. Whether he was aware of it or not, he was paraphrasing and updating Flaubert's remarks on authorship and style. The book (or the film) would seem to be unauthorized, to be coming from nowhere. What this implies, however, is the construction of a text which exempts the author from a level of irony which would include Him. Like a deist God, he has just set things in motion, leaving his imperfect creatures to sort things out for themselves.

Flaubert, in his other most quoted remark, said that he would so much like to write a book that would not be about anything at all, a book without 'content'. Perhaps, relatively speaking, Rohmer succeeded there more than Flaubert. Hardly anything happens in *Maud*. People meet up for various reasons, they eat, drink, go to concerts and masses — and Marie insists on seeing the Christmas lights. But mostly they just talk or look. There are just there, imagining that they know why. Or sometimes admitting that they do not.

It is a response to the actual that is always relevant, but only as statement of inadequacy. That, ultimately, is the point of references to literary analogies. They make us rethink both the novelistic and the cinematic. They make us think again about the classic realist text, imposing a reinsertion of irony and how it functions politically within a hierarchy or discourses, recognizing its presence when there is, authorially speaking, nothing else to be done. For all his aestheticism, we can thank Rohmer for that. He signals a gap which moral pretensions and pious thoughts can never fill.

NOTES

1. There is a well-chosen selection of reviews in *Avant-Scène Cinéma*, 98, 1969.
2. Pierre Billard, writing in *L'Express*, 9 June 1969.
3. Gilles Jacob, *Les Nouvelles littéraires*, 22 May 1969.
4. *Le Monde*, 7 June 1969.

SELECTED BIBLIOGRAPHY

Clouzot, Claire (1972) *Le Cinéma français depuis la nouvelle vague*, Paris, Nathan.
Collet, Jean (1972) *Le Cinéma en question*, Paris, Editions du Cerf.
Crisp, Colin (1977) 'The Ideology of Realism. Eric Rohmer: *Celluloid and Marble* and *My Night with Maud*', *Australian Journal of Screen Theory*, 2, 3-32.
Elsaesser, Thomas (1974) 'The Cinema of Irony', *Monogram*, 5, 1-2.
Etudes Cinématographiques (1985-1986), 146-152 (Eric Rohmer I and II).
Magny, Joël (1986) *Eric Rohmer*, Paris, Rivages.
Monaco, James (1976) *The New Wave*, New York, Oxford University Press.
Rohmer, Eric (1974) *Six contes moraux*, Paris, Lherne.
Vidal, Marion (1977) *Les Contes moraux d'Eric Rohmer*, Paris, Lherminier.

For a more complete bibliography and for details of Rohmer's writings and interviews, see Magny, Vidal and *Monthly Film Bulletin*, December 1976.

SCRIPT

Rohmer, Eric (1969) *Ma nuit chez Maud*, *Avant-Scène Cinéma*, 98.

APPENDIX

Eric Rohmer (1920—): filmography

1950 *Journal d'un scélérat* (short)
1951 *Charlotte et son steack* (short)
1952 *Les Petites filles modèles* (short)
1954 *Bérénice* (short)
1954 *La Sonate à Kreutzer* (short)
1958 *Véronique et son cancre* (short)
1959 *Le Signe du lion*
1960 *La Boulangère de Monceau* (short)
1963 *La Carrière de Suzanne* (short)
1964 *Nadja à Paris* (short)
1965 *Paris vu par* (episode)

1966 *Une étudiante à Paris* (short)
1967 *La Collectionneuse*
1968 *Fermière à Montlaucon* (short)
1969 *Ma nuit chez Maud* (*My Night with Maud*)
1970 *Le Genou de Claire* (*Claire's Knee*)
1972 *L'Amour l'après-midi* (*Love in the Afternoon*)
1976 *La Marquise d'O*
1978 *Perceval le Gallois*
1980 *La Femme de l'aviateur* (*The Aviator's Wife*)
1982 *Le Beau mariage*
1983 *Pauline à la plage*
1984 *Les Nuits de la pleine lune* (*Full Moon in Paris*)
1986 *Le Rayon vert* (*The Green Ray* [UK]; *Summer* [USA])
1986 *Quatre aventures de Reinette et Mirabelle*
1987 *L'Ami de mon amie*

Other films cited in the text

Deux ou trois choses que je sais d'elle (*Two or Three Things I Know about Her*),
    Jean-Luc Godard (1966)
L'Enfant Sauvage (*The Wild Child*), François Truffaut (1970)
La Femme infidèle, Claude Chabrol (1968)
Vent d'est, Jean-Luc Godard (1970)

18. ' Liberté! Egalité! Paternité': Jean-Luc Godard and Anne-Marie Miéville's *Sauve qui peut (la vie)* (1980)

CLAIRE PAJACZKOWSKA

> 'In what way can psychoanalysis cast light on the cinematic signifier?' (Christian Metz)[1]

> 'I hate cinema.' (Anne-Marie Miéville)[2]

Sauve qui peut (la vie) marked Jean-Luc Godard's return to filmmaking following a five year period in video and television production. He describes it as 'my second first film; as at the time of the New Wave I am simultaneously proposing a language and an analysis of that language'.[3] This essay discusses the film in relation to three main problems, first the question of authorship, second the question of the representation of women, and third the question of narrative.

Since 1974, Godard has worked in close collaboration with Anne-Marie Miéville, with whom he co-founded the SonImage production company, following a return to his native Switzerland at the close of the Dziga-Vertov period. 'She is at least 50% of this film' Godard has said in interviews, and Miéville is credited with editing the film and co-scripting it (with Jean-Claude Carrière, Buñuel's scriptwriter). Their collaboration is an interesting one, marking many changes in the themes of Godard's work. Whereas the earlier post-1968 films (the Godard-Gorin and Dziga-Vertov period), focused almost exclusively on narrowly defined political and social issues, the SonImage projects have broadened both the range of themes and the range of analyses. Some notable changes have included a wider recognition of 'significant' people, to include children, families, the middle-aged and the elderly, with fewer photogenic young revolutionaries; and an increasing focus on the filmmaker's 'self' as an object of potential knowledge and criticism.

Miéville's work as a filmmaker can give us some idea of the kind of influence she may have had on Godard's change of direction. Her film *Le Livre de Marie*, a study of the effects of parental divorce on the emotional life of a young girl, is an empathic and thoughtful observation on the rights and needs of children. Miéville seems to work within a tradition of women's values, so that where Godard's *Je vous salue Marie* shocked the Pope, Miéville's *Le Livre de Marie* illuminated the ordinary anguish of adolescence.

Their first collaboration was *Ici et ailleurs*, then came *Numéro deux,* an analysis of the family as a social institution, of the division between the spheres of home and work, and of the relationship between the sexes. Godard included himself, as filmmaker, within the field of vision and included the decisions, demands and contradictions of filmmaking within the diegetic space. *Sauve qui peut (la vie)* resumes the analysis of these themes — and adds to them the opposition between country and city. But it is mostly a study of Godard's 'self'; either intentionally, or by virtue of a crisis of identity and a quest for self-knowledge, or a combination of both. *Sauve qui peut (la vie)* is an observation of how the 'self' is constructed through actions and reactions, desire, vision, the reciprocity of language and representation. It is especially an exploration of relationships created in, or blocked by, violence.

These themes are now fairly common in independent cultural production, since feminism has required of men a greater measure of self-awareness and personal responsibility. And also since psychological and psychoanalytic theory has been added to the means we have for trying to understand our 'selves' and the outside world, and the relation between these. Whereas, traditionally, there was one set of codes for representing the world of personal relationships, melodrama, and another for representing the world of social or external reality, the documentary, Godard creates new combinations of both sets of codes to represent 'the fiction of the reality and the reality of the fiction'. For example, *Sauve qui peut (la vie)* works with constant references to music, its presence or absence on the soundtrack is monitored by the characters who ask 'What is that music?', certain characters can or cannot hear it. Peter Harcourt[4] has suggested that only some of the women characters hear the orchestral (non ambient sound) music, which would seem to reinforce the cultural associations between music, melodrama and 'women's pictures'. Cityscapes, industrial landscape and urban interiors are represented in documentary codes, with ambient sound, non actors, and fewer close-up shots. Also the codes of pornography (possibly a sub-category of the documentary), are used in several sequences.

What is particularly interesting about *Sauve qui peut (la vie)* is that the standard themes of contemporary filmmaking, such as the use of formal self-reflexivity to represent and analyse personal self-knowledge, and the ways in which gender, inner reality and social reality are interconnected, are here centred on one particular man's 'self'. It is the life of Paul Godard (the name of Jean-Luc's father) that is central to the web of interconnecting relations; and it raises the interesting problem of how to represent one man's struggle for meaning without misrepresenting it as simply 'everyman's' struggle, or overdramatizing it as a unique tragedy.

Critics' assessment of the film is quite divided on this issue, many see Godard as the 'great barometer', as does Richard Roud, others claim him as *auteur*, which is more usual in art cinema.

> *Sauve qui peut* is the film of a man at the end of his tether,
> and a perfect reflection of the times in which we live:
> chaotic, pessimistic, fragmentary. The world today seems

hell bent on going to hell in a handcart and Godard, the great
barometer, has portrayed that in his film.[5]

Here the filmmaker, as recipient of the external environment, or as gauge
of a social climate, is more or less passive in the relation of transmitting
meaning from world to spectator. Alternatively, John Coleman:

> I find something painfully autobiographical and undigested
> in Godard's oeuvre. It is possible that this is what I am
> supposed to be doing. But if honesty is the best policy it is not
> inevitably interesting.[6]

This view accords the *auteur* a more active role in the generation of the
film's meaning, although 'undigested' implies that it may be the result of
unintentional as well as intentional meaning. Godard himself[7] has been quite
vocal in denouncing the auteurist policies of the New Wave, claiming that these
were formulated by the group of young filmmakers through sheer
self-interest. But whatever the claims of the New Wave *auteurs* themselves, the
concept of auteurism has developed an autonomous existence as part of a
critical method. From Sarris' construction of the auteur theory to the more
systematic analyses of auteur-structuralism, the concept of auteurism in
cinema is a fundamental part of film analysis. Just as the concept of authorship
has been a source of heated controversy in the adjacent fields of literary
analysis and art history, the textual analysis of film has sought to understand
the process of authorship. The puzzle of trying to formulate the interrelations
between author, textual structure, social structure and reading or spectating
subject, remains unresolved, enigmatic and compelling. In *Sauve qui peut (la
vie)* the question of authorship is further complicated by the fact of
co-production. And besides having taken on the name of his father, in an
Oedipal gesture, Godard's text represents the 'death of the author' as a literal
event when Paul Godard is run over by a car at the close of the narrative. The
symbols and meanings of authorship and paternity in the film are certainly
over-determined, as we shall see.

If Godard started out with the belief that the meaning of his films was
self-generated, he later changed his mind entirely and considered film as
'society communicating with itself'. The *politique des auteurs* in its most naïve
form may well have been defensive; it seems unlikely that the young, and
mostly male, filmmakers in 1950s France could have been the cause of the
New Wave phenomenon that brought them such sudden and loud acclaim.
They, in their youth and masculinity, may well have been the signifiers of an
idealized excitement, potential, hope and glamour, characteristic of the despair
of an older generation of French men and women who had survived through
two world wars and under German occupation. The older generation may
have been colluding with the narcissism of the sons, combining a denial of
their own suffering with hope for their children's futures. Like tragic heroes,
unaware of the forces that created the manic upswing of the New Wave, they

believed in the autonomy of a self that, after all, seemed to be confirmed by their environment, or at least its media. Many of the New Wave filmmakers continued their careers in the film industry, with critical acclaim and media recognition, although not quite of the same intensity as the initial upsurge. Godard, however, turned to Marxism, predicted and participated in the uprisings of 1968, and replaced the *auteur* with the collective, to remake film according to the model of Revolutionary Communism. The idea of a film crew was replaced by the political cell, a revolutionary history was rediscovered and Dziga-Vertov's working name adopted. At the same time Godard identified himself as belonging to a generation of 'Marx and Coca-Cola'. Authorial intention went from the driving seat to being a mere cipher, the subject was conceived of as a refraction of media imagery, becoming unified and significant only in and through class struggle. *Le Gai savoir* depicts the excitement and bewilderment of starting from a degree zero of language, using Situationist syntheses of politics and Surrealism, and proposing simultaneously 'a language and an analysis of that language'.

Sauve qui peut (la vie) recapitulates these earlier forms of authorship. Godard is collaborating with Miéville in a deliberate and politically informed way, making the collaboration a theme of the film itself in the relationship between Paul Godard and Denise Rimbaud (played by Jacques Dutronc and Nathalie Baye), and yet maintaining the role of director or, as he has termed it, 'composer'. Whereas Denise and Paul's collaboration is represented as violent and 'impossible', Godard and Miéville collaborated successfully. The question of authorship raised within the film seems to be. 'What is it that prevents men and women from working and living together as equals?' From where does the 'impossibility' of progressive collaboration emanate?

The film, having no unifying narrative or narratives, has five sections which are named and numbered in sequence. Each section is the 'story' of one of the central characters, presenting what might be called their predicament. Within these sections the characters create and break relationships with one another in a series of points in time that are loosely connected or unconnected. The main characters are Paul Godard, a filmmaker, Denise Rimbaud his co-worker and lover, and Isabelle Rivière (Isabelle Huppert) a country girl arriving in the city and setting up as a stylized prostitute.

The first section is numbered zero and called *La Vie*, it opens on blue sky, an airplane's vapour trail and orchestral music. The landscape is rural Switzerland and Denise Rimbaud is framed riding her bike through the country. The easy rhythm of the cutting and the feel of her freedom of movement is interrupted by an unexpected intrusion of the film's form, stop-motion photography.

The second section (1) *L'Imaginaire*, is Denise's 'story', she is leaving the city and her work in television to move to the country. She is leaving her flat and is leaving Paul Godard. When framed in the city she is often arguing with Paul and is almost always active, when in the country she is often portrayed as reflective, writing, listening, or as free, cycling across open spaces. She is self-absorbed in writing something that 'may be part of a novel'.

Sauve qui peut (la vie) — above: Isabelle Huppert and Jacques Dutronc; centre: Isabelle Huppert; below: Jean-Luc Godard in front of poster representing Sylvie Vartan.

The third section (2) *La Peur*, fear, is Paul's 'story'. He is seen living alone, framed as constrained by the walls of his dimly lit hotel room; the emptiness of his space is underscored by the booming voice of a female opera singer which invades his privacy until he bangs on the wall to 'stop the noise'. Paul's body is framed so that it seems insignificant and lost within architectural space. A 'foreign' hotel employee wants to touch him, professing to love him, homosexuality appears as an alien threat which imposes itself from the outside. Paul meets and argues with Denise; one stop-motion sequence shows a depressing meal time, the stasis between the couple is violently interrupted as Paul lunges at Denise in a fantasy gesture which is both erotic and aggressive. Paul is also seen meeting with his ex-wife and their daughter, and he experiences them as making excessive (financial) demands on him. In another stop-motion sequence the daughter, Cecile, is catching and throwing a ball, absorbed in a relation of reciprocity from which Paul is excluded, except as voyeur; and the voice-over soundtrack is of two men discussing perverse, incestuous desires for their daughters. In a later sequence, Paul listens to Cecile telling him about how the blackbird has adapted to city life, as if this is a metaphor for the corruption of innocence he feels his perverse fantasy might be. Paul's complete inability to be a father to his child is probably the most tragic of all the inadequate relationships depicted, but it is not represented as such. Paul's fear is located as part of a more general masculine predicament, along with the 'arrogance and terminal despair' of the businesman-technocrat, and the violence of the motorbikers later on. David Denby notes that the film is full of images of men brutalizing women in the most casual ways. In the scene with the motorbikers, another of the stop-motion sequences, one biker symbolically clad in black leather, slaps a woman's face from side to side trying to make her choose between the two men. She repeatedly refuses to make a choice, an ironic comment on how men 'coerce women into exercising free will'.[8]

Isolation and fear are also present in Paul's workplace. When he teaches a class about film (and Godard, since the Dziga-Vertov period, has seen film as a form of education rather than entertainment) he is framed alone against the blackboard. On the blackboard is written 'Cain and Abel, Cinema and Video'; the filmmaker alone with his conflicts, and his decisions.

Furthermore it transpires that Paul is only present at this screening/seminar because Marguerite Duras refuses to be, he is a stand-in for the 'mother' of the avant-garde. This mysterious scene in which Jean-Luc pays homage to Duras, but only *by putting himself in her place* is crucial for understanding Godard's central fantasy about himself as filmmaker. He is unable to work *with* Denise as a woman and filmmaker, and can only learn from women by taking their place. In making this identification with Duras/Mother he loses the capacity to speak for himself and becomes her voice.

The fourth section (3) is *Le Commerce* — the 'story' of Isabelle Rivière in which themes of prostitution and pornography are explored. Godard has often used the theme of prostitution as a metaphor. In *Vivre sa vie* and *Deux ou trois choses que je sais d'elle* it serves as a description of the condition of women in our society, exchanging sex, love, domestic labour for money, power or security. Then again, as part of a French tradition of Romantic artists, Godard uses prostitution as a metaphor for the predicament of the artist in capitalist society, where the pure concerns of Art must be debased and commodified. Godard had proclaimed, somewhat melodramatically, 'I myself am a whore, fighting against the pimps of cinema', and a scene in *Sauve qui peut (la vie)* shows Isabelle punished by her pimps for having tried to work without them, being spanked and forced to repeat 'Only the banks are independent'. The metaphor of the prostitute when used to symbolize the predicament of the artist in capitalist society is popular but inappropriate. It tends to obscure the fact that most artists receiving state or commercial sponsorship are men, but more fundamentally it tends to eroticize the nature of the exchange between the funding agency and artist. If Isabelle's humiliation is a metaphor for Godard's relation to 'the banks', this erotic fantasy conceals the artist's more ambivalent anger or guilt about the inadequacy of his own resources. Also, as Laura Mulvey has noted,[9] throughout his films Godard has tended to use the image of woman as a signifier of sexuality, guilt and shame, which is the basis of this metaphor.

Thirdly, prostitution and pornography are representative of a kind of alienated sexuality, where the self has separated from the body. As Isabelle nonchalantly acts out her clients' scenarios of male fantasy, her inner monologue, talking about affectionate friendships with women, is heard on the soundtrack. Alternative readings of Isabelle's predicament have been suggested: Angela Carter sees Isabelle as one who 'sells her body but retains her integrity',[10] the *Camera Obscura* editors find the impassive nonchalance more sinister and disturbing.[11] Julia Kristeva sees this character as typifying something 'cold and calculating' in many of Godard's women characters.[12]

Le Commerce contains what may be the most memorable of the film's sequences, a parody of a Sadean orgy, orchestrated by a businessman in his office. Robert Stam describes, and interprets, the scene:

> We are shown a technocrat's wet dream — the Taylorisation of sexual production. Sex is programmed and disciplined by the science of management. The boss monopolizes the information, plans the work, and sets the procedures. Like a filmmaker he assigns precise movement and attitudes to the 'actors' (his assistant, a secretary and a prostitute). The image taken care of, he concentrates on the soundtrack. Each participant is assigned a dipthong ('ai', 'ei') — presumably the signifier of rampaging lust — to be repeated at regular intervals. The orgy participants, like assembly line workers, are reduced to well-defined jerks, twists, moans and quivers. The *cinéaste*-patron literally oversees a hierarchy of domination. The sightlines are arranged by him and work to his benefit. Yet, ultimately he cannot enjoy his power.

Isabelle reads his face and finds 'dark pride, terminal despair, arrogance and fear'.[13]

The scene is both very funny and sinister, it certainly conveys a forceful critique of industrial mechanization, as an expression of the destructive potential of a need for absolute control. It gives a dramatic enactment of the psychoanalytic view of cinema as a perverse form of voyeurism, the businessman-*cinéaste* might also represent the spectator of the classic-realist film demanding that the diegesis should be a system of moving parts, to form a circuit of projection and introjection between the screen and the self. Kristeva has suggested that this scene represents an unconscious fantasy of a man being both sexes simultaneously, an auto-erotic omnipotence fantasy. This key scene, like the scene in which Paul Godard identifies himself with Marguerite Duras, clearly articulates a fundamental male fantasy, that of being a woman or *the only* woman, Mother. It is probably this fantasy that gives meaning to the character of Isabelle, the debased woman or prostitute, who is also used by Jean-Luc Godard as a self-image.

The final section of the film, (4) *La Musique*, takes the place of narrative closure. It is the orchestration of the themes initiated earlier, and, despite the strongly anti-narrative structure, gives a sense of some desultory resolutions. The space vacated by Denise, as she leaves the corruption of the city, is taken over by Isabelle who initiates her sister into selling her body. The co-worker with integrity is replaced by a perverse and calculating girl, leaving Paul Godard bereft. Worse still, in a dramatic closing scene Paul Godard is left by his ex-wife and Cecile only to be run over by the pimp's Mercedes; 'Isn't that Daddy?' Cecile asks her mother, 'Cela ne nous regarde pas' ('It's none of our business'), replies her mother, displaying the same indifference to suffering that has traditionally been typical of men vis-à-vis women. The film's main theme music wells up, and, as the camera follows mother and daughter through an urban landscape, we see the orchestra, in formal dress, playing. Is it Jean-Luc Godard's bid to free us from the emotional manipulation of melodrama, to distance us, and himself, from Paul Godard's masochistic fantasy that he will die if he is not loved? The *form* of death is significant I would argue. Not only is being run over commonly referred to as 'se faire écraser' — being crushed (as metaphorically in the experience of losing hope or suffering a narcissistic blow), but there were also two real road accidents that featured significantly in Jean-Luc Godard's life, his own accident in 1970, and his mother's death in a car crash in 1954. This particular form of narrative closure is over-determined, but its emotional significance has been displaced and only the violence remains.

Godard has said of the film's title, 'If the film has a double title it is because I wanted to give it a title that would be at once commercial and classical, "Sauve qui peut" — Every Man for Himself — is a formula, and a simultaneous desire to call it "life" or "joy", the sky, passion, or something like that.' Here again are the ambivalence, and ambiguity, that run throughout the film, in its themes — such as commerce versus truth or art, love embattled with violence, being related or being isolated, hope versus despair — and in its formal structure, particularly the narrative coherence and incoherence. 'Sauve qui peut' *is* formulaic but it is also, traditionally, the cry of despair of a shipwrecked and drowning man, so another narrative closure is potentially present in a different metaphor, in 'drowning', that is in grief.

In using an auteurist method one might interpret the film's script, themes, title and stories, as a symptomatic text, as a kind of body, or a form of manifest content of Jean-Luc Godard's unconscious conflicts. But the film has two authors and Godard has insisted that it is a product of their collaboration.

Moreover, Christian Metz and Laura Mulvey have argued that a psychoanalysis of cinema has more to offer as a method of investigating the cinematographic apparatus, to show how the mechanism of identification works to articulate psychic and social reality.

Drawing from both these methods one can find, through the imagery and narrative structure of *Sauve qui peut*, traces of a fantasy of an escape from the Oedipus complex, and so can connect the meaning of the film's violence to the 'impossibility' of a relation between the sexes.

As MacCabe and Mulvey have noted:

> Godard's perception of women in the economy is simultaneously illuminating and obscurantist [...] Godard's films conflate woman and sexuality. It is as though woman can be of interest only through her sexuality [...] woman, once again becomes the sign for the sexual desires and fears of men [...] an image of mystery, essential otherness and, very often, violence and deceit.[14]

When Isabelle moves into Denise's flat she is framed against a window, a familiar Godardian motif. She looks at two photographs fixed to the wall to her right. Above is a smiling Chinese child holding up a can of Coca-Cola. Below is a photograph, either documentary or pornographic, of a naked couple copulating. Now that Maoist children happily drink from the symbol of US imperialism, Marx and Coca-Cola, one time polar opposites like Daddy and Mummy, have merged into the same reality. And if we are no longer the generation of Marx and Coca-Cola, then are Isabelle/Godard/we merely the by-product of the body's need to discharge sexual tension, the children of physical reproduction? Isabelle's enigmatic inner world is as hidden from vision as her body is exposed to it. It exists on the soundtrack as an inner monologue, the *parole de femme* or woman's speech that signifies the invisible truth of a real but inner world. This scene suggests that socio-political reality and physical reality can have meaning only when connected through the subjective world of the 'self'.

This scene is unusual. In most of Godard's films women are presented as girls, sexual and beautiful in a childlike way. With a few exceptions they are, as MacCabe and Mulvey suggest, the embodiment of male desires and fears. Jean Seberg's boyish haircut, Anna Karina's round face, Juliet Berto's pouting mouth and high pitched voice, were the precursors of the more recent nymphets in school vests. Godard gets older but his women never grow up, in fact they seem to get younger.

The forms of sexuality portrayed in the films, and especially in *Sauve qui peut (la vie)*, are almost always perverse — anality, orality, exhibitionism, voyeurism, violence, sado-masochism, fetishism and narcissism are everywhere, so that ordinary coitus seems insignificant if not non-existent. In *Weekend, Vent d'est, La Chinoise, Le Gai savoir*, even simple explanations of the workings of capitalist economy were not free from images of naked women signifying the dehumanization effect of the commodity production of the 'consumer society's' use of woman as spectacle. Not unlike a magician's assistants, or the 'lovely gals' on a TV game show, Godard's women handed round copies of the Little Red Book, or sat naked decoratively signifying patriarchal oppression.

The one time when a woman was represented as actively engaged in meaningful work — Jane Fonda as Susan, reporting a strike in *Tout va bien* — Godard and Gorin later retracted the implicit support with a brutal sequel in *Letter to Jane*. Kristeva has argued that Godard represents women's motivation as somewhere 'beyond the pleasure principle':

> The question is whether this *beyond the pleasure principle* is a place from which they can thereby speak the truth about sexuality and male fantasy [...] or whether this *beyond the pleasure principle*, with its tendency towards violence, death and *jouissance* is the depth of repression.[15]

It seems to me that there are two types of female character in *Sauve qui peut (la vie)*. There are the girls like Cecile, Isabelle, Denise and the woman being hit by the biker, whose faces or bodies are the objects of an obsessive and tactile gaze, usually marked by stop-motion photography. These are fetishized and sexualized women who are objects of desire and violence. The second type of female character is, of course, the mother. But these mothers are all absent. As in the enigmatic absence of Marguerite Duras from her screening, the absent mother becomes transformed into a metaphor, a symbol. In a spectacular contradiction, as a stand-in for Duras, Paul Godard tells the audience 'Every time you see a truck (*camion*) go by, say to yourself *c'est une parole de femme*', referring to Duras' novel and film *Le Camion*. Not unlike the Roman Catholic doctrine of the assumption of the Holy Virgin Mother who rose to heaven, Paul Godard sublimates Duras through the presence of her words in writing, but also carries the additional meaning of the absence, the death, of Jean-Luc Godard's own mother, who died in a road accident. This absence leads Godard to speak, to symbolize, to make films, to replace the absent mother in some way himself. Similarly, the businessman-technocrat's ultimate consolation is his omnipotent fantasy of being both sexes simultaneously, the phallic mother. And another scene which symbolizes the absent mother is Paul Godard's disappearance under the wheels of the pimp's

Mercedes, which could be seen as a fantasy of being the mother in a masochistic primal scene in which copulation is mistaken for death. The violence in the film clearly is a replacement for loss and mourning.

The perverse child-woman as other, as signifier of male desire, is the alternative to identifying with woman as mother and being dead. The point of perverse sexuality, as the psychoanalyst Janine Chasseguet-Smiregel suggests, is to deny coitus, to deny the Oedipus complex and to deny difference, using pregenital sexualities to replace genitality. Genitality entails an acknowledgement of sexual maturity, and the need for a partner who is one's sexual other. This is represented as castration, the loss of a self that needs recognize no other. Often in Godard's films perverse child-women are pregenital substitutes protecting the man from an encounter with the other and with reality. Similarly the *identification* with the mother, with Godard as Duras or with the phallic mother, may also be a form of avoiding an encounter with difference, a narcissistic short-circuit to avoid reality.

But perhaps this fetishistic escape from reality is inherent in the film medium, as the apparatus of identification and the cinematic textual system is based on the activation of perverse partial drives and their corresponding fantasies, as Mulvey has explained.[16]

Godard's films have always been part of the experimental avant-garde, and like Brecht, the Soviet Formalists and the Situationists he combines poetic formalism with political analysis to forge an alternative to classic realism. The jump cuts in *A bout de souffle*, the episodic narrative of *Masculin-féminin*, the spiral movement of *Le Gai savoir*, were all aspects of what Peter Wollen has defined as counter-cinema,[17] a textual practice that combines signifying elements in new, unexpected and self-reflexive ways. The codes of classic realism, that is the conventions of illusionism, narrative transitivity leading to closure and the denial of authorial enunciation, were seen as collusive with middle-class ideology which obscures historical contradiction. The critique of cinematic illusionism has taken many forms: some filmmakers concentrate on the image or viewing context, which makes film an equivalent to painting and the visual arts, others on the sound/image relation, others on narrativity. The most extreme of the latter denounced narrative transitivity as 'fascist', although from the outset the danger of setting up an opposition between inherently good or bad forms had been signalled by Wollen. What a radical formalism was intended to create was a freedom for the spectator, to loosen the ties (the etymological origin of the term ana-lyse) binding the spectator to the fantasies depicted on the screen, and thus to enable spectators to understand and eventually enjoy the process by which the film creates meaning. Counter-cinema was to facilitate a state of 'passionate detachment'[18] for the spectator, as a freedom from fascination.

The inevitable and understandable confusion and frustration of those spectators unfamiliar with the codes of counter-cinema were to be taken into account by filmmakers at some level of their practice, by offering alternative satisfactions, by offering truth, and by expecting limited audiences. Godard uses all of these and often uses humour and irony, such as in *Sauve qui peut (la vie)* where the 'orgy' scene offers intellectual pleasure which counteracts the anxiety and unease of the imagery. The numbered sequences provide a beat which is echoed in the rhythm of the editing, replacing a story with a pulse.

In theory, the destruction of narrative transitivity is intended as an introduction to the construction of new relations of causality. Classic realism is abandoned as a fiction in order to be able to represent truer causal relations such as the effects of history, the economy, social institutions, language and the unconscious.

There are times in Godard's counter-cinema when the attack on narrative coherence does not result in the facilitation of the spectator's capacity to think. There are times when the intensity of the aggression, combined with the distraction of perverse sexual imagery, provokes a withdrawal or counter-attack, obliterating the freedom to think. This experience is different from the frustration or confusion suffered when there is a lack of the kind of textual gratification offered by classic realism. The experience to which I refer involves an attack on linking and on causality itself.

Godard has suggested that a narrative consists of 'a beginning, a middle and an end, but not necessarily in that order' and that 'cinema is not one image after another it is one image *plus* another out of which is formed a third, the latter being formed by the viewer the moment he or she makes contact with the film'.[19] At one level this is formal experimentation, courageous and imaginative, but at another level it is an attack, not just on the conventions of realism but on reality itself. To obliterate the temporal axis in favour of a spatial axis is to do away with one of the bases of reality.

By the same token, formalist analyses of narrative which see in it only sequences of paradigms with little or no temporal significance are reductive. The subjective dimension of narrative, as Bruno Bettleheim has demonstrated using the structures of fairy tales, is that it gives form to the Oedipus complex, giving symbolic recognition to what can be represented, metaphorically, as a journey or transition.[20] The journey in question is the transition from infancy and childhood to maturity, and the time that must elapse between the awakening of sexual desires in the Oedipus complex and their possible gratification following maturity. Or, to use a Lacanian model, the trajectory of the subject from the Imaginary — in which difference, time and frustration do not exist — to the Real, in which they do. Narrative transition, from an equilibrium through loss and disruption to a new equilibrium built on the relics of the first, corresponds to the universal need for a symbolic recognition of the Oedipus complex, and stories, when told, recounted or read, or in film, are a necessary part of the Symbolic which facilitates the loss of the Imaginary and the journey towards the Real. To reduce the temporal axis of narrative to a set of paradigmatic combinations is to collapse the Symbolic back into the Imaginary, and so deny reality.

The ambivalence which is characteristic of many Godard films, and especially *Sauve qui peut (la vie)* exists in both the imagery of women and in the narrative structure. It is not only the product of anger directed at an exploitative economy, oppressive social institutions or manipulative textual systems (this aspect of Godard is well documented), but is also unconscious aggression at the Oedipus complex as a fact of reality.

The film's central predicament, like those of its characters, revolves around a man's need for self-knowledge and self-love in order to be able to love and work with others.

Returning to the initial quotations, psychoanalysis suggests that unless Oedipal conflict is understood for what it is, the unconscious fears and desires will tend to be projected by the self on to the outside world, or on to another.

In *Sauve qui peut (la vie)* Godard and Miéville have explored this tendency to project sexuality on to 'woman', and violence on to an external cause. If the film claims that a progressive and productive collaboration between men and women is 'impossible', it nevertheless explores the effects of that impossibility on the masculine self, and represents these as a combination of despair and violent eroticism. Although traces of irony and a self-mocking kind of humour indicate the film's critical awareness of the contemporary masculine predicament, the *work* of mourning the loss of 'possibilities' is largely unrepresented. Grief, loss and a respect for psychic pain are replaced by images of violence or eroticism. Although the film does represent the reality of subjectivity, alongside social reality and textual reality, the exploration of masculine subjectivity stops short of recognizing the Oedipus complex. Instead the film attacks the idea of a productive and meaningful relationship between men and women, which, in the unconscious, is an attack on the Oedipal parents. I have argued that the film's narrative fragmentation and its images of women are both examples of attacks on the Oedipus complex and reality itself.

The Godard-Miéville collaboration has nonetheless been progressive and productive; and throughout this time Anne-Marie Miéville has continued to make her own films too. If *Sauve qui peut (la vie)* is proof of the possibility of some kind of productive collaboration, we could ask what the film reveals about the difficulties of such work. The most basic difficulty, clearly shown in the film, is that of recognizing and accepting the full extent of subjective reality and its influence on external reality. The unconscious meaning of the mother has a particularly significant effect on male subjectivity, and unless the Oedipus complex is recognized and accepted as a subjective reality men will continue to misrecognize and to misunderstand women.

And if it is true that the cinematic signifier, as described by Metz, is too closely bound up with fantasy, voyeurism, sadism and the specular world of the Imaginary to be capable of symbolizing the possibility of a productive and progressive collaboration between men and women, then Anne-Marie Miéville's hatred of cinema is not only justified but sadly illuminating.

NOTES

1. Christian Metz (1982) *Psychoanalysis and Cinema*, London, Macmillan, 25.
2. Anne-Marie Miéville, Report by Colin MacCabe, The *Guardian*, 1 October 1980.
3. Godard, Interview with Jean de Baroncelli, *Le Monde*, 22 May 1980.

4. Peter Harcourt (1981-2) 17-27.

5. Richard Roud (1980) *Sight and Sound*, 50 (1), 40-45.

6. John Coleman, *New Statesman*, 10 October 1980.

7. Lawrence Cohn, 'Auteur Theory Called Fraud', *Variety*, 8 October 1980.

8. David Denby, *New York Magazine*, 20 October 1980.

9. Colin MacCabe and Laura Mulvey (1982).

10. Angela Carter, *The Sunday Times Magazine*, 8 September 1983.

11. *Camera Obscura* (1982) 8/9/10, Special Issue on Godard: Elisabeth Lyon 'La Passion c'est pas ça', 7-10; Constance Penley 'Pornography, Eroticism', 13-18; Janet Bergstrom 'Violence and Enunciation', 21-30.

12. Julia Kristeva (1984-5) 4, Special Issue on Godard *Art Press*.

13. Robert Stam (1981) 194-199.

14. Colin MacCabe and Laura Mulvey (1982) 94-95.

15. Julia Kristeva, 1984-5, 31.

16. Laura Mulvey (1975) 'Visual Pleasure and Narrative Cinema', *Screen*, 17 (3).

17. Peter Wollen (1983) 'Godard and Countercinema: *Vent d'est*', *Readings and Writings*, London, Verso.

18. Laura Mulvey in MacCabe and Mulvey (1982).

19. Nick Grant, *The Leveller*, October 1980.

20. Bruno Bettelheim (1976) *The Uses of Enchantment*, London, Thames and Hudson.

SELECTED BIBLIOGRAPHY

Harcourt, Peter (1981-2) 'Le Nouveau Godard', *Film Quarterly*, 35 (2).

MacCabe, Colin and Mulvey, Laura (1982) *Godard: Sounds, Images, Politics*, London, Macmillan.

Milne, Tom (ed.) (1972), *Godard on Godard*, London, Secker and Warburg.

Roud, Richard (1970) *Godard*, London, Secker and Warburg.

Stam, Robert (1981) 'Jean-Luc Godard's *Sauve qui peut (la vie)*, *Millenium Film Journal*, 10-11.

Williams, Christopher (1977) 'Politics and Production', *Screen Reader One*, SEFT.

Camera Obscura, Special Issue on Godard, 1982, 8/9/10.

Frame Work, 1980, 13.

Undercut, 1981, 2.

Framework, 1983, 21.

APPENDIX

Jean-Luc Godard (1930—): filmography

See chapter 15, on *A bout de souffle*, for full filmography.

Anne-Marie Miéville (1945—): filmography

1977 *Papa comme maman*
1980 *L'Amour des femmes*
1983 *How Can I Love?*
1984 *Le Livre de Marie*
1986 *Faire la fête*

Jean-Luc Godard and Anne-Marie Miéville: filmography

1970-4 *Ici et ailleurs*
1975 *Numéro deux*
1976 *Comment ça va? — Du passif à l'actif*

1976 *Six fois deux (sur et sous la communication)*
1978 *France/tour/détour/deux enfants*
1980 *Sauve qui peut (la vie) (Slow Motion* [UK]; *Everyman for Himself* [USA]).

Other films cited in the text

A bout de souffle (*Breathless*), Jean-Luc Godard (1959)
La Chinoise, Jean-Luc Godard (1967)
Le Camion, Marguerite Duras (1977)
Deux ou trois choses que je sais d'elle (*Two or Three Things I Know about Her*),
     Jean-Luc Godard (1966)
Le Gai savoir, Jean-Luc Godard (1968)
Letter to Jane, Jean-Luc Godard (1972)
Masculin-féminin (*Masculine-Feminine*), Jean-Luc Godard (1966)
Tout va bien, Jean-Luc Godard (1972)
Vivre sa vie (*It's My Life* [UK]; *My Life to Lead* [USA]), Jean-Luc Godard (1962)
Vent d'est, Jean-Luc Godard (1970)
Weekend (*WeekEnd*), Jean-Luc Godard (1968)

19. Therapeutic realism: Maurice Pialat's *A nos amours* (1983)

GINETTE VINCENDEAU

Among the recent wave of postmodern young directors steeped in international image culture, Maurice Pialat may well be the last *French auteur* according to the definition handed down by the New Wave. Recently described by Alain Bergala as 'without any doubt, Renoir's true heir today' (*Cahiers du cinéma* 354, 21), Pialat is an artisan who works uneasily within as well as against the mainstream industry, a brilliant filmmaker with a recognizable style, and above all someone seen to be reworking, from film to film, deeply personal matters. Yet Pialat's films also show an almost ethnographic concern with areas of French society not usually associated with *auteur* cinema. His works have generally portrayed working-class milieux and looked at deprived childhood (*L'Enfance nue*), difficult adolescents (*Passe ton bac d'abord*), and semi-hooligans (*Loulou*), as well as unglamorous subjects such as the bitter breakdown of a couple (*Nous ne vieillirons pas ensemble*) and cancer (*La Gueule ouverte*). Even though he has made forays into genre cinema with *Police* and literary adaptation with *Sous le soleil de Satan*, his cinema as a whole retains this dual focus: an emphasis on the painfully personal on the one hand, and a *cinéma-vérité* approach to French society on the other. Nowhere is this truer than in *A nos amours*.

A nos amours has generated a large amount of journalistic and critical material which has tended to centre on the conflictual interaction of personal and professional relationships: between director and scriptwriter, director and actors, and even actors among themselves.[1] While this is inherent to the myth of *auteur* cinema which stresses the romantic pains of creation, the problems surrounding the making of *A nos amours* have more than scandal value; they are inscribed in the very fabric of the film, both as determining factors and as reworked material.

From Langmann's script to Pialat's film

The narrative of *A nos amours* focuses on Suzanne (Sandrine Bonnaire), an adolescent living in contemporary Paris with her parents (played by Maurice Pialat and Evelyne Ker), both artisans in the fur trade, and her brother Robert (Dominique Besnehard), also working in the trade but with ambitions as a writer. Suzanne leads a free sexual life but has difficulties in forming lasting relationships with men. Her father's desertion of the home early on in the film has a traumatic effect on the rest of the family who quarrel violently after his departure. Suzanne eventually marries Jean-Pierre (Cyril Collard) but even that relationship is short-lived and at the end of the film she leaves for the USA with Michel (Christophe Odent). *A nos amours* as it stands now is the result of a series of displacements, both sexual and temporal: from a woman's autobiographical script to a male-directed film, from a text sociologically anchored in the late 1960s to a filmic statement on the 1980s, from the mental universe of a man in his fifties to the existential angst of an 18-year-old girl.

A nos amours is based on Arlette Langmann's script *Les Filles du faubourg,* an autobiographical account of her adolescence in the Parisian Jewish rag trade milieu of the 1960s, and written in the mid-1970s as the basis for a film to be directed by Pialat. Financial considerations delayed the making of that film, but Langmann[2] and Pialat worked jointly on many other projects: she edited most of his films and scripted *Loulou,* in which she also appears briefly. Their collaboration, both intense and fruitful, culminated with *A nos amours* (which demanded complex re-writings) and simultaneously came to an acrimonious end.[3] Pialat's career is littered with such occurrences, where working and personal matters collide, though he is obviously able to create strong enough professional loyalties to overcome emotional rifts: he and Gérard Depardieu, after their well-publicized clashes on *Loulou,* collaborated harmoniously for *Police* and *Sous le soleil de Satan.* Pialat's ex-wife Micheline heads their production company *Les Films du Livradois* which produced *Passe ton bac d'abord* and *A nos amours,* while their previous joint production company, *Lido Films,* produced *Nous ne vieillirons pas ensemble* and *La Gueule ouverte.*

The transition from Langmann's *Filles du faubourg* to Pialat's *A nos amours* has more than anecdotal interest, it has narrative consequences. Pialat, who himself plays the part of the father, was reluctant to 'die'. Though the film as it stands still deals with the theme of patriarchal abandonment, this significantly altered the story, since Langmann's text had been written partly as a way of coming to terms with the death of her father. But a more crucial change is from the plural of *les filles* to the concentration on a single heroine. While this change emerged extra-textually out of the unexpected discovery of Sandrine Bonnaire's striking talent as an actress (she had answered an advertisement to play an extra), it also put a different emphasis on the film, altering in the process the sociological impact of Langmann's text. Though some scenes retain a semi-documentary feel in their depiction of Suzanne and her gang of friends — for instance at the holiday camp, in the café before going to school, at their party — *A nos amours* is neither a French 'brat pack' movie, nor the portrait of a group of adolescents in the sense that *Passe ton bac d'abord* was. Nor is it a document on a stratum of French society; the rag trade background, the parents' Polish origins, are 'given', to be immediately dropped; traces of the Jewishness of the milieu permeate some of the casting, Bernard and Michel for instance, but this is not in any way emphasized. At the same time, however, the 1960s haunt the film, producing curious discrepancies in the depiction of family relationships. The attempts by Suzanne's parents to be strict are of that era, as are the expressed concerns with what the young men are 'doing', the father's anger at Suzanne going out in the evening, her mother's disapproval of her sleeping naked in bed, and the order to come back 'before midnight'. Yet Suzanne and her friends' free sexual life seems far more in tune with the 1980s; it is as if pre-1968 parents were trying to deal with early 1980s adolescents.

In the transformation from Langmann's original text to the final film, *A nos amours* also changed from a feminine self-exploration to the reworking of a classic motif of male *auteur* cinema: the 'puzzle' of a beautiful, problematic, idealized (if not idolized) young woman. In this shift the subject of Langmann's script was changed into the object of the quest of a different narration. Suzanne functions, in an obvious way, as an object of spectatorial desire, like the young heroines of Godard's *Je vous salue Marie*, Rohmer's *Les Nuits de la pleine lune*, or Doillon's *La Tentation d'Isabelle*. The fact that she is constructed in such a way is inscribed from the very beginning of the film. After a semi-documentary pre-credit sequence set in the holiday camp, which shows Suzanne and her friends rehearsing a play, the film shifts register to show her standing alone at the prow of a boat, clad in pure white against the intense blue of the Mediterranean sky and sea and Purcell's *Cold Song* on the soundtrack. This is shot in a series of long takes on which the credits are superimposed. We hardly need the reverse shot of Robert and his two friends — Michel and Jacques (Jacques Fieschi) — and his comment that 'my sister is beautiful, isn't she?' to recognize that feminine beauty is the object of our gaze. But in addition to this classic voyeuristic structure, within the framework of a type of cinema which privileges the personal, she also functions, like the protagonists of the films mentioned above, as a site of cross-gender identification in the way she articulates some of the key thematic concerns of the film, such as anxiety and despair, which accumulate on her far in excess of her explicit characterization as a 'normal', realistic, contemporary Parisian schoolgirl. Thus Suzanne in *A nos amours* bears the traces of the *filles* as well as the burden of the film's angst; she is both Langmann's heroine and Pialat's 'hero'.

Family dinners

Though Pialat frequently declared himself 'fed up with realism', his cinema is best defined as the meeting place of different historical traditions of realism. *A nos amours*, like his other films, fuses the New Wave concern with location shooting and contemporary setting with the ethnographic inspiration of forms of direct cinema, the humanist slant of Neo-Realism, as well as the 'intimate', psychological, realism championed both by the New Wave and by Central European cinema in the 1960s. Underlining all these different traditions are basic realist strategies which Pialat draws on, such as the use of non-professional or little-known actors (sometimes mixed with stars, as in *Loulou* and occasionally including Pialat himself, Renoir-style), the frequent recourse to improvisation, and the attention to colloquial language, as well as hand-held camerawork and the use of available light (as in the night street scenes between Suzanne and Bernard — Pierre-Loup Rajot — and later Suzanne and Jean-Pierre), all strategies traditionally aimed at producing a sense of immediacy and spontaneity, an effect of authenticity. But rather than working towards greater transparency, Pialat's realism in *A nos amours* tends towards the self-conscious and on occasions the creation of a sense of malaise. This technically arises out of a predominance of indoor scenes shot in claustrophobic medium close-ups, and the deliberate inclusion of 'flawed' episodes, of moments of rupture or tension in the film, both as ways of capturing 'the truth' of characters or situations at given privileged moments, but also as stylistic motifs. The latter, it seems, is a conscious choice on Pialat's part: 'Suddenly there are abrupt changes in tone or rhythm, fleeting occurrences which are not as realist as all that. They produce emotions of a different order which are, in my opinion, as valid as those arising out of more classical filmmaking' (Pialat 1984, 12).

A striking example of this is the party meal in Suzanne's home, the penultimate scene of the film. The main characters include Suzanne, her mother and her brother Robert, her husband Jean-Pierre and Robert's friend Michel. Among characters new to the spectator at this point are Marie-France (Valérie Schlumberger), who turns out to be Robert's new wife, and her brother Jacques (Jacques Fieschi), whom we have fleetingly seen on the boat during the opening credit sequence. This is a celebratory meal, with champagne and cakes, but, out of an initially friendly atmosphere, tensions emerge, particularly between Jacques and Jean-Pierre, over their views on art. Jacques, mocked as an 'intellectuel de gauche' by Robert, has an air of superior knowledge and references are made to his (and his sister Marie-France's) class difference from the rest of the party — the intellectual grande-bourgeoisie versus Jewish rag-trade money. As the meal is reaching its end, the surprise arrival of the estranged father (Pialat) — ostensibly to show the flat to a prospective buyer — stuns the whole party and creates an upheaval, particularly when he virulently attacks the values of the fine arts magazine Jacques edits, and when the mother, outraged and at the end of her tether, ends up violently slapping him and throwing him out.

It is perhaps with this meal that Pialat shows best a less obvious but possibly deeper allegiance to another, older, tradition of realism, that of the French cinema of the 1930s. He has often explicitly acknowledged his 'debt' to Renoir and, especially, Pagnol. In some ways, his working methods, shooting as a tight group, involving actors and technicians, recall those of Pagnol; it is no accident that during that traumatic conversation at the end of the meal, the father refers to his son's — in his view ruined — potential as a 'new Pagnol'. One of *A nos amours'* directors of photography, Jacques Loiseleux, summed up the way Pialat associates his collaborators very closely with the whole filmic process: 'You don't experience just the mechanics of shooting, rather, you are integrated in the group of actors'(*Cinématographe* 94, 13). (Other members of the technical crew actually appeared in the film as actors too: Dominique Besnehard, who plays Robert, also worked on the casting of the

A nos amours — Suzanne (Sandrine Bonnaire)

film, Cyril Collard — Jean-Pierre — was one of the assistant directors, and Valérie Schlumberger — Marie-France — worked on the costumes.) There is a long tradition in French cinema of focusing on meals, and the 1930s particularly made use of it: the cooperative celebrating at the end of Renoir's *Le Crime de Monsieur Lange*, the picnic in *Partie de campagne*, the Communion meal at the beginning of Carné's *Hôtel du Nord*, or the family lunch in Pagnol's *Le Schpountz*, are only a few of the best known examples. To such famous precedents Pialat had already added his own piece of anthology with the justifiably notorious lunch in *Loulou*. But whereas in the 1930s films the meals were occasions for celebrating the cohesion of the family or the community, with the disrupting forces safely outside (this is spatially clearest in *Le Crime de Monsieur Lange*), in *A nos amours,* as in *Loulou,* the meals function more ambiguously. They are, rather, attempts at affirming or re-creating the cohesion of the family, while at the same time providing a stage for its most violent tensions to emerge: the lunch in *Loulou* nearly ends in murder, the party in *A nos amours* degenerates into verbal and physical assaults. Before the final party meal discussed here, another scene had foreshadowed the symbolic link between meals and family. A routine family dinner in Suzanne's home shortly before her father's desertion shows friends unable to stay for it, the brother who cannot be bothered to come to table, and Suzanne leaving in a huff after her father's remarks about her make-up. As the mother bitterly puts it, 'I cook, but nobody eats'. By contrast, Suzanne and her friends eat heartily their own junk food (the spaghetti at their party).

The last meal is central to the film in other respects. It is also a forum for the expression of ideological and ethical conflicts. It is not irrelevant that Jacques is played by Jacques Fieschi, the editor of the film journal *Cinématographe,* now extinct, but thriving in 1983 when the film was made. The father's attack on the unethical attitude displayed in Jacques' journal towards Robert's work is a direct reference by Pialat to his own anger at a *Cinématographe* interview with the cinematographer Pierre-William Glenn disparaging one of his films. This is not just anecdotal. Behind a personal settling of accounts lie larger issues to do with the place of *auteur* cinema in France and its relationship to criticism. Pialat may be unreasonable in his intransigent attitude, the fact remains that most film journals of repute (and in particular *Cahiers du cinéma* and *Positif*) now function, in France, as a support system for French auteur cinema, playing a vital role as its place in the French and international market-place becomes increasingly threatened by Hollywood, by French and European big-budget co-productions, and of course by television.[4] What is at stake here is no less than the place of auteur films as cultural products, the settling of accounts with Fieschi/Cinématographe is an attempt at a reckoning on a larger scale, a way of reaching the whole profession beyond one film journal.[5]

It is also relevant to know that the actors involved in the scene had no idea Pialat would suddenly re-appear, ghost like, during the meal. While before his arrival they clearly ad lib part of their dialogue (the scene was not planned in the original script), improvisation takes on a more radical meaning upon Pialat's turning up as an unexpected guest. As he put it himself, 'it's not just improvisation, more like surprise' (*Cahiers du cinéma* 354, 14). This, again, is more than a piece of gossip. Pialat as director in this scene inscribes himself bodily on his film, but also on his own working and aesthetic project, highlighting some of its inherent problems. A closer look at the scene reveals a contradiction between the desire to capture the immediacy of 'reality', the revealing spontaneity of looks and gestures — as for instance in the reactions of guests around the table, aghast at his sudden appearance — and the constraints of continuity editing (whatever liberties Pialat might take with it) which demands *reverse* angles. Even if we did not have extra-textual evidence, such as Jacques Fieschi's testimony (*Cinématographe* 94, 18-19), it is obvious in terms of the spatial construction of the scene that some shots caught 'in the act' had to be intercut with rehearsed ones; unsurprisingly Pialat reserved those for himself and, in his barbed exchange with Fieschi, filmed the shots of his own reactions after the event, while Fieschi was put on the spot without any warning. The textual inscription of *mise-en-scène* through the dual part of actor/director played by Pialat also extends to the direction of actors. While the decision to let the actors improvise gives them a hand in the *mise-en-scène*, it also necessarily threatens the director's sole claim to authorship. Isn't Pialat's on-the-spot anticipating of Evelyne Ker's reactions ('I know you, you're going to say ...') a disguised order for the course of events for her to follow? Such an authoritarian attitude coupled with a method akin to psychodrama reaps its rewards in powerful emotional impact but contains its own dangers: Evelyne Ker's violent slapping of Pialat, also unplanned, is both her revenge at the violence inflicted on her character, and (not negligeably) on her person, and can also be seen as the symbolic, though ultimately 'recuperated', revenge of the whole cast against an overbearing, doubly patriarchal, figure. The issue of violence in *A nos amours* is one that needs to be taken further.

The Oedipal stage as boxing ring

In Godard's *Pierrot le fou*, Sam Fuller defined cinema as 'a battleground'. Pialat's conception of filmmaking, by comparison, might be accurately described as belonging to the boxing ring. On a thematic level, his films repeatedly proclaim a preference for situations where people have rows, where they clash, where there is 'trouble'. Conflict is the preferred element of his films, and moreover a type of conflict which always assumes a great physicality. The body is constantly at the centre of Pialat's films, whether in love-making, in death, or in actual punch-up; flesh is the focus of the *mise-en-scène*. Not, however, the flesh of titillating sexiness. Though there is quite a lot of nudity in *A nos amours*, it is not on the whole erotically coded. Flesh in Pialat's films is also often victimized, and female flesh particularly so in *A nos amours*. It could also be called 'sad'; though Suzanne claims that she likes sex, the scenes featuring her making love (always, in fact, the moments *after* love-making) produce little sense of pleasure; an index of this is given early on during the holiday scene, when at the end of a long close-up of her face — she is lying on the grass, with the American boy still on top of her — Suzanne blandly replies 'don't mention it, it's free' to his 'thank you'. Although the physical is a strong element of *A nos amours* both in thematic terms and in the *mise-en-scène*, pleasures of the flesh — food and sex — appear rather joyless. Real contact is more likely to be made through violence than tenderness, and ultimately, though perversely, real love rests with the family.

A nos amours looks squarely at the family as the prime locus of violence; the boxing ring overlaps with the Oedipal stage. Suzanne is slapped in the face by her father and hit by her mother. The greatest violence though originates with the father's desertion. After he has gone, Suzanne, her mother and her brother, start an infernal and seemingly endless round of confrontations of incredible violence, matched by their language. The 'raw' impact of these scenes is based on the immediacy of the painful emotions unleashed and some degree of improvisation on the part of the actors who were physically deeply implicated in these scenes (Evelyne Ker continued acting in the second major family row, although she was bleeding for real). Paradoxically though, for all their 'heat', these scenes produce a sense of coldness, of distance: we are watching, literally, a 'scene'. This has to do first with their excess which turns them into melodramatic tableaux (it is worth noting here that both parents have no names, they are just the archetypal 'mother' and 'father') but also with questions of *mise-en-scène*. The stage-like aspect of the flat, its large open doors, the fluidity of camera movements and the use of staging in depth, larger shot scale and longer takes — contrasting with the tight static medium close-ups of most of the film — all this makes its different rooms into one large set while it remains a recognizably real nineteenth-century Parisian bourgeois flat. Finally, the jarring quality of these family rows, compared to the rest of the film, is an effect of the uneven progression of the narrative as a whole. In emphasizing these moments at the expense of overall causality, *A nos amours* breaks the rules of classical narrative. Its temporal development is uneven, syncopated, with gaps and ellipses; for instance between the holiday camp sequence and the next scene between Suzanne and Henri (Eric Viellard); another example of a disconcerting ellipse occurs just before the first major family row, which seems to run on without a time gap from the preceding scene (though, in fact, there is one night betwen the two), in which Suzanne and her mother share a rare moment of tenderness. In one sense this is a fundamental feature of European 'art' cinema. In another, it is consistent with Pialat's method which tends to look for narrative development as filming goes on: often working without a shooting script (*découpage*), deliberately filming 'wastage' material while including unplanned or technically flawed passages (as for instance with the sub-standard lighting of the scenes in the holiday café). This narrative remodelling often continues at the editing stage. Yann Dedet, one of the editors of the film, gave a perceptive definition of Pialat's editing which could serve as a comment on his whole work: 'it [...] tends more towards emotion than comprehension' (*Cinematographe* 94).

The desire to privilege 'emotion' over 'comprehension' helps understand the importance given to the family rows in the overall narrative. *A nos amours* unfolds along two different temporalities. The cause and effect chain of the narrative such as it is (the father leaving home, Suzanne's trajectory through a succession of men, her marriage, her leaving for the USA) grinds to a halt during the scenes of family quarrels, to which the characters, as we do, obsessively keep coming back; the compulsive repetitiveness of these scenes is evocative of the patient, the hysterical family, going to the analyst for a cure, the realistic *mise-en-scène* becomes a therapy. The theatricality of these scenes is enhanced by their setting, an overdetermined domestic and work space, redolent of '20 years of work', as the mother puts it both proudly and bitterly. It is also *her* space *par excellence*. In this respect, the positioning of her figure in these scenes is crucial — as the family rows begin, she can always be seen,

immobile in one corner of the frame, in almost identical postures, slightly
hunched — she is there, *waiting*, for either Suzanne or her brother to come, as
she is metaphorically waiting for the husband who deserted the home after 20
years of communal life.

Evelyne Ker's paroxytic acting has been noted by many, even criticized
as excessive and 'hysterical', including by Pialat. But the inflection Evelyne
Ker gives the character and her extraordinary bodily movements seem apt for
the expression of the frustration and anger of a woman protagonist who is
repeatedly defined as useless, full of love that is no longer needed. There again
the metaphor of the meal — cooked but not eaten — is proper for her
characterization by the film, which is undoubtedly misogynistic but
nevertheless revealing of the 'family drama'; it is indicative that the film
inflected Langmann's text in yet another way, that is in the direction of
violence. As Evelyne Ker said, 'in the script, after the violent scenes there
were moments of love and tenderness which have completely disappeared in
the film. The mother is nothing but a castrating and hysterical woman. *A nos
amours* has become a version of "the unloved one" (*la mal-aimée*)' (Pialat
1984, 155). Many spectators find these scenes, and Evelyne Ker's performance
in particular, difficult to watch, distasteful even. Could it be that, familiar as
we are with routine externalized male violence in genre films such as the
western or the thriller, we cannot cope with the spectacle of the greatest
violence of all, that which exists within the family, and the havoc it wreaks on
women, particularly the mother?

* * *

A nos amours, however, is the story of Suzanne, a fundamentally split
character. On one level, this is a function of the shifts outlined at the beginning
of this essay: though a child of the 1960s in her original delineation and in her
relationship to her parents, she is also a 'typical' adolescent of the 1980s in
terms of surface realism: her clothes, her relationship to her friends, to men,
especially her language. But two unexpected (in Pialat's work) intertextual
references accentuate the split between the naturalistic input in Suzanne's
character and other concerns of the film: Musset on the one hand, and Purcell
on the other. The film opens with Suzanne rehearsing the part of Camille in
Musset's *On ne badine pas avec l'amour* (written in 1834). The Romantic
drama functions as a 'warning' to Suzanne and a signpost to the spectator:
Suzanne/Camille does, indeed, 'trifle' with love, dangerously so for all
concerned. At the same time, and in contrast to the passions aroused in
Musset's play, and in the people who surround Suzanne in the film (men, but
also her mother), she is presented as 'cold'. She has, as she puts it, 'a dry heart'.
These elemental differences are at the centre of Purcell's *Cold Song*, first
heard over the credit sequence ('I can scarely move, or draw my Breath, Let
me, let me, Freeze again to Death'), taken from his drama *King Arthur* from
the passage where Cupid tries to awaken the Ice Genius. The music is repeated
later in the film in the scene where Suzanne is under a bus shelter in the rain
after seeing Luc with her girl friend (and again over the end credits). And it is

here, with the use of the poignant music, that the gap between the excess of meaning condensed on Suzanne, compared to her ostensible depiction as a contemporary adolescent, is perhaps most evident. Suzanne in the bus shelter suffers from more than seeing her ex-boy-friend with her 'best friend'. She carries the burden of a far more generalized despair, that of the 'father' of the film.

For Suzanne may have a 'dry heart', it still belongs to one man, her father. The real moment of intimacy in the film is not in any of the love-making scenes, but in a sequence which focalizes the privileged aspect of the father-daughter relationship: the scene in the flat at night when Suzanne's father tells her that he is leaving the family; by contrast his announcement of the same decision to his wife and son is left off-screen. The fact that the scene is filmed in classical shot/reverse-angle-shot continuity with a concentration on close-ups proclaims the rapport to be the most important emotional relationship of the film and ensures spectator identification, as opposed to the family rows whose *mise-en-scène* tends to distance the viewer, as mentioned earlier. The centrality of the father is also reinforced by casting — the men in Suzanne's life are coded as fairly insignificant, and often, particularly in the case of Michel and Bernard, look confusingly alike, against the charisma of Pialat as an actor. The father's 'confession' condenses many different levels in the film: it is a moment of obvious complicity between two characters, between two actors, and between an actress and her director (there is no need to insist on the duplication of symbolic roles between father/director and daughter/actress since it has such a long history in *auteur* cinema). This complicity is renewed later in the last scene of the film when Suzanne is taken to the airport by her father: she looks intensely at him, but gazes vacantly in the plane, next to Michel. This particular Oedipal relationship is here strongly connoted as erotic: both Suzanne and her father at one point in the film express erotic fantasies about each other — the father 'I was imagining you with Bernard Trévi', Suzanne 'when I meet a new man I cannot help thinking of my father'.[6] But equally important are structural similarities between them. In contrast with the immobility of the others, and the mother in particular, Suzanne and her father are the two characters who leave, who move on. They are both anguished, and they both have the power to inflict the greatest pain on others. The two of them are dissatisfied, in other words are desiring subjects, but in the case of Suzanne, despite her overt dual role as object and subject of desire, there is little sense of what she actually 'wants'. This is the point, perhaps, where the dual concerns of the film most obviously clash. The realistic project of *A nos amours* (the traces of Langmann's autobiography, the surface realism, and the gesture to capture the spontaneity of 'moments') struggles to assert itself against the representation of Suzanne as locus of others' projections and particularly the *auteur*'s textual and extra-textual personal concerns. The fact that this cuts across gender divisions in a highly over-determined way is only one (crucial though it is) aspect of the question.

Another important aspect of this duality takes us back to larger questions of realism and their interaction with the notion of the *auteur* as organizing principle of a film. The ethnographic impulse traditionally implies a distance, the position of a detached observer. By inscribing himself so intensely on *A nos amours*, Pialat is bidding to establish control and inflect the material in ways which appear to contradict, or at least distort, the sociological 'truth' of the given situations presented in the film. The tearing apart of the family in *A nos amours* may seem excessively bleak and hopeless, it nevertheless points to deeply felt transformations in the traditional family unit in France. In its continuing portrait of French milieux, Pialat's *mise-en-scène* acts both as a magnifying glass for some of their least palatable aspects, but also points nostalgically to deeply rooted but endangered traditions. It is thus, paradoxically, in this very distortion that the effect of ethnographic realism ultimately resurfaces. Through its intense reworking of the personal, *A nos amours* highlights, in an admittedly excessive and melodramatic way, some key shifts in contemporary French society.

NOTES

1.   See Pialat (1984) *A nos amours*. This 'book of the film' includes a transcription of the dialogues as well as a collection of testimonies and interviews with personnel involved in the making of the film. See also *Cinématographe* 94 (1983) which contains interviews with Pialat, Jacques Loiseleux and Yann Dedet, and a text by Jacques Fieschi on his experience of working on *A nos amours; Positif* 275 (1984), *Image et son, La Revue du cinéma* 389 (1983), and *Cahiers du cinéma* 354 (1983).
2.   Arlette Langmann's brother is the director Claude Berri (and hence a distant model for the character of Robert), who worked with Pialat on one of his early television films, *Janine* (1961).
3.   Pialat, who had allegedly offered to share directorial credit with Langmann in recognition of her input, ended up almost totally repressing her contribution upon the film's release. For more details, see Langmann's testimony in Pialat 1984.
4.   Although the relationship between *auteur* cinema and television in France is altering fast and in ways that are not wholly negative (for example television takes an increasing part in the financing and exhibiting of *auteur* films), the fact remains that French filmmakers still tend to display a deep distrust of television.
5.   It should be said here that Pialat's standing in the French film profession altered drastically after the success of *A nos amours* (which was awarded the prix Louis Delluc). The budgets of *Police* and *Sous le soleil de Satan*, his two subsequent films, were much larger than those of any of his preceding films; *A nos amours* was shot for FF 6m, whereas *Police* had a budget of FF 30m.
6.   At the risk of labouring the point, this father-daughter axis is a central narrative axis of French cinema. See my essay on Pagnol's trilogy in this volume, 80, note 5.

SELECTED BIBLIOGRAPHY

Very little has been published on Maurice Pialat and his films, outside journalistic sources (for these see footnote 1 above). Below is some useful material.

Ciment, Michel (1982) 'Maurice Pialat' in Cowie, Peter (ed.) *The International Film Guide 1982,* London, Tantivy Press, 20-24.
Pialat, Maurice (1984) *A nos amours,* Paris, Lherminier.

Prédal, René (1984) *Le Cinéma français contemporain,* Paris, Editions du Cerf.
Wilson, David (1980) 'Maurice Pialat', in Roud, Richard (ed.)*Cinema: A Critical Dictionary. The Major Filmmakers*, New York, Viking, London, Secker & Warburg.

SCRIPT

Pialat, Maurice (1984) *A nos amours,* Paris, L'Herminier. This book (mentioned above) is not a script, strictly speaking, but a transcription of dialogue from the film, with some indications of *mise-en-scene* (though there is no shot-by-shot breakdown).

APPENDIX

Maurice Pialat (1925—): filmography

1960 *L'Amour existe* (short)
1961 *Janine* (for television)
1962 *Maître Galip* (for television)
1967 *L'Enfance nue*
1970-1 *La Maison des bois* (television series)
1972 *Nous ne vieillirons pas ensemble*
1974 *La Gueule ouverte*
1978 *Passe ton bac d'abord*
1979 *Loulou*
1983 *A nos amours*
1985 *Police*
1987 *Sous le soleil de Satan (Under Satan's Sun)*

Other films cited in the text

Le Crime de M. Lange (*The Crime of M. Lange*), Jean Renoir (1935)
Hôtel du Nord, Marcel Carné (1938)
Je vous salue Marie (*Hail Mary*), Jean-Luc Godard (1984)
Les Nuits de la pleine lune (*Full Moon in Paris*), Eric Rohmer (1984)
Une Partie de Campagne (*A Day in the Country*), Jean Renoir (1936)
Pierrot le fou, Jean-Luc Godard (1965)
Le Schpountz, Marcel Pagnol (1938)
La Tentation d'Isabelle, Jacques Doillon (1985)

20. Representing the sexual impasse: Eric Rohmer's *Les Nuits de la pleine lune* (1984)

BERENICE REYNAUD

At an anonymous, deserted suburban intersection, with a bleak and low horizon in the background, two cars enter our field of vision, cross and disappear. The camera sweeps past another car parked in front of a row of small grey buildings, then stops for a moment in front of the entrance of one of them. The title of the film, *Les Nuits de la pleine lune*, appears on this image. A literal translation would be 'Nights with a Full Moon', and not *Full Moon in Paris*, as the film was released in English-speaking countries, probably to capitalize on Rohmer's fashionable 'Frenchness'. As this essay hopes to demonstrate, this translation is a misinterpretation, since the film's argument rests on the contrast between the space of Paris and that of the suburb, and the heroine's essential displacement.[1]

A woman is seen leaving the building, then the camera resumes its panning, upwards against the outside wall. The text of a proverb[2] appears on the film strip: 'Who has two wives loses his soul. Who has two houses loses his reason'; then there is a cut. On the next shot, another superimposition: 'November'; we are inside the building; a young man in shorts (Tchéky Karyo) is working out. A new cut brings us into a bedroom where a young woman (Pascale Ogier), lying down on a bed, is in the middle of a telephone conversation. Then she hangs up and rushes down the stairs, which are made simply of wooden boards so that, by placing the camera under the stairs, it is possible to see the person climbing up or down, with a sort of 'stripped' effect reminiscent of the famous Venetian blinds in *film noir* (or in Stroheim's *Foolish Wives*): Rohmer will use these stairs as an essential prop throughout the movie.

Downstairs, the woman, Louise, meets the man, Rémi: they are lovers and share a domestic relationship. However, their initial mode of introduction emphasizes the separateness of their space, their lifestyle. In the next shots, we see Louise in the suburban street, wearing a flamboyant red scarf that contrasts sharply with the grey that surrounds her — then at the station — and finally on the train. In a succession of quick, elliptic shots, we see her in Place des Victoires, a fashionable neighborhood in Paris, and in an office located in a former grand-bourgeois apartment. Rohmer does not dwell on Louise at work, nor Louise's relations with her co-workers. We will only learn later in the film that she works in an interior design agency, having recently graduated from art school.

Significantly, the first third of the film ('November') keeps the heroine increasingly on the move: picked up at her office by a friend, Octave (Fabrice Luchini), she first invites him to her studio in Paris where she changes her clothes, then is taken by him to his apartment 'to check the babysitter'. They finally go together to a party, where she quarrels with Rémi, and is brought home by her friend Camille, who lives in a nearby suburb.

In the following sequence, Louise is seen as she enters her building through a glass door, climbs the stairs, opens the door of the apartment, and, once inside, looks up: light appears under the bedroom door, proof that Rémi is awake. After a violent scene with Rémi, who physically injures himself in his anger, Louise runs upstairs; once again, the stairs in the apartment function as a sign of the separateness between the couple. In the next shot, it's already morning; Louise comes downstairs, in a skimpy 'baby doll', and joins Rémi, who has been lying on the living room couch. There, she informs him of her decision to move back one night a week to her studio in Paris, and they painstakingly manage to reach an agreement.

Their 'discussion' is not, however, a real verbal exchange: Louise, in a situation of inferiority, instead of trying to explain herself, is mostly cautious not to offend Rémi, and, saying things like 'Promise you won't be angry... I'm doing this *for* you, not *against* you', she sounds like the insincere *femme fatale* she is not (though probably envisioned as such by Rémi).

It is not to Rémi, but to Octave, that Louise attempts to formulate what she is and what she wants, but there, she is hardly more successful. Early in the film, she endeavours to have a 'serious conversation' with him, but Octave, a writer, a married man with a child, keeps trying — and none too subtly, in spite of their 'old friendship', to seduce her. Not only does he listen merely to what he wants to, but he systematically tries to insert himself into the gaps of her discourse to formulate the expression of his own desire.[3] While Louise tries to explain that she '[has] not been alone a single day since [she was] fifteen', because there had been 'no transition between [her] boyfriends', and she now feels the need to 'experience loneliness' — Octave interprets this as an expression of her dissatisfaction with the quality, not only of her current lover, but of all the former ones as well: 'You love men who are beneath you.' What Louise strives to express is the basic contradiction of her own desire (which formulates the classical plight of the hysteric, according to Freud and Lacan): both a feeling of being 'crowded' by men — 'I am too much loved' ('On m'aime trop') — and her utter dependence on the Other's desire — 'It's the other's desire that causes mine.' When she talks of her relation with Rémi she uses the same parameters, centering her discourse on *her* perception of Rémi's desire for her: 'He loves me *too much*. When I am loved too much, I love less.' But she adds, 'a woman never remains unmoved when a man makes an effort'. So what links her to Rémi is also what estranges her from him. Interestingly enough, Rémi's desire, taken for granted throughout the movie remains opaque until the end, when he finally states clearly what *he* wants, after having been presented mostly through what he *did not* want (going out, dancing, spending too much time separated from Louise, living in Paris, etc...).

As for Octave, his perception of Louise as an object of desire is also contradictory, and rests on the half-formulated question of how *he* fits within *her* desire (Octave's relation to women is not based on 'What do women want?' but 'Do women want *me*?'). What baffles Octave is that, while Louise seeks his company and spends a lot of time with him, she refuses to sleep with him. 'Carnal relationships do not interest me', she says, adding 'I like you, but I'm not *attracted* to you.' Octave's response is revealing: 'There's something virginal in you. I cannot stand having another man touch you. Especially the ones you go out with, who are of an absolutely pathetic bestiality.' Like Molière's Dom Juan, who, talking of a happily married young bride he intends to seduce, comments 'My love sprang out of jealousy', Octave's desire for Louise is supported by other men's desire for her. His character seems also to have been inspired by the seducer in Alfred de Musset's *Les Caprices de Marianne* (himself called Octave), who deserts the heroine at the end, after the man who really loved her has been killed; this reference adds another tragic overtone to the end of the film: will Octave remain Louise's friend, now that she has experienced rejection?

Early in the film, Octave declares that he is fascinated by the 'physical, practical, material' aspect of Louise's personality, which he assumes he is the only one to perceive. As in the triangle described by literary critic Girard, 'for a vain man to desire an object, it is enough for him to be convinced that this object is already desired by a third party... . The mediator is a *rival* produced by vanity... whose desire... makes the object infinitely desirable to the subject' (1961, 20-21). Octave desires Louise because of all the other men who desire her, but at the same time is conceited enough to think that he is the only one to see her 'as she is'. However, in order to keep himself in this position of high priest of Venus, he cannot touch her. This is probably the position where Louise, consciously or not, wants him, for she needs his desire to be kept at a certain distance, to feel wanted as a woman. This precarious equilibrium is constantly threatened by Octave's jealousy, addressed to Louise's other sex partners: 'It's intolerable that you grant others what you refuse *me*', he says, as she prepares to go on a date with the saxophone player. 'It drives me mad that a part of you escapes me.' 'It's only a little part...' answers Louise. She knows that Octave does *not* desire her; what he wants in her is what 'the others' have — or think they have: the 'little part' she denies Octave is what would satisfy his vanity and, hence, is not part of herself at all.[4]

While Louise feels 'crowded' by Rémi's love for her, she feels denied by Octave's 'mediated desire' (Girard 1961, 33). In both cases they want 'too much': Rémi loves her 'too much' — and, since love is a demand for love, he wants too much love — and Octave wants to possess 'the whole of her' — i.e. some imaginary projection created out of his vanity — which, in both cases, is an impossibility.

Rémi in his confusion between demand (which can be fulfilled) and desire (which cannot) imprisons Louise in a network of contradictory demands which she cannot meet (it is the typical ordeal imposed by the obsessional upon the hysteric). He wants Louise to give him *what she has* (her time...), while in love one can only give what one does not have. Lacan summarizes this situation as follows: 'I love you, but because inexplicably I love in you something more than you — the *objet petit a* — I mutilate you.' (Lacan 1978, 268) and its corollary: 'I give myself to you, but this gift of my person — Oh, mystery! — is changed inexplicably into a gift of shit' (ibid.). Symptomatically, he is totally unprepared to accept her giving him what she wants to give him — a teapot she bought on her 'day off' in Paris — even though (and maybe *because*) he *needs* a teapot. 'How much do I owe you?' he says, unwrapping the present.

Octave, on the other hand, suffers from the paradox of Dom Juan: he intends to take (*mille e tre*) women one after the other, but does not understand that, being 'not-whole', they resist ultimate possession. For Lacan, this essential 'not-wholeness' of 'the woman' is caused by the fact that there is always something in her which escapes phallic *jouissance*, and gives her access to a non-phallic, 'other', jouissance. He develops this in his commentary of Zenos' paradox of the 'impossible' race between Achilles and the tortoise (as applied to the 'non-relation' between Achilles and the captive Briseis in Homer's *Iliad*): 'When Achilles has stepped forward, scored with Briseis, the latter, like the tortoise, has advanced a bit, because she is *not-whole*, not wholly his. Something remains of her ' (1975, 13).

In addition, in the later scene in the café, Octave displays a sort of hysterical identification with Louise by sharing with her the 'anxiety' caused in her by the presence of nature (contextually, 'nature' means suburb, as opposed to Paris; psychoanalytically, they both express a common 'fear of the void'). So Octave's unconscious strategy ends up in a double denial of sexual difference: 1) Louise is, like a man, *wholly in* a place where he could successfully reach her, *if only she would let him*; and 2) Octave is, like a woman, subjected to an hysterical need of filling the void (in the discourse of others).

As for Louise, 'devoured' as she is by these two contradictory sets of desires, her only possible escape, beyond her desire to 'experience loneliness' — which may or may not be 'fake'[5] remains hysteria, whose particular plight for the woman is to deny men's castration *in her body*, to provide a sort of support for the foibles of men's desire. In the case of Louise, she physically breaks down in tears, first with Rémi — in the scene after the party, when his 'too-much-desire' ('trop-de-désir'), suffocates and angers her, then, at the end, when she has to face his lessened desire ('moins-de-désir') for her — and then in an extremely significant moment with Octave, when the latter tries to rape her verbally and physically to prevent her from meeting the saxophone player.

If I have, at the beginning of this essay, insisted on the multiple displacements of the heroine up and downstairs, in the street, in the train, in cars (always driven by others), etc... it is because these various moves in space constitute the axis of the film, and, while Rohmer's superbly mastered style eliminates all 'unimportant' moments, he has carefully kept those when Louise is 'in transit'. Even in the important scene when she encounters Rémi in a café

Les Nuits de la pleine lune — above: Louise (Pascale Ogier) and Rémi (Tchéky Karyo); below: Louise and Octave (Fabrice Luchini).

in Paris, she has to climb down the stairs that lead to the bathroom to see him in the telephone booth, while, to catch sight, at the same moment, of the unknown woman, all Octave has to do is to remain seated at his table. Not only is Louise 'commuting' between Paris and the suburb — between her job and social life, on the one hand, her domestic cohabitation with Rémi, on the other — but she is perpetually, essentially displaced, as the last sequence of the movie proves.

Her date with the saxophone player itself is shown as a series of displacements (on the young man's motorbike) between various locations: a bar, a disco. But the essential is that he 'takes her places', before she 'takes him home': in other words, the saxophone player does exactly what the sedentary, homebound Rémi does not do. But, once sex is over, while he is asleep, Louise is restless and cannot close her eyes. She finds it unbearable to stay in the same room as the young man. When trying to explain her dilemma to the insomniac illustrator she meets in the café where she is waiting for the first train to Marne-la-Vallée, she says 'I am claustrophobic.' But what makes her so, if not the too-violent expression of the desire of the Other? Significantly enough, the only Friday night when she feels like returning to the suburban apartment, is when Rémi does not want her any more, when there is no longer another's desire to suffocate her. 'The direction's inverted now', she adds. 'The exile is here [in Paris], the centre there [in the suburb].' But the centre, as she will discover, is nothing but a void that she will flee from by the first available train.

Louise's displacement is not anecdotal, but structural. It is as a woman, in her relationship with men, that she is essentially displaced. Rémi represents a certain form of patriarchal, patrilocal relation to space: he lives where he works, or rather has transported his home to the town where he works (as an urban development executive); he has put his young lover in his home, and expects from her companionship, domesticity (even in a modern, 'yuppie' form where it would consist, for example, of playing tennis with him every Saturday morning as Marianne — the woman he eventually falls in love with — probably does) — in brief, the traditional male expectations. Even though Louise tries to creatively inhabit the space by putting a work table where she pursues her 'own work' as a designer, she is only 'passing through' a space where she has no real right and has to leave as soon as the relation breaks up.[6]

The second form of displacement is the one performed by Octave's fantasies, which cast Louise both as a virgin and as a sexless being who could be entirely possessed, a position that is literally untenable.

But why is that? Gayatri Chakravorty Spivak notes that 'throughout his work, Derrida asks us to notice that *all* human beings are irreducibly displaced although, in a discourse that privileges the centre, women alone have been diagnosed as such' (1983, 170). The reason, once again, has to be found in Freud:

> The boy-child is irreducibly and permanently displaced
> from the mother, the object of his desire. But the girl-child

is doubly displaced. The boy is born as a subject that desires to copulate with the object... , The little girl is born an uncertain role-player — a little man playing a little girl or vice versa. The other she desires is 'wrong' and must be changed. (Spivak 1983, 172-173)

But, as Spivak points out, 'the deconstructive discourse of man (like the phallocentric one) can declare its own displacement [as the phallocentric its placing] by taking the woman as object or figure....' (ibid., 173)

So the correct question that a feminist should ask is: 'what is man that the itinerary of his desire creates such a text?' (ibid., 186). By contrast, the question that haunts Louise — 'what do men want from me' — does not allow her to address men's desire correctly. In her self-centredness (she tries to deny the Other's desire), she does not understand that her only possible centre is a void, because she is essentially displaced. As the man she meets in the bar at night reminds her, 'in each of these apartments you have a man. But these men, *they must have their word to say in the matter*.' Such is Louise's mistake: she was so busy defending herself against a certain representation she had of masculine desire ('I'm loved too much') that the reality of *her* alienation in Rémi's desire totally escaped her. In his discussion of the 'non-relation' between Achilles and Briseis/the tortoise (a metaphor for *sexual impasse*), Lacan concludes that it is through a conceptualization of this operation in space that mankind has been able to quantify the real. The mathematic notion of 'real numbers', for example,[7] has been defined through a study of the 'smaller and smaller' steps that the two actors of the fable take without ever meeting, 'except in infinity' (1975, 13). Till the bitter 'return of the real' of the ending, Louise keeps missing this infinity because, as a woman, she is seduced, and even mesmerized, by men's fetishizing gaze. She lets them define her as an object of their desire, and, as such, lets herself be posited within the phallic function, where, being both inside and outside — not wholly in, says Lacan — she is constantly rejected at the periphery, dislocated, denied, displaced.

Alain Philippon astutely notes that 'Louise joins the list of the women losers in Rohmer's cinema.... . As such, she still partakes of a cinema that posits itself in the post-feminist discourse and libertarian utopias and fetishizes woman's body only to signify its defeat' (1984, 42). He adds that he does not read this as 'misogyny, but generalized bitterness' (ibid.) as applied to the 1980s. But it is true that, when their desire confronts that of men, women usually lose in Rohmer's movies, and are often ridiculed (Maud, Haydée the collector, Chloé, Sabine who wants a beautiful wedding, etc.), while man's own desire is measured *to the extent* he resists, or denies that of the woman. The only exception is the luminous ending of *Le Rayon vert* where Marie Rivière's ridiculous stubbornness eventually pays off. In contrast to Louise at the beginning of the film, Marie has experienced loneliness, as she perceives the Other's desire as a lack (although she has her moments of hysteria, too). Knowing how awkward she is with others, but still going on, Marie is a comical character *à la* Keaton, while Louise, who thinks (because men led her to think so, in a game of mutual deception) that she masters the rules of the game, is never ridiculous, but superbly tragic.

The difference between Marie and Louise is both scandalous and simple: Marie has grace ('a la grâce'), while Louise does not. For Rohmer, the difficult question of grace is an ethical problem, not a religious one. As early as 1953, discussing the cinema of Renoir, Hitchcock and Rossellini, he wrote: 'If art is, finally, moral, it is not by discovering the way to an abstract equality of liberty, but exalting the exception, made only possible by the rule, and... everybody's inequality with regards to fate, even salvation'(1984, 73).[8] Rohmer's originality has been to address this classical issue as a *modern* concern, in purely cinematic terms. For him, the interest of cinema is to create a new ontology: not to show things differently, but show different things. And, instead of describing cinema as an art of illusion, he postulates the notion of *truth*: 'from the confrontation of [my] discourse with the characters' discourse and behaviour, a certain truth is born, different from the literality of texts and gestures: the truth of the film' (ibid., 90).

Louise's alienation from grace can best be read in the situations where (in contrast to Marie, who might be obnoxious, but never cheats) she is guilty of a certain *mauvaise foi* — whose expression is not to be found in the character's discourse (we agree with her) nor in a certain falseness conveyed by the performance (the actress is absolutely, breathtakingly, tragically *sincere*, and Pascale Ogier's interpretation is one of the beauties of the film), but in the heroine's relationship to the off-screen space (*le hors-champ*).

From this point of view, two scenes are crucial. In the first, Louise is in her studio, on a Friday night, alone. Through a telephone call, her date for the evening (with an unnamed person) is cancelled. She then tries, unsuccessfully, to contact Octave, and two other men. Finally, she resorts to reading in bed for the rest of the evening. There is a fade-out, and the next shot shows her having breakfast in bed, while playing a sentimental record by Edith Piaf. Octave returns her call, and she explains to him how much she welcomed the opportunity to spend an evening alone, for a change.

The way the previous sequence is directed, however, contradicts her. I am reminded of two other films where the collaboration between a director and an actress manages to convey, through very subtle signs, the growing anxiety and distress of a woman trapped alone *in her own space*. One is the long, static shot of Jean Eustache's *La Maman et la putain*, where Bernadette Lafont remains in her living room, listening to an old record, after Jean-Pierre Léaud and Françoise Lebrun have departed together. The other is the scene when Delphine Seyrig in Chantal Akerman's *Jeanne Dielman* waits for a customer (who may or may not be late: we will never know). Suddenly the space these women inhabit, which, in all three cases, is specifically shown as their emotional base, becomes too small: since they have mentally projected themselves into an outside where, at this specific moment, they are not wanted. Their own imaginary, so to speak, devours the frame of the image: the space they are left with is no longer the space of their desire, which is outside, and extends within the boundaries of the frame, as if the inside was 'emptied' by the outside. Significantly, all three women try to conceal to themselves this displacement from their own centre, but Louise is the one whose *mauvaise foi* is the most apparent, since it is due more to vanity than courage.

The second scene occurs in the second third of the film ('December'): Louise's life becomes more and more dependent on what happens off-screen while she continues to deny that this is so. In the café, while she is in the ladies room, there is a significant shot showing Octave looking with surprise at something we never see. Later, in his conversation with Louise, we will learn it was a woman, and possibly Camille, which would have made her the partner of Rémi's unexpected Parisian rendez-vous. Louise's *mauvaise foi* is obvious in the next scene, where Camille comes to visit her in Marne-la-Vallée. Since she denies to herself (and to Octave), until the end, that Rémi could have a sex life outside her own field of vision,[9] Louise cannot confront her friend, but she is haunted by what might have happened, at another place and another time, between Rémi and her. In directing their encounter, Rohmer remembered the lessons learnt in watching Hitchcock's films: the bus ride undertaken by Sylvia Sydney's kid brother in *Sabotage*, for example, becomes a real nightmare for the spectator because we know there is a time bomb in his satchel: the invisible 'contaminates', so to speak, the visible. We have a similar situation in Louise's encounter with Camille: the banality of the gestures and words becomes the signifier of Louise's anxiety, which revolves not about the here and now, but the unfathomable space off-screen. *Mauvaise foi*, again: Louise wants so much to be reassured that she will gratefully accept *any* sort of explanation: Camille's new boyfriend is not Rémi, but some man whom we never see. The anxiety generated in the off-screen space of the Other is allayed by some mere signifiers (Camille's story about her trip to Italy) emitted from the same space.[10]

Trapped within her own imaginary, Louise forgets that she was initially misled by Octave, and that the real question is not: who is Camille's new boyfriend? — but: who was the woman with Rémi that day?

The issue of Louise's exclusion from grace, her *mauvaise foi*, her displacement, can also be addressed if one substitutes *language* for *grace*. The question of grace in its relation to women has been of particular interest to Rohmer throughout his career as a critic and filmmaker, expecially since his discovery of Roberto Rossellini's *Stromboli* (1950), about which he wrote, in 1950: 'I have seen very few contemporary works that exalt so magnificently, so directly, the Christian idea of grace ... that proclaim more openly *man*'s misery without God' (1984, 135, my stress). But this *man* is actually a woman, Ingrid Bergman, upon whom is thrown the burden of *visually representing* this misery. 'It is quite meaningful', adds Rohmer, 'to compare *Stromboli* to [Alfred Hitchcock's] *Under Capricorn* ... where we see the same performer climbing the long path that connects despair and self-loathing to peace and a restored good conscience' (ibid.,136-7). But Bergman's erotic attractiveness in both films is more apparent before than after the redemption, and we know that there is no 'salvation' for most of Rohmer's heroines who, left to their own devices, fail in what they are doing, and are excluded from what they want most.

It seems, thus, that the image of the woman has to be understood as a signifier whose function is cinematically to represent the desire of the filmmaker. I do *not* mean — as a more classical feminist analysis would — the object of his desire, but *his desire itself*, which opens up an entirely different set of identifications. Desire being born in language, its visual representation is highly problematic. The more traditional way of doing it — which I will call the 'fetishistic approach' — is based on the notion of 'visual pleasure' (to quote a well-known interpretation) and consists in glamorizing the traditional objects of male desire: women's bodies, as wholes (in narrative movies), or as collections of parts (in pornographic cinema). From this point of view — which I do not want to exclude, since cinematic perception operates on different, simultaneous levels — the 'defeat' of the woman has a specific meaning: a woman is never so desirable (for the spectator) as when she is crying (waiting to be comforted) or in jeopardy (waiting to be saved). Her defeat means she is lacking something, that only a man (and/or the Grace of God) can provide.

Rohmer's films, however, are not confined to this primitive, fetishistic level. Instead of presenting his heroines as pure objects of desire, he makes desiring subjects out of them and it is their desire — and not the man's — that constitutes the motor of the fiction. The prospective groom in *Le Beau mariage*, or Rémi in *Les Nuits de la pleine lune*, do not speak until the end of the film, while the aviator in *La Femme de l'aviateur*, or the playboy in *Pauline à la plage*, never express clearly what they want. In Rohmer's films, it is the women who act the filmmaker's desire. And how is desire best represented? — in its failure. Not only because 'there is no sexual relation' (Lacan 1975, 35) and, as such, it 'cannot be *written*' (ibid., my stress). But also because of the specificity of cinematic representation, its use of space and time:

> Desire is one of the most fertile themes in cinema: it requires the spreading before our eyes of the whole spatial and temporal distance which lies between hunter and prey. The act of waiting is enjoyed in itself ['l'attente jouit d'elle-même'], and the tender whiteness of a throat,[11] or, as in Stroheim's *Greed*, the sparkling of gold, are adorned with a seduction forever renewed for the impotent desire. This is something that we, the spectators, repeatedly experience in front of these impalpable and fleeting images that arrest our gaze, both gratifying and deceiving it. (Rohmer 1984, 57)

Once desire is fulfilled, not only is the object of desire destroyed as such — it is now an 'object of possession', much less interesting to represent — but also the aesthetic perspective, when 'the act of waiting [which] is enjoyed for itself", no longer exists. This is what Proust expresses in a well-known passage of *Swann's Way*:

> And it was Swann who, before she allowed her [face], as though in spite of herself, to fall upon his lips, held it back at a little distance, between his hands... . Perhaps ... he was fixing upon the face of an Odette not yet possessed, nor even kissed by him, which he was seeing for the last time, the comprehensive gaze with which, on the day of his departure, a traveller hopes to bear away with him in memory of a landscape he is leaving forever. (Proust 1981, 255)

However, while it is possible, in a literary work, to represent a man's desire as perpetually frustrated (Werther, Swann), when the same thing happens in film, the man becomes a highly comical character (the tradition of the 'Hollywood clowns', for example, is based on that assumption) — hence the difficulty of adapting a romantic novel for the screen without being mildly ridiculous. The filmic signifiers are organized around the phallic determination of the gaze: what a man sees, he wants, and what he wants, he gets (and if he does not get it, he does not dwell on it, but burns his house, and disappears from the deigetic space, like John Wayne in John Ford's *The Man Who Shot Liberty Valance*). Conversely, when desire, with its avatars, pains and failures, is born by a woman, she becomes a tragic figure, an immense source of aesthetic enjoyment.[12] It is not possible, however, to use a woman's image to express a man's desire without substantially altering the parameters of this desire. For one thing, the image of the woman, being so often used to signify the object of desire, and not its subject, retains some of this determination, and thus expresses a contradictory statement: 'I want, but I am wanted as well' (and not necessarily by the same person) — a position that Louise, like most heroines of fiction, finds untenable. It is untenable, because it is not real. In *Les Nuits de la pleine lune*, we see a fictional character struggling to have the right to exist on her own terms, to extricate herself from the representations thrown upon her by men: Rémi, Octave, Rohmer. Louise's plight (to have her independence and her man at the same time) is real enough; but what is at stake is not the defeat of 'a real woman', but the essential limit (what Lacan calls 'la butée') of desire itself. As is often the case, the image of a woman is used to suture a system of representation:

> In so far as the system closes over that moment of difference or impossibility, what gets set up in its place is essentially an image of the woman [...]The system is constituted as a system or whole only as a function of what it is attempting to evade and it is within this process that the woman finds herself symbolically placed ...

says Jacqueline Rose (1986, 219), who adds, quoting Lacan: 'On the one hand the woman becomes, or is produced, precisely as what [man] is not, that is, sexual difference, and on the other as what he has to renounce, that is *jouissance*' (Lacan 1970-1, 9-10).

Is it not, then, because Louise says to Octave: 'I have more fun than [Rémi] does' that she 'has to' be punished at the end? This surplus of *jouissance* (for which she will pay dearly) is also what irritates Octave. His desire for her being perpetually frustrated, he tries to fill the void opened by this frustration with a constant flow of words and rationalizations (another example of *mauvaise foi*). In his hysterical identification with the young woman, he wants to keep her virginal, wants her desire to be as unfulfilled as his (this is why he tries to convince her that the objects of her enjoyment are worthless).

Three operations are taking place here: 1) Rémi will actually frustrate Louise's desire because she does not conform to his definition of an object of desire; 2) Octave wants to reduce Louise, whose 'excess of jouissance' he cannot stand, to the same state of unsatisfaction as his; 3) Rohmer has to posit Louise's desire as impossible to satisfy, in order to make her the tragic figure that represents his desire (all desires) as an object of aesthetic contemplation. In other words, at three different narrative levels, Louise's character is produced as that of an hysteric. This is a classical suture derived from the clinical discourse, where the woman's excess of *jouissance* is evacuated as *lack*, and made implicitly responsible for the sexual impasse. But Lacan — even before identifying, in *Encore* (1975, 17) the phallic function as the main obstacle to sexual jouissance — raised 'the specific question of why [the hysteric] can sustain her desire only as an unsatisfied desire, "a question" [left] entirely out of the psychoanalytic field', and out of all systems of representation as well, a flaw that can be attributed only to 'some kind of original sin in analysis' (1978, 12). [13]

Women are, as always, paying for this original sin — they are neither within, nor without the symbolic order: language, grace etc... . This is especially true for the defeated heroines of Rohmer's movies. They bear the burden of representing the sexual impasse, the non-communication between the sexes, and men are for them, at best, a lost object. [14]

Translations of Rohmer quotations are by the author.

NOTES

1. The representation of the suburb is rare in French, and this is why *Les Nuits de la pleine lune* is also important at a sociological level. Significantly, Rohmer's latest film, *L'Ami de mon amie*, takes place entirely in the suburbs, except for a few, nondescript scenes: it is Paris that represents an alien, vaguely 'boring' space.
2. The credits state that the film is the fourth in the series 'Comedies and Proverbs'. Rohmer likes to connect his films in 'series'. The first (from *La Boulangère de Monceau*, to *L'Amour l'après-midi*) is entitled 'Moral Tales'. 'Comedies and Proverbs' ('proverb', in this case, meaning a short comedy developing the moral applications of a proverb) started with *La Femme de l'aviateur*.

My films generate each other within a closed system, like in the 'Moral Tales', in which I had pre-decided the ending. The 'Comedies and Proverbs' are also a closed system, even if the ending is not pre-decided. The 'Moral Tales' were films in which I started with a theme and created variations upon it, the 'Comedies and Proverbs' are films in which I have looked for a theme. It happens that I have more or less found the theme of the first four 'Comedies and Proverbs' [*La Femme de l'aviateur, Le Beau mariage, Pauline à la plage, Les Nuits de la pleine lune*], you can see the similitude of the situations, the character always fails in his [sic] attempt, and the film begins in the place where it ends. Now, I would like to direct [...] a new series of 'Comedies and Proverbs' that will have an open ending, i.e. there wouldn't be a final failure, nor a return to the departure point. (Rohmer 1985, 92)

3. This is a paradigmatic situation that Lacan describes as such: 'A lack is encountered by the subject in the Other, in the very intimation that the Other makes to him in his discourse. In the intervals (gaps) of the discourse of the Other, this is what emerges... *He is saying this to me but what does he want?*' (1978, 214)

4. 'The real Madame de Rénal is the one Julien desires. The real Mathilde the one he does not. In the first case, we are dealing with passion; in the second with vanity' (Girard, 1961, 33).

5. For want of space, I refer the reader to the article by G. C. Spivak mentioned in the bibliography, for further consideration of the relationship between women's 'fake orgasm' and their displacement. I have also addressed similar issues in a research paper, 'Briseis' Desire', presented in April 1983 at the Whitney Museum, New York.

6. It seems almost trivial to say so, but unfair not to mention it ... *Les Nuits de la pleine lune* can be read as an homage to Virginia Woolf's pertinent conclusions in *A Room of One's Own*.

7. The mathematic notion of 'real numbers' expresses *quantities*, as opposed to imaginary numbers. It is the progress (or failure) of desire that makes space quantifiable for the mathematician, as it makes it an aesthetic category for the filmmaker (see Rohmer 1984, 57).

8. The films discussed in Rohmer's essay (1984 — initially published in *Cahiers du cinéma* under the name of Maurice Scherer) are Renoir's *Le Carrosse d'or*, Hitchcock's *I Confess*, and Rossellini's *Europe 51*.

9. Because of that naïve belief, Louise will be totally blind to the presence of her future rival. The first time Marianne appears in the cinematic field, it is as an anonymous, attractive young woman, dressed in white, standing in the centre of the frame when Louise and Octave arrive at the party. But they do not see her, and greet Louise's friend Camille who is dancing next to her. Later, Marianne will be identified as a friend of Camille's, and briefly introduced to a sulking Rémi, before disappearing once again from the frame. Finally, when Camille drives Louise back home, Marianne is sitting silently in the back of the car. While Louise discusses the difficulties of her relationship with Rémi, and even suggests to Camille that she goes out with the latter, the shot is a point of view shot from the car's windshield, and Marianne is kept out of our field of vision, as she is from Louise's. This precision is important to underline Louise's 'emotional blindness' (she does not want to see), but also to explain the function of the off-screen space in Rohmer's cinema, which is never arbitrary, but constructed from elements already presented, albeit in a deceptive manner, in the cinematic field. In his analysis of Marcel Carné's *Les Portes de la nuit*, for example, he writes: 'in the warehouse scene, Prévert's text [the dialogue between Yves Montand and Natalie Nattier] is weak because it depends, like a theatre narration, on an imaginary world located 'beyond' that of the film [...] One has to find a way to integrate the word, not inside the world which is filmed, but *inside the film itself*' (1984, 39, my stress). Rohmer has understood particularly well that the 'imaginary field' in cinema is created through a constant dialectic between the visible and the invisible.

10. For Lacan the Other is the guarantee of the truth. But 'there is no Other of the

Other', i.e. nobody to guarantee that the Other is telling the truth. Camille's story, of course, cannot really be checked.

11. This excerpt comes after a long discussion of Murnau's *Nosferatu* (1922).

12. Mary Ann Doane notes that, in some cases, the burden of representing desire can be borne by a man: 'In the love story, the male undergoes a kind of feminization by contamination — in other words, he is to a certain degree emasculated by his very presence in a feminized genre. As Roland Barthes claims (in *A Lover's Discourse* [1978] translated by Richard Howard, New York, Hill and Wang, 14) there is always something about the lover which is 'feminized': 'in any man who utters the other's absence, *something feminine* is declared' (Doane 1987, 97).

13. Since I was not entirely satisfied with Sheridan's translation, I substituted mine (in the italicized part of the sentence).

14. This conclusion represents only part of a work in progress I am currently undertaking about the representation of women in cinema. The first part of this research was presented in lecture form at the Whitney Museum on 12 May 1987, under the title 'Delacroix's *Death of Sardanapalus*: A Careful Misreading'.

Special thanks to David Jacobson for reading the first draft and for his help in locating references, and to Jackie Raynal.

SELECTED BIBLIOGRAPHY

Doane, Mary Ann (1987) *The Desire to Desire*, Bloomington and Indianapolis, Indiana University Press.
Girard, Raymond (1961) *Mensonge romantique et vérité romanesque*, Paris, Grasset.
Lacan, Jacques (1970-1) *Le Séminaire XVIII: D'un discours qui ne serait pas du semblant*, unpublished typescript.
Lacan, Jacques (1975) *Encore*, Paris, Le Seuil.
Lacan, Jacques (1978) *The Four Fundamental Concepts of Psychoanalysis*, trans. Alan Sheridan, New York, Norton.
Philippon, Alain (1984) 'Les Fantômes de la liberté', *Cahiers du cinéma*, 364.
Proust, Marcel (1981) *Swann's Way*, trans. C. K. Scott Moncrieff and Terence Kilmartin, New York, Vintage.
Rohmer, Eric (1984) *Le Goût de la beauté*, (ed.) A. Narboni, Paris, Editions de l'Etoile.
Rohmer, Eric (1985) 'Secrets de Laboratoire', *Cahiers du cinéma*, 371/372.
Rose, Jacqueline (1986) *Sexuality in the Field of Vision*, London, Verso.
Spivak, Gayatri C. (1983) 'Displacement and the Discourse of Woman', in M. Krupnick (ed.), *Displacement: Derrida and After*, Bloomington, Indiana University Press.
Woolf, Virginia (1929) *A Room of One's Own*, London, Harcourt, Brace and Janovitch.

APPENDIX

Eric Rohmer (1920—): filmography

See chapter 17, on *Ma nuit chez Maud*, for full filmography.

Films cited in the text

L'Ami de mon amie, Eric Rohmer (1988)
Le Beau mariage, Eric Rohmer (1982)
Le Carrosse d'or (*Golden Coach*), Jean Renoir (1952)
La Femme de l'aviateur, Eric Rohmer (1980)
Foolish Wives, Erich von Stroheim (1921)
Europe 51, Roberto Rossellini (1952)
Greed, Erich von Stroheim (1923)

I Confess, Alfred Hitchcock (1953)
Jeanne Dielman, 23 quai du Commerce, 1080 Bruxelles, Chantal Akerman (1975)
La Maman et la putain (*The Mother and the Whore*), Jean Eustache (1973)
The Man Who Shot Liberty Valance, John Ford (1961)
Les Nuits de la pleine lune (*Full Moon in Paris*), Eric Rohmer (1984)
Pauline à la plage, Eric Rohmer (1983)
Les Portes de la nuit (*Gates of the Night*), Marcel Carné (1946)
Le Rayon vert (*The Green Ray* [UK]; *Summer* [USA]), Eric Rohmer (1986)
Sabotage, Alfred Hitchcock (1949)
Stromboli, Roberto Rossellini (1950)
Under Capricorn, Alfred Hitchcock (1949)

21. Beyond the gaze and into *femme-filmécriture*: Agnès Varda's *Sans toit ni loi* (1985)

SUSAN HAYWARD

Agnès Varda's filmic production has been little heralded by feminist critics, least of all by those in the United States and the United Kingdom where her work has been dismissed by such critics as the late Claire Johnston as reactionary and certainly not feminist.[1] Curiously, Varda's work is often passed over in silence in anthologies on women's film — and yet she herself claims to be an avowed feminist. The debate here, however, is not going to centre around the global issue of a feminist cinema but rather will endeavour to demonstrate how Varda's latest film *Sans toit ni loi* is as much political as it is — *and because it is* — feminist in its conception and message.

Implicit in Jacqueline Rose's discussion (1986, 203 ff.) of Comolli and Metz's current film theory is the idea that, for film to be political, it must eschew its mainstream proclivity to reproduce an 'imaginary identity' (203). In other words cinema which 'appears as a type of analogical machine for the programming of identity' (203) cannot be political. In a somewhat similar vein, Claire Johnston argues that '[t]he camera was developed in order to accurately reproduce reality and safeguard the bourgeois notion of realism which was being replaced in painting' (1976, 214). She also points out that a direct consequence in cinema of this 'law of verisimilitude' is 'the repression of the image of woman as woman and the celebration of her non-existence' (211). Elsewhere, but very much connected to this notion of non-existence, Maureen Turim defines film as a presence which speaks and hides absence (1986, 234). Film, unlike theatre, is the absent spectacle — the spectacle of absence. In this respect, therefore, it would seem to provide the perfect vehicle of expression for women as filmmakers and makers of feminist films. As Jutta Brückner so astutely points out: 'the cinema offers us a place to focus our own desires for particular images, to explore our own experience of linguistic and visual absence, for we have always been made into images instead of acquiring our own' (1985, 121) Similarly, Johnston proposes that feminist film cannot rely purely and simply on a retransmission of women's issues, it has to go further and take male and Hollywood iconography to task. And in essence this sums up her reproach to Varda in the past — i.e. that her filmmaking practices could be recuperated into the dominant ideology.[2]

Sans toit ni loi is a reinscription of an original and real text. Varda's first idea — to make a film about road people/vagrants (male and female) in the winter, who perish from the cold — became substantially modified when she encountered a hitchhiking vagabond, Settina. The starting point, then, is this young woman's experience. However, the representation of this experience — through a series of flashbacks which, at times even, become imbricated — is intentionally non-realistic. Essentially the structure of the film, which is made up of 47 episodes, takes to task the issue of image construction or, as Tim Corrigan puts it, 'the fetishizing action of the male perspective' (1986, 267). By extension, Varda's cinematic writing — *cinécriture*[3] as she terms it — goes counter to the established canons of western filmmaking practices.

Let us take the issue of image construction first. The film is about a young woman, Mona, who has perished from the cold. Upon this corpse, numerous persons attempt to transfix a meaning (already a contradiction). Eighteen visions of Mona are presented by those who saw her. However, as the film makes transparently clear, Mona refuses to be coopted into any image. In her refusal of all social discourses — which her preponderant mutism serves to reinforce — she defies identification, will not be made other. Her peripatetic and solitary existence is a deliberate choice ('being alone is good', 'champagne and the road, that's good', 'I move') and functions metonymically for her unfixability and unnamability.[4] Her rejection of social and sexual productivity, which her choice implies, erases the hegemonic image of women — she leaves no trace, as Varda's voice-over comments: 'this death leaves no traces.' The film is a series of gazes, of one-way exchanges from different specular positions. Each contributor fixes their gaze not on Mona but on their perception of Mona as a figure of their desire. As such, each portrait offered up to the spectator is revealing of the relator and not of the one related. The effect is to empty the mirror of ascribed meanings. Male discourses (whether uttered by men or women) cannot produce her identity. Mona's independence from a fixed identity is an assertion of her *altérité* (her otherness); her autonomy from male fetishization is an obligation to recognize her *différence* — woman as an authentic and not a second sex.[5] As an authentic sex, Mona both attracts and repels — meanwhile she remains indifferent, impassive to the violence of these responses. On a basic level these two responses originate from our sense of smell — and indeed sex and smell are very closely interrelated. Symbolic of Mona's indifference to others' reactions is her very filth, her uncleanliness and smelliness. And it is in Jean-Pierre's flashback-'portrait' of her that we can perceive most clearly what Varda is saying about image construction.

His 'narration' is imbricated first (about half-way through the film) in the 'narration' of the paleontologue Mme Landier (the tree specialist who is also his boss) and then latterly (towards the very end of the film) in Yolande's (the maidservant to his aunt) 'narration'. His initial meeting with Mona is via his boss who tells him to go and have a look at her, as if she were a specimen (one of *her* specimens). Mona steps out of Mme Landier's car — Jean-Pierre has just circled halfway round it peering in as if she were in a specimen glass — her filthy hair whips around her face in the wind (she looks almost Medusa-like) and she asks him if she frightens him. The next shot is of Jean-Pierre in his apartment with his wife, Eliane. She has just emerged from a bath(!) and is wrapped around with a towel. Jean-Pierre tells her about Mona and how her hair reminded him of his wife's; at this juncture he is fondling her hair — Eliane rightly reads the subtext and refuses to make love, obliging him instead to attend to her toenails.

To Mona's filth is immediately contrasted Eliane's pristine cleanliness. The sexual transference speaks for itself: physically aroused by Mona he attempts to gratify his desire through his wife. What attracted him? Doubtless, Mona's evident availability so sharply contrasted with his wife's persistent refusals. Conversely, what prevented him from acting? Mona's refusal, through her filth, to signify for him his image of woman. And there is a further connotation, transpiring in this instance from the similitude in their hair — to which *he* draws attention — for it implies a very fixed image of woman in his mind (i.e. one woman is very much like another).

In the closing part of the film, he re-encounters Mona — who is flipped out on drugs — at Nîmes railway station. This time it is he who is in the glass container: he holds up in the telephone booth both to hide away from her and to call Mme Landier who is desperately seeking Mona; and it is now Mona who roves around outside the 'specimen' cabinet. She is, however, oblivious to his identity. At this point he shouts out (not even down the receiver which he is waving about quite hysterically) 'she frightens me because she disgusts me'. This scene is in direct counterpoint to the earlier meeting when he had seen her as object. Now she is subject ('she frightens me', rather than 'I am frightened of her'), he is object — the specimen in the glass cabinet. The contrast here is between his total awareness of her identity, which frightens him because it is beyond *his* control, and her complete denial of him through her oblivion. She is presence, he is absence.

Mona assumes her filth just as she assumes her marginality, she answers to no one and thanks no one. In so doing she creates her own image and simultaneously destroys the 'Image of Woman'. Equally, her speechlessness — which is in direct contrast to the volubility of those who would fix her — points to the moment pre-linguistic (that period of life which precedes the institution of patriarchal language) where the locus is the body-female in all its 'intimated reality of sensuousness' (Brückner 1985, 121).

By now it should be becoming clear that Varda bases her films on contrast and counterpoint, she also structures them around the dialectics of alternation and the theme of replacement (Audé 1981, 142). Thus she says: 'this dialectic, this ambiguity, this contradiction between the filmic negatives of one's inner life and the actual images of life as it is lived, this is the subject matter of all my films' (Audé 1981, 141). And in talking about *Sans toit ni loi* she again states this dialectic inside/outside: 'there are people who are 'inside' in the warmth, comfortably installed and others outside, in the cold, with not much idea of where they will sleep' (*Cinéma 85*, 332, 2).

Evidently her *cinécriture* reflects this structuring of 'a reality' — a first aspect of which is the use of the shifting point of view (employed as early as her first film *La Pointe Courte*). And in this film there are eighteen different points of view. This replacing of one vision by another, this proliferation of points of view, around one object, Mona, has a threefold effect. In the first instance it causes a disengagement from the story — thus preventing it from becoming an ideological film about vagrancy; [6] this is not a film about 'les nouveaux pauvres' (the new poor) but — amongst other things — about how a particular vagrant woman lives her solitude. In the second instance, the effect is to unfix the gaze, to render it inoperable. Because there are so many points of view, Mona cannot be caught in any of them. In this criss-crossing of gazes, Mona has already moved on or has not yet arrived. Varda represents this phenomenon visually through the contrasting images of Mona's wanderings and her speculators' immobilism, and, structurally, through alternately imbricating or fragmenting the portraits. Thirdly and finally, through this contrast of movement versus immobilism, Varda subverts the traditional codes of classical narrative cinema which depict man as the gender on the move and woman as static.

Interestingly, the structuring of the portraits finds a ready reflection in Varda's use of the tracking shot. The tracking shot is Mona's sign, as is the music that accompanies it. Of the fourteen tracking shots employed, all frame Mona at some juncture and all but three are accompanied by her theme. And here the parallels between shot and portrait become striking. With regard to the 'orchestrated' tracking shots there are three different compositions, in terms of the spoken portraits there are three types. And just as there are unorchestrated tracking shots so too there are silent portraits, most remarkably Assoun's.

The composition of the 'orchestrated' tracking shots is as follows: in the first instance, either the camera and frame 'abandon' Mona and go on to focus on an object, or she exits the frame; in the second, through her positioning in the frame she splits the horizontal tracking shot line either by crossing it (moving from the back to the foreground and exiting front-frame), or by remaining stationary as the camera continues its tracking movement and stops on an object; and in the third instance, both camera and Mona stay in tandem and come to a halt together. Two further points — both pointing to the contingency of her existence — Mona is rarely at the beginning of the tracking shot, she either walks in or is picked up by the camera and, equally significant, in all of these tracking shots she and the camera, when on the tracking shot line, move from right to left — this movement serving as a metaphor for both the flashback and, even more significantly, death.

This visual representation of the flashback, then, points predominantly to the idea of discontinuity — only the last two orchestrated tracking shots are in tandem and therefore continuous. This discontinuity is similarly present in the portraits — all of which are forms of flashback, but most of which are fragmented. There are just six stories where the portrait and images are in tandem (i.e. Mona arrives and the person whose path she has crossed immediately picks up the description). Otherwise they assume two forms. The first form is flashforward within a flashback, that is to say, we see the end of

Sans toit ni loi — above: Mona (Sandrine Bonnaire); below: Mona hitchhiking.

the story or encounter before we perceive the occurrence which preceded or brought about that encounter. For example, towards the very beginning of the film the demolition man tells the truck driver of his encounter with Mona (he discovers her in some derelict chalets he is about to raze to the ground) and there is a flash-shot of him peering in on her; much later, about halfway through the film, we see Mona arriving at these chalets and adopting them as her shelter.

The second form, far more digressive in fact, is a form whereby an initial flashback is interrupted by the insertion of other flashbacks only to be picked up again at some later juncture. Either the interruption is felt as a complete cut, as in the goat farmer's story (in an episode in the first half of the film, we see Mona arrive, stay and leave the farm and then some twelve episodes later in the latter half of the film we see and hear the goat farmer's summing up of the encounter). Or the flashback becomes fragmented by the imbrication of another portrait within the existing one. In this instance both get interrupted by a further flashback or series of flashbacks. Yolande's story and Mme Landier's are the two exemplars of this most dense of all digressive structures.

The tracking shot is a natural icon for a road movie as are the stops in between (think for example of *Easy Rider*). Thus when Varda states in an interview that 'the whole film is one long tracking shot ... we cut it up into pieces, we separate the pieces and in between them are the "adventures"' (*Cinématographe*, 114, 1985, 19) it might seem that she is following the canons of this particular genre. However, from its very inception this film goes counter to the canonic laws. First, it is filmed going backwards down the road (the tracking from right to left); second, the narration is a series of flashbacks all interwoven rather than an ordered sequence of events which lead inexorably to a bad end (*Easy Rider*) or a reasonable resolution (*Paris, Texas*) — furthermore, in Varda's film the spectator and the speculators already know the end; third, the tradition is for the point of view to be that of the roadster(s), but in this film it is everyone else's but Mona's that is given; fourth, the roadster is in this instance a woman on her own; fifth, a road movie implies discovery, obtaining some self-knowledge — but this is not the purpose here: in her filth and her solitude, Mona has acquired her identity, her marginality, and gazes uninterestedly past the others — including us. And her death, which she finally stumbles upon by tripping over an irrigation pipe, leaves us silent in its irony, coming as it does to she who emerged Aphrodite-like from the sea and whose pursuit of and longing for drinking water punctuates the entire film.

As with all texts — be they myths, allegories, film genres, whatever — whenever Varda makes reference to them she does so dialectically and contrapuntally. Thus water is not just an agent of cleansing and irrigation or refreshment, it is also a source of life and death. Water is immediately within this film associated with the birth of Aphrodite, the goddess of desire who yields to Dionysus the god of the vine. She is also the death-in-life goddess who every year, in remembrance of destroying the sacred king, bathes in the sea and rises again renewed. After her first bathe in the sea, Mona only seeks out water for refreshment; 'other women bathe (Eliane and Mme Landier), Mona doesn't'. Thenceforth, Mona roams the vineyards of the Hérault encrusting herself in her dirt. But unlike Aphrodite she will not yield to the pagan dionysians whose assault on her own filth with their *lie-de-vin* she cannot accept. This 'rape' of her identity, this sullying by another, is untenable — hence her reaction. This patriarchal pagan rite (only the men can dress-up as the wine gods and daub the women) is not the cause of her death, but is a contributing factor and for two reasons. First, the male rite withdraws sustenance (as a result of the festivities she cannot obtain any bread). Second, the violence of her rejection of their ritual practices and of the implicit tyranny of the gaze (she blockades herself in a telephone booth and screams, counterpointing her earlier reduction to a specimen by Mme Landier and again Jean-Pierre's own violent reaction to her at his loss of identity) aggravates her already advanced stage of hypothermia.

When we first see Mona's body it is covered with reddish stains, looking very much like blood. There is then a flash-shot of people mopping down a telephone booth (by now this object is becoming a pertinent symbol of enclosure rather than of an opening up of the horizons of communication) which is covered in red stains of some indistinguishable sort. Only the end shots of this film make clear what that red is. The series of flashbacks which separates these two sets of shots serves — through the images of Mona's living gestures — to show how her filth is accrued and her clothing diminished; and the last memorable trace on her body, the red stains, is the last to receive elucidation. We know as early as the beginning of the film that foul play has been ruled out, thus the film's structure is also an uncovering of how her body got there and in that state.

An entire film in flashback to explain a death or murder is part of the classical canon (*Murder, My Sweet*) but an entire film in flashback to elucidate one shot is not. To suffuse one shot with so much signification is to impregnate it with geological proportions of textural significance whose structures are as deep as they are dense, and whose references within those structures traverse discourses ancient and modern. I mentioned earlier the digressive structure of Varda's flashback construction and the analogically digressive composition of her tracking shots. These are aspects of her feminist *cinécriture* which are political because — as with feminist writing[7] which refuses to inscribe contours — in their digressiveness they go counter to dominant male filmmaking practices and are, therefore, counter-cinematic. And it is also true that her particular approach of textural intertextualization (a *mise-en-abyme* of different textures: painting, sculpture, photography, etc., *cinépeinture* as she calls it) is equally counter-cinematic in that it works 'in opposition to the naturalized dominant male discourse to produce textual contradictions which would de-naturalize the workings of patriarchal ideology' (Cook 1985, 198). These textual contradictions create gaps in representation 'into which woman's representation can insert itself' (ibid.). Varda makes frequent reference to the painterly quality of her films and to her desire to leave gaps, *des creux*. And certainly her painterly references stretch from the quattrocento to the realism of Courbet and Millet. Similarly, her filmic references are drawn from the silent era and also from contemporary cinema — and, as we have already indicated, many genres are re-represented.

Let us now consider the opening shot of the film — a very slow zoom. I will use this one shot to show how it establishes immediately the notion of intertextuality and the function of textual contradiction, both of which run throughout the film. Traditionally, a zoom transports the viewer from one space to another (and therefore one time to another) in such a way that perspectival time and space are dissolved. Varda, in slowing it down as she does, makes both time and space perspectival, and in so doing creates the intervals, the spaces or gaps in between which are not normally perceptible. The slowness of the zoom allows time in between to perceive the shifting of planes from foreground to background. Through this counter-cinematic practice, the zoom becomes de-naturalized and does not conform to the dominant ideology. Colliding with this technological subversion is the implicit subversiveness of the painterliness of Varda's shot. From the lighting (a luminous pale blue) to the slow tracerly movement across the terrain — from the trees in the foreground to those in the background upon a rounded hillock — this shot is reminiscent of Piero della Francesca's fresco *Resurrection of Christ* (1474?) with the hill of Golgotha[8] in the background — the hill where Jesus was crucified. The reference to Francesca, the greatest Italian painter of the quattrocento,[9] is particularly vital because he too subverted the then dominant painterly practices. He was the discoverer of a new vision in painting with a precise definition of volumes in space, a sense of interval, and a new treatment of light. Not only was he a canon-breaker on the visual front, he also took the chronological nature of aesthetic religious narration to task. Eschewing the prevalent formalistic and diegetic representation of the biblical allegories, he chose rather, for the sake of symmetry and a sense of interval, as in the fresco *Legend of the True Cross* (1452-59), to group his scenes out of chronological sequence. Through the slow zoom, Varda refers back to this vital subversiveness of the quattrocento and also towards her own filmmaking practices. Similarly, the *mise-en-scène* is both ancient and modern. It is Golgotha of the crucifixion — the Christian myth of life and death; and it is equally Van Gogh's canvas *La Route aux cyprès* (1890) — perceived later in both Mona's and Mme Landier's collection of postcards. Finally, it is also — through this last reference — an intertextualization-through-inversion of Alain Resnais' documentary *Van Gogh* (1947). In his film, Resnais uses zooms, pans and tracking shots of Van Gogh's paintings themselves to recreate the life of the artist. In her film, Varda inverts Resnais' initial oxymoron of painting as the cinematic shot (whereby stasis becomes movement and in so doing creates a life — in this instance, Van Gogh's), and in *Sans toit ni loi*, movement becomes stasis (i.e. the shot as painting) signifying death.

In just this single shot, texts and intertexts are immediately juxtaposed for the purpose of contradiction — so too are their textural representations (i.e. the plasticity of paint as a texture is distinct from that of celluloid). Simultaneously, these textual contradictions cause a constant shifting and thus indeed a rift between the multi-layered planes of time and space. These contradictions unfix rather than transfix meaning and the whole of the film is similarly infused with this unease of the *insaisissable*. Visual presence is made absence: that which is there cannot be seized — there are no contours which define.

Varda treats objects in a similar intertextual and dialectical fashion. A brief look at how she reworks the signification of certain objects will show how they serve to intensify the digressive texturality of her *cinécriture*. In this instance, I shall focus on the representation of death which is, after all, a dominant discourse within the film.

Trees are amongst the many objects that link or punctuate the film and, as with most of the other objects, are more readily associated with violence and death than with regeneration and life. Trees are framed as Mona is raped. Trees (plane trees) have been 'colonized'/'raped' by a deathly American-imported fungus (gift of World War II). Mona immediately identifies with their destiny: 'si *elles* crèvent, pensez à moi' ('if they perish, think of me'), she says (my stress).

Walls, doors and shutters almost invariably shut Mona out, only at best do they conceal her from the police. They are symbolic of her numerous evictions, the last of which is fatal. In accidentally setting fire to her refuge (a derelict house shared with other drop-outs), David — a former acquaintance of hers — deprives her of her protection from the cold. Incidentally, this eventuality is foreshadowed in an earlier episode when David — who was then shacked up with Mona in an unlived-in mansion — gets into a fight with robbers and drops his oil lamp. That time the house miraculously does not catch fire. In this second occurrence, however, it is David's violence (he attacks the squatters who owe him money) which causes the fire. In film culture, it is women who are most often associated with fire — that most obvious of death symbols. Here it is associated with David and not Mona — he brings the fire and plunders her home. Moreover, David is allegorically associated with death and with the imagery of the opening shot of the film. For he is the wandering Jew. The one who insulted Christ on his way to Golgotha and who was condemned to wander about the world until Christ's second coming.

Plastic tents and cloches, intended to warm the earth for growth and germination, offer poor comfort to Mona and will ultimately serve to encase her corpse. Indeed, in the closing episode we are reminded of the symbolism of the greenhouse in Renoir's *La Règle du jeu* where it is the site of André Jurieu's death (in fact Mona's twitching movements as she lies dying are very reminiscent of Jurieu's).

Death also crosses Mona's path in the form of the gravedigger whose hooded cloak masks his face. Cloaked and masked as he is he recalls the character of Death in Bergman's *Seventh Seal*. Earlier, there is another reference to this same film, this time to the sound and image construct of its opening sequence. In Bergman's film, the Knight awakens and washes himself in the sea, the sound-track is Bergman in voice-over reading from the book of Revelations. In Varda's film, we hear her voice-over — the only voice-over of the film — accompanying the shot of Mona emerging, cleansed, from the sea. At this point she is also Botticelli's *Birth of Venus* (1485). Thus, again the dialectical tension of life and death is represented and, too, tension in a textural sense because of the simultaneous reference to two contrasting modes of visual imagery. As was pointed out above, to place a painterly reference alongside a cinematic one is to represent immobilism and movement simultaneously. But this oxymoron gathers even further layers of contradictions when one considers that both Botticelli's painting and Bergman's film are inscribed within yet another text or even series of texts: the fictionalized documentary of Settina's/Mona's story/portrait.

Fact and fiction, documentary, a road movie in flashback, Greek, pagan and Christian myths, contrastive visual discourses — just so many texts all interwoven and rewritten within a digressive structure that, in the end, the film itself maintains the enigmatic mystery of an incomplete (in the sense that it cannot be completed) jigsaw puzzle. We cannot fix the film any more than we can fix Mona and it is in this de-fetishization of the text as well as the body-female that Varda asserts her own brand of feminist filmmaking practices.

NOTES

1.   See her article, 'Women's cinema as counter-cinema' (1976). And also Louise Heck-Rabi (1984), who provides a very comprehensive study of Varda's critical acclaim.

2.   This is a point of view I do not share incidentally and one which I have argued against elsewhere (*ASMCF Review*, 33, 1988).

3.   Interview, *24 Images*, 27, 1986.

4.   The original title of this film was going to be *A saisir*, obviously intended ironically (see Sheila Johnston's review in *Films and Filming*, 380, 1986, 41).

5.   For further discussion on the authentic sex, see Sigrid Weigel's article 'Double focus', (1985) 78-79.

6.   Olivier Dazat makes this particular point in comparing this film to earlier forms of the road movie. See his article in *Cinématographe*, 1985, 11.

7.   Luce Irigaray and Hélène Cixous both speak of the necessity for 'feminine' writing to traverse discourses and thus 'set fire to fetishized words, appropriate terms, well-constructed forms' (Weigel 1985, 75).

8.   Jean Decock (*Visions*, 35, 1986) identifies the symbolism of the hill but I believe he gets the painterly reference wrong. It is almost certainly not an Italian primitive as he claims, but a direct reference to the quattrocento. See also note 9.

9.   As early as her first film, *La Pointe Courte*, Varda refers to the painterliness of the film and makes specific reference to Piero della Francesca (interview in *Cahiers du cinéma*, 165, 1965).

SELECTED BIBLIOGRAPHY

Audé, Françoise (1981) *Ciné-modèles Cinéma d'elles: situation des femmes dans le cinéma français 1956-1979*, Lausanne, l'Age d'Homme.
Brückner, Jutta (1985) 'Women behind the camera', in Gisela Ecker (ed.), *Feminist Aesthetics*, London, The Women's Press, 120-124.
Cook, Pam (ed.) (1985) *The Cinema Book*, London, British Film Institute, 202.
Corrigan, Timothy (1986) 'The tension of translation: Handke's *The Left-handed Woman*', in Eric Rentschler (ed.), *German Film and Literature: Adaptations and Transformations*, New York and London, Methuen, 260-275
Heck-Rabi, Louise (1984) *Women Filmmakers*, Metuchen, New Jersey and London, The Scarecrow Press, 322-352.
Johnston, Claire (1976) 'Women's cinema as counter-cinema', in Bill Nichols (ed.), *Movies and Methods*, Berkeley, University of California Press, 208-217.
Pingaud, Bernard (1963) 'Agnès Varda et la réalité', in Raymond Bellour (ed.), *Un cinéma réel*, ArtSept, 1.
Rose, Jacqueline (1986) *Sexuality in the Field of Vision*, London, Verso.
Turim, Maureen (1986) 'Textuality and theatricality in Brecht and Straub/Huillet: *History Lessons*', in Eric Renschler (ed.), *German Film and Literature: Adaptations and Transformations*, New York and London, Methuen, 231-245.
Weigel, Sigrid (1985), 'Double Focus: On the history of women's writing', in Gisela Ecker (ed.), *Feminist Aesthetics*, London, The Women's Press, 59-80.

APPENDIX

Agnès Varda (1928—): filmography

1954 *La Pointe Courte*
1957 *O saisons, ô châteaux* (short)
1958 *L'Opéra Mouffe* (short)
1958 *Du côté de la côte* (short)
1961 *Cléo de 5 à 7*
1963 *Salut les Cubains* (short)
1965 *Le Bonheur*
1966 *Elsa et la rose* (short)
1966 *Les Créatures*
1967 *Loin du Vietnam* (sketch in collective film)
1968 *Uncle Yanco* (short)
1968 *Black Panthers* (short)
1969 *Lions Love*
1970 *Nausica*
1975 *Daguerreotypes*
1975 *Réponses de femmes* (short)
1976 *Plaisir d'amour en Iran* (short)
1980 *Murs, murs* (short)
1981 *Documenteur* (short)
1982 *Ulysse* (short)
1983 *Une Minute pour une image* (170 two minute films)
1984 *Les Dites cariatides* (short)
1984 *Sept pièces, cuisine, salle de bain, à saisir* (short)
1985 *Sans toit ni loi*
1987 *Jane B. vue par Agnès V.*
1987 *Kung Fu Master*

Other films cited in text

Easy Rider, Denis Hopper (1969)
Murder My Sweet/Farewell My Lovely, Edward Dmytryck (1944)
Paris, Texas, Wim Wenders (1984)
La Règle du jeu (*Rules of the Game*), Jean Renoir (1939)
The Seventh Seal, Ingmar Bergman (1957)
Van Gogh, Alain Resnais (1948)

SELECTED BIBLIOGRAPHY ON FRENCH CINEMA

The following is a *selection* of works in book form on French cinema or relevant to the study of French cinema, published in French and in English. Additional material on the individual films and directors considered in this book can be found under each chapter.

Reference

Chirat, Raymond (1975) *Catalogue des films français de long métrage, films sonores de fiction, 1929-1939,* Brussels, Cinémathèque Royale de Belgique. An illustrated edition of the same catalogue was published in 1981 (same publisher).
Chirat, Raymond (1981) *Catalogue des films français de long métrage, films de fiction, 1940-1950,* Luxemburg, Imprimerie Saint-Paul.
Chirat, Raymond and Icart, Roger (1984) *Catalogue des films français de long métrage, films de fiction, 1919-1929,* Toulouse, Cinémathèque de Toulouse.
Chirat, Raymond and Romer, Jean-Claude (1984) *Catalogue des films français de fiction de 1e partie 1929-1939,* Bois d'Arcy, Service des Archives du Film, Centre National de la Cinématographie.
Cowie, Peter (yearly since 1964) *The International Film Guide,* London, Tantivy Press.
Franju, Georges (1982) *De Marey à Renoir: trésors de la Cinémathèque Française 1882-1939,* Paris, *Avant-Scène Cinéma,* 279-280.
Icart, Roger (n.d.) *Pour Vous, Ciné-Miroir, Cinémonde, 1929-1940, Index 1, films français de long métrage et de fiction,* Toulouse, Documents de la Cinémathèque de Toulouse.
Image et magie du cinéma français: 100 ans de patrimoine (1980), no specified author, Paris, Conservatoire National des Arts et Métiers.
Katz, Ephraïm (1980) *The International Film Encyclopedia,* London, Macmillan.
Lyon, Christopher (ed.) (1984) *The Macmillan Dictionary of Films and Filmmakers, I: Films, II: Filmmakers,* London, Macmillan.
Mitry, Jean (1980-1982) *Filmographie universelle,* 26 vols, Bois d'Arcy, Service des Archives du Film.
Passek, Jean-Loup *et al.* (1986) *Dictionnaire du cinéma,* Paris, Larousse.
Pinel, Vincent (1985) *Filmographie des longs métrages sonores du cinéma français produits et présentés commercialement sur grand écran entre 1930 et 1984 (à l'exception des films classés 'X'),* Paris, Cinémathèque Française.
Roud, Richard (ed.) (1980) *Cinema: A Critical Dictionary, The Major Filmmakers,* 2 vols, New York, Viking, London, Secker and Warburg.
Sabria, Jean-Claude and Busca, Jean-Pierre (1985) *L'Index du film français — 1944-1984: 40 ans de cinéma en France, Répertoire des films de A à Z,* Paris, Cinéma de France.
Tulard, Jean (1982) *Dictionnaire du cinéma, 'Les Réalisateurs',* Paris, Laffont.
Tulard, Jean (1984) *Dictionnaire du cinéma, Acteurs-Producteurs- Scénaristes-Techniciens',* Paris, Laffont.
Wakeman, John (1987-1988) *World Film Directors,* 2 vols, New York, H. W. Wilson.

Film history: general

(with special emphasis on French film history)

Bardèche, Maurice and Brasillach, Robert (1948) *History of the Film,* trans. and ed. by Iris Barry from 1st French edition (1935), London, Allen and Unwin.
Bardèche, Maurice and Brasillach, Robert (1954) *Histoire du cinéma (Nouvelle édition définitive en deux volumes),* Paris, André Martel.
Beylie, Claude and Carcassone, Philippe (1983) *Le Cinéma,* Paris, Bordas.

Le Cinéma (grande histoire illustrée du 7e art) (1982-1984), no specified author, 10 vols, Paris, Atlas.

Deslandes, Jacques and Richard, Jacques (1966) *Histoire comparée du cinéma, I: 1826-1896,* Paris, Casterman.

Deslandes, Jacques and Richard, Jacques (1968) *Histoire comparée du cinéma, II: 1896-1906,* Paris, Casterman.

Ford, Charles (1972) *Femmes cinéastes, ou le triomphe de la volonté,* Paris, Denoël.

Jeanne, René and Ford, Charles (1947-1962) *Histoire encyclopédique du cinéma,* 5 vols, Paris, Robert Laffont (I) and SEDE (II to V).

Lamartine, Thérèse (1985) *Elles Cinéastes ad-lib 1895-1981,* Montréal, Editions du Remue-Ménage.

Langlois, Henri (1986) *Trois cents ans de cinéma,* Paris, Cahiers du Cinéma and Cinémathèque Française.

Lejeune, Paule (1987) *Le Cinéma des femmes,* Paris, Atlas.

Leprohon, Pierre (1961-1963) *Histoire du cinéma,* 2 vols, Paris, Editions du Cerf.

Mitry, Jean (1967-1980) *Histoire du cinéma, art et industrie,* 5 vols, Paris, Editions Universitaires.

Moussinac, Léon (1967) *L'Age ingrat du cinéma,* Paris, Editeurs Français Réunis.

Philippe, Claude-Jean (1984) *Le Roman du cinéma, I: 1928-1938,* Paris, Fayard.

Philippe, Claude-Jean (1986) *Le Roman du cinéma, II: 1938-1945,* Paris, Fayard.

Rhode, Eric (1976) *A History of the Cinema,* New York, Farrar, Straus and Giroux.

Sadoul, Georges (1946-1954) *Histoire générale du cinéma,* 5 vols, Paris, Denoël. Reprinted (1973-1975) with a few amendments.

French cinema: history and criticism

Some books dealing with other national cinemas or other topics have been included under this heading if of sufficient relevance to French cinema.

1. General

Agel, Henri (1958) *Miroirs de l'insolite dans le cinéma français,* Paris, Editions du Cerf.

Andrew, Dudley (1978) *André Bazin,* New York, Oxford University Press.

Andrew, Dudley (1984) *Film in the Aura of Art,* Princeton, Princeton University Press.

Armes, Roy (1985) *French Cinema,* London, Secker and Warburg.

Arnoux Alexandre (1946) *Du muet au parlant: mémoires d'un témoin,* Paris, Nouvelle Edition.

Bandy, Mary Lea (ed.) (1983) *Rediscovering French Film,* New York, Museum of Modern Art (contains substantial bibliography).

Bazin, André (ed.) (1984) *La Politique des auteurs,* Paris, Cahiers du Cinéma, Editions de l'Etoile.

Borga, J.-M. and Martinand, B. (1977) *Affiches du cinéma français,* Paris, Delville.

Boulanger, Pierre (1975) *Le Cinéma colonial,* Paris, Seghers.

Braunberger, Pierre (1987) *Cinémamémoire,* Paris, Centre Georges Pompidou, Centre National de la Cinématographie.

Brieu, Christian and Ikor, Laurent and Viguier, Jean-Michel (1985) *Joinville, le cinéma: le temps des studios,* Paris, Ramsay.

Brunius, Jacques-Bernard (1954) *En marge du cinéma français,* Paris, Arcanes.

Buss, Robin (1988) *The French Through Their Films,* London, Batsford.

Cadars, Pierre (1982) *Les Séducteurs du cinéma français (1928-1958),* Paris, Henri Veyrier.

Chantal, Suzanne (1977) *Le Ciné-monde,* Paris, Grasset.

Chevallier, Jacques (ed.) (1963) *Regards neufs sur le cinéma,* Paris, Editions du Seuil.

Chirat, Raymond and Barrot, Olivier (1983) *Les Excentriques du cinéma français (1929-1958),* Paris, Henri Veyrier.

Chirat, Raymond and Barrot, Olivier (1986) *Inoubliables! Visages du cinéma français: 1930-1950*, Paris, Calmann-Lévy.
Comes, Phillppe de and Marmin, Michel (1984) *Le Cinéma français: 1930-1960*, Paris, Editions Atlas.
Cottom, J. V. (1983) *Ce monde fou-fou du cinéma français*, Bruxelles, J. M. Collet.
Courtade, Francis (1978) *Les Malédictions du cinéma français*, Paris, Alain Moreau.
Daniel, Joseph (1972) *Guerre et cinéma - Grandes illusions et petits soldats*, Paris, Armand Colin.
Daquin, Louis (1960) *Le Cinéma notre métier*, Paris, Editeurs Français Réunis.
Des Femmes de Musidora (1976) *Paroles... elles tournent*, Paris, Des Femmes.
Devailleux, Claire (1981) *Les Acteurs au travail*, Paris, Hatier.
Diamant-Berger, Henri (1945) *Destin du cinéma français*, Paris, Imprimerie de Montmartre.
Ducout, Françoise (1978) *Les Séductrices du cinéma français, 1936-1956*, Paris, Henri Veyrier.
Frank, Nino (1950) *Petit cinéma sentimental*, Paris, La Nouvelle Edition.
Guérif, François (1981) *Le Cinéma policier français*, Paris, Henri Veyrier.
Guillard, Gilbert (1983) *Le Cinéma français de 1930 à 1981*, Munich, Manz Verlag.
Hammond, Paul (ed.) (1978) *The Shadow and its Shadow: Surrealist Writings on Cinema*, London, British Film Institute.
Harcourt, Peter (1974) *Six European Directors, Essays on the Meaning of Film Style*, Harmondsworth, Middlesex, Penguin Books.
Hillairet, Prosper *et al.* (1985) *Paris vu par le cinéma d'avant-garde*, Paris, Centre National Georges Pompidou.
Jeanne, René and Ford, Charles (1961) *Le Cinéma et la presse 1895-1960*, Paris, Armand Colin.
Jeanne, René and Ford, Charles (1969) *Paris vu par le cinéma*, Paris, Hachette.
Kyrou, Ado (1963) *Le Surréalisme au cinéma*, Paris, Terrain Vague.
Lacassin, Francis (1972) *Pour une contre-histoire du cinéma*, Paris, UGE (10/18).
Lapierre, Marcel (ed.) (1946) *Anthologie du cinéma*, Paris, La Nouvelle Edition.
Lapierre, Marcel (1948) *Les Cent visages du cinéma*, Paris, Grasset.
Lebrun, Dominique (1987) *Paris-Hollywood, les Français dans le cinéma américain*, Paris, Hazan.
Leprohon, Pierre (1954) *50 ans de cinéma français (1895-1945)*, Paris, Editions du Cerf.
Martin, Marcel (1971) *France*, London, Zwemmer, New York, Barnes.
Mazeau, Jacques and Thouart Didier (1983) *Acteurs et chanteurs*, Paris, PAC.
Michalczyk, John (1980) *The French Literary Filmmakers*, Philadelphia, The Art Alliance Press, London, Associated University Presses.
Prédal, René (1972) *La Société française (1914-1945) à travers le cinéma*, Paris, Armand Colin.
Prédal, René (1980) *80 ans de cinéma: Nice et le 7e art*, Nice, Serre.
Reader, Keith (1981) *Cultures on Celluloid*, London, Quartet.
Richebé, Roger (1977) *Au-delà de l'écran*, Monte-Carlo, Pastorelly.
Roud, Richard (1983) *A Passion for Films, Henri Langlois and the Cinémathèque Française*, London, Secker and Warburg.
Roux, Jean and Thévenet, René (1979) *Industrie et commerce du film en France*, Paris, Editions Scientifiques.
Sadoul, Georges (1953) *French Film*, London, Falcon Press.
Sadoul, Georges (1979) *Chroniques du cinéma français:1 1939-1967*, Paris, UGE (10/18).
Sadoul, Georges (1981) *Le Cinéma français: 1890-1962*, Paris, Flammarion.
Siclier, Jacques (1957) *La Femme dans le cinéma français*, Paris, Editions du Cerf.
Thiher, Allen (1979) *The Cinematic Muse: Critical Studies in the History of French Cinema*, Columbia and London, University of Missouri Press.
Truffaut, François (1975) *Les Films de ma vie*, Paris, Flammarion.
Truffaut, François (1978) *The Films in My Life*, trans. Leonard Mayhew, New York, Simon and Schuster.

Védrès, Nicole (1945) *Images du cinéma français,* Paris, Editions du Chêne.
Virmaux, Alain and Odette (eds) (1975) *Colette: au cinéma,* Paris, Flammarion.
Virmaux, Alain and Odette (1976) *Les Surréalistes et le cinéma,* Paris, Seghers.
Virmaux, Alain and Odette (eds) (1981) *Colette at the Movies,* trans. by Sarah W. R. Smith,
    New York, Ungar.
Weil-Lorac, Roger (1977) *50 ans de cinéma actif,* Paris, Dujarric.
Witta-Montrobert, Jeanne (1980) *La Lanterne magique: mémoires d'une script,* Paris,
    Calmann-Lévy.

2. Silent cinema

Abel, Richard (1984) *French Cinema: The First Wave, 1915-1929,* Princeton, Princeton
    University Press.
Bordwell, David (1980) *French Impressionist Cinema: Film Culture, Film Theory, and Film
    Style,* New York, Arno.
Coissac, Georges-Michel (1925) *Histoire du cinématographe: de ses origines jusqu'à nos
    jours,* Paris, Editions du 'Cinéopse'.
Fell, John (1983) *Film Before Griffith,* Berkeley and Los Angeles, University of California
    Press.
Fescourt, Henri (1959) *La Foi et les montagnes,* Paris, Paul Montel.
Hughes, Philippe de and Marmin, Michel (1986) *Le Cinéma français, le Muet,* Paris, Atlas.
Leprohon, Pierre (1982) *Histoire du cinéma muet 1895-1930,* Plan-de-la-Tour, Editions
    d'Aujourd'hui (reprint of 1961 edition, Editions du Cerf).
Monaco, Paul (1976) *Cinema and Society: France and Germany During the Twenties,* New
    York, Elsevier.

3. The 1930s

Barrot, Olivier and Jeancolas, Jean-Pierre (1973) *Les Français et leur cinéma, 1930-1939,*
    Créteil, Maison de la Culture, Losfeld.
Bessy, Maurice (1987) *Histoire du cinéma français: encyclopédie des films 1935-1939,*
    Paris, Pygmalion.
Beylie, Claude (ed.) (1983) *Cinémagazine 1930,* Paris, Avant-Scène (reprint of original
    articles).
Chirat, Raymond (1983) *Le Cinéma français des années 30,* Paris, Hatier.
Chirat, Raymond (1987) *Atmosphères: sourires, soupirs et délires du cinéma français des
    années 30,* Paris, Hatier.
Garçon, François (1984) *De Blum à Pétain: cinéma et société française (1936-44),* Paris,
    Editions du Cerf.
Grelier, Robert *et al.* (eds) (1986) *Mémoires d'en France 1936-1939,* Paris, Aimo.
Guillaume-Grimaud, Geneviève (1986), *Le Cinéma du Front Populaire,* Paris, Lherminier.
Jeancolas, Jean-Pierre (1977) 'Cinéma d'un monde en crise', *La Documentation française,*
    special dossier.
Jeancolas, Jean-Pierre (1983) *15 ans d'annés trente, le cinéma des Français, 1929-44,*
    Paris, Stock.
Lagny, Michèle, Ropars, Marie-Claire and Sorlin, Pierre (1986) *Générique des années
    trente,* Saint-Denis, Presses Universitaires de Vincennes.
Léglise, Paul (1970) *Histoire de la politique du cinéma français, Tome I: Le Cinéma et la IIIe
    République,* Paris, Lherminier.
Martin, John W. (1983) *The Golden Age of French Cinema, 1929-39,* Boston, G. K. Hall.
Peyrusse, Claudette (1986) *Le Cinéma méridional 1929-1944,* Toulouse, Eché.
Renaitour, Jean-Michel (1937) *Où va le cinéma français?,* Paris, Baudiniaire.
Strebel, Elizabeth Grottle (1980) *French Social Cinema of the Nineteen-Thirties: A Cinematic
    Expression of Popular Front Consciousness,* New-York, Arno.

Vincendeau, Ginette and Reader, Keith (1986) *La Vie est à nous, French Cinema of the Popular Front, 1935-1938,* London, British Film Institute.

4. The Occupation

Bazin, André (1975) *Le Cinéma de l'Occupation et de la Résistance,* Paris, UGE (10/18).
Bazin, André (1981) *French Cinema of the Occupation and Resistance,* trans. Stanley Hochman, New York, Ungar.
Bertin-Maghit, Jean-Pierre (1980) *Le Cinéma français sous Vichy, les films français de 1940 à 1944,* Paris, Ça Cinéma.
Bonny, Maurice (1986) *Histoire du cinéma français; encyclopédie des films 1940-1950,* Paris, Pygmalion.
Chirat, Raymond (1983) *Le Cinéma français des années de guerre,* Paris, Hatier.
Ehrlich, Evelyn (1985) *Cinema of Paradox: French Filmmaking under the German Occupation,* New York, Columbia University Press.
Garçon, François (1984) *De Blum à Pétain: cinéma et société française (1936-1944),* Paris, Editions du Cerf.
Halimi, André (1976) *Chantons sous l'occupation,* Paris, Olivier Orban.
Jeancolas, Jean-Pierre (1976) 'Cinéma d'un monde en guerre', *La Documentation française,* special dossier.
Jeancolas, Jean-Pierre (1983) *15 ans d'annés trente, le cinéma des Français, 1929-1944,* Paris, Stock.
Kaplan, Alice Yeager (1986) *Reproductions of Banality (Fascism, Literature, and French Intellectual Life),* Minneapolis, University of Minnesota Press (contains a long interview with Maurice Bardèche).
Léglise, Paul (1977) *Histoire de la politique du cinéma français, Tome II: Le Cinéma entre deux Républiques (1940-1946),* Paris, Lherminier.
Peyrusse, Claudette (1986) *Le Cinéma méridional 1929-1944,* Toulouse, Eché.
Rebatet, Lucien (F. Vinneuil) (1941) *Les Tribus du cinéma et du théatre,* Paris, Nouvelles Editions Françaises.
Régent, Roger (1975) *Cinéma de France, de 'La Fille du puisatier' aux 'Enfants du paradis',* Paris, Editions d'Aujourd'hui (reprint of 1948 edition).
Siclier, Jacques (1981), *La France de Pétain et son cinéma,* Paris, Veyrier.

5. French cinema since WW2

Agel, Henri *et al.* (1953) *Sept ans de cinéma français (1945-51),* Paris, Editions du Cerf.
Armes, Roy (1976) *The Ambiguous Image: Narrative Style in Modern European Cinema,* London, British Film Institute.
Audé, Françoise (1981) *Ciné-modèles, Cinéma d'elles, situations de femmes dans le cinéma français 1956-1979,* Lausanne, L'Age d'Homme.
Barboni, Laurette (1986) *Cinéma d'aujourd'hui: images de cinéma, images de société,* Sèvres, Centre International d'Etudes Pédagogiques de Sèvres.
Barrot, Olivier (1979) *L'Ecran français 1943-1953, histoire d'un journal et d'une époque,* Paris, Les Editeurs Français Réunis.
Bazin, André (1983) *Le Cinéma français de la Libération à la Nouvelle Vague (1945-1958),* Paris, Cahiers du Cinéma, Editions de l'Etoile.
Bessy, Maurice (1986) *Histoire du cinéma français: encyclopédie des films 1940-1950,* Paris, Pygmalion.
Bonnel, René (1978) *Le Cinéma exploité,* Paris, Editions du Seuil.
Borde, Raymond, and Buache, Freddy and Curtelin, Jean (1962) *Nouvelle Vague,* Premier Plan, Lyon, Serdoc.
Bredin, Jean-Denis (1982) *The Bredin Report: On the Future of the French Cinema,* London, British Film Institute.
Buache, Freddy (1987) *Le Cinéma français des années 60,* Paris, Hatier.

Charensol, Georges (1946) *Renaissance du cinéma français,* Paris, Editions du Sagittaire.
Chirat, Raymond (1985) *La IVe République et ses films,* Paris, Hatier.
Clouzot, Claire (1972) *Le Cinéma français depuis la nouvelle vague,* Paris, Fernand Nathan.
Collet, Jean (1972) *Le Cinéma en question* (Rozier, Chabrol, Rivette, Truffaut, Demy, Rhomer), Paris, Editions du Cerf.
Degand, Claude (1972) *Le Cinéma, cette industrie,* Editions Techniques et Economiques.
Douin, Jean-Luc (ed.) (1983) *La Nouvelle Vague 25 ans après,* Paris, Editions du Cerf.
Durgnat, Raymond (1963) *Nouvelle Vague, The First Decade,* Loughton, Essex, Motion Publications.
Ford, Charles (1977) *Histoire du cinéma français contemporain 1945-1977,* Paris, France-Empire.
Goldmann, Annie (1971) *Cinéma et société moderne, le cinéma de 1958 à 1968,* Paris, Anthropos.
Graham, Peter (ed.) (1968) *The New Wave,* London, Secker and Warburg.
Harvey, Sylvia (1978) *May '68 and Film Culture,* London, British Film Institute.
Hennebelle, Guy (1975) *Quinze ans de cinéma mondial, 1960-1975,* Paris, Editions du Cerf.
Hillier, Jim (ed.) (1985) *Cahiers du cinéma 1: the 1950s, Neo-Realism, Hollywood, The New Wave,* London, Routledge and Kegan Paul, British Film Institute (trans. of selection of original *Cahiers du cinéma* articles).
Hillier, Jim (ed.) (1986) *Cahiers du cinéma 2: 1960-1968,* London, Routledge and Kegan Paul, British Film Institute (ditto).
Horton, Andrew S. and Magretta, Joan (eds) (1981) *Modern European Filmmakers and the Art of Adaptation,* New York, Ungar.
Jacob, Gilles (1964) *Le Cinéma moderne,* Lyon, Serdoc.
Jeancolas, Jean-Pierre (1974) *Le Cinéma des Français, 1969-1974, les années Pompidou,* Créteil, Maison de la Culture.
Jeancolas, Jean-Pierre (1979) *Le Cinéma des Français — la Ve République, 1958-78,* Paris, Stock.
Leenhardt, Roger (1986) *Chroniques de cinéma,* Paris, Cahiers du Cinéma, Editions de l'Etoile.
Maarek, Philippe J. de (1979) *De mai 68 aux films X: cinéma, politique et société,* Paris, Dujarric.
Martin, Marcel (1984) *Le Cinéma français depuis la guerre,* Paris, Edilig.
Monaco, James (1976) *The New Wave,* New York, Oxford University Press.
Noguez, Dominique (1982) *Trente ans de cinéma expérimental en France (1950-1980),* A.R.C.E.F.
Pivasset, Jean (1971) *Essai sur la signification politique du cinéma,* Paris, Cujas.
Prédal, René (1984) *Le Cinéma français contemporain,* Paris, Editions du Cerf.
Siclier, Jacques (1961) *Nouvelle vague?,* Paris, Editions du Cerf.
Société des Réalisateurs de films (1978) *La Règle du jeu: situation du cinéma français: 1968-1978,* Paris, Albatros.

6. Theoretical works

This is a selection of French theoretical works as well as general theoretical works which we consider relevant to French film theory and history, and/or the analysis of French films.

Allen, Robert C. and Gomery, Douglas (1985) *Film History, Theory and Practice,* New York, Knopf.
Aumont, Jacques and Leutrat, Jean-Louis (1980) *La Théorie du film,* Paris, Albatros.
Aumont, Jacques *et al.* (1983) *L'Esthétique du film,* Paris, Fernand Nathan.
Bailbé, Claude, and Marie, Michel and Ropars, Marie-Claire (1975) *Muriel,* Paris, Galilée.
Bazin, André (1958-1962) *Qu'est-ce que le cinéma?,* 4 vols, Paris, Editions du Cerf.
Bazin, André (1967) *What is Cinema?,* 2 vols, trans. Hugh Gray, Berkeley, University of California Press (NB: some French articles are omitted in the English translation).

Bordwell, David (1985) *Narration in the Fiction Film,* London, Methuen.
Bordwell, David and Thompson, Kristin (1986) *Film Art: An Introduction,* 2nd edition, New York, Knopf.
Burch, Noël (1969) *Praxis du cinéma,* Paris, Gallimard.
Burch, Noël (1973) *Theory of Film Practice,* New York, Praeger.
Chion, Michel (1982) *La Voix au cinéma,* Paris, Cahiers du Cinéma, Editions de l'Etoile.
Chion, Michel (1985) *Le Son au cinéma,* Paris, Cahiers du Cinéma, Editions de l'Etoile.
Chion, Michel (1988) *La Toile trouée (la parole au cinéma),* Paris, Cahiers du Cinéma, Editions de l'Etoile.
Collet, Jean *et al.* (1977) *Lectures du film,* Paris, Albatros.
Cook, Pam (ed.) (1985) *The Cinema Book,* London, British Film Institute.
Durand, Jacques (1958) *Le Cinéma et son public,* Paris, Sirey.
Dyer, Richard (1979) *Stars,* London, British Film Institute.
Ferro, Marc (1976) *Analyse de films, analyse de sociétés,* Paris, Hachette.
Ferro, Marc (1977) *Cinéma et histoire,* Paris, Denoël-Gonthier.
Ferro, Marc (1984) *Film et histoire,* Paris, Editions de l'Ecole des Hautes Etudes en Sciences Sociales.
Haskell, Molly (1974) *From Reverence to Rape, The Treatment of Women in the Movies,* New York, Rinehart and Winston.
Kaplan, E. Ann (1983) *Women and Film: Both Sides of the Camera,* London, Methuen.
Kay, Karin and Peary, Gerald (1977) *Women and the Cinema: A Critical Anthology,* New York, Dutton.
Kuhn, Annette (1982) *Women's Pictures, Feminism and Cinema,* London, Routledge and Kegan Paul.
Mast, Gerald and Cohen, Marshall (eds) (1979) *Film Theory and Criticism,* New York, Oxford University Press.
Metz, Christian (1968-1972)*Essais sur la signification au cinéma,* 2 vols, Paris, Klincksieck.
Metz, Christian (1971) *Langage et cinéma,* Paris, Larousse.
Metz, Christian (1974a) *Film Language: A Semiotics of the Cinema,* trans. of *Essais sur la signification au cinéma* by Michael Taylor, New York, Oxford University Press.
Metz, Christian (1974b) *Language and the Cinema,* trans. of *Langage et cinéma* by Donna Jean Umiker-Sebeck, The Hague, Mouton.
Metz, Christian (1977) *Le Signifiant imaginaire, psychanalyse et cinéma,* Paris, UGE (10/18).
Metz, Christian (1982) *The Imaginary Signifier: Psychoanalysis and the Cinema,* trans. Celia Britton, Anhwyl Williams, Ben Brewster and Alfred Guzzetti, Bloomington, Indiana University Press.
Mitry, Jean (1966-1968) *Esthétique et psychologie du cinéma, I: Les Structures, II: Les Formes,* Paris, Editions Universitaires.
Mitry, Jean (1987) *La Sémiologie en question,* Paris, Editions du Cerf.
Morin, Edgar (1956) *Le Cinéma ou l'homme imaginaire, essai d'anthropologie sociologique,* Paris, Les Editions de Minuit.
Morin, Edgar (1957) *Les Stars,* Paris, Editions du Seuil.
Morin, Edgar (1960) *The Stars,* trans. R. Howard, New York, Grove Press.
Nichols, Bill (ed.) (1976) *Movies and Methods,* Berkeley, University of California Press.
Nichols, Bill (ed.) (1985) *Movies and Methods,* vol. II, Berkeley, University of California Press.
Ropars-Wuilleumier, Marie-Claire (1970a) *L'Ecran de la mémoire, essai de lecture cinématographique,* Paris, Editions du Seuil.
Ropars-Wuilleumier, Marie-Claire (1970b) *De la littérature au cinéma: génèse d'une écriture,* Paris, Armand Colin.
Ropars-Wuilleumier, Marie-Claire (1981) *Le Texte divisé,* Paris, P.U.F.
Sarris, Andrew (1973) *The Primal Screen: Essays on Film and Related Subjects,* New York, Simon and Schuster.
Screen Reader 1 (1977) Cinema/Ideology/Politics.

Screen Reader 2 (1981) Cinema and Semiotics.
Short, K. R. M. (ed.) (1981) *Feature Film as History*, Beckenham, Croom Helm.
Simon, Jean-Pierre (1979) *Le Filmique et le comique,* Paris, Albatros.
Sorlin, Pierre (1977) *Sociologie du cinéma, ouverture pour l'histoire de demain,* Paris,
    Aubier.
Sorlin, Pierre (1980) *The Film in History (Restaging the Past),* Oxford, Blackwell.
Wollen, Peter (1969) *Signs and Meaning in the Cinema,* London, Secker and Warburg.
Zimmer, Christian (1984) *Le Retour de la fiction,* Paris, Editions du Cerf.
Zimmer, Christian (1974) *Cinéma et politique,* Paris, Seghers.

INDEX OF FILMS